LIBRARY OF HEBREW BIBLE/
OLD TESTAMENT STUDIES

578

Formerly Journal for the Study of the Old Testament Supplement Series

CROSSING THE JORDAN

Diachrony Versus Synchrony in the Book of Joshua

Eun-Woo Lee

B L O O M S B U R Y
NEW YORK • LONDON • NEW DELHI • SYDNEY

Bloomsbury T&T Clark
An imprint of Bloomsbury Publishing Plc

50 Bedford Square
London
WC1B 3DP
UK

175 Fifth Avenue
New York
NY 10010
USA

www.bloomsbury.com

First published 2013

British Library Cataloguing-in-Publication Data
A catalogue record for this book is available from the British Library.

ISBN: HB: 978-0-567-38067-8

Library of Congress Cataloging-in-Publication Data
A catalogue record for this book is available from the Library of Congress.

Typeset by Forthcoming Publications Ltd (www.forthpub.com)
Printed and bound in Great Britain

Dedicated with love and affection to:

Mi-Ran
Life companion, immortal friend

and

Ha-Neul, Dong-Hee, Ha-Yim
God's present, joy of their parents

CONTENTS

Acknowledgments xiii
Abbreviations xv

Chapter 1
INTRODUCTION 1

Chapter 2
SYNCHRONIC READINGS OF JOSHUA 3–4 14
2.1. Polzin, *Moses and the Deuteronomist* 14
2.2 Hawk, *Every Promise Fulfilled* 22
2.3. Mitchell, *Together in the Land: A Reading of the Book of Joshua* 29
2.4. Winther-Nielsen, *A Functional Discourse Grammar of Joshua* 34
2.5. Conclusion 41

Chapter 3
POLZIN AND TEXT-CRITICAL ANALYSIS OF JOSHUA 3–4 42
3.1. Introduction 42
3.2. Text-Critical Analysis of Joshua 3–4 43
3.2.1. LXX^{B} Retroversion of LXX *Vorlage*, and MT of Joshua 3–4 43
3.2.2. Text-Critical Analysis of Joshua 3–4 54
3.2.3 Conclusion of Text-Critical Study 66
3.3. Conclusion 68

Chapter 4
READING JOSHUA 3–4 AS PART OF THE DEVELOPING ARK NARRATIVE 69
4.1. Introduction 69
4.2. The Ark in the Old Testament 70
4.3. Preliminary Analysis: The Literary History of Joshua 3–4 in the Context of the Parallel Ark Narratives 71
4.3.1. Designations for the Ark in the Parallel Ark Narratives 71

4.3.2. The Verbs Describing the Movements of the Ark in the Parallel Ark Narratives 78
4.3.3. Levites and Priests in the Parallel Ark Narratives 84
4.3.4. Divine Epithets in the Parallel Ark Narratives 87
4.3.5. כל־ישראל and כל־העם in the Parallel Ark Narratives 90
4.3.6. Additional Evidence 93
4.3.6.1. War Motif 93
4.3.6.2. The Placement of 2 Samuel 5:11–25 and 2 Chronicles 14 94
4.3.6.3. The Transportation of the Ark and the Playing of Musical Instruments 96
4.3.6.4. רוע / תרועה in Numbers 10:5, 6, 7, 9, Joshua 6:5, 10, 16, 20, 1 Samuel 4:5, 6, 2 Samuel 6:15// 1 Chronicles 15:28aαβ 99
4.3.6.5. The Problem of Geographical Names Between Kiriath-jearim and Baale-judah 99
4.3.6.6. עד היום הזה (2 Samuel 6:8//1 Chronicles 13:11; 1 Kings 8:8//2 Chronicles 5:9; Joshua 4:9; 6:25; 1 Samuel 5:5; 6:18) 100
4.3.6.7. יד יהוה (Joshua 4:24; 1 Samuel 5:6, 9) 101
4.3.6.8. (כ)מתמול שלשים (Joshua 3:4; 4:18); אתמול שלשים (1 Samuel 4:8) 101
4.3.6.9. התקדשו and יתקדשו (Joshua 3:5; 1 Chronicles 15:12; 2 Chronicles 5:11) 101
4.3.6.10. נפלאתיו (Joshua 3:5; 1 Chronicles 16:9, 12, 24) 102
4.3.6.11. וישכמו (Joshua 6:15; 1 Samuel 5:3, 4) and וישכם (Joshua 3:1; 6:12) 102
4.3.6.12. קציר־חטים (LXX Joshua 3:15; 1 Samuel 6:13) 103
4.3.6.13. מלמעלה (Joshua 3:13, 16; 1 Kings 8:7// 2 Chronicles 5:8) 103
4.3.6.14. מחר (Joshua 3:5; 4:6, 21); מחרת (1 Samuel 5:3, 4) 103
4.3.6.15. מהר (Joshua 4:10; 1 Samuel 4:14) 104
4.3.6.16. אוצר יהוה (Joshua 6:19); אוצר בית־יהוה (Joshua 6:24); באוצרת בית יהוה (1 Kings 7:51)// באוצרת בית האלהים (2 Chronicles 5:1) 104
4.3.6.17. הענן in 1 Kings 8:10b//2 Chronicles 5:13b; 1 Kings 8:11//2 Chronicles 5:14; Numbers 10:34; cf. 9:15–23; 10:11–12 104
4.3.7. Summary 105
4.4. The Literary Historical Reading of Joshua 3–4 in the Context of the Parallel Ark Narratives 106

4.4.1. Ark Stories in the Books of Samuel–Kings and Chronicles (1 Samuel 4:1b–7:2, 2 Samuel 6// 1 Chronicles 13–16, 1 Kings 7:51–8:11// 2 Chronicles 5) 107
4.4.1.1. The Ark's Arrival to the Temple in Jerusalem (1 Kings 7:51–8:11//2 Chronicles 5) 111
4.4.1.2. The Ark Is Carried to Jerusalem (2 Samuel 6// 1 Chronicles 13–16) 113
4.4.1.3. The Ark Is Carried to Kiriath-jearim (1 Samuel 4:1b–7:2) 126
4.4.2. The Literary History of Joshua 3–4 128
4.4.3. The Literary History of Joshua 6: The Ark in the Conquest Story of Jericho (Joshua 6:1–27) 129
4.4.4. The Movement of the Ark in the Wilderness (Numbers 10:33–36) 132
4.5. Conclusion 134

Chapter 5
READING JOSHUA 3–4 IN THE CONTEXT OF EXODUS 13:17–14:31 AND 2 KINGS 2 136
5.1. Introduction 136
5.2. Preliminary Analysis of the Study of the Literary History of Exodus 13:17–14:31, Joshua 3–4, 2 Kings 2 136
5.2.1. Shared Words 136
5.2.1.1. Words That Are Used in the Same Way in all Three Passages 136
5.2.1.1.1. חרבה (Exodus 14:21; Joshua 3:17, 4:18; 2 Kings 2:8) 136
5.2.1.2. Words That Are Used in All Three Passages, But Are Used Differently 137
5.2.1.2.1. רום (Exodus 14:8, 16; Joshua 4:5; 2 Kings 2:13) 137
5.2.1.2.2. חמשים (Exodus 13:18; Joshua 4:12; 2 Kings 2:16) 137
5.2.1.3. Words That Appear Only in Exodus and Joshua 137
5.2.1.3.1. יבשה (Exodus 14:16, 22, 29; Joshua 4:22, 23) 137
5.2.1.3.2. שוב (Exodus 14:26, 27, 28; Joshua 4:18) 138
5.2.1.3.3. ים סוף (Exodus 13:18; Joshua 4:23) 138
5.2.1.4. Words That Appear Only in Exodus and Kings 138
5.2.1.4.1. רוח (Exodus 14:21; 2 Kings 2:9, 15, 16) 138

5.2.1.5. Words Which Appear Only in Joshua and Kings 138
5.2.1.5.1. עבר (Joshua 3:1, 2; 4:10, 11, 12; 2 Kings 2:8) 138
5.2.2. Shared Themes 139
5.2.2.1. Succession Narratives 139
5.2.2.2. War Motif 139
5.2.2.3. The Route to the Water 141
5.2.2.4. Water: הים (Exodus 14:2, 9, 16, 21, 22, 23, 26, 27, 28, 29, 30), מי הירדן (Joshua 3:8, 13; 4:7, 18, 23), המים הירדים (Joshua 3:13, 16), הירדן (2 Kings 2:6, 7, 13), המים (2 Kings 2:8, 14) 142
5.2.2.5. The Shape of the Divided Water 142
5.2.2.6. The Media Used to Perform a Miracle: Moses' Staff, (the Feet of the Priests Carrying) the Ark, and Elijah's Mantle 143
5.2.2.7. The Pillar of Cloud and Fire, and the Ark: The Symbols of Yahweh's Presence 144
5.2.3. Summary of the Preliminary Analysis 145
5.3. Conclusion 146

Chapter 6
THE LITERARY HISTORY OF JOSHUA 3–4 148
6.1. Introduction 148
6.2. The Textual History of Joshua 3–4: Comparison Between the OG *Vorlage* and the MT 149
6.2.1. The Pluses in MT and the OG *Vorlage* Joshua 3–4 149
6.2.1.1. The Pluses in MT Joshua 3–4 150
6.2.1.1.1. הוא וכל בני ישׂראל, "he and all the sons of Israel" (3:1) 150
6.2.1.1.2. לאמר (3:6), ויאמר אל־בני ישׂראל (4:21) 150
6.2.1.1.3. כי (3:7) 151
6.2.1.1.4. ויאמר יהושע (3:10) 151
6.2.1.1.5. לפניכם (3:11) 151
6.2.1.1.6. כפות (3:13; 4:18) 151
6.2.1.1.7. מלמעלה ו--- נד אחד (3:13) 151
6.2.1.1.8. הכן (3:17) 151
6.2.1.1.9. לכם (4:2, 3) 152
6.2.1.1.10. איש־אחד (4:2) 152
6.2.1.1.11. ממצב רגלי הכהנים (4:3) 152
6.2.1.1.12. יהושע (4:5) 152
6.2.1.1.13. ארון (4:5) 152
6.2.1.1.14. אלהיכם (4:5) 153

6.2.1.1.15. תוך (4:9, 10, 18) 153
6.2.1.1.16. ככל אשר־צוה משה את־יהשע (4:10) 153
6.2.1.1.17. את־אבותם, מחר (4:21) 154
6.2.1.1.18. הזה (4:22) 154
6.2.1.2. The Pluses in the OG *Vorlage* Joshua 3–4 154
6.2.1.2.1. ---ינו ו--- (3:3) 154
6.2.1.2.2. למחר (3:5) 155
6.2.1.2.3. חטים (3:15) 155
6.2.1.3. Conclusion on the Pluses in the OG *Vorlage* and MT Joshua 3–4 155
6.2.2. Other Divergences Between the OG *Vorlage* and MT in Joshua 3–4 155
6.2.3. Conclusion: Differences Between the OG *Vorlage* and the MT Joshua 3–4 161
6.3. Literary-Critical Analysis of Joshua 3–4 161
6.3.1. Introduction 161
6.3.2. Literary-Critical Analysis of Joshua 3–4 Based on the Retroversion of the LXX *Vorlage* 163
6.3.2.1. Departure from Shittim (3:1) 163
6.3.2.2. Preparation for Crossing the Jordan (3:2–4) 164
6.3.2.3. Institutions from Joshua (3:5–6) 166
6.3.2.4. Yahweh Addresses Joshua and Joshua Prepares His People (3:7–11) 167
6.3.2.5. Choose Twelve Men (3:12) 169
6.3.2.6. Descent and Passing Over on "Dry Ground" (3:13–17) 170
6.3.2.7. Carrying Twelve Stones Over to the Other Side of the Jordan (4:1–8) 171
6.3.2.8. Erecting Memorial Stones in the Middle of the Jordan (4:9) 175
6.3.2.9. The Priests Standing in the Middle of the Jordan (4:10a) 175
6.3.2.10. Peoples' Passing Over in Haste (4:10b–11a) 175
6.3.2.11. The Crossing Over of the Ark and the Stones (4:11b) 176
6.3.2.12. Eastern Tribes Crossing the Jordan (4:12–13) 176
6.3.2.13. The Exaltation of Joshua (4:14) 177
6.3.2.14. The Ark of the Covenant of the Testimony of Yahweh (4:15–16) 177
6.3.2.15. Ascent and Arrival at Gilgal (4:17–19) 177
6.3.2.16. Stones at Gilgal and the Confession (4:20–24) 178

6.3.2.17. The Examination of the Result of Literary-Critical Analysis Based on the Hebrew *Vorlage* of LXX Joshua 3–4 179
6.3.2.18. Conclusion: Literary Critical Analysis of Joshua 3–4 Based on the Hebrew Retroversion of the LXX *Vorlage* 184
6.3.3. Literary-Critical Analysis of Joshua 3–4 Based on the Final Shape of the MT 185
6.3.3.1. Preparation for Crossing the Jordan (3:1–4) 185
6.3.3.2. "Sanctify yourselves" (3:5–6) 186
6.3.3.3. Yahweh Addresses Joshua and Joshua Prepares His People (3:7–11) 186
6.3.3.4. Choose Twelve Men (3:12) 187
6.3.3.5. Descent and Passing Over on "Dry Ground" (בחרבה) (3:13–17) 187
6.3.3.6. Carrying Twelve Stones Over to the Other Side of the Jordan and Erecting Twelve Memorial Stones in the Middle of the Jordan (4:1–9) 188
6.3.3.7. The Succession of Joshua to Moses (4:10–14) 189
6.3.3.8. The Ark of the Testimony (4:15–16) 190
6.3.3.9. Ascent and Arrival at Gilgal (4:17–19) 190
6.3.3.10. Stones at Gilgal and Confession (4:20–24) 191
6.3.3.11. The Examination of the Result of Literary-Critical Analysis Based on the Final Shape of the MT 191
6.3.3.12. Conclusion: Literary-Critical Analysis of Joshua 3–4 Based on the Final Shape of the MT 202

Chapter 7
CONCLUSION 204
7.1. The Most Probable Literary History of Joshua 3–4 204
7.2. Polzin, the Textual and Literary History, and MT Pluses in Joshua 3–4 209

Bibliography 212
Index of References 220
Index of Authors 236

Abbreviations

AB	Anchor Bible
ABD	*Anchor Bible Dictionary*. Edited by D. N. Freedman. 6 vols. New York, 1992
AOTC	Apollos Old Testament Commentary
ASTI	*Annual of the Swedish Theological Institute (Leiden)*
ATD	Das Alte Testament Deutsch
BARev	*Biblical Archaeology Review*
BDB	Brown, F., S. R. Driver, and C. A. Briggs. *A Hebrew and English Lexicon of the Old Testament*. Oxford, 1907
BEATAJ	Beiträge zur Erforschung des Alten Testaments und des antiken Judentum
BHK	*Biblia Hebraica*. Edited by R. Kittel. 3d ed. Stuttgart, 1937
BHS	*Biblia Hebraica Stuttgartensia*. Edited by K. Elliger and W. Rudolph. 4th ed. Stuttgart, 1990
Bib	*Biblica*
BKAT	Biblischer Kommentar Altes Testament
BTH	The Book of Two Houses
BZAW	Beihefte zur Zeitschrift für die alttestamentliche Wissenschaft
CBC	Cambridge Bible Commentary
CBQ	*Catholic Biblical Quarterly*
CTA	*Corpus des tablettes en cunéiformes alphabétiques découvertes à Ras Shamra-Ugarit de 1929 à 1939*. Edited by A. Herdner. Mission de Ras Shamra 10. Paris, 1963
CTM	*Concordia Theological Monthly*
DCH	*Dictionary of Classical Hebrew*. Edited by D. J. A. Clines. Sheffield, 1993–2011
EvT	*Evangelische Theologie*
FOTL	Forms of the Old Testament Literature
FRLANT	Forschungen zur Religion und Literatur des Alten und Neuen Testaments
HAR	*Hebrew Annual Review*
HAT	Handbuch zum Alten Testament
HSM	Harvard Semitic Monographs
HTR	*Harvard Theological Review*
HUCA	*Hebrew Union College Annual*
JBL	*Journal of Biblical Literature*
JNES	*Journal of Near Eastern Studies*

JSOT	*Journal for the Study of the Old Testament*
JSOTSup	Journal for the Study of the Old Testament: Supplement Series
LHBOTS	Library of Hebrew Bible/Old Testament Studies
LXX	Septuagint
LXX^{A}	Septuagint (Codex Alexandrinus)
LXX^{B}	Septuagint (Codex Vaticanus)
LXX^{L}	Septuagint (Lucianic recension)
MT	Masoretic Text
NCBC	The New Century Bible Commentary
NICOT	New International Commentary on the Old Testament
NIV	New International Version
NJPS	New Jewish Publication Society Translation (1985)
NRSV	New Revised Standard Version
OG	Old Greek
OTG	Old Testament Guides
OTL	Old Testament Library
OTS	*Oudtestamentische Studiën*
RB	*Revue biblique*
SBLDS	Society of Biblical Literature Dissertation Series
SBT	Studies in Biblical Theology
SJOT	*Scandinavian Journal of the Old Testament*
SJT	*Scottish Journal of Theology*
SOTSMS	Society for Old Testament Study Monograph Series
SSN	Studia Semitica Neerlandica
TDOT	*Theological Dictionary of the Old Testament*. Edited by G. J. Botterweck and H. Ringgren. Translated by J. T. Willis, G. W. Bromiley, and D. E. Green. 8 vols. Grand Rapids, 1974–
Tg	Targum
ThWAT	*Theologisches Wörterbuch zum Alten Testament*. Edited by G. J. Botterweck and H. Ringgren. Stuttgart, 1970–
TOTC	Tyndale Old Testament Commentaries
Vg	Vulgate
VL	Vetus Latina (Old Latin)
VT	*Vetus Testamentum*
VTSup	Vetus Testamentum Supplements
WBC	Word Biblical Commentary
ZAW	*Zeitschrift für die alttestamentliche Wissenschaft*

Acknowledgments

To write a book is a large project that cannot be completed without the assistance of many people who have accompanied me on the journey of life and who have laid a precious foundation for me and profoundly influenced my life. It is now my pleasure to express my gratitude to them.

First of all, I would like to reserve my special gratitude for Professor A. Graeme Auld for his penetrating criticism balanced by generous encouragement during the process of this research. Through scholarly enthusiasm and personal warmth, he showed me what a teacher's life should be. I also thank Dr David J. Reimer and Professor Timothy H. Lim for their constant interest and consideration, and Professor Hans Barstad and Professor Hugh Pyper for their guidance and helpful advice for further scholarly study.

I am indebted to the high quality of teaching staff in my home school, the Presbyterian College and Theological Seminary (PCTS), Seoul, Korea, in particular, to the Old Testament scholars, who, in addition to their professional expertise, taught me many valuable lessons: Professor Joong-Eun Kim taught me respect for the biblical texts and church; Professor Sa-Moon Kang, love for the weak and scholarly way to go; Professor Young-Il Chang, the way to use historical criticism respecting both scholarly integrity and faith; the late Professor Dong-Soo Lee, the stylishness of silence and respect for others; Professor Dong-Hyun Park, love for human beings and justice.

I would also like to thank Rev Hoon Ko and Ansan 1 Church, Rev Yeo-Min Yun and Song-Cheon Church, Ai Dasom for their scholarship and prayer. Without their assistance, this project would not have been completed. I also wish to thank Professor Kyung-Jin Min, my seminary senior and a comrade while on national service, who not only consoled the frustration and despair of a young man in a divided country, but also introduced me into the deep and challenging world of the Old Testament.

I also want to thank my dear friends in Edinburgh—too many to mention—without whose friendship and kindness my time in Edinburgh would have been much the poorer. In particular, I would like to mention a few names: Ishbel Coy, June Percival, the Ashforth family, and house group members who have been my family's real friends like parents in a foreign country and the late Sheila Masterton, a great missionary, who showed concern for me and cared for me with all her heart at the age of 80 when I was alone in Edinburgh at the first stage of my study and who will be wearing a beautiful smile in heaven to celebrate the completion of my studies.

I also feel strong obligation to express my appreciation to my proof readers, to whom I am also indebted as a non-native English speaker: Robin and his wife at the earlier stage of my study and Laura Joffe at the latter stage of my study. They offered high quality English language revisions in various stages of my research and considerate hospitality whenever I visited them never making me feel that I imposed upon them. I also thank Andrew Mein and Claudia Camp, the editors of the Library of Hebrew Bible/Old Testament Studies, and to Duncan Burns, my copy editor.

My parents and parents-in-law also deserve my special gratitude for their self-sacrificing love and unfailing prayer. Especially heartfelt thanks should be given to my brothers, sisters, and sisters-in-law for their support and devotion, and even for all the small but very important ways in which they helped our family to live in a foreign country.

Finally, I am grateful to my dear son, Dong-Hee Lee and dear daughter, Ha-Yim Lee, who were born during my study in Edinburgh and have brought delight to all my family members. I am also greatly thankful to my dear daughter, Ha-Neul Lee, who, since birth, has suffered many painful procedures and operations, but who has overcome those ordeals with joy and has rather encouraged her father to complete his project. I have a guilty conscience where she is concerned because she has had to be deprived of precious time with her father because of his studies. Thus, I sincerely dedicate this book to my angel-like daughter. Above all, optimum appreciation beyond expression should be given to my dear wife, Mi-Ran Oh, who supported me with an immeasurable depth of love and infinite sacrifice which can never be repaid..

Eun-Woo Lee
At the Skirt of Acha Mountain

Chapter 1

INTRODUCTION

This study seeks to present a test case for diachronic and synchronic approaches in the book of Joshua, especially in Josh 3–4. This complicated text, Josh 3–4, could be a good example for readers who are interested in the synchronic–diachronic question.

Since Polzin's epoch-making synchronic study of the book of Joshua,[1] a number of sympathetic readings have appeared.[2] These studies have shown a new direction for those who want to make sense out of the final

1. R. M. Polzin, *Moses and the Deuteronomist: A Literary Study of the Deuteronomistic History* (New York: Seabury, 1980). For more of his study, see *Samuel and the Deuteronomist: A Literary Study of the Deuteronomistic History* (San Francisco: Harper & Row, 1989); idem, *David and the Deuteronomist: A Literary Study of the Deuteronomistic History* (Bloomington: Indiana University Press, 1993); idem, "Curses and Kings: A Reading of 2 Samuel 15–16," in *The New Literary Criticism and the Hebrew Bible* (ed. J. C. Exum and D. J. A. Clines; JSOTSup 143; Sheffield: JSOT, 1993), 201–26. For reviews of his study, see J. Keating, Review of Polzin, *Samuel and the Deuteronomist*, *Faith and Mission* 7 (1989): 89–90; D. Jobling, "Book Review on Polzin's *Samuel and the Deuteronomist*," *Int* 44 (1990): 416; M. T. Davis, Review of Polzin, *Samuel and the Deuteronomist*, *Theology Today* 46 (1990): 458–60; B. L. Johnson, Review of Polzin, *Samuel and the Deuteronomist*, *WThJ* 54 (1992): 368–70; D. Edelman, Review of Polzin, *Samuel and the Deuteronomist*, *JNES* 52 (1993): 306–8.

2. For synchronic research on Joshua, see P. P. Saydon, "The Crossing of the Jordan, Josue 3 and 4," *CBQ* 12 (1950): 194–207; Polzin, *Moses and the Deuteronomist*; B. Peckham, "The Composition of Joshua 3–4," *CBQ* 46 (1984): 413–31; L. D. Hawk, *Every Promise Fulfilled: Contesting Plots in Joshua* (Literary Currents in Biblical Interpretation; Louisville: Westminster John Knox, 1991); G. Mitchell, *Together in the Land: A Reading of the Book of Joshua* (JSOTSup 134; Sheffield: JSOT, 1993); J. Svensson, *Towns and Toponyms in the Old Testament, with Special Emphasis on Joshua 14–21* (CB[OT] 38; Stockholm: Almqvist & Wiksell, 1994); N. Winther-Nielsen, *A Functional Discourse Grammar of Joshua: A Computer-assisted Rhetorical Structure Analysis* (OTS 40; Stockholm: Almqvist & Wiksell, 1995); R. D. Nelson, *Joshua* (OTL; Louisville: Westminster John Knox, 1997).

form of the text. However, how can their methodologies be applied to Josh 3–4, one of the most complex texts in Joshua? This research attempts to probe the methodology of those synchronic readers who have dealt with this complicated text. One important test is the relevance of their approach to the two different descriptions concerning the twelve stones set up in the middle of the Jordan and on the other side of the river.

The large number of text-critical issues in this text also makes it difficult to read only from the final form of the MT.[3] A further difficulty is which text we should follow among the MT, the LXX, and the *Vorlage* behind the Greek text. The impossibility of simple answers drives us to sympathize with a diachronic approach.

According to Winther-Nielsen, since Wellhausen proposed the theory that the Gilgal stone narrative was copied from the Jordan stone narrative, diachronic research has dominated the study of these chapters.[4] This has been mainly focused on the MT.

3. For the text-critical issues of this text, see especially S. Holmes, *Joshua, the Hebrew and Greek Texts* (Cambridge: Cambridge University Press, 1914); R. G. Boling and G. E. Wright, *Joshua* (AB 6; New York: Doubleday, 1982); J. A. Soggin, *Joshua* (2d ed.; OTL; London: SCM, 1982); T. C. Butler, *Joshua* (WBC 7; Waco: Word, 1983); L. J. Greenspoon, *Textual Studies in the Book of Joshua* (HSM 28; Chico: Scholars Press, 1983); J. Gray, *Joshua, Judges and Ruth* (NCBC; London: Marshall, Morgan & Scott, 1986); K. Bieberstein, *Joshua–Jordan–Jericho. Archäologie, Geschichte und Theologie der Landnahmeerzählungen Josua 1–6* (OBO 143; Göttingen: Vandenhoeck & Ruprecht, 1995); J. Moatti-Fine, *Jésus (Josué). Traduction du texte grec de la Septante, Introduction et notes* (La Bible d'Alexandrie 6; Paris: Eisenbrauns, 1996); S. Sipilä, "The Septuagint Version of Joshua 3–4," in *VII Congress of the International Organization for Septuagint and Cognate Studies: Leuven 1989* (ed. C. E. Cox; SBLSGS 31; Atlanta: SBL, 1991; idem, *Between Literalness and Freedom: Translation Technique in the Septuagint of Joshua and Judges Regarding the Clause Connections Introduced by* ו *and* כי (Publications of the Finnish Exegetical Society 75; Göttingen: Vandenhoeck & Ruprecht, 1999); E. Tov, "The Growth of the Book of Joshua in the Light of the Evidence of the LXX Translation," and "Midrash-Type Exegesis in the Septuagint of Joshua," in *The Greek and Hebrew Bible: Collected Essays on the Septuagint* (VTSup 72; Leiden: Brill, 1999); M. N. van der Meer, *Formation and Reformulation: The Redaction of the Book of Joshua in the Light of the Oldest Textual Witnesses* (VTSup 102; Leiden: Brill, 2004); A. G. Auld, *Joshua, Moses and the Land: Tetrateuch–Pentateuch–Hexateuch in a Generation of Study Since 1938* (Edinburgh: T. & T. Clark, 1980); idem, *Joshua Retold: Synoptic Perspectives* (Edinburgh: T. & T. Clark, 1998); idem, *Joshua: Jesus, Son of Nauē, in Codex Vaticanus* (Septuagint Commentary Series; Leiden: Brill, 2005).

4. Winther-Nielsen, *A Functional Discourse Grammar of Joshua*, 169.

Driver and Cooke held that this narrative was composed of three layers: P, JE, and a Deuteronomic editor.[5] In contrast, Eissfeldt rejected P and D as editors and substituted them with J, E, and L.[6]

Unlike previous scholars' attempts to find older Pentateuchal sources in Joshua, Rudolph suggested a new direction in studying first Genesis, then Exodus to Joshua. Denying the existence of E, he divided Josh 3–4 into the following: a basic J narrative of the Crossing of the Jordan (3:1, 5–6, 14–17; 4:9, 10b, 11a, 12–13, 15–18, 11b, 19b); its first expansion of Joshua's magnification by an editor of J (3:7–11, 13; 4:14); a secondary account (3:12; 4:1b–5, 3b, 8a^{b}b, 10a, 20); Deuteronomic additions, explaining and emphasizing the role of the ark and the lesson from the crossing (3:2–4, 10; 4:6–8a^{a}, 21–24); and later glosses (3:4ab^{a}; 4:1a, 19a).[7]

Some scholars argue that Noth was influenced by Rudolph's viewpoint and accepted his literary theory. Noth came to believe that the failure of the literary-critical research in Joshua was caused by the assumption that the contents of this book are simply a continuation of those in the Pentateuch. For him, such a thing as the "Hexateuch" never existed in any form. He rejected the existing literary-critical method in this narrative as well, because "das Verschwinden des Jordanwassers deutlich genug nur einmal berichtet wird."[8] According to his 1938 edition of *Das Buch Josua*, this narrative is divided into "den ursprünglichen Bericht and die deuteronomistische und spätere Redaktion."[9] In the 1953 edition, he breaks down this narrative even further. The purpose of this narrative was to explain "die Steine im Jordanbett und die Steine in Gilgal." These two stories "vielleicht durch Umordnungen im Text vereinigt wurden [von dem Sammler]." Then the Dtr (3:2–4, 6–10; 4:6, 7, 10aβ, 12, 14, 21, 22, 24) and post-Dtr (4:15–18a) *Zuwachs* followed.[10] Noth replaced Rudolph's documentary hypothesis with his own theory, and made a large contribution in developing the conception of a so-called Dtr history and its theology in the study of this narrative.

5. S. R. Driver, *An Introduction to the Literature of the Old Testament* (9th ed.; Edinburgh: T. & T. Clark, 1913), 105; G. A. Cooke, *The Book of Joshua* (The Cambridge Bible; Cambridge: Cambridge University Press, 1918), 17; Saydon, "The Crossing of the Jordan, Josue 3 and 4," 194.

6. O. Eissfeldt, *Hexateuch-Synopse* (Leipzig: Hinrichs, 1922), 206–9.

7. W. Rudolph, *Der "Elohist" von Exodus bis Josua* (BZAW 68; Berlin: Töpelmann, 1938), 169–78.

8. M. Noth, *Das Buch Josua* (HAT 1/7; Tübingen: J. C. B. Mohr, 1938), 11 (2d ed., 1953, 31).

9. Noth, *Das Buch Josua* (1938), vii–xv, 10–13.

10. Noth, *Das Buch Josua* (1953), 7–17, 25–37.

Keller rejected Noth's historical and literary theories, arguing that only the Gilgal stone version is original and that all other accounts of Joshua, the ark, the priests, and the command and its execution are secondary.[11]

Dus, thoroughly indebted to Noth, changed his view into five successive layers: first, a fragmentary aetiology of the twelve stones in the Jordan; second, "die um die Ätiologie der Gilgalsteine und der zwölf אנשים"; third, *ein Sammler*, who incorporated them into an account of the *Landnahmeerzählung*; fourth, a deuteronomistic interpolator, who was particularly concerned with the ark; and finally, *ein priesterlicher Bearbeiter*, who transposed the aetiology of the stones in the Jordan from its original connection with the crossing to its present association with the Gilgal aetiology.[12]

According to Vogt, the text is composed of two narratives, one historical and the other liturgical and ritual. In this analysis, he implied two editions of the Dtr history.[13] Although Vogt followed Noth in making Dtr an editor rather than the author of the history, he seemed to try to avoid the excessive application of convergent theories.

Langlamet divided the materials in Josh 3–4 into nine sub-divisions:[14] (1) the aetiology of the stones of Gilgal without the figure of Joshua (4:2, 3, 8); (2) a Shittim-Gilgal story (3:1, 5, 14a, 16; 4:19); (3) an "ark" narrative (3:9–11, 13, 15a; 4:7, 10b); (4) an aetiology of the stones in the Jordan (4:9); (5) a "Joshua" version of the aetiology of the Gilgal stones (4:4–5, 20); (6) two Gilgal catechisms (4:6–7, 21–24); (7) a first Deuteronomistic redaction (3:6, 8, 12, 13, 14b, 15b, 17; 4:1, 2, 9, 10, 11, 15–18, 21); (8) the texts of the Deuteronomistic historian or his school (3:2–3, 7, 17; 4:11b–12, 14); (9) brief later additions (3:3, 4, 4:13). Langlamet supplied most detailed divisions on this narrative and paid close attention to its literary and tradition-historical problems without having recourse to the kind of source-criticism which Noth rejected.[15]

Repudiating previous literary theory and historical aetiology, Soggin maintained that the ritual reference is derived from the Exodus account of the Passover and the crossing of the Reed Sea. For him, the narrative

11. C. A. Keller, "Über einige alttestamentliche Heiligtumslegenden II," *ZAW* 68 (1956): 85–97.

12. J. Dus, "Die Analyse zweier Ladeerzählungen des Josuabuches (Jos 3–4 und 6)," *ZAW* 72 (1960): 106–34.

13. E. Vogt, "Die Erzählung vom Jordanübergang, Josue 3–4," *Bib* 46 (1965): 125–48.

14. F. Langlamet, *Gilgal et les récits de la traversée du Jourdain* (Cahiers de la Revue Biblique; Paris: Gabalda, 1969).

15. Auld, *Joshua, Moses and the Land*, 43.

is divided into two parts, pre-Dtr material and easily recognizable Dtr additions.[16]

Boling tried to reduce the complexity of this narrative by applying the so-called Deuteronomistic double redaction theory. He argues that to the story of the "crossing from Shittim to Gilgal" (3:1–16; 4:10–14) was inserted the ancient aetiology (3:17–4:8), then 4:9 and 4:15–18 were added by Dtr_2.[17]

Van Seters holds that J and P were secondarily added into the original Dtr, which was influenced by Assyrian reports of military campaigns.[18] According to him, the Dtr Historian interpreted the tradition of the entrance into the land as a great military conquest. Furthermore, he maintains that the Dtr narrative has a basic similarity to the accounts of such military campaigns in the Assyrian annals and to the "letters to the god." These pay special attention to a few major battles or conquests of important cities while summarizing the overthrow of many others in a stereotyped series. They sometimes highlight the overcoming of a special barrier, such as a river in flood or a mountain range. The king receives an oracle of salvation before an important battle from a deity who promises victory from the enemy. Sometimes envoys come from afar to sue for peace and submit to terms of servitude in order to avoid destruction. General descriptions of sieges or military strategies; lists of participants of coalitions, kings defeated, or cities; enumerations of casualties and the amount of booty; dedications of victory and of spoils to the god—all these occur with great regularity.[19] From the complex narrative Van Seters first separates the basic Dtr account of the conquest, which, according to him, has been made to correspond with the literary pattern of military campaigns in the Assyrian royal inscriptions: 3:2–3, 6–7, 9–11, 13–16; 4:10b, 11a, 12–14. Then, the Gilgal stone story (J) was added: 3:8, 12, 17; 4:1–5, 8, 20–24. Finally, the priestly writer's concern for the ark and memorial stones in the middle of the Jordan (P) was inserted: 3:1, 4–5; 4:6–7, 9–10a, 11b, 15–19.[20] However, Van Seters dates the sources differently to most scholars. The date of D is ca. 625 B.C.E., while that of J is likely exilic (ca. 540 B.C.E.), and P postexilic (ca. 400 B.C.E.).[21] His attempt to compare Josh 3–4 with Neo-Assyrian accounts

16. Soggin, *Joshua*, 43–67.

17. Boling and Wright, *Joshua*, 179–81.

18. J. Van Seters, *In Search of History* (New Haven: Yale University Press, 1983), 325–30.

19. Ibid., 330–31.

20. Ibid., 325–27.

21. J. Van Seters, "The Pentateuch," in *The Hebrew Bible* (ed. S. L. McKenzie and W. P. Graham; Louisville: Westminster John Knox, 1998), 3–49.

appears to form a new category of literary studies and to broaden the way to approach this complex literary composite.

Peckham suggests that Dtr_2 mainly interprets the event as a skillful author and only vv. 5, 10b, 16b in ch. 3 belong to Dtr_1.[22] He follows the double redaction theory, but only Dtr_2 plays an important role in his idea. Thus, his theory seems to be close to that of the so-called single deuteronomistic authorship.

According to Fritz, the final form of this narrative "ist das Ergebnis eines langen Wachstumsprozesses, bei dem mehrere Stufen der Redaktion unterschieden werden können." For him, "[d]ie ursprüngliche Fassung" is 3:1, 14a, 15a, 16; 4:11a, 18, 19, in the middle of which "steht der Durchzug des Volkes." Then, this narrative form "wurde durch eine redaktionelle Überarbeitung ergänzt, in der die Rolle der Lade stärker betont wird, 3:10, 11, 13, 14b, 17; 4: 9, 10." This emphasis of the ark in the wonder of the Jordan belongs to the deuteronomistic redactor (RedD). Third, in the narrative of passing over the Jordan was "eine Erzählung von der Mitnahme der zwölf Steine" from the riverbed and their "Aufstellung am Ort des Lagers eingearbeitet 4:1–8, die durch 4:20–23 neu interpretiert worden ist." Here "der nachpriesterschriftliche Einschub (4:15–17)" and "die weiteren redaktionellen Zusätze" (3:2–4, 5, 6, 7, 8, 9, 12, 15b; 4: 11b, 12, 13, 14, 24) followed.[23] Fritz tends to follow the traditional historical-critical approach and seems to be especially influenced by Noth. However, since he starts the literary history with the first Deuteronomist, Fritz shows a different position from Noth, for whom there was a substantial contribution from an earlier *Sammler*.

Nelson mainly tries to find a pattern which emphasizes the unity of this narrative in synchronic perspective,[24] but he recognizes the existence of different materials beneath this complex text. According to him, this part is composed of pre-deuteronomistic material, deuteronomistic redaction, and P-like expression (3:4a; 4:16, 19),[25] but there is no evidence of the

22. Peckham, "The Composition of Joshua 3–4," 418–31.

23. V. Fritz, *Das Buch Josua* (HAT 1/7; Tübingen: Mohr–Siebeck, 1994), 1–9, 41–56.

24. Nelson, *Joshua*, 1–24, 53–75. In synchronic perspective, Nelson finds a pattern of narrative action interwoven with associated speech (command, prediction, and explanation): command (3:3, 5a, 6, 8; 4:2, 3, 5, 15–17), prediction (3:5b, 13), explanation (3:4, 11; 4:6–7, 14, 21–24). That is, "an inner circle of speeches focus on the story at hand. Similarly, an outer circle of (deuteronomistic) sentences splice the narrative into the larger story of Joshua: 3:2, 7, 9–10; 4:12–14. Yet another set of phrases connects what happens at the Jordan back to the exodus experience" (3:16; 4:19, 22–23).

25. Ibid., 1–24, 53–75.

second Deuteronomist in this narrative.[26] First, the main narrative line, which embodies the original story, is 3:1, 5, 11, 13–17. He holds that the ark is certainly part of this pre-deuteronomistic material.[27] Second, he indicates the contribution of the Deuteronomic Historian (DH) to this narrative with some confidence. The designation "carriers of the ark" (3:15a) has been supplemented from a deuteronomistic perspective by "the levitical priests" (3:3) and then simply by "the priests" (3:13, 14, 15, 17; 4:9, 10, 18). Other deuteronomistic contributions are the appearance of the priests in 3:6, 8,[28] the concern for the two and half tribes in 4:12,[29] the title "the ark of the covenant" (3:3, 6, 8, 11, 14, 17),[30] and the expanded terminology for the ark in 4:7, 9, 18.[31] The three-day chronology and "the officers" of 3:2 could be connected back to 1:10–11 and Joshua's correlation to Moses in 3:7 and 4:14 to 1:5 and 7, which are the concerns of DH. Another characteristic deuteronomistic interest is the education of future generations (4:6–7, 21–24).[32] Third, priestly redactional interests (3:4a; 4:16, 19) played a role in the creation of the final form of this narrative, but to link this P-like redactional activity with the Priestly writing in the Pentateuch is to go beyond the evidence.[33] However, he maintains that further attempts to reconstruct the literary history of this narrative, beyond this recognition of deuteronomistic redaction and the conspicuous P-like redaction, are doomed to failure.[34]

On the other hand, there have been some scholars, who noted a great number of differences between MT and LXX Josh 3–4. These interpreters have tried to consider the challenges from the LXX more seriously.

In his 1914 study, *Joshua*, Holmes pointed out that the differences between the Hebrew and Greek texts are not the result of textual errors in the Hebrew text underlying the Greek translation, but those of a systematic revision on the MT side.[35] According to him, since the MT is longer in many places, it is the result of a deliberate and later revision.[36] Having established the priority of the LXX over the MT in Josh 3–4,

26. Ibid., 6.
27. Ibid., 56.
28. Ibid.
29. Ibid., 66.
30. Ibid., 56.
31. Ibid., 66.
32. Ibid.
33. Ibid., 9.
34. Ibid., 57.
35. Holmes, *Joshua, the Hebrew and Greek Texts*.
36. Ibid., 3.

Holmes raised the possibility that the Greek text represented the original Hebrew text, while the MT was the result of subsequent additions.

Auld supports Holmes' position on the priority of the LXX, but unfolds his theory on a much bigger scale. He pays attention to the literary-critical problems in the book of Joshua, and suggests new literary relations between Joshua and the Pentateuch on the one hand, and the book of Chronicles on the other.[37] However, these literary-critical problems should be taken into account with the large number of text-critical issues represented by LXX Joshua. For him, the generally shorter Greek text is a better witness than the MT to that common original from which have both diverged.[38] Auld noticed that among Langlamet's nine layers in Josh 3–4, the last three redactional layers are MT pluses.[39] According to him, the much longer MT Josh 3–4 is the result of "progressive supplementation"[40] or "expansion."[41]

Tov also pays close attention to the differences between the LXX and the MT of Joshua in the broader context of the Hebrew Bible.[42] He holds that the numerous divergences between MT and LXX Joshua should be understood as the result of a re-editing of the book.[43] His study on Josh 3–4 also focuses on the pluses in the MT which are much more frequent than its minuses. He classifies those large number of pluses in the MT under the headings of "additions of MT whose secondary nature is evident from the context," "additions in MT whose secondary nature is evident from their formulation," "small elucidations," "harmonizing additions," "contextual additions," "emphasis," "substantial additions," "theological corrections," and the "influence of Deuteronomy."[44] According to him, the pluses in MT Josh 3–4 are contextually secondary and exegetical additions.[45] The LXX Josh 3–4 also contains some pluses, which may have been omitted from the MT. The minuses and pluses of the *Vorlage* of LXX Josh 3–4 make the MT and LXX into two parallel editions.[46] This

37. Auld, *Joshua, Moses and the Land.*

38. Auld, *Joshua Retold*, 19.

39. Auld, *Joshua, Moses and the land*, 91.

40. Auld, *Joshua Retold*, 24.

41. A. G. Auld, "Studies in Joshua: Text and Literary Relations" (Ph.D. diss., University of Edinburgh), 119.

42. See E. Tov, *Textual Criticism of the Hebrew Bible* (Minneapolis: Fortress, 1992), 313–49; idem, *The Text-Critical Use of the Septuagint in Biblical Research* (2d ed.; JBS 8; Jerusalem: Simor, 1997), 237–63.

43. Tov, "The Growth of the Book of Joshua," 385–96.

44. Ibid., 389–94.

45. Ibid., 394.

46. Ibid., 395.

explains his leading principle of literary growth in the book of Joshua. Unlike preceding scholars such as Holmes and Auld, Tov also pays attention to the internal evidence of the book of LXX Joshua. For this purpose, he examines the translator's word choice as well as the word order and consistency in the translation. Thus, the translation technique of LXX Joshua is important for the evaluation of the LXX. According to Tov, even though the translation technique of the LXX ranged from "relatively free" to "relatively literal," it remained sufficiently close to the Hebrew to establish the translator's faithfulness to his source. This could be supported by the fact that the pluses of the LXX are Hebraistic in diction and can be retroverted easily into Hebrew.[47]

Even though Sipilä pays attention to the translation technique of LXX Joshua in his recent book *Between Literalness and Freedom*[48] and skillfully evaded the burden of answering the question of whether the Greek translator worked from a different Hebrew *Vorlage* by excluding those passages where the MT and LXX differ from his study,[49] in his earlier study on Josh 3–4 he discussed textual variants between MT and LXX Josh 3–4 closely.[50] In all, he deals with 120 cases within Josh 3 and 4 where the LXX and the MT differ from each other.[51] Above all, he first pays attention to the translation technique of the LXX. As Hebrew differs a lot from Greek, the translation differs in many cases from the *Vorlage*. The translator sometimes changed or modified the Hebrew wording and structure. However, most of the cases where his/her translation does not follow the wording of the *Vorlage* are connected with purely linguistic problems. Even though the translator did not always produce fluent Greek, he/she was capable of handling most of the difficulties.[52] Here he points out Noth's mistakes in arguing that the LXX *Vorlage* was actually the same as the MT and that all the deviations from the MT had been caused by the LXX Translator,[53] since we now know that the *Vorlage* really differed from the MT.[54] Second, he considers corruptions in the MT.[55] In these cases the MT has eleven additions, four corrections and four mistakes within Josh 3–4, which attests to the *Vorlage* being more original than the MT. The corruptions include the MT copyist's attempts

47. Ibid., 388.
48. Sipilä, *Between Literalness and Freedom*.
49. Ibid., 17.
50. Sipilä, "The Septuagint Version of Joshua 3–4," 63–74.
51. Ibid., 64.
52. Ibid., 65.
53. Noth, *Das Buch Josua* (1938), 7.
54. Sipilä, "The Septuagint Version of Joshua 3–4," 66.
55. Ibid., 68.

to clarify the texts, which were in some way strange or vague, and theological corrections.[56] Third, he also maintains that there were corruptions in the LXX *Vorlage*.[57] According to him, there are 16 corruptions in the Hebrew *Vorlage* of LXX Josh 3–4, which can be divided into ten corrections, three additions and three mistakes. The reasons for the correction in the *Vorlage* are mainly for the clarification of the context; and they are sometimes connected with a formula or actualization of the text. At any rate, the MT is more original in this case.[58] Therefore, for Sipilä, both the opinions that the MT is the only relevant text (e.g. Noth's viewpoint) and that the LXX is the better and more original text (e.g. Holmes' viewpoint) are criticized. Rather, according to him, the *Vorlage* is as good or as original as the MT.[59]

Another contribution to the debate is provided by Van der Meer, who critiques Holmes, Auld, and Tov in his book *Formation and Reformulation*.[60] He tries to prove the priority of the proto-MT over the *Vorlage* of the LXX. According to him, the evidence from the biblical scrolls from the Dead Sea and also the LXX is not sufficient to support the priority of the LXX *Vorlage*.[61] Even though there is some possibility of reconstructing an editorially different Hebrew version behind LXX Josh 20, in all other cases one cannot claim an editorial priority of the LXX over the MT.[62] He holds that not the LXX but the MT attests to the final stage of the literary formation of Joshua.[63] Thus, his conclusion is that the study of the literary formation of the Hebrew text should be in its own right and that of the ancient versions in their own context.[64] Following established so-called deuteronomistic theory, he divides the redactional history of the book of Joshua into three stages: (1) a Deuteronomistic reformulation of older pre-Deuteronomistic narratives, (2) a nomistic redaction of the Deuteronomistic sections; and (3) a Priestly redaction.[65] He reaches this position by dealing with Josh 1, Josh 5:2–12, Josh 8:1–29, and Josh 8:30–35 in his four major chapters. But he does not study Josh 3–4 closely, which contains a number of textual and literary-critical issues, and which seems not to accord with his position. He simply mentions

56. Ibid., 68–69.
57. Ibid., 69.
58. Ibid., 71.
59. Ibid., 72.
60. Van der Meer, *Formation and Reformulation*.
61. Ibid., 115.
62. Ibid., 115–16.
63. Ibid., 523.
64. Ibid., 156–59.
65. Ibid., 115–53.

that 4:21–5:8 is the Deuteronomistic version of the Joshua narratives and that 4:19 is part of a Priestly redaction of the book of Joshua.[66]

As we saw above, the diachronic research on Josh 3–4 so far has been proceeding in two directions. On the one hand, there have been some attempts to find various layers of material behind the text giving priority to and based solely on the MT. On the other hand, there have been attempts to reconstruct the textual and literary history of this narrative, considering a number of differences between the MT and LXX, and accepting those challenges raised by the LXX. However, the former shows the limitation of not paying attention to the differences between the MT and LXX, but tracing the literary history of this complicated narrative only from the final form of the MT. In addition, almost all of their studies are indebted to the existing so-called deuteronomistic theory raised by Noth.[67] While the latter have merits in the point that they note the divergences between the MT and LXX, and adequately consider those

66. Ibid., 536.

67. Of course, his theory has been revised and complemented by R. Smend and his Göttingen school and by F. M. Cross and his Harvard school, but they are indebted in the point that they still recognize some kind of "Deuteronomist or Deuteronomists." For Smend and his Göttingen school, see R. Smend Jr., "Das Gesetz und die Völker. Ein 'Beitrag zur deuteronomistischen Redaktionsgeschichte,'" in *Probleme biblischer Theologie. Gerhard von Rad zum 70. Geburtstag* (ed. H. W. Wolff; Munich: Kaiser, 1971); idem, *Die Entstehung des Alten Testaments* (Stuttgart: Kohlhammer, 1981), 110–25; Walter Dietrich, *David, Saul und die Propheten* (BWANT 7/2; Stuttgart: Kohlhammer, 1987); Ernst Würthwein, *Studien zum deuteronomistichen Geschichtswerk* (BZAW 227; Berlin: de Gruyter, 1994); Auld, *Joshua, Moses and the Land*; idem, *Joshua Retold*. In the case of Auld, after long period of his study on the "so-called Deuteronomistic history," he started to think negatively about the existence of Deuteronomist. For this, see A. G. Auld, "The Former Prophets," in McKenzie and Graham, eds., *The Hebrew Bible*, 53–68; idem, "The Deuteronomist Between History and Theology," in *Congress Volume: Oslo, 1998* (ed. A. Lemaire; Leiden: Brill, 2000), 353–67; idem, "The Deuteronomist and the Former Prophets, or What Makes the Former Prophets Deuteronomistic?," in *Those Elusive Deuteronomists* (ed. L. S. Schearing and S. L. McKenzie; JSOTSup 268; Sheffield: Sheffield Academic, 1999), 116–26; idem, "Samuel, Numbers, and the Yahwist-Question," in *Abschied vom Jahwisten* (ed. Jan Christian Gertz, Konrad Schmid and Markus Witte; Berlin: de Gruyter, 2002), 233–46.

For F. M. Cross and his Harvard school, see F. M. Cross, *Canaanite Myth and Hebrew Epic: Essays in the History of the Religion of Israel* (Cambridge, Mass.: Harvard University Press), 1973; R. D. Nelson, *The Double Redaction of the Deuteronomistic History* (Sheffield: JSOT, 1981); B. Peckham, *The Composition of the Deuteronomistic History* (Atlanta: Scholars Press, 1985); G. N. Knoppers, *Two Nations Under God: The Deuteronomic History of Solomon and the Dual Monarchies* (2 vols.; HSM 52–53; Atlanta: Scholars Press, 1993–94).

challenges raised by the LXX, even such investigations do not supply detailed explanation on the literary history of Josh 3–4. In particular, they have not explained clearly a good number of repetitions, discontinuities, and inconsistencies in the text. Furthermore, they do not offer any detailed and distinct analysis of the literary history and of the various strata of materials existing behind this text. Even though this kind of study succeeds in highlighting the importance of the LXX and in showing the priority of the LXX at some points, it has not attempted to produce a retroversion of the Hebrew *Vorlage* of LXX Josh 3–4, nor has it tried to reconstruct the literary history of this narrative from the OG *Vorlage* or find layers of materials in this text.

Therefore, the purpose of the present study is to reconstruct the literary history of Josh 3–4, and find out the various layers of materials behind this text, while thoroughly considering those challenges provided by OG *Vorlage*.

In this book, we will also discuss one of the recent trends in the diachronic way of reading the text. P. Volz and W. Rudolph attempted to show the non-existence of E,[68] and in a recently published book, *Abschied vom Jahwisten*, A. G. Auld, J. Blenkinsopp, E. Blum, J. C. Gertz, W. Johnstone, R. G. Kratz, T. C. Römer, K. Schmid, and M. Witte reject the existence of a Yahwist (J). They prefer to call material which does not belong to P simply "non-Priestly," and suggest new directions for literary criticism.[69] One of these specific features is to read the Pentateuch and the Former Prophets in reverse order. According to Blum and Van Seters, the non-Priestly portions of Genesis–Numbers were written on the basis of Deuteronomy and the Former Prophets. Van Seters keeps the name "Yahwist" but his Yahwist is also post-Deuteronomistic.[70] For Auld, "The Book of Two Houses" (the story of the house of David in Jerusalem and of the house that Solomon built for Yahweh there) is the root work of the story of Israel before the monarchy.[71]

For the purpose of investigating these recent challenges and reading the literary history of Josh 3–4 in a diachronic way, the writer proceeds to the next two studies.

68. P. Volz and W. Rudolph, *Der Elohist als Erzähler: Ein Irrweg der Pentateuchkritik?* (Giessen: Töpelmann, 1933); Rudolph, *Der "Elohist" von Exodus bis Josua*.

69. Gertz, Schmid and Witte, eds., *Abschied vom Jahwisten*.

70. Van Seters, "The Pentateuch," 3–49.

71. Auld, "The Former Prophets," 53–68; idem, *Kings Without Privilege* (Edinburgh: T. & T. Clark, 1994); idem, "The Deuteronomist Between History and Theology," 353–67; idem, *I & II Samuel* (OTL; Louisville: Westminster John Knox, 2011), 9–14.

First, what position does this text hold in the setting of the wider Old Testament? Especially, how do we compare the ark story in this text with that in the Pentateuch[72] and other Former Prophets and Chronicles?[73]

Second, how do we compare this text with the crossing of the Reed Sea in Exod 13:17–14:31 and with Elijah and Elisha crossing the river in 2 Kgs 2?

There are a number of issues which need to be resolved before we read this literary composite.

Chapter 2 introduces the synchronic reading of the text by Polzin, Hawk, Mitchell, and Winther-Nielsen, and attempts to uncover the problems in applying their methods to this complicated text, while offering some critique for sympathetic readings.

Chapter 3 investigates the differences between the MT and the LXX of Josh 3–4 through text-critical analysis. It reconstructs the Hebrew *Vorlage* of LXX Josh 3–4.

As a preliminary study to read the literary history of Josh 3–4 in a diachronic way, my aim here is to consider what position this text holds in the setting of the wider context of the ark narrative and water-crossing stories in the Old Testament.

Chapter 4 compares the ark story in this text with that in the Pentateuch and other Former Prophets and Chronicles.

Chapter 5 compares this text with the crossing of the Reed Sea in Exod 13:17–14:31 and with Elijah and Elisha crossing the river in 2 Kgs 2.

With the help of the above investigations, Chapter 6 attempts to read the literary history of Josh 3–4 based on the Hebrew *Vorlage* and the MT of Josh 3–4. One other major purpose of this chapter is to find materials which exist behind the text of the MT and LXX, via a diachronic route, revealing a literary history. This study aims to find in this complex narrative various layers of materials in much the same way as archaeologists or geologists explore the strata they study.

In conclusion, my aim here will be to identify the layers of Josh 3–4 in the context of existing academic research. I will also discuss the limitations of Polzin's synchronic study, which is regarded as one of the best sympathetic readings of the Joshua text, in that it reads only from the final text of the MT.

72. Exod 25:10–22; 33:1–6; 37:1–9; Num 10:33–36; Deut 10:1–9.

73. 1 Sam 4:1b–7:2; 2 Sam 6//1 Chr 13–16; 1 Kgs 8:1–11//2 Chr 5.

Chapter 2

Synchronic Readings of Joshua 3–4

Since Polzin opened new horizons in biblical research, there have been many synchronic studies attempting to prove the consistency and unity of theme in the book of Joshua. In this chapter, we will examine the methodologies of some notable holistic readers, namely, Polzin, Hawk, Mitchell, and Winther-Nielsen, the differences and similarities between them, and whether the other three go through the door which Polzin opened. Furthermore, we will investigate how their methodologies are applied to Josh 3–4, one of the most complex texts in the book of Joshua, and how they explain the two different descriptions of the stones in the middle of the Jordan and on the other side of Jordan. Finally, we will examine to what extent these holistic readers recognize the differences between the MT and the LXX versions of our text.

2.1. *Polzin,* Moses and the Deuteronomist[1]

In his book *Moses and the Deuteronomist*, Polzin presents a literary analysis of *Deuteronomy*, *Joshua*, and *Judges*. His book contains the description of a debate between traditional historical and contemporary literary criticism. In this volume, Polzin holds that while a diachronic historical-critical analysis of biblical texts is necessary for an adequate understanding (p. 3), a preliminary literary analysis of biblical material is necessary for a scholarly understanding of what this ancient text means (p. 5). According to him, "[t]he priority of synchrony (in the dynamic sense emphasized especially by the Russian Structuralists) over diachrony is not in rank but only in operation" (p. 6). Citing Krystyna Pomorska, he asserts that "if we move in the opposite direction, basing synchronic analyses on historical studies, *we always run a risk of applying ready-made theories to them*" (p. 6, Polzin's italics). He maintains that we have to make a literary analysis the starting point of our efforts

1. R. M. Polzin, *Moses and the Deuteronomist: A Literary Study of the Deuteronomistic History* (New York: Seabury, 1980).

to gain an intimate knowledge of the literary work (p. 6). He writes that his assumption is not based upon previous historical-critical analysis. However, from the beginning he assumes that the Deuteronomistic History (DH) is a unified literary work (p. 18). For him, the so-called Deuteronomist means a person or persons fulfilling an authorial or editorial role, who is/are responsible for the final form of the DH (p. 18). He goes so far as to argue that a "prophet like Moses" is the so-called Deuteronomist himself (p. 61).

Following Voloshinov's linguistic analytical method, Polzin applies the distinction of direct and indirect discourse to the so-called DH. He contends that almost all of the book of Deuteronomy is composed of *reported speech*, mostly in direct discourse and mostly of Moses. On the other hand, Joshua–2 Kings predominantly consist of *reporting speech*, that of the narrator, with a significantly smaller amount of reported speech (p. 19). In reported speech what God has prophesied concerning Israel is emphasized, while in reporting speech how God's word has been exactly fulfilled in Israel's history is underscored by the narrator (p. 19).

Polzin suggests that the reader should distinguish voices, for example, Yahweh's, Moses', a prophet's, and the narrator's (who delivers their voices).

According to Polzin,

> ...on the basic plane of a work's ideology, a proposed framework ought to be able to describe which of the text's utterances or words express its dominant ideological voice(s), which its subordinated or dependent ideological voice or voices, and which utterances express both kinds of voices. (p. 24)

Based on the Russian Bakhtin's formalist theory, Polzin appears to maintain that when a narrator's and hero's voice overlap each other, a distinct ideological perspective is claimed. Polzin argues that it is possible to find an "ultimate semantic authority" which could either be a single voice or two or more voices, by analyzing the composition of the text (p. 20).

According to Polzin, in the book of *Deuteronomy*, Moses is both God's mouthpiece and the hero of the book. Here, the narrator, who delivers Moses' word to the people of Israel plays the important role of the author of the so-called Deuteronomic history. He holds that there can be a tension between the voice of Moses and that of the narrator, with the result that the narrator's words weaken Moses' authority (p. 35). By inserting editorial expressions such as "to this day" (Deut 2:22) when he conveys Moses' word, the narrator intercepts the flow of the passage and makes the readers bend an ear to his evaluation. Polzin asserts that the voice, in support of Moses' authority, has an ideological tendency that emphasizes God's mercy. Nevertheless, the voice that weakens Moses' authority involves an ideological tendency highlighting Yahweh's justice (p. 39). Polzin insists that the book of *Deuteronomy*, in its ideological and surface composition, provides the reader with a bird's-eye view of the so-called DH (p. 72).

Polzin observes that the book of Joshua is composed by the formation of direct discourse between Yahweh and Joshua delivered indirectly through the agency of the narrator. He insists that the purpose of the book of Joshua is to show how Moses' law is applied. That is to say, in the course of Joshua's conquest of the land the narrator states the estrangement of the people from Yahweh's word (p. 144). Using the Russian formalist Uspensky's perspective, Polzin analyzes the narratives in the book of Joshua in the dimension of phraseological, spatio-temporal, psychological, and ideological aspects (pp. 73–145). Polzin states that the ultimate and semantic authority of the book of Joshua can be established by finding a dominant ideological trend in the complex composition of various voices. Polzin contends that Israel's identity as both citizen and alien supplies the interpretive clue to the dominant ideological perspective of the book of Joshua. The constant concern of the text with "exceptional outsiders," (Rahab, the exempted animals of Ai, the trickster Gibeonites, the women, dependants, Levites, or especially the transjordanian tribes of Israel), shows their functional role throughout the story as *types of Israel* (p. 145). According to Polzin, God's mercy and justice function together. He claims that the relationship between God's mercy and justice can be understood by Israel's self-understanding as both citizen and alien within the community of the Lord. As the narrative describes Israel settling within the land, it emphasizes how much of the "outside," both communally and territorially is "inside" Israel. Doubtless the Deuteronomic narrator's audience, which appears from the text to be situated outside Israel-the-land, could take comfort in the realization that they had always been outsiders, even when inside the land. At the same time, the experience of the Transjordanian tribes could offer a model for an Israelite community, even though they lived outside the land that God had given to their fathers. Thus, in spite of all their deficiencies, the fact that the community of Israel was still alive is the gist of all of the ideological aspects of the story. This confusing fact was something that authoritarian dogmatism could not explain easily (p. 145).

In the postscript, which is the fifth part of the book, Polzin traces the hermeneutical implications of his study. According to him, the so-called Deuteronomist, who does not always support Moses' authority, does not allow immediacy, transparency, and univalency for the text: subsequent revisionary interpretation not only does not recover the original word of

God, but makes clear that that is impossible (p. 206). Polzin holds that modern historical criticism has a Hirschian perspective, which is to say, that a text has a single meaning that is the intent of the original author (p. 211). On the contrary, Gadamer, like Deuteronomy, allows for freedom, multivalence, and contradictory meanings. By applying Gadamer's theory, he appears to argue that the text is open to any possible meaning. However, it seems to be that each text has its own distinct meaning within its special situation. Furthermore, there may be layers of both long tradition and redaction lying under a text. The research on Josh 3–4, one of the most complex texts in the book of Joshua, reveals more about these questions.

Polzin devotes "...an inordinate amount of space to an analysis of Josh 3:1–5:1"[2] (p. 92) and pays "special attention to this narrative to illustrate how powerfully it can affect and effect the ideological perspectives of the book" (p. 94). He contends that "the ritual nature" of 3:1–5:1 allows the Deuteronomist to construct a highly intricate and amazingly precise compositional structure. According to him, the programmed and stylized aspects of *a cultic procession* offer the narrator a vast array of literary devices that interconnect the various surface points of view of the story to a degree that approaches geometric precision (p. 94).[3] Maintaining that the chronological discrepancy between 3:2 and 4:19 is not a "crucial problem," and does not play a "key role," he insists that it is not so meaningful to invest hermeneutic energy in this question (pp. 91–92). He regards the event of crossing the Jordan as a cultic procession based on the chronological contents in this narrative and 4:19.

Following the Russian formalist Uspensky's view, he analyzes the temporal, spatial, psychological, and phraseological aspects of this narrative and pays attention to "...the highly complex nature of the literary interconnections that [seem to] make up its unity" (p. 94).

First, he tries to explain the complexity of this text by "a frequent and often puzzling shift in temporal point of view" (p. 94). The narrative of 3:1–5:1 shifts back and forth in its temporal perspective. According to Polzin, the narrative in these two chapters is composed of a "chain of eleven representative events":

1. Journey from Shittim to the Jordan;
2. Procession to the river bank;
3. The priests carrying the Ark enter the river;

2. Polzin attaches Josh 5:1 to the "Jordan crossing story." For this, see the next chapter.

3. Here Polzin does not consider textual issues raised by scholars. For this, see Chapter 6.

4. The waters pile up;
5. The people enter the river;
6. The priests stop in the middle of the river;
7. The people cross over;
8. Joshua has twelve stones set up at Gilgal;
9. Joshua has twelve more stones set up in the middle of the Jordan;
10. The priests carrying the Ark come up out of the Jordan;
11. The waters of the Jordan return to their place.

And these events are divided into five episodes:

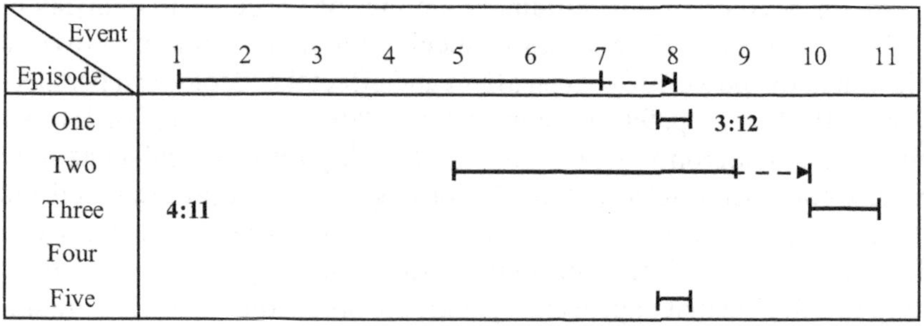

The first seven events in ch. 3 (from the story that "all Israelites set out from Shittim and came to the Jordan" [3:1] to the report that "all Israel passed over on dry ground until the whole nation had crossed the river" [3:17]) constitute the first episode. Event 8 (4:1–8) is the second episode, related to God's command to choose twelve men (4:2) and the setting down of the twelve stones in the Israelite camp. Here he argues that 3:11–12 prefigures episode 2 and thus creates a literary connection between the two episodes (p. 95). The material in 4:9–14 comprises the third episode. He says that "[t]he temporal limits of this third episode extend both before and beyond those of the second episode." Furthermore, this episode retraces certain events that had occurred within the first two episodes. Here again, he contends that 4:11 is also "...a literary foreshadowing of the central event of the fourth episode (4:15–18), that is, the priests carrying the ark coming out of the Jordan" (p. 96).[4] Finally, the fifth episode (4:19–5:1) comprises the same eighth event as the second event. Polzin argues that this is a temporal shift backwards to replay 4:1–8 from different spatial and psychological points of view (p. 97). According to him, 3:12 and 4:11 are also "literary signals" that

4. There are some major textual differences between MT and LXX Josh 3:12; 4:2, 11. We will discuss this in Chapters 3 and 6.

shift in time to highlight the setting up of the twelve stones (4:1–8) and the coming up of the priests (4:15–18) (p. 97).

Further to the above point, Polzin notices two examples of temporal shift in point of view that are directly reflected on the phraseological level of the text (p. 97). Noticing the shift of verbal form from the perfective to an imperfective of עבר in 3:17 and 4:10, Polzin insists that in Josh 3, mobility, change, and transition are emphasized, while Josh 4 is focused on the stationary status of the ark and the priests (98–9).

Second, the shift of the narrator's spatial point of view can also explain the incongruities of this story (Josh 3:1–5:1). According to Polzin, in 3:1–4:14 the narrator takes his perspective from the point of view of the Israelites entering the land, but then in 4:15–5:1 he takes his narrating position from the point of view of a non-Israelite watching the progress of this miraculous procession (p. 101). For this purpose, he especially focuses on the second episode of 4:1–8. Noticing the threefold indication, "from here," "from the middle of the Jordan," and "where the priests' feet stand firm," Polzin asserts that, although it is not clear where Yahweh is while speaking to Joshua in 4:3, Joshua and the twelve men must be together with the priests, where he should command the men to carry the twelve stones to the camp (p. 99–100).[5] Additionally, holding that in 3:1–4:14 the narrator looks at the Israelites from inside the Promised Land and in 4:15–5:1 from outside (p. 101), he tries to explain the discontinuity between those two parts.

His attempt to explain the text from a spatial point of view is closely related to his third attempt to understand it from a psychological point of view. According to Polzin, 3:1–4:14 is narrated from the perspective of the Israelites, who take part in the procession of crossing the Jordan and 4:15–5:1 from the invaded non-Israelites, who are observing this miraculous event.

Fourth, according to Polzin, the phraseological composition of this narrative, that is, the pattern of prediction/fulfillment, command/fulfillment, and prefiguration/fulfillment can also help to explain the intricacy of this text. Putting it another way, he argues that all three variations are repetitive structures of the type "anticipation/confirmation." He also says that the *antiphonal pattern* of the story mirrors the ritual nature of this narrative (p. 105).

Fifth, the ambiguities of this narrative cannot be resolved by only one of these elements. Polzin contends that the interrelationships between the various compositional planes (temporal, spatial, psychological, and

5. Polzin again oversees some differences between the MT and the LXX in this verse. For this, see Chapters 3 and 6.

phraseological analyses) offer important instances where the various surface planes of the story concur (p. 107). According to him, in this narrative there is no theme of God's justice and mercy. The issues are limited to the hermeneutic problems involved in the fulfillment of God's word (p. 110). Here, finally, he tries to explain the difficulty of the twelve stones set up in the middle of the Jordan in 4:9. He holds that even though it is forbidden to add or take away from what God commanded in Deut 13:1, the voice of "critical traditionalism" neutralizes the dogmatic voice of 13:1 and "every interpretation of God's word is an adding to it or a taking away from it." Thus, the stones Joshua set up in the Jordan without God's command are "a testament to the necessity of change and mobility in the understanding, interpretation, and application of God's word" (p. 109).[6]

As we examined above, by using Russian literary theory, especially Uspensky's theory, Polzin adequately explains many of the complicated problems in the narrative of Josh 3–4. His attempt to read one of the most difficult and complex texts in the book of Joshua from the perspective of temporal, spatial, phraseological, and psychological aspects demonstrates the merit of synchronic methodology. His literary theory explains a lot of problems in this narrative comparatively well and defends the text plausibly.

However, his literary reading reveals some problems in understanding this text. In his study of this narrative, the temporal aspect is quite important. In addition, he regards the event of crossing the Jordan as a cultic procession based on the chronological contents in this narrative and 4:19, as we have seen in the previous section. Yet he fails to pay proper attention to the chronological discrepancy between 3:2 and 4:19, and by investing no hermeneutic energy into finding a solution, he stands at variance with his own understanding of this narrative. Problematically, he seeks to read the final form of this narrative as a literary unity without noticing the problems behind the text. Furthermore, Polzin claims that the shift from perfective to imperfective use of עבר in 3:17 and 4:10 signifies mobility, change and transition in Josh 3 and the stationary status of the ark and the priests in Josh 4. However, we learn that in 3:17 the ark and the priests are stationary and in 4:15–18 the priests come up from the water, which contradicts Polzin's argument. In fact, in his previous explanation of the shift of temporal point of view, he held that 4:11 anticipates 4:15–18 and emphasized the coming up of the priests and the ark. Therefore, even though his attempt to identify the temporal

6. Here again, Polzin does not pay attention to the difference between MT and LXX Josh 4:9. We will discuss this further in Chapters 3 and 6.

shift in verbal form is new, it is an oversimplified understanding of these two chapters.

Furthermore, his attempt to explain the incongruities of this story from the shift of the narrator's spatial and psychological point of view also has some weak points. Focusing on 4:1–8, Polzin holds that in 3:1–4:14 the narrator takes his position from the point of view of the Israelites entering the land, but in 4:15–5:1 from the point of view of a non-Israelite watching the miraculous procession. For this purpose, he especially focuses on the second episode of 4:1–8; however, the LXX does not support Polzin's theory.[7] In addition to this critical issue, a careful reading of 4:10b–11 reveals that until all that Moses commanded was completed, the priests stood firm and the people crossed in a hurry. Although in 4:1–8 it seems that the people are already on the western side of the river, in 4:10b–11a they are in the middle of the Jordan with the priests while the commands are completed. There is a distinct discrepancy in a spatial point of view between these two sections.

Moreover, Polzin's position that 3:1–4:14 is narrated from the Israelites' perspective and 4:15–5:1 from that of the invaded non-Israelites, also reveals some problems. If we read 4:15–18 again, focusing on the dialogue between Yahweh and Joshua, the narrator describes the coming up of the priests from the perspective of Israel. In 4:19–24 also, noticing the communication between Joshua and the Israelite ("You"), the narrator explains the miraculous event of crossing the Jordan from the Israelite perspective. The expression "all people on earth," which Polzin argues shows a non-Israelite perspective, is that of the third person, which is referred to from an Israelite perspective. It is also difficult to hold that 5:1 is written from a non-Israelite perspective. In this part foreign kings are expressed in the third-person form as "all the kings of the Amorites that were beyond the Jordan to the west, and all the kings of the Canaanites that were by the sea." In 5:1, the Israelite narrator tries to highlight God's power by the event of crossing the Jordan which would ultimately make Israel respect and fear Yahweh. The above points show that Polzin's attempt to explain this text from a psychological perspective based on Uspensky's literary theory is also problematic.

Thus, one must insist that his attempt to read 3:1–4:14 and 4:15–5:1 as a consistent and coherent text from temporal, spatial, and psychological points of view is quite implausible. The relationship between 3:1–4:14 and 4:15–5:1, especially that between 4:1–8 and 4:20–24 will be examined in Chapters 5 and 6 on literary history, in relationship with Exod 13:17–14:31. In addition, Polzin's explanation of the twelve stones

7. We will discuss these text-critical issues further in Chapter 3 and 6.

in the middle of the Jordan and on the bank of the Jordan is insufficient. Holding that the stones Joshua set up in the Jordan without God's command show the necessity of flexibility in understanding, interpretation, and application of God's word, he makes a good attempt to explain the twelve stones in the middle of the Jordan figuratively. However, his explanation cannot cover all the problems of the two different stone stories. He seems to evade the difficulties of these two parts in an allegorical way. An expression similar to ושתים עשׂרה אבנים of 4:9 appears in 4:20, namely, ואת שׁתים עשׂרה האבנים האלה. The stories of twelve stones at Gilgal and in the Jordan are remarkably different and 4:9 appears to have been added to this part by a redactor.[8] Above all, one of the biggest problems in Polzin's study is that he overlooks the text-critical issues in this text. By not considering the differences between the MT and the LXX in Josh 3–4 at all and by trying to apply a literary reading only from the final shape of the MT text instead, he fails to read properly this complex narrative.

In conclusion, Polzin seems to suggest an epoch-making direction to biblical research in order to understand and interpret the text as it is through literary reading. He applies his intricate methodology to Josh 3–4 and explains rather well a number of problems in this Jordan-crossing story. However, he reveals some problems in attempting to explain the inconsistencies and discrepancies in Josh 3–4 *only* by synchronic literary reading and fails to understand the literary history behind the ancient document, especially by not considering the differences between the MT and the LXX. Therefore, one can concur that his study provides, as he says, a "preliminary" basis for the understanding of a complex biblical text quite well. However, his study is limited in that he does not suggest any "adequate" and "diachronic" reading to be followed.

2.2. *Hawk,* Every Promise Fulfilled[9]

In his book *Every Promise Fulfilled*, Hawk also adopts a literary approach. He rejects using the traditional historical-critical methodology, with its understanding of the book of *Joshua*'s "incoherence as a consequence of a complex history of composition" (pp. 15–16). By confining his reading to the plot, he tries to see more clearly the relationship between the configuration of the story and its tensions in order to develop a strategy for understanding them (p. 17). In tracing the plot(s)

8. This will also be discussed further in Chapters 3 and 6.

9. L. D. Hawk, *Every Promise Fulfilled: Contesting Plots in Joshua* (Literary Currents in Biblical Interpretation; Louisville: Westminster John Knox, 1991).

of Joshua, he tries to keep three levels of plot in mind: the framework, the arrangement of incidents and patterns, and the underlying structure which is to be understood in terms of the mind that does the organizing (p. 19).

According to Hawk, the dynamic quality of a plot is not limited to the text. The interpretive processes take place between text and reader, and the efforts to achieve agreement between events appear on the reader's side (pp. 26–27). He uses Paul Ricoeur's theory, which describes the operation of plot in terms of a three-fold mimesis: $mimesis_1$–prefiguration, $mimesis_2$–emplotment, $mimesis_3$–refiguration (p. 27). Hawk holds that by these three aspects, one can better understand the way a plot operates. The first reason is that plot offers a design, which shows the significance of each event and its relationship to the whole (p. 28). Plot also supplies causality, which is the primary means of connection. Second, plots give time the impression of being an ordered sequence of events and thus satisfy the human demand for coherence (p. 32). Finally, a plot gives a clear sense of an ending—it leads events toward an end or resolution (p. 28). Utilizing Kermode's view of plot endings to enhance his examination, Hawk argues that the end supplies a destination for the configuration of events, a goal toward which the plot is directed. This movement toward the end provides the plot with its dynamism (p. 35).

Now, having described these three aspects of the plot, Hawk goes on to deal with some other elements. He says that all narratives contain some element of obscurity (p. 36) for pragmatic reasons: tension and suspense are important elements for capturing and holding a reader's interest. The feints and detours, the obstacles and indeterminacies are also parts of a plot that mirror our experience of the world in which answers and meanings are rarely explicit (p. 36). Furthermore, Hawk introduces the notion of desire as "a primary metaphor for understanding the operation of plot in Joshua" (p. 40). In reading Joshua, he is concerned with two fundamental questions: "[W]hat form does desire assume?… [H]ow does desire shape the contours of its plots?" (p. 40). In order to answer these questions, he pays attention to the issues of explicit commentary on the story, to repetition of motifs and key terms, to the presentation and resolution of the disruptive aspects of the story, and to the way the story is brought to a close (p. 40).

In Chapters 3 to 6 of his study, Hawk gives his specific analysis of the plot of the book of Joshua. By paying attention to "the conquest story of the land" (chs. 1–12), he starts to apply his theory to the book of Joshua (p. 43). Hawk argues that the two summary texts on victories in Northern Canaan (11:12–15) and conquests west of the Jordan (11:16–23) present "the configurational agenda which characterizes the entire book" (p. 43).

The tension here is between a desire to depict Israel's complete success on the one hand, and disruptive information which reports significant failures on the other (p. 51). By this, Hawk identifies two different kinds of plots: *ostensive plots* and *opposing plots* (p. 53). Ostensive plots orient the story "in the direction of fulfillment." The ostensive plot is that of obedience and integrity. Unlike the former, opposing plots are composed of "dissonant patterns which oppose the movement toward fulfillment." The type of opposing plot is that of disobedience and of fragmentation (p. 53). Overall, Hawk contends that the dynamic created by ostensive and opposing plots is a struggle to gain mastery over textual dissonances so that concordance may be established and the desired end achieved (p. 53).

The story of Rahab is a good example of the distinctiveness of his idea. While modern scholars have viewed Rahab in a positive light (p. 60), Hawk maintains that Rahab, a woman of Canaan and a prostitute, plays a threatening role towards Israel in this book (p. 61). Hawk sees the story of Rahab as evidence of disobedience to Yahweh's command that all the inhabitants of Canaan be destroyed by Israel. At the same time, according to Hawk, the story of the crossing of the Jordan shows the plot of obedient Israel as it enters the land to obtain Yahweh's promise (p. 71). The episodes of Achan and the Gibeonites also show the two conflicting lines, which "compete and move the text along, mirroring the contest between Israel and Canaan" (p. 92). These stories oscillate between obedience and disobedience, and in the process create a sense of ambiguity and tension about the fulfillment of the promise (p. 93).

Hawk also discusses the plot in terms of integrity and fragmentation. According to him, the plot of integrity points to the desired end of fulfillment and rest in the land. A fragmenting plot, however, leads to a different end—an end in which Israel fails to possess all the Promised Land. This plot is apparent by disruptive notes about the presence of non-Israelite peoples within the borders of Israel. The disruptions of this fragmenting counter-plot are distinct throughout Josh 13–21 (p. 100).

Furthermore, Hawk discusses the endings and ambiguity in the book of Joshua. He asserts that in a story's ending, conventionally, patterns are completed, connections between events clarified, and tensions resolved. However, as Joshua moves toward a conclusion, tensions are actually intensified, not diminished. In the final part of the book (Josh 22–24), these discords are finally given explicit expression, and the contest of plots moves into the foreground (p. 117). Here, Hawk introduces the structuralist analyses of Polzin and Jobling on the report of the eastern tribes' return and their erection of an altar. They show that a concern with the integrity of Israel is operative at a deeper level (p. 120). In Polzin's view, the central problem of the narrative is the question of who belongs to Israel. Jobling also notes that the episode is really concerned with the integrity of Israel and that building the altar is therefore disobedient as well as divisive (p. 121). According to Hawk, the altar is an ambiguous symbol. The book of Joshua concludes with a short appendix, a series of burial reports (24:29–33) (p. 138). The closure of the book of Joshua comes with the death of Joshua and ostensibly affirms the fulfillment of desire; an obedient Israel is now settled in the land (p. 139). However, the end of the ostensive plots is not entirely successful in bringing about the sense of an ending. The many examples of transgression, division, and apathy, as well as the predictions of Joshua and Moses, point out that the ending yet resides in the future (pp. 139–40). The gap between fulfillment and unfulfillment challenges the reader and exposes the desire for coherence and satisfaction (p. 140).

In his concluding chapter, Hawk concentrates on the nature of the book of Joshua, especially from the perspective of *desire*. He maintains that within the context of the story, Israel's clear desire is for the land (p. 141). However, as soon as Israel enters the land, Israel begins to succumb to its temptations (p. 143). Yahweh's desire is for Israel, especially for Israel's loyalty. This desire appears throughout the narrative and is apparent in Yahweh's endurance; even though Israel breaks some prohibitions, Yahweh nevertheless continues to aid Israel. The narrator's desire appears to be an ending that affirms an obedient Israel dwelling without rivals in the Promised Land. Yet the narrator also supplies instances of Israel's disobedience and fragmentation, often immediately after affirmations of success or obedience. These metaphors become increasingly difficult as the story develops (pp. 143–44).

According to Hawk, such operation of plots in the book of Joshua mirrors one's own investment in coherent representations of reality. An ostensible framework is provided, incoherences are repeatedly countered, and an affirmative ending is offered. Hawk insists that the operation of plot in Joshua, in a sense, reflects the difficulty of applying dogma to the experience of life (p. 145).

Hawk pays some attention to Josh 3–4 and tries to apply his theory to this narrative. Explaining the elements of plot and the plot as design, Hawk contends that Josh 3–4 is an allusion (and the account of Israel's crossing the Jordan contains many allusions, implicit and explicit) to the Exodus and events on Mount Sinai. In connection with the crossing of the Reed Sea, the narrator expands the meaning of the present Jordan crossing in its current context. The experiences of the present generation of Israelites, for example, are connected with those of their parents and their ancestors. The narrator makes these linkages by thematic allusions to Sinai (the erection of twelve stones, the three days' wait, the call to consecration) and by means of speeches (Joshua's connection of the crossing of the Reed Sea and the Jordan) (pp. 29–30).

Next, Hawk observes the portrait of the obedient Israel in this narrative. According to him, "...Israel crosses the Jordan in strict obedience to the words of Moses..." (p. 71): this story counters the portrait of the disobedient Israel in Josh 2 by the most powerful image of strict obedience to the words of Moses. This episode is structured by a detailed command/execution framework which reinforces and advances the plot of obedient Israel. At various points in this narrative, Joshua gives commands and instructions (or Yahweh gives commands through Joshua), and the narrator describes the execution of these commands. The obedience of Israel is also stressed by the ark of the covenant, which is given central place in the narrative. As Israel follows the ark, the symbol of Yahweh's leadership, into the Jordan, its obedience is likewise symbolized and affirmed. The drying up of the Jordan and the return of the waters by the entrance and departure of the ark confirm again the connection between Israel's obedience and the successful appropriation of the promise of the land; a connection which Joshua explicitly confirms in 3:10–13 (pp. 71–72). Here, like Polzin, Hawk also pays attention to the verb עבר, but in different ways. The root עבר, which means "to cross over or through," occurs 20 times in Josh 3 and 4. Of course, given the context, its general meaning is not surprising. However, the word can also mean a darker crossing—the transgression of the covenant with Yahweh (Josh 7:11, 13; 23:16; Judg 2:20; 2 Kgs 18:12). Its repetition, therefore, is a reminder that the disobedience of Israel concerning Rahab still causes tension between God and Israel and is still to be resolved (p. 72).

Furthermore, the narrative of crossing the Jordan symbolizes the desire for integrity. Hawk maintains that in the account of the Jordan crossing (3:1–4:24) the struggle between integrity and fragmentation is apparent. The crossing is undertaken by "all Israel" (3:1, 7, 17; 4:14), "the entire nation" (3:17; 4:1, 11). Israel must enter the land as one unit, even if it should be divided later so that some may return to the Transjordan (p. 94). The event of crossing the Jordan also symbolizes Israel's transformation into a nation of ordered people. Hawk argues that by crossing the Jordan, Israel moves from the place of chaos to the place of order (p. 95). However, the sense of integrity is muddled by the way in which the narrative describes this event, which is apparent in the erection of the twelve stones.[10] He asks: "How many events does the

10. Hawk admits that "Nowhere is the confusion more apparent than in the erection of the twelve stones" (p. 96).

narrative refer to, one or many? And where is the memorial? At Gilgal? In the middle of the Jordan?" (p. 96).

He continues to say that, textually speaking, the fact that the Jordan is crossed not once but many times is more significant. Instead of describing the crossing in a straightforward way, the narrator appears to take the reader back and forth across the Jordan (p. 96). The many textual crossings of the Jordan introduce ambiguity. This move is accomplished by the shift of perspective, by emphasizing "the other side." The movement back and forth across the Jordan blurs its function as a boundary (p. 97).

In the Jordan crossing, the reader encounters an apparently climactic event in which Israel shows complete accord with Yahweh. However, incoherence and incongruity continue in this narrative, creating a sense of ambiguity and disorientation. The episode reaches its conclusion, not by a straightforward and purposeful advance, but in an intermingled way filled with intricacies and repetitions. Beneath the surface of the text the contesting plots of integrity and fragmentation push the narrative towards disparate conclusions (p. 98).

Like Polzin's synchronic perspective, examined above, Hawk also suggests new directions for research on the book of Joshua. Hawk explains the difficulties and complexities of the book by applying literary theory and paying attention to the conflicting plots: conquest and compromise, obedience and disobedience, integrity and fragmentation, endings and ambiguity. Here, his research is quite practical in comparison with the old historical reading. He does not try to harmonize and resolve those inconsistencies, but just holds that the plot tensions show the difficulty of applying dogma to the experience of life. His study is quite plausible, but does not appear to satisfy readers who want a clear literary closure of the book of Joshua.

Hawk does not provide a detailed analysis of every unit in the book of Joshua. He only focuses his study on the units closely related with his main concern of contesting plot. He also supplies a unique interpretation of a particular unit, with which others would sometimes not agree.

His reading also shows some similarities with Polzin's and in some parts seems to be based on his work. Both of them make use of literary theory when interpreting a biblical text. Though Polzin borrows the methodologies from the Russian structuralist and formalist literary interpretation theories, Hawk mainly focuses his study on the way the plot functions. In explaining the endings and ambiguity in the book of Joshua, Hawk introduces the structuralist theory of Polzin. Therefore, Hawk's approach seems to have had some point of contact with Polzin's structuralist theory. As well as that, they both use a specific hermeneutic method: Polzin uses Gadamer's theory and Hawk employs Paul Ricoeur's theory. However, more than anything else, they are very much similar in that both of them focus on how Moses' law, especially חרם, is applied in the book of Joshua. Of course, there is some partial difference in how Polzin understands the success and failure in the application of חרם from the perspective of God's justice and mercy, whereas Hawk looks upon them as the difference between obedience and disobedience, and fulfillment and lack of fulfillment. Polzin expresses the relationship between fulfillment and lack of fulfillment of Moses' law as the difference between authoritative dogmatism and traditional criticism. Hawk understands it from the perspective that applying dogma to one's life is difficult. These two opinions are the converse of each other, in that authoritative dogmatism demands the perfect application of dogma in life, whereas traditional criticism recognizes a gulf between dogma and life.

Hawk applies his general plot-focused approach in the book of Joshua to the complex narrative of crossing the Jordan and has some merit in understanding this text in the context of contesting plot. However, he shows some limitations in reading this narrative: first, he seems to be greatly indebted to Polzin. Hawk pays attention to a detailed command–execution framework. Polzin also applied the framework of prediction–fulfillment, command–fulfillment, prefiguration–fulfillment to understand Josh 3–4. Hawk shows some interest in the Hebrew verb עבר, as does Polzin. But his explanation is quite extraordinary. It remains to be seen whether other scholars will agree with his argument that עבר can also mean a darker crossing—the transgression of the covenant with Yahweh and reminds us of the disobedient Israel in the previous episode of Rahab. He also pays attention to the repetition of crossing the Jordan by the shift of perspective, which appears to be influenced by Polzin's temporal, spatial, phraseological, and psychological shift in perspective. Second, he does not suggest any clear explanation of this complex narrative, especially regarding the two different stories of the twelve stones in the middle and on the other side of the Jordan. He explains this complex story as a symbol of integrity. The sense of integrity is, however, confused by the conflicting reports of the whereabouts of the twelve stones. Hawk asks some important questions regarding where the memorial is and how many events the narrative refers to, but he does not provide any solution to them. Third, he does not consider the differences between the MT and the LXX at all, but applies his literary method only to the final form of the MT. Like Polzin, this is another limitation of Hawk's plot-based approach. We will discuss this further in Chapters 3 and 6.

2.3. *Mitchell,* Together in the Land: A Reading of the Book of Joshua[11]

Mitchell begins his study on the book of Joshua by highlighting a puzzling contradiction. According to him, in the book of Joshua there are, on the one hand, commands to slaughter all of the inhabitants of the land, descriptions of complete destruction and statements recording the success of the conquest; on the other hand, Rahab's family, the Gibeonites and others continue to live in the land (p. 13). Presenting a brief recent research history on the book of Joshua, Mitchell holds that his methodology could relate the mutually contradictory references concerning foreigners to each other in the context of the whole book, while, at the same time, accounting for the history behind the text (p. 17). Unlike most other scholars, his study concentrates on the manner in which the narrative is developed within the compositional framework (p. 18). Mitchell divides his study according to the contradiction of the text: in the first part of his book, Chapters 1 to 5, he first deals with the statement "[t]hey occupy the land and all of them are to be killed," then in the second part (from Chapter 6 to 8), with "Some survive" (p. 19).

Mitchell argues that in the first five chapters of Joshua (1:1–5:15) there is a gradual introduction of warlike themes, even though little attention is paid to the nations occupying the land which Israel is to conquer (p. 22). He goes on to say that these themes express Israel's attitude to the aliens in their midst: the nations are to be engaged in battle and eliminated from the land (p. 22). Mitchell examines words relating to battles, especially the meanings of חרם. In the Assyrian annals, complete annihilation is usually related to punishment for rebellion whereas sometimes the victors show mercy on the defeated enemy (p. 54). However, even though there are parallels between חרם and the language of destruction in the annals, the meaning of חרם in the narrative of Joshua is quite different (p. 54). Quoting H. W. F. Saggs, Mitchell holds that the battle reports in the Hebrew Bible, especially when חרם is used, express brutality quite differently from the literature of the surrounding nations (pp. 54–55).

In chs. 6 and 7 of Joshua also, חרם is the key concept and is first used to describe the complete destruction of Jericho and its inhabitants. However, if it is considered in the context of ch. 7, it denotes a test of obedience (p. 81). According to Mitchell, the survival of Rahab and her

11. G. Mitchell, *Together in the Land: A Reading of the Book of Joshua* (JSOTSup 134; Sheffield: JSOT, 1993).

family is in contrast with the destruction of Achan as well as with the destruction of Jericho (p. 81).[12]

Mitchell looks at the compositional structures connecting the battle reports in Josh 8:30–12:24. According to Mitchell, the repetitive form "and he did to city B and its king as he had done to city A and its king" signifies the connection of the stories of total destruction (p. 83). However, the pace of conquest suddenly slows down in the stories of Mount Ebal and results in the trickery of the Gibeonites and the covenant (p. 98). The story of the Gibeonites is similar to that of Rahab, in which the word חרם is first mentioned (p. 86). Mitchell notices that although attention has been paid to destroying the enemy, there is a discernible shift of focus in chs. 11–12 to the occupation of the land itself, and the language of ch. 1 returns (p. 98). In this part, the main theme is taking the land in the sense of it becoming Israel's inheritance (p. 94).

Then, Mitchell pays attention to two somewhat contradictory statements in chs. 13–21: "(1) the period of warfare is over; and (2) there has been a partial failure to conquer and settle" (p. 99). These statements constitute the major theological reflection in 13:1–23:1. Mitchell contends that while the contradiction between statements of complete conquest and incomplete conquest is accounted for as the result of a variety in the source or redactional contribution, this problem cannot be easily solved until it is possible to relate it to the contradictions in the compositional structure of the book of Joshua as a whole (p. 109).

Moreover, Mitchell examines the destruction and loss of the land: one important aspect of the conclusion of the book of Joshua, which presents the possibility that Israel could experience the same fate as the nations who lived in Canaan before the Israelites (p. 110). The concluding three chapters warn that illicit worship will result in the failure of the conquest, and Israel will share the fate of the nations (p. 119).

In the second half of his book Mitchell explores expressions related to the enemy nations in the land. In chs. 1–12 the nations are mentioned as those who are to be exterminated. In order to stress the conflict and thoroughness of destruction, the nations are described in comprehensive categories: "all the inhabitants of the land," "Canaanites" or "Amorites." Lists of nations or kings also appear. The expression כל־ישבי הארץ is unique to the book of Joshua for denoting the totality of nations. According to Mitchell, in the DH, they are used as a particular category

12. Mitchell argues that "...[in] the stories of the defeat of the Israelites at Ai and the thorough destruction of Achan, Israel is treated no differently from the occupants of the land... This conclusion is unavoidable because of the symmetry between the narratives concerning Rahab the Canaanite and Achan the Israelite" (p. 82).

of nations—the pre-Israelite occupants of the land. They serve as the opponents of YHWH and are symbols of all that Israel must avoid (pp. 140–41). However, in chs. 13–22, the nations are listed as individuals shattered in the course of settlement (p. 137). Their loss of power and glory is made obvious by the fact that they are no longer mentioned in association with their kings (p. 141). Subsequently, in the last two chapters of Joshua, the language returns to comprehensive titles such as "all the enemies" (כל־האיבים), "all the nations" (כל־הגוים), and "all the peoples" (כל־העמים). Therefore, the expressions relating to the nations are carefully provided in the overall narrative. Each major shift is constituted by a complementary change in the formulas denoting the nations (p. 141).

Mitchell also examines some important verbs, to which other prominent scholars pay little attention (p. 144). According to Mitchell, hearing (שמע) plays an important role in the compositional and theological structures of Joshua. Usually in the book of Joshua, the nations "hear" (שמע) and "fear" (ירא), but Israel "sees" (ראה) and "knows" (ידע) (pp. 144–48). However, the reverse case also happens: sometimes the nations know, and Israel hears and fears.

Then, Mitchell closely examines the contrast between the nations' dwelling in Israel's midst and their complete destruction. Here, he surveys all the notes to designate the role of the nations that remain in the midst of Israel: Rahab, the Gibeonites, the Geshurites and Maacathites (13:13), the Jebusites (15:63), the Canaanites of Gezer (16:10), Beth-shean, Ibleam, Dor, Endor, Taanach, Megiddo and all their villages (17:12–13). The contrast between the pre-Israelite nations in Israel's midst and their complete destruction is a feature of all the references to the nations which remain (p. 184). The two contrasting elements are closely related.

In his conclusion, Mitchell reveals that his reading of Joshua focuses on the role of the nations. In the book of Joshua they are prominent, both in the compositional structures and in the stories themselves. The survival of some of the nations is in tension with God's command to destroy all the inhabitants of the land, and further serves to focus attention on the nations (p. 185). Furthermore, he argues that the juxtaposition of these ideas is a feature of the compositional arrangement in Joshua (p. 188). Moreover, חרם can also be understood in the light of the ambiguity. The ambiguities in the Rahab and Gibeonite stories become a feature of the conquest in general when the stories are considered in the context of the overall narrative (p. 189). The Rahab and Gibeonite stories clearly present both the command to destroy the nations, as well as the fact of their partial survival (p. 190). In the last part, Mitchell tries to solve these ambiguities by introducing the concept of "dream" and "reality." There is a dream of a land that is occupied by only one, holy nation. However, the inescapable reality is that foreigners remain. The narrative moves between "dream" and "reality." The narrative is an attempt to reconcile the desire for a land free from foreigners and from the challenge of living together with others in the Promised Land.[13]

Mitchell refers to the crossing of the Jordan briefly as part of the gradual introduction of warlike themes into the narrative (p. 22). He argues that the lengthy and slow-moving account of the river crossing dominates the early chapters. While in Josh 1 the conquest is symbolized by the prefigured river crossing, here the emphasis is on the crossing itself (p. 40). Even though he is not interested in source-critical approaches, he presents Otto's two-source account of this literary puzzle, which argues that one group of the twelve representatives comes from the east bank and the stones are set in the Jordan, while the other group of the twelve representatives who were already on the west bank removes the stones from the river and set them up on the west bank. This is an example of the symmetrical relationship between Cisjordan and Transjordan that occurs throughout the book of Joshua (pp. 40–41). However, by simply mentioning that by means of repetition the river crossing itself is stressed (p. 41), he evades examining the history of this literary composite and moves on quickly to another topic. Comparing this narrative to many other passages in the Hebrew Bible (e.g. Pss 24; 33:7; 65; 74; 89; 104:8–9; 114; Gen 1:9; Isa 51:10; etc.) which deal with crossing and with primeval waters, he maintains that the crossing means a shift, an entrance into an ordered world while leaving behind the wasteland of chaos (p. 41). He also pays attention to the miraculous character of the crossing. According to him, the Lord alone is the cause of events. This is supported by the parallel drawn with the Reed Sea crossing in Josh 4:21–24 (p. 42). Thus, the connection with the Reed Sea crossing serves to emphasize the miraculous character of the Jordan crossing in which miracle is understood in its liturgical and mythological dimensions (p. 43). Then, his concern is focused on the relationship between the cultic and the military in the river crossing. He holds that 3:10, in which the enemy is briefly mentioned, links the successful river crossing with the Lord's forthcoming successful defeat of the occupants

13. Mitchell contends that "For a people living under colonial rule, tales set in a distant age before they have been alienated from their land, and which describe the death of the kings, offer a vision of the future which makes the present bearable. A powerless people is able to find consolation" (p. 190).

of the land (p. 44). Verse 5:1, in which fear on the part of the occupants of the land is referred to, further serves to introduce a military mood to the narrative. The sense of battle is also suggested in 3:5, in which, prior to the crossing, the Israelites are told to sanctify themselves. Mitchell holds that this is a preliminary feature of the holy war. According to him, "...the amount of attention devoted to the crossing itself suggests that it cannot simply be likened to the first of the battles or understood as the first stage of conquest, but is a description of the conquest as a whole" (p. 45).

As we observed above, Mitchell's research is unique in that his study is focused on the compositional framework of the book of Joshua. Mitchell's study is also different from that of Polzin and Hawk in that he pays attention to the holy war, whose form is similar to the Assyrian annals while its use in the Hebrew text is different. He also provides at points analyses of some important Hebrew vocabulary related to war.

However, his study seems to oversimplify the book of Joshua by focusing exclusively on the contradictory statement "they occupy the land and all of them are to be killed, but some survive." He also reads the book of Joshua from the perspective of the application of חרם as Polzin and Hawk do. Even although his position does differ from that of Polzin and Hawk in the sense that Mitchell understands the gap between the full application of חרם and its failure as the difference between "dream and reality," it seems to be indebted to that of Polzin, who understands it as the difference between authoritative dogmatism and traditional criticism, and that of Hawk, who understands it as the difficulty of applying dogma to the daily lives of people. Authoritative dogmatism dreams of the perfect application of dogma to the real life, but traditional criticism stresses the impossibility of it. Furthermore, even though he assumes a DH, he does not explain who Dtr is and what the relationship is between Joshua and the other former prophets.

Mitchell also notes the problems of repeated and different reports of the river crossing in the text of Josh 3–4. However, he does not appear to succeed in applying his general theory to this narrative because his interest is limited to the question of whether this narrative is cultic or military, and evades other issues. By merely quoting Otto's opinion on the two different references to the stones in the middle of the Jordan and on the bank of the Jordan, which seem to be from two different materials, he fails to provide his own explanation of them. Moreover, Mitchell shows his limitations by reading the narrative only from the final form of the MT.

2.4. *Winther-Nielsen,* A Functional Discourse Grammar of Joshua[14]

Winther-Nielsen tries to demonstrate a textual and thematic unity in the book of Joshua from a unique direction. He applies modern linguistic theory and methodology to the analysis of ancient Hebrew grammar and text. Winther-Nielsen's book *A Functional Discourse Grammar of Joshua* has brought significant progress in the application of linguistics to the description of Biblical Hebrew grammar and narrative structure.

According to him, diachronic and synchronic readings before him share a common trait of linguistic inadequacy (p. 10). Therefore, there is an urgent need for a new textual analysis of Joshua based on solid linguistic norms (p. 10). His study proposes a functional grammar for Hebrew, which explains linguistic rules and principles in terms of their functionality (p. 1). This functional grammar begins with a structural syntax emptied of meaning, as well as with generative semantics loaded with interpretation (p. 14). It has a discourse-pragmatic orientation in the sense that it is interested in the sequencing and placing of atomic propositions within a wider communicative context. These grammatical elements are brought together within a theory of discourse grammar (p. 1). In order to deal with clause connections within a whole book, Winther-Nielsen uses a computer-assisted description of relations between clauses and an analysis of rhetorical structure among the related regions of text (p. 1). Although he pays attention to some scholars' argument of the variations between the MT and the LXX, he suggests that the MT should be used for grammatical analysis, and only obvious scribal errors should be corrected prior to that analysis (pp. 21–22).

Winther-Nielsen offers a model for discourse-pragmatic analysis within a functional grammar. He maps the territory by developing his linguistic theory. Functionalism and discourse-pragmatics have been increasingly placed at the heart of linguistic study because of the growing awareness of the communicative aspects of language by scholars (p. 29).[15] Functional grammar posits some major levels of grammatical

14. N. Winther-Nielsen, *A Functional Discourse Grammar of Joshua: A Computer-assisted Rhetorical Structure Analysis* (OTS 40; Stockholm: Almqvist & Wiksell, 1995).

15. Winther-Nielsen says that "Functional grammar is a pragmatic theory which assumes that the mutual knowledge shared by senders (S) and addressees (A) shapes their communicative interplay…" This communicative use of language also affects its view of discourse as "the record (text) of a dynamic process in which language was used as an instrument of communication in a context by a speaker / writer to express meanings and achieve intentions (discourse)" (ibid., 29).

organization: intraclausal, interclausal, and discourse levels (p. 32). First, at the intraclausal level, a functional grammar must account for how semantics and pragmatics influence the syntactic structure of the clause (p. 33). This can be explained by semantic relations between types of verbs and nouns: the internal clause-syntax is decided by the extent to which certain types of predicates (mainly verbs) dominate the semantic functions of their co-occurring arguments (mainly nouns) (p. 33). Then, the theory of the layered structure of the clause explains the internal structure of the Hebrew predicate (p. 44) and the function of the Hebrew verb at the intraclausal level (p. 52).

Second, at the interclausal level, functional grammar recognizes three main domains of cross-clausal grammar: clause combining, participant reference and temporal sequencing of predicates (p. 53). No clause is totally independent on its immediate clausal context and the strands of discourse coherence always entail some grammatical concomitants in clause-combining syntax (p. 53). Other interclausal links depend on pragmatic or rhetorical relations within the sentences (p. 62). Referential coherence also ties connected chains of clauses together by references to participants or themes (p. 62). The key issues are how referents are made active in memory and context, at which level they occur, and how prominent they are in subsequent discourse (p. 63). Another major strand of interclausal information is made up by sequential coherence, or action-event sequencing of predicates (p. 70). In Hebrew, the system of sequential coherence is fundamentally formed by *wayyiqtol*-clause chaining, and its corollary in chain initial, medial and final constructions (pp. 73–74).

Third, the final level to be considered in the discourse-pragmatic grammar is discourse organization (p. 79). The grammatical analysis of discourse organization is mainly a matter of the segmentation of larger stretches of discourse into chunks or spans of connected text and "…the relations of such parts to the whole and of the parts to each other" (p. 79).[16] Pragmatic rhetorical analysis contributes to discourse analysis. The Rhetorical Structure Theory describes how texts are organized beyond grammatical mechanisms of interclausal linkage and coherence. It presents an independent, user-oriented and descriptive basis for the analysis of clause combining and textual coherence (pp. 87–88). It offers an independent pragmatic procedure for the discovery of grammatically

16. According to Winther-Nielsen, "…discourse organization can be explained in the terms of the grammar of macrostructure, constituent structure, superstructure, peak structure and dialogue structure. Discourse grammar assumes that semantic discourse structure is syntactically varied for pragmatic purposes" (ibid., 87).

or lexically unmarked relationships. It can be used to check which regions of a text present the topics of the discourse (p. 96). A computer-assisted syntactic analysis can carry out the pragmatic analyses of Rhetorical Structure Theory in order to check the structural description of interclausal relations (p. 96). It analyzes related pieces of information successively upwards in the grammatical hierarchy from morpheme to text. The analyses are composed of five stages: morphological analysis, semantic analysis, phrase structure analysis, clause division and clause relations (p. 97). In this research, a grammar of Joshua can benefit from a carefully checked phrase structure database with clause demarcation added. Clause-combining computer programs can then work out the syntactic hierarchical relations (p. 101).

After employing the illustration of the linguistic theories and the analytical strategy, Winther-Nielsen closely examines the narrative of Josh 2 in order to demonstrate the coherence of rhetorical relations, interclausal syntax and thematic unity. One noticeable point in his argument regarding Josh 2 is that this story is an exception to the policy of the extermination of foreigners in Moses' law (p. 162).

Winther-Nielsen applies the same techniques to investigate a larger section of the text, Josh 3–8, with special attention to the episode structure, the internal grammatical coherence and the thematic role of dialogue. According to him, the discourse markers of 5:1 (ויהי כשמע כל־מלכי) and 9:1 (ויהי כשמע כל־מלכים) separate the story of the crossing of the Jordan (3:1–4:24) from the stories of the circumcision and Passover celebration at Gilgal (5:2–12) and the stories of Jericho (5:13–6:26) and the story taking place at Ai (6:27–8:29) (p. 165). According to Winther-Nielsen, the thematic statement in the story of Jericho is that everything should be dedicated to Yahweh (6:17b) (p. 210). Like the other holistic readers, he pays attention to the application of חרם. He argues that the case of Rahab and her family (6:17b-c) is an exception from חרם: their lives were spared as the spies swore (p. 210). The above-mentioned stories have quite similar features. Long instructions in dialogue (3:2–5, 6–13; 6:2–5, 6–10; 7:3, 6–15; 8:1–9) follow their initiating stages (3:1; 5:13; 6:27–7:1). Each of them has double peaks describing the marvelous crossing of the Jordan, the miraculous conquest and cunning battle tactics (3:14–17; 4:18; 6:16–20b, 20c–21; 8:13b–16, 17–24). All of them end in distinct time closures (4:19–24; 6:26; 8:28–30) (p. 235). However, the stories also differ in their plots and thematic macrostructures. The Jordan story has an elaborate flashback (3:1, 2–5) and an inter-peak episode of stone picking (4:1–10). The divine commander story (5:13–15) heralded the Jericho incident (ch. 6). The introductory stage of the Ai story is a thematic preview that leads to the embedding of the stories of the defeat (7:2–5) and of the execution of Achan (7:6–25) (p. 235).

Winther-Nielsen tries to apply the procedures and the validity of his findings in Josh 2–8 to the structure of the whole book of Joshua (p. 241). Through his constituent analysis, he highlights the significance of the main boundary markers placed by the aging of Joshua (13:1; 23:1). Accordingly, the book of Joshua is divided into three episodes: the conquest (1:9–12:24), the distribution (13:1–22:34) and the covenant (23:1–24:28), framed by stage and closure (p. 264). The constituent structure of the total work can also account for the role of several minor parts (p. 264). Winther-Nielsen contends that the coherence of the book of Joshua can be supported by its constituent structure.[17]

He pays special attention to the grammatical functions of the Hebrew verb, especially in relation to the aspects. There are two aspectual features in Hebrew verbal morphology: perfectivity and sequentiality (pp. 277–78). The combination of these aspectual features produces four finite forms: *qatal*, *yiqtol*, *wayyiqtol*, and *wᵉqatal*. Hebrew has four sub-systems of syntactic chaining through the clustering of *wayyiqtol* (N[18]), *wᵉqatal* (D[19]), *wᵉqatal* (lists) and *wᵉyiqtol* (D) in descending order of priority (p. 283). Grammatical results of discourse organization and interclausal coherence are useful in tracing the thematic aspects of the book of Joshua and its superstructure (p. 293). The opening paragraph in 1:1–9 and the closing story in 24:29–33 influence the whole ideological perspective of the discourse in Joshua (p. 293). Winther-Nielsen holds that the theme of Joshua's servanthood of Moses, God and obedience sets the framework for the themes of conquest, distribution and lifelong success. The promise and fulfillment is the driving power for Joshua's

17. He says that "The closure of the conquest discourse in Josh 12 has a mirror-image in the East Jordanian tribal allotment in the stage of the distribution (13:7b–14:5). Together they form a tail–head linkage between the two major episodes of Joshua. The latter unit previews the dismissal of the eastern tribes and the return to their lot in the closure of the distribution (22:1–34). The closure in Josh 22 with convocation of tribes and a speech on obedience by Joshua is also strikingly similar to the stage of the covenant episode in Josh 23. The distribution-address (22:1–8) and the covenant-address (23:1–15) thus form a second discourse-level tail–head linkage. Finally, the covenant episode of Josh 23–24 can be viewed as a unity pervaded by didactic dialogue discourse. As a final episode on loyalty, it brings central themes of the completed conquest and distribution to a forceful conclusion" (p. 264).

18. N: Narrative.

19. D: Discourse.

service in a Mosaic fashion (p. 296). According to Winther-Nielsen, the key linguistic expressions show the central themes in the book of Joshua: עבר ("cross," 1:2b), נתתיו ("I have given," v. 3a), גבולכם ("your border," v. 4b), and לא־יתיצב איש לפניך כל ימי חייך ("nobody shall hold stand against you all the days of your life," v. 5a) (p. 316).

In conclusion, Winther-Nielsen maintains that most previous diachronic readings of the book of Joshua are irrelevant for grammatical analysis—inconclusive at best and invalid at worst. However, the linguistic reading of Joshua presents more important challenges for us to face in our extant data and to push genetic matters aside for quite some time. The synchronic investigations often supply close readings that are relevant from a linguistic point of view. Modern readings should look for the linguistic structure of the text by writers in specific situations (p. 326). Finally, Winther-Nielsen says that "the most interesting aspects of a functional discourse grammar is that it enables the linguist to establish the textual integrity and thematic unity of individual stories, groups of connected stories and complete works" (p. 326).

Unlike his explanation of Josh 2, Winther-Nielsen does not seem to involve himself greatly in the explanation of Josh 3–4. Yet he does try here to apply functional discourse grammar to read this complex story. According to him, 5:1, which refers to the terror-stricken Canaanites, is an introduction to the following story, also a tail–head linkage in line with 2:24, and does not belong to the story of the crossing of the Jordan (p. 165). First, he examines the boundary markers in order to analyze the structure of this narrative. According to him, וישכם יהושע בבקר (3:1a) clearly marks the opening of a new discourse (p. 172). He argues that הוא וכל־בני ישראל[20] in 3:1 broadens the agent reference to include all the Israelites following the restricted focus of Josh 2, and the shift of verb form to plural and the syntax are not awkward (p. 173). A time reference, ויהי, in 3:2a opens the first episode. Moreover, ויאמר is used as a boundary marker in 3:6a (Episode 2), in 4:15a (Episode 6). 3:14a (Episode 3), 4:1a (Episode 4),[21] and 4:11a (Episode 5) are also markers of episode boundaries opened by ויהי. Thus, the grammatical evidence for episode boundaries divides Josh 3–4 as follows: the march to Jordan (3:1, stage), preparatory orders (3:2–5, Episode 1), crossing orders (3:6–13, Episode 2), descent (3:14–17, Episode 3), orders regarding the stones (4:1–10, Episode 4), crossing lead (4:11–14, Episode 5), emerging on the other side of water (4:15–18, Episode 6), arrival at Gilgal (4:19–24, closure) (p. 175).

20. However, the LXX does not represent this phrase.
21. Only MT Josh 4:1a represents this word.

Furthermore, Winther-Nielsen pays attention to the problem of the internal consistency of this narrative. According to him, following Polzin's way of tracing a temporal thread, or a "chain of representative events," is one way to argue for the coherence of the story (p. 175). Then he applies discourse grammar to explore the continuity of this story (p. 176). His analysis is especially focused on 3:14–17. He argues that this section anticipates the miracle by commenting that the Jordan overflows during the time of harvest (p. 177). Verse 4:18 has structural similarities with this section. In the episode of the return of the waters, the heightened grammar twists the action into descriptive mode (p. 178). Both 3:14–17 and 4:18 describe miraculous situations with dramatic pauses that occur at the climaxes (p. 179). Winther-Nielsen contends that the coherence of Josh 3–4 is shaped stylistically by miraculous high points in 3:14 and 4:18, and by grammatical repetition in 4:9–10 and 4:11–15 (p. 182). Additionally, he spends some time explaining the two stories of the stones in the middle of the Jordan and on the other side of the Jordan. According to him, these two stories are not dissimilar. In 4:9a, no new information is added.[22] It merely stresses that Joshua was ultimately responsible for erecting the stones in Gilgal (p. 181).

After his efforts to plot the episodes and their internal coherence, Winther-Nielsen tries to trace the themes elaborated in the dialogue structure (p. 182). Here, noting Polzin's observation on the "anticipation/confirmation" structure, he applies discourse-pragmatics by paying attention to the use of highly marked dialogue introducers (p. 183). In conclusion, he argues that a functional discourse grammar discloses a unified structure, a clear sequence of events and a strong conquest theme in Josh 3–4. According to him, a discourse grammar can support the readings of this narrative in its original or final shape (p. 190).

As with other synchronic readers, Winther-Nielsen's application of functional discourse appears to make good attempts to establish the textual integrity and thematic unity of the book of Joshua. By closely analyzing the grammar, syntax, and rhetorical issues of the Hebrew text, and by applying solid linguistic norms and modern linguistic theory, Winther-Nielsen makes a significant contribution to the literary study on the book of Joshua.

However, in his linguistic analysis, it is sometimes unclear whether his claims are based on general linguistic theory or on specific Hebrew syntax. He also does not provide enough grammatical examples, other than those of Joshua. If he had offered more Hebrew evidence in Chapter

22. Here, Winther-Nielsen does not pay attention to the differences between MT and LXX Josh 4:9.

2, his theory might have been more persuasive. Moreover, it is not certain whether he succeeded in establishing the textual integrity and thematic unity of the book of Joshua, because even to understand his theory is difficult, let alone to examine whether it is applied properly. In addition, like other holistic readers (Polzin, Hawk, Mitchell), Winther-Nielsen also notices the extermination policy of foreigners in Moses' law in the book of Joshua and pays attention to the application of חרם.

Winther-Nielsen's general approach seems to be applied to the literary composite of Josh 3–4 properly at some points. By paying attention to whether a functional grammar can explain some of the complexity and support the unity of the story by an analysis of constituents, coherence and content, he examines the story of crossing the Jordan in Josh 3–4 and proposes a unified and sequential structure as a whole plausibly.

However, he does not suggest a plausible explanation of the two different descriptions of the twelve stones in the middle of the Jordan and on the other side of the Jordan. He merely ambiguously contends that the Jordan stone story highlights that Joshua was ultimately responsible for erecting the stones in Gilgal and that these two stories are not dissimilar. Yet, if we read 4:9 and 4:20–24 closely, there are stones set in the middle of the Jordan and also stones on the bank of the Jordan.

His study also has some similarities to that of Polzin, and sometimes he seems to be indebted to him. Like Polzin, he analyzes the story of the crossing of the Jordan by dividing the narrative into episodes. He also pays attention to a temporal thread, or chain of representative events, to argue for the unity of this story in the same way as Polzin does.[23] By paying attention to dialogue introducers, another dimension of discourse-pragmatics, Winther-Nielsen tries to trace the themes elaborated in the dialogue structure, and seems to get some insight from Polzin. To explain dialogue and theme structure in this narrative, Winther-Nielsen quotes Polzin's "command/fulfillment"[24] and "anticipation/confirmation" structures "as the working out of an antiphonal pattern"[25] (pp. 182–83).

In addition, Winther-Nielsen also reveals some limitations in that he does not note the differences between the MT and the LXX in this narrative and only tries to read in a linguistic and literary way only in the final form of the MT.

23. Winther-Nielsen quotes Polzin's view (*Moses and the Deuteronomist*, 95–97) closely in his explanation of the coherence and style structure of Josh 3:1–4:24 (*A Functional Discourse Grammar of Joshua*, 175–76).

24. Polzin, *Moses and the Deuteronomist*, 104.

25. Ibid., 105.

2.5. *Conclusion*

Synchronic studies by Polzin, Hawk, Mitchell, and Winther-Nielsen have suggested a new and interesting direction in the research of the book of Joshua. In their view, while diachronic scholars divide the text, classify layers of material, and reconstruct the text rather impetuously, they value and respect the text. Initially, they do their best to understand what this ancient text means, even when the meaning is difficult to determine. This seems to be the merit of their methodology.

However, no less than the diachronic critics, their approaches also seem to be quite divergent. Although Polzin, Hawk, Mitchell, and some of Winther-Nielsen's works have similarities, mainly in that the others are indebted to Polzin, their methodologies and the results of their studies are quite different from one another. Since each uses a rather different technical terminology, it is not clear to what extent they can speak to one another. They seem to speak past each other, meaning that they would need an interpreter before they can come into dialogue. The divergence and the intricacy of their investigations are not so different from those of diachronic studies. They also show difference in chapter division: Polzin and Mitchell attach 5:1 to the Jordan-crossing story, while Hawk and Winther-Nielsen attach the verse to the stories of circumcision and Passover celebration at Gilgal.[26] Furthermore, although Polzin explained the complex narrative of Josh 3–4 from various aspects and dimensions quite well, the approaches of others are quite trivial, being focused on just some narrow point, while failing to cover every problem in this literary composite. Besides, even Polzin, to whom others are indebted and whose study on this narrative is better than that of the others, does not supply a clear explanation of the two different descriptions of the twelve stones in the middle of the Jordan and on the bank of the Jordan. In addition, his research is limited insofar as he does not pay attention to the differences between the MT and the LXX, but reads only from the final form of the MT. Although Polzin does not disparage diachronic research and says that synchronic study must come first, he does not offer any diachronic attempt on Josh 3–4. This being the case, what sort of diachronic work on Josh 3–4 should follow Polzin's synchronic efforts? In the next chapter, we will investigate some text-critical issues in this complex narrative.

26. For this, see the next chapter.

Chapter 3

Polzin and Text-Critical Analysis of Joshua 3–4*

3.1. *Introduction*

In the previous chapter, we examined some notable synchronic readings by Polzin, Hawk, Mitchell, and Winther-Nielsen, and looked at the strengths and weaknesses of their methodologies regarding the complex narrative of Josh 3–4. Through the examination above, we have come to know that Polzin uses one of the best methodologies to explain a number of complicated problems in this text. Nevertheless, his study has limitations in that he applies his literary method to this narrative only from the final shape of the MT. How could the result be different if he read from the final form of the LXX?

In this chapter, we will investigate the differences between the MT and LXX of Josh 3–4 through text-critical analysis and examine the limitations of Polzin's synchronic study in reading only from the final form of the MT. First, we will try to note differences between the major Greek editions (Margolis, Rahlfs, and Auld) and retrovert Hebrew *Vorlage* of the LXX. Second, through text criticism, we will analyze the differences between the MT and LXX, and investigate the cause(s) of these differences. Furthermore, we will study the limitations caused by Polzin's lack of attention to the text of the LXX.

* The later division attached Josh 5:1 to the previous chapter. The noun "dry ground" (יבשה) in 4:22 is related to the verb "dried up" (הוביש) in 4:23 and 5:1; and some could hold that this shows 5:1 is linked with 4:22–24. However, the older marginal division of B starts a new section here (see Auld, *Joshua: Jesus, Son of Nauē*, 121). Furthermore, this kind of unity by the Canaanite kings introduces a new narrative in Josh 9. Thus, 5:1 seems to belong to the circumcision and the keeping of the passover (5:2–12).

3.2. *Text-Critical Analysis of Joshua 3–4*

3.2.1. *LXX^B^ Retroversion of LXX* Vorlage, *and MT of Joshua 3–4*

Table 1

	LXX^B^-Josh3–4 (ed. Auld)	*Retroversion of LXX* Vorlage *Josh 3–4*	*MT Josh 3–4*
3:1	καὶ ὤρθρισεν Ἰησοῦς τὸ πρωί καὶ ἀπῆρεν(1) ἐκ Σαττειν(2) καὶ ἤλθοσαν ἕως τοῦ Ιορδάνου καὶ κατέλυσαν ἐκεῖ πρὸ τοῦ διαβῆναι	וישכם יהושע בבקר ויסע מהשטים ויבאו עד־הירדן וילנו שם טרם יעברו: ס	וַיַּשְׁכֵּם יְהוֹשֻׁעַ בַּבֹּקֶר וַיִּסְעוּ מֵהַשִּׁטִּים וַיָּבֹאוּ עַד־הַיַּרְדֵּן הוּא וְכָל־בְּנֵי יִשְׂרָאֵל וַיָּלִנוּ שָׁם טֶרֶם יַעֲבֹרוּ׃
3:2	καὶ ἐγένετο μετὰ τρεῖς ἡμέρας διῆλθον οἱ γραμματεῖς διὰ τῆς παρεμβολῆς	ויהי מקצה שלשת ימים ויעברו השטרים בקרב המחנה:	וַיְהִי מִקְצֵה שְׁלֹשֶׁת יָמִים וַיַּעַבְרוּ הַשֹּׁטְרִים בְּקֶרֶב הַמַּחֲנֶה׃
3:3	καὶ ἐνετείλαντο τῷ λαῷ λέγοντες ὅταν ἴδητε τὴν κιβωτὸν τῆς διαθήκης Κυρίου τοῦ θεοῦ ἡμῶν καὶ τοὺς ἱερεῖς ἡμῶν(1) καὶ τοὺς Λευείτας(2) αἴροντας αὐτήν ἀπαρεῖτε ἀπὸ τῶν τόπων ὑμῶν καὶ πορεύεσθε(3) ὀπίσω αὐτῆς	ויצוו את־העם לאמר כראותכם את ארון ברית־יהוה אלהינו וכהנינו והלוים נשאים אתו תסעו ממקומכם והלכתם אחריו	וַיְצַוּוּ אֶת־הָעָם לֵאמֹר כִּרְאוֹתְכֶם אֵת אֲרוֹן בְּרִית־יְהוָה אֱלֹהֵיכֶם וְהַכֹּהֲנִים הַלְוִיִּם נֹשְׂאִים אֹתוֹ וְאַתֶּם תִּסְעוּ מִמְּקוֹמְכֶם וַהֲלַכְתֶּם אַחֲרָיו׃
3:4	ἀλλὰ μακρὰν ἔστω ἀνὰ μέσον ἡμῶν(1) καὶ ἐκείνης ὅσον δισχιλίους πήχεις στήσεσθε μὴ προσεγγίσητε αὐτῇ ἵν' ἐπίστησθε τὴν ὁδόν ἣν πορεύεσθε(2) αὐτήν οὐ γὰρ πεπόρευσθε τὴν ὁδὸν ἀπ' ἐχθὲς καὶ τρίτης ἡμέρας	אך רחוק יהיה בינינו ובינו כאלפים אמה תעמדו אל־תקרבו אליו למען אשר־תדעו את־הדרך אשר תלכו־בה כי לא עברתם בדרך מתמול שלשום: ס	אַךְ רָחוֹק יִהְיֶה בֵּינֵיכֶם וּבֵינָו כְּאַלְפַּיִם אַמָּה בַּמִּדָּה אַל־תִּקְרְבוּ אֵלָיו לְמַעַן אֲשֶׁר־תֵּדְעוּ אֶת־הַדֶּרֶךְ אֲשֶׁר תֵּלְכוּ־בָהּ כִּי לֹא עֲבַרְתֶּם בַּדֶּרֶךְ מִתְּמוֹל שִׁלְשׁוֹם׃ ס

3:5	καὶ ειπεν Ἰησοῦς τῷ λαῷ ἁγνίσασθε εἰς αὔριον ὅτι αὔριον ποιήσει ἐν ἡμῖν[1] Κύριος θαυμαστά	ויאמר יהושע אל־העם התקדשו למחר כי מחר יעשה יהוה בקרבנו נפלאות:	וַיֹּאמֶר יְהוֹשֻׁעַ אֶל־הָעָם הִתְקַדָּשׁוּ כִּי מָחָר יַעֲשֶׂה יְהוָה בְּקִרְבְּכֶם נִפְלָאוֹת׃
3:6	καὶ ειπεν Ἰησοῦς τοῖς ἱερεῦσιν ἄρατε τὴν κιβωτὸν τῆς διαθήκης Κυρίου καὶ προπορεύεσθε τοῦ λαοῦ καὶ ηραν οἱ ἱερεῖς τὴν κιβωτὸν τῆς διαθήκης Κυρίου καὶ ἐπορεύοντο ἔμπροσθεν τοῦ λαοῦ	ויאמר יהושע אל־הכהנים שאו את־ארון ברית יהוה ועברו לפני העם וישאו הכהנים את־ארון ברית יהוה וילכו לפני העם: ס	וַיֹּאמֶר יְהוֹשֻׁעַ אֶל־הַכֹּהֲנִים לֵאמֹר שְׂאוּ אֶת־אֲרוֹן הַבְּרִית וְעִבְרוּ לִפְנֵי הָעָם וַיִּשְׂאוּ אֶת־אֲרוֹן הַבְּרִית וַיֵּלְכוּ לִפְנֵי הָעָם׃ ס
3:7	καὶ ειπεν Κύριος πρὸς Ἰησοῦν ἐν τῇ ἡμέρᾳ ταύτῃ ἄρχομαι ὑψῶσαί σε κατενώπιον πάντων υἱῶν Ισραηλ ἵνα γνῶσιν καθότι[1] ἤμην μετὰ Μωυσῆ οὕτως ἔσομαι καὶ μετὰ σοῦ	ויאמר יהוה אל־יהושע היום הזה אחל גדלך בעיני כל־בני ישראל אשר ידעון כאשר הייתי עם־משה כן אהיה גם עמך:	וַיֹּאמֶר יְהוָה אֶל־יְהוֹשֻׁעַ הַיּוֹם הַזֶּה אָחֵל גַּדֶּלְךָ בְּעֵינֵי כָּל־יִשְׂרָאֵל אֲשֶׁר יֵדְעוּן כִּי כַּאֲשֶׁר הייִתִי עִם־מֹשֶׁה אֶהְיֶה עִמָּךְ׃
3:8	καὶ νῦν ἔντειλαι τοῖς ἱερεῦσιν τοῖς αἴρουσιν τὴν κιβωτὸν τῆς διαθήκης λέγων ὡς ἂν εἰσέλθητε ἐπὶ μέσου[1] τοῦ ὕδατος τοῦ Ιορδάνου καὶ ἐν τῷ Ιορδάνῃ στήσεσθε	ועתה תצוה את־הכהנים נשאי ארון־הברית לאמר כבאכם עד־קצה מי הירדן ובירדן תעמדו: ס	וְאַתָּה תְּצַוֶּה אֶת־הַכֹּהֲנִים נֹשְׂאֵי אֲרוֹן־הַבְּרִית לֵאמֹר כְּבֹאֲכֶם עַד־קְצֵה מֵי הַיַּרְדֵּן בַּיַּרְדֵּן תַּעֲמֹדוּ׃ פ
3:9	καὶ ειπεν Ἰησοῦς τοῖς υἱοῖς Ισραηλ προσαγάγετε ὧδε καὶ ἀκούσατε τὸ ῥῆμα Κυρίου τοῦ θεοῦ ἡμῶν[1]	ויאמר יהושע אל־בני ישראל גשו הנה ושמעו את־דבר יהוה אלהינו:	וַיֹּאמֶר יְהוֹשֻׁעַ אֶל־בְּנֵי יִשְׂרָאֵל גֹּשׁוּ הֵנָּה וְשִׁמְעוּ אֶת־דִּבְרֵי יְהוָה אֱלֹהֵיכֶם׃

3:10	ἐν τούτῳ γνώσεσθε ὅτι θεὸς ζῶν ἐν ὑμῖν καὶ ὀλεθρεύων ὀλεθρεύσει ἀπὸ προσώπου ἡμῶν[1] τὸν Χαναναῖον καὶ τὸν Χετταῖον καὶ τὸν Φερεζαῖον καὶ τὸν Ευαῖον καὶ τὸν Αμορραῖον καὶ τὸν Γεργεσαῖον καὶ τὸν Ιεβουσαῖον	בזאת תדעון כי אל חי בקרבכם והורש יוריש מפנינו את־הכנעני ואת־החתי ואת־הפרזי ואת־החוי ואת־האמרי ואת־הגרגשי ואת־היבוסי:	וַיֹּאמֶר יְהוֹשֻׁעַ בְּזֹאת תֵּדְעוּן כִּי אֵל חַי בְּקִרְבְּכֶם וְהוֹרֵשׁ יוֹרִישׁ מִפְּנֵיכֶם אֶת־הַכְּנַעֲנִי וְאֶת־הַחִתִּי וְאֶת־הַחִוִּי וְאֶת־הַפְּרִזִּי וְאֶת־הַגִּרְגָּשִׁי וְהָאֱמֹרִי וְהַיְבוּסִי:
3:11	ἰδοὺ ἡ κιβωτὸς διαθήκης κυρίου πάσης τῆς γῆς διαβαίνει τὸν Ιορδάνην	הנה ארון [1]ברית אדון כל־הארץ עבר בירדן:	הִנֵּה אֲרוֹן הַבְּרִית אֲדוֹן כָּל־הָאָרֶץ עֹבֵר לִפְנֵיכֶם בַּיַּרְדֵּן:
3:12	προχειρίσασθε ὑμῖν δώδεκα ἄνδρας ἀπὸ τῶν υἱῶν Ισραηλ ἕνα ἀφ' ἑκάστης φυλῆς	קחו לכם שני עשר איש מבני ישראל איש־אחד לשבט:	וְעַתָּה קְחוּ לָכֶם שְׁנֵי עָשָׂר אִישׁ מִשִּׁבְטֵי יִשְׂרָאֵל אִישׁ־אֶחָד אִישׁ־אֶחָד לַשָּׁבֶט:
3:13	καὶ ἔσται ὡς ἂν καταπαύσωσιν οἱ πόδες τῶν ἱερέων τῶν αἰρόντων τὴν κιβωτὸν τῆς διαθήκης κυρίου πάσης τῆς γῆς ἐν τῷ ὕδατι τοῦ Ιορδάνου τὸ ὕδωρ τοῦ Ιορδάνου ἐκλείψει τὸ δὲ ὕδωρ τὸ καταβαῖνον στήσεται	והיה כנוח רגלי הכהנים נשאי ארון הברית אדון כל־הארץ במי הירדן מי הירדן יכרתון המים הירדים יעמדו:	וְהָיָה כְּנוֹחַ כַּפּוֹת רַגְלֵי הַכֹּהֲנִים נֹשְׂאֵי אֲרוֹן יְהוָה אֲדוֹן כָּל־הָאָרֶץ בְּמֵי הַיַּרְדֵּן מֵי הַיַּרְדֵּן יִכָּרֵתוּן הַמַּיִם הַיֹּרְדִים מִלְמָעְלָה וְיַעַמְדוּ נֵד אֶחָד:
3:14	καὶ ἀπῆρεν ὁ λαὸς ἐκ τῶν σκηνωμάτων αὐτῶν διαβῆναι τὸν Ιορδάνην οἱ δὲ ἱερεῖς ἦρσαν τὴν κιβωτὸν τῆς διαθήκης[1] πρότεροι τοῦ λαοῦ	ויסע העם מאהליהם לעבר את־הירדן והכהנים נשאו את־ארון הברית לפני העם:	וַיְהִי בִּנְסֹעַ הָעָם מֵאָהֳלֵיהֶם לַעֲבֹר אֶת־הַיַּרְדֵּן וְהַכֹּהֲנִים נֹשְׂאֵי הָאָרוֹן הַבְּרִית לִפְנֵי הָעָם:

3:15	ὡς δὲ εἰσεπορεύοντο οἱ ἱερεῖς οἱ αἴροντες τὴν κιβωτὸν τῆς διαθήκης ἐπὶ τὸν Ιορδάνην καὶ οἱ πόδες τῶν ἱερέων τῶν αἰρόντων τὴν κιβωτὸν τῆς διαθήκης Κυρίου ἐβάφησαν εἰς μέρος τοῦ ὕδατος τοῦ Ιορδάνου ὁ δὲ Ιορδάνης ἐπλήρου καθ᾽ ὅλην τὴν κρηπῖδα αὐτοῦ ὡσεὶ ἡμέραι θερισμοῦ πυρῶν	וכבוא הכהנים נשאי ארון הברית עד־הירדן ורגלי הכהנים נשאי ארון ברית יהוה בלו בקצה מי הירדן נט והירדן מלא על־כל־גדותיו כימי קציר חטים:	וּכְבוֹא נֹשְׂאֵי הָאָרוֹן עַד־הַיַּרְדֵּן וְרַגְלֵי הַכֹּהֲנִים נֹשְׂאֵי הָאָרוֹן נִטְבְּלוּ בִּקְצֵה הַמָּיִם וְהַיַּרְדֵּן מָלֵא עַל־כָּל־גְּדוֹתָיו כֹּל יְמֵי קָצִיר׃
3:16	καὶ ἔστη τὰ ὕδατα τὰ καταβαίνοντα ἄνωθεν ἔστη πῆγμα ἓν ἀφεστηκὸς μακρὰν σφόδρα σφοδρῶς ἕως μέρους Καθιαιρειν[1] τὸ δὲ καταβαῖνον κατέβη εἰς τὴν θάλασσαν Αραβα θάλασσαν ἁλός ἕως εἰς τὸ τέλος ἐξέλιπεν καὶ ὁ λαὸς ἱστήκει[2] ἀπέναντι Ιερειχω[3]	ויעמדו המים הירדים מלמעלה קמו נד־אחד הרחק מאד מאד העיר אשר מצד קרית יערים והירד ירד על ים הערבה ים־המלח עד־תם נכרת והעם עמדו נגד יריחו:	וַיַּעַמְדוּ הַמַּיִם הַיֹּרְדִים מִלְמַעְלָה קָמוּ נֵד־אֶחָד הַרְחֵק מְאֹד מֵאָדָם הָעִיר אֲשֶׁר מִצַּד צָרְתָן וְהַיֹּרְדִים עַל יָם הָעֲרָבָה יָם־הַמֶּלַח תַּמּוּ נִכְרָתוּ וְהָעָם עָבְרוּ נֶגֶד יְרִיחוֹ׃
3:17a	καὶ ἔστησαν οἱ ἱερεῖς οἱ αἴροντες τὴν κιβωτὸν τῆς διαθήκης Κυρίου ἐπὶ ξηρᾶς ἐν μέσῳ τοῦ Ιορδάνου	ויעמדו הכהנים נשאי ארון ברית־יהוה בחרבה בתוך הירדן: ס	וַיַּעַמְדוּ הַכֹּהֲנִים נֹשְׂאֵי הָאָרוֹן בְּרִית־יְהוָה בֶּחָרָבָה בְּתוֹךְ הַיַּרְדֵּן הָכֵן וְכָל־יִשְׂרָאֵל עֹבְרִים בֶּחָרָבָה עַד אֲשֶׁר־תַּמּוּ כָּל־הַגּוֹי לַעֲבֹר אֶת־הַיַּרְדֵּן׃
3:17b	καὶ πάντες οἱ υἱοὶ Ισραηλ διέβαινον διὰ ξηρᾶς ἕως συνε τέλεσεν πᾶς ὁ λαὸς διαβαίνων τὸν Ιορδάνην	וכל־בני ישראל עברים בחרבה עד אשר־תמו כל־העם לעבר את־הירדן:	

4:1	καὶ ἐπεὶ συνετέλεσεν πᾶς ὁ λαὸς διαβαίνων τὸν Ιορδάνην καὶ ειπεν Κύριος τῷ Ἰησοῖ λέγων	ויהי כאשר־תמו כל־העם לעבור את־הירדן ויאמר יהוה אל־יהושע לאמר:	וַיְהִי כַּאֲשֶׁר־תַּמּוּ כָל־הַגּוֹי לַעֲבוֹר אֶת־הַיַּרְדֵּן פ וַיֹּאמֶר יְהוָה אֶל־יְהוֹשֻׁעַ לֵאמֹר:
4:2	παραλαβὼν ἄνδρας ἀπὸ τοῦ λαοῦ ἕνα ἀφ᾽ ἑκάστης φυλῆς	קח לך אנשים מן־העם איש־אחד משבט:	קְחוּ לָכֶם מִן־הָעָם שְׁנֵים עָשָׂר אֲנָשִׁים אִישׁ־אֶחָד אִישׁ־אֶחָד מִשָּׁבֶט:
4:3	σύνταξον αὐτοῖς καὶ[1] ἀνέλεσθε ἐκ μέσου τοῦ Ιορδάνου ἑτοίμους δώδεκα λίθους καὶ τούτους διακομίσαντες ἅμα ὑμῖν καὶ[2] αὐτοῖς θέτε αὐτοὺς ἐν τῇ στρατοπεδίᾳ[3] ὑμῶν οὗ ἐὰν παρεμβάλητε ἐκεῖ τὴν νύκτα	וצוה אותם ושאו מתוך הירדן הכין שתים־עשרה אבנים והעברתם אותם עמכם ואותם הנחתם אותם במלון אשר־תלינו בו הלילה:	וְצַוּוּ אוֹתָם לֵאמֹר שְׂאוּ־לָכֶם מִזֶּה מִתּוֹךְ הַיַּרְדֵּן מִמַּצַּב רַגְלֵי הַכֹּהֲנִים הָכִין שְׁתֵּים־עֶשְׂרֵה אֲבָנִים וְהַעֲבַרְתֶּם אוֹתָם עִמָּכֶם וְהִנַּחְתֶּם אוֹתָם בַּמָּלוֹן אֲשֶׁר־תָּלִינוּ בוֹ הַלָּיְלָה: ס
4:4	καὶ ἀνακαλεσάμενος Ἰησοῦς δώδεκα ἄνδρας τῶν ἐνδόξων ἀπὸ τῶν υἱῶν Ισραηλ ἕνα ἀφ᾽ ἑκάστης φυλῆς	ויקרא יהושע אל־שנים העשר איש אשר הכין מבני ישראל איש־אחד משבט:	וַיִּקְרָא יְהוֹשֻׁעַ אֶל־שְׁנֵים הֶעָשָׂר אִישׁ אֲשֶׁר הֵכִין מִבְּנֵי יִשְׂרָאֵל אִישׁ־אֶחָד אִישׁ־אֶחָד מִשָּׁבֶט:
4:5	ειπεν αὐτοῖς προσαγάγετε ἔμπροσθέν μου πρὸ προσώπου Κυρίου εἰς μέσον τοῦ Ιορδάνου καὶ ἀνελόμενος ἐκεῖθεν ἕκαστος λίθον ἀράτω ἐπὶ τῶν ὤμων αὐτοῦ κατὰ τὸν ἀριθμὸν τῶν δώδεκα φυλῶν τοῦ Ισραηλ	ויאמר להם עברו לפני לפני יהוה אל־תוך הירדן והרימו משם איש אבן אחת לשאת על־שכמו למספר שנים עשר שבטי ישראל:	וַיֹּאמֶר לָהֶם יְהוֹשֻׁעַ עִבְרוּ לִפְנֵי אֲרוֹן יְהוָה אֱלֹהֵיכֶם אֶל־תּוֹךְ הַיַּרְדֵּן וְהָרִימוּ לָכֶם אִישׁ אֶבֶן אַחַת עַל־שִׁכְמוֹ לְמִסְפַּר שִׁבְטֵי בְנֵי־יִשְׂרָאֵל:
4:6	ἵνα ὑπάρχωσιν ὑμῖν οὗτοι εἰς σημεῖον κείμενον διὰ παντός ἵνα ὅταν ἐρωτᾷ σε ὁ υἱός σου αὔριον λέγων τί εἰσιν οἱ λίθοι οὗτοι ὑμῖν	למען תהיה זאת אות בקרבכם תמיד כי־ישאלך בנך מחר לאמר מה האבנים האלה לכם:	לְמַעַן תִּהְיֶה זֹאת אוֹת בְּקִרְבְּכֶם כִּי־יִשְׁאָלוּן בְּנֵיכֶם מָחָר לֵאמֹר מָה הָאֲבָנִים הָאֵלֶּה לָכֶם:

4:7	καὶ σὺ δηλώσεις τῷ υἱῷ σου λέγων ὅτι ἐξέλιπεν ὁ Ιορδάνης ποταμὸς[1] ἀπὸ προσώπου κιβωτοῦ διαθήκης κυρίου πάσης τῆς γῆς ὡς διέβαινεν αὐτόν καὶ ἔσονται οἱ λίθοι οὗτοι ὑμῖν μνημόσυνον τοῖς υἱοῖς Ισραηλ ἕως τοῦ αἰῶνος	ואתה אמרת לבנך לאמר אשר נכרת מי הירדן מפני ארון ברית־אדון כל־הארץ בעברו והיו האבנים האלה לזכרון לבני ישראל עד־עולם:	וַאֲמַרְתֶּם לָהֶם אֲשֶׁר נִכְרְתוּ מֵימֵי הַיַּרְדֵּן מִפְּנֵי אֲרוֹן בְּרִית־יְהוָה בְּעָבְרוֹ בַּיַּרְדֵּן נִכְרְתוּ מֵי הַיַּרְדֵּן וְהָיוּ הָאֲבָנִים הָאֵלֶּה לְזִכָּרוֹן לִבְנֵי יִשְׂרָאֵל עַד־עוֹלָם׃
4:8	καὶ ἐποίησαν οὕτως οἱ υἱοὶ Ισραηλ καθότι ἐνετείλατο κύριος τῷ Ἰησοῖ καὶ λαβόντες δώδεκα λίθους ἐκ μέσου τοῦ Ιορδάνου καθάπερ συνέταξεν κύριος τῷ Ἰησοῖ ἐν τῇ συντελείᾳ τῆς διαβάσεως τῶν υἱῶν Ισραηλ καὶ διεκόμισαν ἅμα ἑαυτοῖς εἰς τὴν παρεμβολὴν καὶ ἀπέθηκαν ἐκεῖ	ויעשו־כן בני־ישראל כאשר צוה יהוה אל־יהושע וישאו שתי־עשרה אבנים מתוך הירדן כאשר דבר יהוה אל־יהושע בתם בני־ישראל לעבר ויעברום עמם אל־המלון וינחום שם:	וַיַּעֲשׂוּ־כֵן בְּנֵי־יִשְׂרָאֵל כַּאֲשֶׁר צִוָּה יְהוֹשֻׁעַ וַיִּשְׂאוּ שְׁתֵּי־עֶשְׂרֵה אֲבָנִים מִתּוֹךְ הַיַּרְדֵּן כַּאֲשֶׁר דִּבֶּר יְהוָה אֶל־יְהוֹשֻׁעַ לְמִסְפַּר שִׁבְטֵי בְנֵי־יִשְׂרָאֵל וַיַּעֲבִרוּם עִמָּם אֶל־הַמָּלוֹן וַיַּנִּחוּם שָׁם׃
4:9	ἔστησεν δὲ Ἰησοῦς καὶ ἄλλους δώδεκα λίθους ἐν αὐτῷ τῷ Ιορδάνῃ ἐν τῷ γενομένῳ τόπῳ ὑπὸ τοὺς πόδας τῶν ἱερέων τῶν αἰρόντων τὴν κιβωτὸν τῆς διαθήκης Κυρίου καί εἰσιν ἐκεῖ ἕως τῆς σήμερον ἡμέρας	ושתים עשרה אבנים אחרות הקים יהושע בו בירדן תחת מצב רגלי הכהנים נשאי ארון ברית יהוה ויהיו שם עד היום הזה:	וּשְׁתֵּים עֶשְׂרֵה אֲבָנִים הֵקִים יְהוֹשֻׁעַ בְּתוֹךְ הַיַּרְדֵּן תַּחַת מַצַּב רַגְלֵי הַכֹּהֲנִים נֹשְׂאֵי אֲרוֹן הַבְּרִית וַיִּהְיוּ שָׁם עַד הַיּוֹם הַזֶּה׃

4:10	ἱστήκεισαν[1] δὲ οἱ ἱερεῖς οἱ αἴροντες τὴν κιβωτὸν τῆς διαθήκης ἐν τῷ Ιορδάνῃ ἕως οὗ συνετέλεσεν Ἰησοῦς πάντα ἃ ἐνετείλατο κύριος ἀναγγεῖλαι τῷ λαῷ καὶ ἔσπευσεν ὁ λαὸς καὶ διέβησαν	והכהנים נשאי ארון הברית עמדו בירדן עד אשר כלה יהושע את־כל־ אשר־צוה יהוה לדבר אל־העם וימהר העם ויעברו:	וְהַכֹּהֲנִים נֹשְׂאֵי הָאָרוֹן עֹמְדִים בְּתוֹךְ הַיַּרְדֵּן עַד תֹּם כָּל־הַדָּבָר אֲשֶׁר־צִוָּה יְהוָה אֶת־יְהוֹשֻׁעַ לְדַבֵּר אֶל־הָעָם כְּכֹל אֲשֶׁר־צִוָּה מֹשֶׁה אֶת־יְהוֹשֻׁעַ וַיְמַהֲרוּ הָעָם וַיַּעֲבֹרוּ׃
4:11	καὶ ἐγένετο ὡς συνετέλεσεν πᾶς ὁ λαὸς διαβῆναι καὶ διέβη ἡ κιβωτὸς τῆς διαθήκης Κυρίου καὶ οἱ λίθοι ἔμπροσθεν αὐτῶν	ויהי כאשר־תם כל־העם לעבור ויעבר ארון ברית ־יהוה והאבנים לפניהם:	וַיְהִי כַּאֲשֶׁר־תַּם כָּל־הָעָם לַעֲבוֹר וַיַּעֲבֹר אֲרוֹן ־יְהוָה וְהַכֹּהֲנִים לִפְנֵי הָעָם׃
4:12	καὶ διέβησαν οἱ υἱοὶ Ρουβην καὶ οἱ υἱοὶ Γαδ καὶ οἱ ἡμίσεις φυλῆς Μανασση διεσκευασμένοι ἔμπροσθεν τῶν υἱῶν Ισραηλ καθάπερ ἐνετείλατο αὐτοῖς Μωυσῆς	ויעברו בני־ראובן ובני־גד וחצי שבט המנשה חמשים לפני בני ישראל כאשר דבר אליהם משה:	וַיַּעַבְרוּ בְּנֵי־רְאוּבֵן וּבְנֵי־גָד וַחֲצִי שֵׁבֶט הַמְנַשֶּׁה חֲמֻשִׁים לִפְנֵי בְּנֵי יִשְׂרָאֵל כַּאֲשֶׁר דִּבֶּר אֲלֵיהֶם מֹשֶׁה׃
4:13	Τετρακισμύριοι εὔζωνοι εἰς μάχην διέβησαν ἐναντίον Κυρίου εἰς πόλεμον πρὸς τὴν Ιερειχω[1] πόλιν	ארבעים אלף חלוצי הצבא עברו לפני יהוה למלחמה אל עיר יריחו:	כְּאַרְבָּעִים אֶלֶף חֲלוּצֵי הַצָּבָא עָבְרוּ לִפְנֵי יְהוָה לַמִּלְחָמָה אֶל עַרְבוֹת יְרִיחוֹ׃ ס
4:14	ἐν ἐκείνῃ τῇ ἡμέρᾳ ηὔξησεν κύριος τὸν Ἰησοῦν ἐναντίον παντὸς τοῦ[1] γένους Ισραηλ καὶ ἐφοβοῦντο αὐτὸν ὥσπερ Μωυσῆν ὅσον χρόνον ἔζη	ביום ההוא גדל[2] יהוה את־יהושע בעיני כל־עם ישראל ויראו אתו כאשר יראו את־משה כל־ימי חייו:	בַּיּוֹם הַהוּא גִּדַּל יְהוָה אֶת־יְהוֹשֻׁעַ בְּעֵינֵי כָּל־יִשְׂרָאֵל וַיִּרְאוּ אֹתוֹ כַּאֲשֶׁר יָרְאוּ אֶת־מֹשֶׁה כָּל־יְמֵי חַיָּיו׃ פ
4:15	καὶ ειπεν κύριος τῷ Ἰησοῖ λέγων	ויאמר יהוה אל־יהושע לאמר:	וַיֹּאמֶר יְהוָה אֶל־יְהוֹשֻׁעַ לֵאמֹר׃

4:16	ἔντειλαι τοῖς ἱερεῦσιν τοῖς αἴρουσιν τὴν κιβωτὸν τῆς διαθήκης τοῦ μαρτυρίου Κυρίου ἐκβῆναι ἐκ τοῦ Ιορδάνου	צוה את־הכהנים נשׂאי ארון ברית עדות יהוה ויעלו מן־הירדן:	צַוֵּה אֶת־הַכֹּהֲנִים נֹשְׂאֵי אֲרוֹן הָעֵדוּת וְיַעֲלוּ מִן־הַיַּרְדֵּן:
4:17	καὶ ἐνετείλατο Ἰησοῦς τοῖς ἱερεῦσιν λέγων ἔκβητε ἐκ τοῦ Ιορδάνου	ויצו יהושע את־הכהנים לאמר עלו מן־הירדן:	וַיְצַו יְהוֹשֻׁעַ אֶת־הַכֹּהֲנִים לֵאמֹר עֲלוּ מִן־הַיַּרְדֵּן:
4:18	καὶ ἐγένετο ὡς ἐξέβησαν οἱ ἱερεῖς οἱ αἴροντες τὴν κιβωτὸν τῆς διαθήκης Κυρίου ἐκ τοῦ Ιορδάνου καὶ ἔθηκαν[1] τοὺς πόδας ἐπὶ τῆς γῆς ὥρμησεν τὸ ὕδωρ τοῦ Ιορδάνου κατὰ χώραν καὶ ἐπορεύετο καθὰ ἐχθὲς καὶ τρίτην ἡμέραν δι᾽ ὅλης τῆς κρηπῖδος	ויהי בעלות הכהנים נשׂאי ארון ברית [1]ויתנו־יהוה מן־הירדן רגליהם על החרבה וישבו מי־הירדן למקומם וילכו כתמול־שלשום על־כל־גדותיו:	וַיְהִי בַּעֲלוֹת הַכֹּהֲנִים נֹשְׂאֵי אֲרוֹן בְּרִית מִתּוֹךְ הַיַּרְדֵּן נִתְּקוּ[1] כַּפּוֹת־יְהוָה רַגְלֵי הַכֹּהֲנִים אֶל הֶחָרָבָה וַיָּשֻׁבוּ מֵי־הַיַּרְדֵּן לִמְקוֹמָם וַיֵּלְכוּ כִתְמוֹל־שִׁלְשׁוֹם עַל־כָּל־גְּדוֹתָיו:
4:19	καὶ ὁ λαὸς ἀνέβη ἐκ τοῦ Ιορδάνου δεκάτῃ τοῦ μηνὸς τοῦ πρώτου καὶ Κατεστρατοπέδευσαν οἱ υἱοὶ Ισραηλ ἐν Γαλγαλοις κατὰ μέρος τὸ πρὸς ἡλίου ἀνατολὰς ἀπὸ τῆς Ιερειχω[1]	והעם עלו מן־הירדן בעשׂור לחדש הראשון ויחנו בני־ישׂראל בגלגל בקצה מזרח יריחו:	וְהָעָם עָלוּ מִן־הַיַּרְדֵּן בֶּעָשׂוֹר לַחֹדֶשׁ הָרִאשׁוֹן וַיַּחֲנוּ בַּגִּלְגָּל בִּקְצֵה מִזְרַח יְרִיחוֹ:
4:20	καὶ τοὺς δώδεκα λίθους τούτους οὓς ἔλαβεν ἐκ τοῦ Ιορδάνου ἔστησεν Ἰησοῦς ἐν Γαλγαλοις	ואת שתים עשׂרה האבנים האלה אשר [1]לקח מן־הירדן הקים יהושע בגלגל:	וְאֵת שְׁתֵּים עֶשְׂרֵה הָאֲבָנִים הָאֵלֶּה אֲשֶׁר לָקְחוּ מִן־הַיַּרְדֵּן הֵקִים יְהוֹשֻׁעַ בַּגִּלְגָּל:

4:21	λέγων ὅταν ἐρωτῶσιν ὑμᾶς οἱ υἱοὶ ὑμῶν λέγοντες τί εἰσιν οἱ λίθοι οὗτοι	לאמר אשר ישאלון בניכם אליכם לאמר מה האבנים האלה:	וַיֹּאמֶר אֶל־בְּנֵי יִשְׂרָאֵל לֵאמֹר אֲשֶׁר יִשְׁאָלוּן בְּנֵיכֶם מָחָר אֶת־אֲבוֹתָם לֵאמֹר מָה הָאֲבָנִים הָאֵלֶּה׃
4:22	Ἀναγγείλατε τοῖς υἱοῖς ὑμῶν ὅτι ἐπὶ ξηρᾶς διέβη Ισραηλ τὸν Ιορδάνην τοῦτον(1)	והודעתם את־בניכם (2)כי ביבשה עבר ישראל את־הירדן	וְהוֹדַעְתֶּם אֶת־בְּנֵיכֶם לֵאמֹר בַּיַּבָּשָׁה עָבַר יִשְׂרָאֵל אֶת־הַיַּרְדֵּן הַזֶּה
4:23	Ἀποξηράναντος Κυρίου τοῦ θεοῦ ἡμῶν(1) τὸ ὕδωρ τοῦ Ιορδάνου ἐκ τῶν(2) ἔμπροσθεν αὐτῶν μέχρι οὗ διέβησαν καθάπερ ἐποίησεν κύριος ὁ θεὸς ἡμῶν(3) τὴν ἐρυθρὰν θάλασσαν ἣν ἀπεξήρανεν κύριος ὁ θεὸς ἡμῶν(4) ἔμπροσθεν ἡμῶν ἕως παρήλθομεν	אשר־הוביש יהוה אלהינו את־מי הירדן מפניהם עד ־עברו כאשר עשה יהוה אלהינו לים־סוף אשר־הוביש יהוה אלהינו מפנינו עד־עברנו:	אֲשֶׁר־הוֹבִישׁ יְהוָה אֱלֹהֵיכֶם אֶת־מֵי הַיַּרְדֵּן מִפְּנֵיכֶם עַד ־עָבְרְכֶם כַּאֲשֶׁר עָשָׂה יְהוָה אֱלֹהֵיכֶם לְיַם־סוּף אֲשֶׁר־הוֹבִישׁ מִפָּנֵינוּ עַד־עָבְרֵנוּ׃
4:24	ὅπως γνῶσιν πάντα τὰ ἔθνη τῆς γῆς ὅτι ἡ δύναμις τοῦ Κυρίου ἰσχυρά ἐστιν καὶ ἵνα ὑμεῖς σέβησθε κύριον τὸν θεὸν ὑμῶν(1) ἐν παντὶ ἔργῳ(2)	למען דעת כל־עמי הארץ את־יד יהוה כי חזקה היא למען יראתם אתם את־יהוה אלהינו (3)בכל־מעשה: ס	לְמַעַן דַּעַת כָּל־עַמֵּי הָאָרֶץ אֶת־יַד יְהוָה כִּי חֲזָקָה הִיא לְמַעַן יְרָאתֶם אֶת־יְהוָה אֱלֹהֵיכֶם כָּל־הַיָּמִים׃ ס

3:1

(1) Margolis' edition of LXX Joshua[1] represents ἀπῆρεν, but Rahlfs' manual edition of the book of Joshua in Greek[2] ἀπῆραν. Rahlfs seems to be affected by the MT, which also attests to the third person plural form.

1. M. L. Margolis, ed., *The Book of Joshua in Greek According to the Critically Restored Text with an Apparatus Containing the Variants of the Principal Recensions and of the Individual Witnesses*. Part 1–4, *Joshua 1:1–19:38* (Publications of the Alexander Kohut Memorial Foundation in Trust at the American Academy for Jewish Research; Paris, 1931–38).

2. A. Rahlfs, ed., *Septuaginta. Id est Vetus Testamentum graece iuxta LXX interpretes* (Stuttgart: Privilegierte Württemberg Bibelanstal, 1935).

(2) Margolis' edition follows the first scribal hand with Σαττειν, but Rahlfs' the second hand with the deletion of ε from Σαττειν.

3:3
(1) Margolis represents ὑμῶν.
(2) Rahlfs has Λευίτας. Ε has been removed secondarily in Rahlfs.
(3) Margolis attests πορεύσεσθε. The σ in Margolis' edition alters present into future. This seems to be secondary editing.

3:4
(1) Margolis and Rahlfs represent ὑμῶν.
(2) Margolis πορεύσεσθε.

3:5
(1) Margolis and Rahlfs ὑμῖν.

3:7
(1) Margolis has ὅτι before καθότι.

3:8
(1) Margolis and Rahlfs represent μέρους.

3:9
(1) Margolis represents ὑμῶν.

3:10
(1) Margolis represents ὑμῶν.

3:11
(1) LXX has one long phrase here (ἡ κιβωτὸς διαθήκης κυρίου πάσης τῆς γῆς) and it is not easy to retrovert it into good Hebrew. Furthermore, the absence of the definite article before διαθήκης in LXX and its presence in MT makes it all the more difficult. For this, see the text-critical analysis on this text below.

3:14
(1) Rahlfs attests κυρίου after διαθήκης. He seems to be influenced by MT.

3:16
(1) Margolis has Καριαθαιν, and Rahlfs Καριαθιαριμ.
(2) Margolis and Rahlfs corrected to εἱστήκει by inserting a small superscript ε.
(3) Margolis attests Ιερειχω, but Rahlfs Ιεριχω.

4:3
(1) Margolis attests Καὶ, but Rahlfs λέγων instead of καὶ. Rahlfs seems to be influenced by MT, which has לאמר.
(2) Rahlfs does not represent καὶ here.

(3) Rahlfs follows the correction to στρατοπεδείᾳ. The manuscript has a small superscript E over the I. LXX used two different words στρατοπεδίᾳ and παρεμβάλητε, which have military connotations, at the end of this verse, but MT has words במלון and תלינו from the same root.

4:7

(1) The Jordan is called a נהר (ποταμὸς) in B as in 5:1, but MT has "waters" in both passages. In Hebrew Joshua, as in Deuteronomy, נהר is used just for the "great" river, the Euphrates.[3] Thus, B seems to show free rendering here. In 5:1, B has the third person plural ἐτάκησαν and κατεπλάγησαν. This also appears to be caused by the Greek translator's free rendering of וימס לבבם.

4:10

(1) Margolis and Rahlfs have corrected with the insertion of a small superscript ϵ (ϵἱστήκϵισαν). Whatever the spelling, the pluperfect form in B, Margolis, and Rahlfs is different from that of MT, which has participle.

4:13

(1) Ιϵριχω in Rahlfs.

4:14

(1) Margolis has a different word order, του παντὸς.
(2) MT uses the same verb גדל as in 3:7. LXX uses a different word αυξανϵιν from υψωσαι in 3:7. While MT seems to emphasize the fulfillment of God's promise given in 3:7, LXX seems to give variety in expression by using different words. Once more LXX renders Hebrew גדל—concerning the Lord's exaltation of Solomon to the heights (2 Chr 1:1).[4]

4:18

(1) και ϵθηκαν could be retroverted to ויתנו instead of נתקו in MT; for כפות is MT plus, ויתנו רגלים would be the correct syntax.

4:19

(1) Ιϵριχω in Rahlfs.

4:20

(1) MT has the third person plural לקחו ("they took"), but LXX has the third person singular verb ἔλαβϵν ("he took"). We can retrovert to לקח in the Hebrew *Vorlage* of LXX.

4:22

(1) Margolis and Rahlfs do not attest this word.
(2) MT represents לאמר but LXX ὅτι. Even though this similar pattern appears several times in Josh 3–4, לאמר after והודעתם is not common in Old Testament Hebrew. The Hebrew *Vorlage* of LXX might have כי.

3. Auld, *Joshua: Jesus, Son of Nauē*, 114.
4. Ibid., 117.

4:23
(1) ὑμῶν in Margolis.
(2) του in Rahlfs.
(3) ὑμῶν in Margolis.
(4) ὑμῶν in Margolis.

4:24
(1) Margolis and Rahlfs have ὑμῶν.
(2) Margolis represents καιρῳ, and Rahlfs χρόνῳ instead of ἔργῳ in Auld.
(3) The only other occurrence of כל־מעשה in the book of Joshua is 24:31. כל־מעשה appears also in Num 31:20; Deut 11:7; 28:12; Judg 2:7; Eccl 8:17; 12:14; Hag 2:14, 17. בכל־מעשה as in OG *Vorlage* Josh 4:24 in Deut 2:7; 14:29; 16:15; 24:19; 30:9; 2 Kgs 22:17; 2 Chr 31:21; Esth 10:2. לכל־מעשה in Eccl 8:9. את־כל־אלה־מעשה in Ezek 16:30. וכל־מעשה in Mic 6:16, etc.

3.2.2. *Text-Critical Study of Joshua 3–4*

3:1. a. *and they set out* (ויסעו). The shift of subject from "Joshua" to "they" makes this verse a bit awkward. LXX^{BL} and Syr^{A} read as singular. The Egyptian group of texts supports these versions, which have Joshua only as the grammatical subject of "set out."[5]

b. *He and all the sons of Israel* (הוא וכל־בני ישׂראל). In LXX, this is lacking, while only בני ישׂראל (the sons of Israel) appears in Syriac.[6] This expression, which describes the leader and all the Israelite people, is quite rare in the Old Testament. Only in Num 27:21 does this expression appear. The usual phrase is "all Israel."[7] This is an MT plus, which tries to solve the clumsiness of this verse caused by the subject shift from the singular "he got up early" to the plural "they went…"

3:3. a. אלהיכם ("your God"). In contrast to MT, LXX^{B} has the inclusive θεοῦ ἡμῶν ("our God"), as do other parts in this narrative.

b. *the Levitical priests* (והכהנים הלוים). The Greek has ἡμῶν ("our") after "the priests" and καὶ between "the priests" and "the Levites." Unlike MT, LXX, Targum and Syriac distinguish between them as in Chronicles.[8] These versions clarify the division between the priests and Levites by inserting a conjunction (ו) between the two words. Butler holds that this understanding is later than that of Deuteronomy and the so-called Deuteronomic History, which emphasizes only one Levitical priesthood.[9] However, another possible reason for MT and B handling

5. Ibid., 102.
6. Boling and Wright, *Joshua*, 156.
7. Holmes, *Joshua*, 22.
8. Soggin, *Joshua*, 47.
9. Butler, *Joshua*, 39.

priests and levites differently in this verse is that "levites" are a secondary addition to each. The Vulgate supports MT (*et sacerdotes stirpis leviticae*). Van der Meer also backs up MT, arguing that the MT reflects the older Deuteronomistic conception in which priesthood and Leviticism are merged, whereas LXX shows the younger Priestly conception in which priesthood is claimed for a specific group within the group of Levites.[10] However, the Greek also seems to understand them as a single group: the ark, and (carrying it) our priests and the levites. If so, one question this understanding has to face is why only the priests are called "our." "Our priests" is a rare biblical phrase, attested to only in Ezra 9:7, 34 and Neh 9:32; 10:1 in MT. The Targums and Syriac stress the LXX distinction here and in 9:2. Likewise, Origen and Josephus follow LXX, but Josephus has the priest bear the ark, while the Levites carry the tent and sacrificial instruments.[11]

c. ואתם. Only MT represents this word.

3:4. a. *between it.* K^{e}thîbh reads ובינו, but Q^{e}rê וביניו. In וביניו the second *yod* is critically doubtful. ביניו occurs three times only in the Masoretic Q^{e}rê for בינו.[12]

b. במדה ("by the measure"). LXX reads this word as στήσεσθε (*ʿim^{e}dû*). Moati-Fine assumes that MT במדה misreads as a Hithpael of עמד.[13] Yet, no one can find such a form in the Hebrew Bible, and the Qal seems to make good sense; במדה appears in Lev 19:35 and 2 Chr 3:3, but not as used here in MT. It would be safer to assume here a *Vorlage* different from MT.[14]

3:5. a. LXX represents εἰς αὔριον ("for tomorrow") after *sanctify yourselves* (התקדשו), which is not in MT. In Num 11:18 also, the rare ἁγνίζειν is used and Moses specifies "for tomorrow." This link between LXX and Numbers seems to explain the literalness of the Greek rendering.[15]

10. Van der Meer, *Formation and Reformulation*, 77.

11. Auld, *Joshua: Jesus, Son of Nauē*, 103. For more on the relationship between the priests and Levites, see M. Leuchter and J. M. Hutton, eds., *Levites and Priests in Biblical History and Tradition* (SBL 9; Atlanta: Society of Biblical Literature, 2011).

12. E. Kautzsch and A. E. Cowley, eds., *Gesenius' Hebrew Grammar* (Oxford: Clarendon, 1909), 304.

13. Moatti-Fine, *J'esus (Jesu'e)*; Auld, *Joshua: Jesus, Son of Nauē*, 104.

14. Auld, *Joshua: Jesus, Son of Nauē*, 104.

15. Ibid.

b. בקרבכם ("among you"). The MT and most LXX witnesses have "you," but LXX^B has ἐν ἡμῖν ("in us"), in which Joshua includes himself among the people.

3:6. לאמר. According to van der Meer, the Greek translator of the Hebrew Bible omitted this word to stylize the redundancy of the Hebrew word, since Greek does not require an introduction to mark direct discourse similar to the Hebrew לאמר.[16] He holds that this is a "strong evidence for the stylistic reorganization of the Hebrew text by the Greek translator."[17] However, לאמר after ויאמר is not usual. Rather, it would be plausible to follow Holmes' suggestion that we have "strong evidence... in support of the faithfulnesses of LXX."[18] This is an MT plus. For more of this, see below on 4:21.

3:7. The Piel form of the Hebrew verb גדל corresponds to αὐξάνω ("to increase") in 4:14, but to ὑψόω ("to exalt") in 3:7, which is used only here in Joshua. The standard Greek translation of the Hebrew root גדל is μεγαλύνω in the Greek Pentateuch and the rest of the Greek Old Testament.[19] Only LXX represents υἱῶν (בני) after *kol* and lacks the counterpart of כי, initiating an object clause in this verse.

3:8. a. ואתה. LXX reads this as ועתה (καὶ νῦν). Since the two terms sound alike, a scribal mistake could have been made in dictation—not from the LXX side, but from the MT side. Verse 12 represents ועתה, which is MT plus. For more on this, see below on v. 12. And at the end of the instructions for the priests, LXX represents καὶ, which seems to emphasize the following words.

3:9. a. *the words of Yahweh* (דברי יהוה). LXX and Vulgate read singular ("the word"). Soggin plausibly maintains that "there may be a dittography: the *yod*, the early abbreviation for *yhwh*, was later confused with the suffix, at a time when the divine name was once again written out in full."[20]

b. Here as well, LXX represents "our" (θεοῦ ἡμῶν) instead of "your" in MT. This seems to support the idea that the LXX is earlier than the MT. This is because the idea to separate religious leadership from the people looks more developed and theologized.

16. Van der Meer, *Formation and Reformulation*, 231.
17. Ibid., 232.
18. Holmes, *Joshua*, 6.
19. Van der Meer, *Formation and Reformulation*, 184.
20. Soggin, *Joshua*, 48.

3:10. a. *And Joshua said* (ויאמר יהושע). In LXX, which lacks these two words, Joshua's speech continues directly.

b. *By this* (בזאת). It is not clear what this word means. Butler holds that "a conditional particle usually follows. [So] it is possible that the הנה clause opening v. 11 introduces the apodosis here, but one could read v. 10b as the apodosis."[21] For this, see Chapter 6.

c. מפניכם ("from before you"). By contrast, LXX has ἀπὸ προσώπου ἡμῶν ("before our face"). That Joshua includes himself among the people is typical in LXX as in v. 9.[22]

d. The order of the list of the seven indigenous nations differs a little in the LXX and MT (cf. Gen 15:20; Exod 3:10; 13:5; 23:23, 28; Num 13:29; Deut 7:1; 20:17; Josh 3:10; 9:1; 11:3; 12:8; 24:11).

3:11. a. הברית. *Zāqēp parvum*, which the Masoretes placed on this word, separates it from the word אדון ('the Lord'). Syriac inserted "Yahweh" after ברית. However, the question of the definite article (ה) in the MT cannot be easily solved. Furthermore, the lack of the article in many Greek witnesses is surprising for the opposite reason. According to Gray, this is "an obvious Deuteronomic interpolation."[23] Yet, Auld makes three necessary comments on v. 11 in B: (a) an accidental omission of τῆς following the τὸς of κιβωτὸς is not impossible; (b) "lord" here is not the divine name, but a common Hebrew noun; (c) if "lord" is a common noun and part of a chain of nouns in a genitive phrase, then it and also the third member, "covenant," should also be preceded by the Greek article.[24] Den Hertog argues that the presence of a redundant article in the corresponding phrase in MT may let the absence of the definite article in B appear original. The interpretation of the Targum agrees with LXX.[25] The problem in MT seems to be caused by MT copyist's insertion of definite article, who thought the absence of it in the Hebrew *Vorlage* of LXX was unusual. This verifies that LXX is earlier than MT. This verse also shows that textual and literary criticism are not divided, but complement each other. We will discuss this further in Chapter 6 on literary history.

before you (לפניכם). LXX lacks this.

21. Butler, *Joshua*, 39.
22. Auld, *Joshua: Jesus, Son of Nauē*, 106.
23. Gray, *Joshua, Judges and Ruth*, 62.
24. Auld, *Joshua: Jesus, Son of Nauē*, 106–7.
25. Ibid., 107.

3:12. a. ועתה. Some scholars insist that MT inserted this word to give some connection to a verse which is clearly out of place. However, it is not clear whether the interpolation of this word caused or corrected the clumsiness of this verse. We will consider the literary history of this verse in Chapter 6.

b. משבטי. LXX has מבני (ἀπὸ τῶν υἱῶν) for this. MT's term (שבטים, "tribes") here may reflect greater theologization. Auld has noted that tribal terminology is much more prevalent in MT than LXX within chs. 13–19, and has argued that this is a secondary development.

3:13. a. כפות. In LXX, "the soles of" does not appear as in 4:18. This is an MT plus.

b. מלמעלה ויעמדו נד אחד. LXX represents only יעמדו. A scribe seems to have added these words from v. 16 to make the two clauses correspond.

3:14. The beginning of v. 14 in LXX is slightly briefer than that in MT. Furthermore, the Hebrew of the MT is unusual: the opening formulaic "and it came to be" is not resumed by any finite verb. The Hebrew *Vorlage* of the Greek should have been modeled on the beginning of the report in Num 10:33–36 regarding the departure of the people from the mountain of Yahweh, with the ark travelling in front of them. Subsequently, MT might have clumsily adapted that *Vorlage*, towards the opening of Num 10:35.[26] And, δε in LXX is copulative. This is the second on S. Sipilä's list of copulative uses of δε.[27]

3:15. a. *those who bore the ark*. LXX includes the specific subject "the priests" (οἱ ἱερεῖς).

b. *water*. LXX has εἰς μέρος τοῦ ὕδατος τοῦ Ιορδάνου ("to a part of the water of Jordan"). τοῦ Ιορδάνου is a Greek plus. The Hebrew *Vorlage* of LXX could have "Jordan" twice or it could have used *midrash*-like freedom.[28]

c. כל ימי קציר ("throughout the time of harvest"). The MT attests to one more Hebrew letter (כימי for כל ימי) and one fewer words ("wheat"). The supralinear addition in 4Qjosh[b] and the paraphrase of this passage in 4Qapocryphon of Joshua[b] also agree with LXX in specifying this harvest time as the period of the wheat harvest.[29] There seems to be exegetical

26. Ibid., 108.
27. Sipilä, *Between Literalness and Freedom*, 37.
28. Auld, *Joshua: Jesus, Son of Nauē*, 107.
29. Bieberstein, *Joshua–Jordan–Jericho*, 152–54.

variation from MT side. MT might have smoothed and generalized the harsh and specified reading of LXX.

3:16. a. באדם. K^e^thîbh reads באדם, but Q^e^rê מאדם. LXX appears to read not מאדם but simply מאד, "extremely." There is no agreed reading of v. 16's geographical description between the MT and other versions. The textual diversities of this verse show the problem of the geographical location of Adam and the emphasis of the miraculous. Here textual history becomes exegetical history.[30] The classical term πῆγμα ἓν is used to describe the stationary water, which appears only here in LXX. However, the cognate πηγνυναι has appeared in Exod 15:8—and twice in the aorist form επαγη ("became congealed or solid").[31]

b. LXX represents a Greek plus κατέβη ("came down").

3:17. a. הארון. As v. 11, this verse contains a grammatical anomaly with the article before the *nomen regens*.

b. הכן ("firmly"). This does not appear in LXX^{BA}. This is an MT plus, added as the last word of v. 17.[32] For more on this word, see below on 4:3.

c. *all Israel*. LXX attests בני as v. 7.

4:1 a. *When all the nation had finished passing over the Jordan.* LXX^{B} starts a new portion one half-verse earlier than the medieval western tradition in 3:17b. Codex Alexandrinus treats it as a single "verse" exactly the western 3:17. The MT puts a פ in the middle of 4:1, recognizing a break at this point. However, 4:1a is a repetition to sum up the crossing story of ch. 3 and pick up a new theme, so 4:1 is a single verse, introducing a new story which continues to v. 8.

4:2. קחו לכם מן־העם שנים עשר אנשים איש־אחד איש־אחד משבט (MT). παραλαβὼν ἄνδρας ἀπὸ τοῦ λαοῦ ἕνα ἀφ' ἑκάστης φυλῆς (LXX). LXX, Vulgate and the Eastern Syriac open with a singular form, considering the context correctly. LXX and the Vulgate do not attest the dative plural pronoun לכם. Tov holds that the plus of this *dativus ethicus* phrase is a small elucidation introduced by the editor of MT.[33] However, we can also guess that the *Vorlage* of B read קח־לך. שנים עשר ("twelve") is also an MT plus to emphasize the number of tribes. LXX shows a different word

30. Butler, *Joshua*, 40.
31. Auld, *Joshua: Jesus, Son of Nauē*, 109.
32. Ibid., 110.
33. Tov, "The Growth of the Book of Joshua," 391.

order by putting ἄνδρας (אנשים) directly after קחו, and represents איש־אחד just once. Again, this shows us that MT's reading is textual exegesis of LXX *Vorlage*.

4:3. a. *command.* For וצוו, see v. 2 (קחו).

b. לאמר שאו (καί ἀνέλεσθε). It is a general rule that direct speech comes only after some form of the verb אמר in Hebrew and LXX normally renders לאמר by some form of λέγων. However, only MT represents לאמר. In addition, the use of καὶ in LXX[B] is rather unusual. LXX[B] may have a different Hebrew *Vorlage* ושאו from MT שאו. The Hebrew corresponding to ἀνέλεσθαι in this verse is נשא, but in v. 5 ἀνελόμενος and ἀράτω are expressed by only one Hebrew word, הרים ("raise high").[34] MT may have changed the Hebrew word to give variety in expression.

c. לכם מזה. These words are MT pluses.

d. ממצב רגלי הכהנים. These three words are lacking in LXX Josh 4:3, but the similar phrase (מצב רגלי הכהנים) does occur in v. 9. Perhaps this part originated from the same idea as v. 9, emphasizing the middle of the river.

e. הכין. To understand this verb is not easy. One might think that this is a rare form of Hiphil infinitive absolute used to express a command, but the absence of the appropriate conjunction makes this idea impossible. Noth and Kaufmann helpfully suggest that it is an analogous form to הכן in 3:17, or perhaps results from dittography.[35] Ετοιμους ("ready" or "steady") renders נכנים, the Hebrew cognate of this word, which is found in similar solemn commands in Exod 19:11, 15 and 34:2, to which there is an even closer parallel below in 8:4.[36]

The Greek words at the end of v. 3 give a more military connotation than the MT Hebrew: στρατοπεδεια ("encampment" or "the position of an army") is explicitly military; and the verb παρεμβαλλειν and its noun παρεμβολη in v. 8 are used in military contexts.[37]

4:5. a. LXX lacks Joshua's name, ארון, אלהיכם and represents ἔμπροσθέν μου ("before me"), "twelve" omitted in v. 2. Holmes argues that the MT pluses ("and Joshua," "the ark") seem to be due to a misunderstanding of the original meaning of v. 5.[38] Here, the Greek expression ἔμπροσθέν μου πρὸ προσώπου Κυρίου seems to read a different Hebrew *Vorlage*, לפני

34. Auld, *Joshua: Jesus, Son of Nauē*, 111.
35. Soggin, *Joshua*, 49.
36. Auld, *Joshua: Jesus, Son of Nauē*, 111.
37. Ibid., 111–12.
38. Ibid., 112.

לפני יהוה. We cannot exclude the possibility of editorial revision by the longer MT. E. Tov argues that ארון and אלהיכם are MT pluses caused by theological corrections.[39] The idea that Yahweh himself stands in the middle of the Jordan was a stumbling block to the MT scribe,[40] and the redundancy of לפני (ἔμπροσθέν μου) was a little awkward for him. Thus, he removed one לפני, interpolated ארון between לפני and יהוה, and changed the idea of this passage. In several places LXX mentioned actions happening "in front of the Lord," referring to the actual presence of the Lord with the ark of the covenant. The original idea, which implies direct contact with God, has been changed in MT by the addition of the words "the ark of": 6:7, 13; 7:6.[41]

4:6. The opening clauses of LXX and MT in this verse are quite different. It is not easy to decide whether LXX renders a *Vorlage* substantially different from MT, or whether LXX has shown freedom in translating the Hebrew text. Only LXX represents κείμενον διὰ παντός in this part.[42]

The son's question in this verse recalls the institution of the feast of the passover and unleavened bread (Exod 13:3–10). LXX has singular ὁ υἱός σου ("your son"), as in Exod 13:14 and Deut 6:20, but MT has plural בניכם ("your sons"). Tov attributes the change from plural to singular in this question to the influence of the Passover Haggadah upon a Hebrew scribe responsible for the Hebrew *Vorlage* of LXX.[43] However, I am not persuaded by his supposition that the Passover Haggadah already existed before the LXX came into being. Rather, it would be safer to assume that as Exod 13:14 and Deut 6:20 attest, LXX's singular is primary and MT exegetically changed later.

4:7. a. *And you shall tell them.* MT reads only plural (ואמרתם), but LXX singular καὶ δηλώσεις and συ, and has τῷ υἱῷ σου for להם in MT.

b. נכרתו מי הירדן. LXX lacks this clause, but it occurs in Targum, Syriac and Vulgate. Soggin holds that this kind of repetition is "common in West and South Semitic."[44] However, some scholars try to reject this as a useless repetition. This is likely to be an editorial insertion by a proto-Masoretic scribe.

39. Tov, "The Growth of the Book of Joshua," 394.
40. Sipilä, "The Septuagint Version of Joshua 3–4," 69.
41. Tov, "The Growth of the Book of Joshua," 394.
42. Auld, *Joshua: Jesus, Son of Nauē*, 113–14.
43. E. Tov, "Midrash-Type Exegesis in the Septuagint of Joshua," in *The Greek and Hebrew Bible*, 161–62.
44. Soggin, *Joshua*, 50.

4:8. a. כאשר צוה יהושע ("as Joshua commanded"). Unlike MT, LXX offers "as Yahweh commanded Joshua" (καθάπερ συνέταξεν κύριος τῷ Ἰησοῖ). In 9:3 as well, the LXX attributes an instruction to Yahweh, but the MT to Joshua. Similar to this, in 4:5 and 5:15 "Joshua" is a plus in the MT. The MT seems to magnify Joshua to compare his leadership to that of Moses.

b. למספר שבטי. Instead, LXX reads εν τῇ συντελείᾳ τῆς διαβάσεως ("at the completion of the passing over"). It is quite difficult to find any connection between "the number of tribes" in MT and "the completion of the passing over" in LXX.

"The place where they lodged" (המלון) in v. 8 repeats the same word as in v. 3. However, LXX uses different words, στρατοπεδεία in v. 3 and παρεμβολή in v. 8. We could consider different explanations as to the divergence between LXX and the MT. First, it is possible that there were dual traditions, so both the MT and the LXX reflect early traditions. Second, the LXX *Vorlage* might have the same word as the MT and the LXX translator used two different words. However, the Greek στρατοπεδεία in v. 3 appears to have a more vivid military connotation than the Hebrew would require. The noun παρεμβολή in v. 8, cognate of the verb παρεμβάλλειν in v. 3, is also often used in military contexts.[45] Therefore, it is more probable that the natural Greek syntax reflects the common original text and the MT changed the word exegetically to show that God's command given in v. 3 was fulfilled in v. 8.

4:9. a. ושתים עשרה אבנים. LXX and Vulgate have ἄλλους ("others") before אבנים and make a clear distinction between the twelve stones on the other side of the Jordan in v. 8 and in the middle of the Jordan in v. 9. Here again, we could also consider possible explanations for the divergence between LXX and the MT. First, there may have been dual traditions, so the proto-MT did not have אחרות but the Hebrew *Vorlage* of LXX did have it. Second, the LXX *Vorlage* might not have read אחרות as the MT, but the LXX translator used this word. Third, אחרות (ἄλλους) in LXX might reflect the common original text, while the MT removed the word exegetically. While it is difficult to decide between these three options, the third seems to be more persuasive. An MT editor may have eliminated this word to bestow the same authority to the stones in the middle of the Jordan as the stones on the other side of the Jordan and to read this verse without discontinuity from those previous verses regarding the twelve stones on the other side of the Jordan. However, it does not seem to be probable that the original story featured two sets of twelve stones. Thus,

45. Auld, *Joshua: Jesus, Son of Nauē*, 111–12.

we can suspect the possibility that the MT and B show differences in dealing with 4:9 because it is a secondary addition. For more of this, see Chapter 6.

b. בתוך. MT plus to emphasize the middle of the river.

4:10. a. *Ark*. Only LXX describes the ark as τῆς διαθήκης ("of the covenant").

b. עד תם כל־הדבר אשר־צוה יהוה את־יהושע ("until everything was finished that Yahweh commanded Joshua"). LXX reads ἕως οὗ συνετέλεσεν Ἰησοῦς πάντα ἃ ἐνετείλατο κύριος ("until Joshua finished all that Yahweh commanded"). In LXX, Joshua is the subject of "complete," and lacks ככל אשר־צוה משה את־יהושע, which seems to be an MT plus to underscore the transmission from Moses to Joshua. Tov maintains that this MT plus is a secondary addition to the Hebrew text attested to by LXX based on Deut 3:28. Here, the shorter LXX is more logical than MT, where Joshua had first been commanded by Yahweh, while this MT plus places the authority in the hands of Moses.[46] This passage shows us the inextricability of textual and literary criticism.[47] We will discuss this further in Chapter 6.

4:11. a. The ark (sg.) is the subject of ויעבר. LXX represents והאבנים (οἱ λίθοι) instead of והכהנים in MT. Some commentators who prefer MT maintain that the translator, or an earlier copyist, simply misread the original Hebrew. However, instructions to the priests are given in v. 16. Auld holds that "it [is] more likely that 'stones' has been adjusted to 'priests' in MT, on the basis of too literal a recollection of the command to the priests in 3:6—'Take up the chest of the covenant, and pass on before the people.' "[48]

4:12. The rare Hebrew word חמשים, which is understood by modern scholars in a military sense as "in battle array," occurs only in Exod 13:18; Josh 4:12 and Judg 7:11 in the Hebrew Bible. The Greek cognate of this word in Josh 4:12 is διεσκευασμένοι ("to be equipped"). In LXX of Exodus and Judges, this word is connected etymologically with חמש in the sense of "five." However, the Greek translator of Joshua suggests a

46. Tov, "The Growth of the Book of Joshua," 389.

47. Tov, *Textual Criticism of the Hebrew Bible*, 327–28. See further H.-J. Stipp, "Textkritik-Literarkritik-Textentwicklung. Überlegungen zur exegetischen Aspektsystematik," *ETL* 66 (1990): 145, and Bieberstein, *Joshua–Jordan–Jericho*, 163.

48. Auld, *Joshua: Jesus, Son of Nauē*, 116.

well-considered and contextually appropriate rendering that emphasizes the military function of the Trans-Jordanian tribes as a vanguard for the Israelite army, in line with Num 32 and Josh 4:13, where in the Hebrew text the synonymous word חלוצים ("equipped for war") occurs.[49] Both the verb διεσκευασμένοι ("to be equipped") in 4:12 and the Greek adjective εὔζωνοι (חלוצים) in 4:13 appear only in LXX Sir 36:26 (τίς γὰρ πιστεύσει εὐζώνῳ λῃστῇ, "for who will trust a well-equipped robber?," for Hebrew מי יאמין גדוד צבא, "who will trust a troop of the army?") and 1 Macc 6:33, respectively.[50]

4:13. a. כארבעים אלף. Giving exact number, LXX and Vulgate do not represent כ (τετρακισμύριοι εὔζωνοι). In this verse, we can also find the reading of LXX, which presents the correct number and seems to be earlier than that of MT, which gives an estimated number and improved reading.

4:16. a. העדות. According to Auld, LXX normally distinguishes between two phrases: "the ark of the covenant" (η κιβωτος της διαθηκης), and "the tent of the testimony" (η σκηνη του μαρτυριου). In Exodus, "covenant" and "testimony" are alternative terms for the Decalogue: that the "testimonies" are to be placed within the "ark" (25:15, 20); and it talks in its final chapter of "the tent of the testimony" being erected and "the chest of the testimony" being put in it (40:2–3). LXX shows simpler style than the MT in these matters: it uses μαρτυριον for MT *moᶜed* (traditionally "meeting" and in connection with "tent") and for *haᶜedut* (traditionally "the testimony" and connected with "ark"). It is not easy to discuss which is the more original in the Pentateuch between the simpler LXX and the more complex MT. Yet, here in 4:16, MT's simpler "the ark of the testimony" seems to be the older text.[51]

4:18. χώρα ("place," "region," "land," "cultivated land") occurs outside the LXX Joshua some 65 times as an alternative rendering of the Hebrew noun ארץ besides the standard equivalent γῆ. However, the Hebrew correspondent to this word in this verse is מקום. Within the Greek version of Joshua, this noun recurs only in 5:12 (χώραν τῶν Φοινίκων). The phrase ὥρμησεν τὸ ὕδωρ τοῦ Ιορδάνου κατὰ χώραν ("the water of the Jordan set in motion in its place") in the corresponding Hebrew clause

49. Van der Meer, *Formation and Reformulation*, 243.
50. Ibid., 244.
51. Auld, *Joshua: Jesus, Son of Nauē*, 118.

וישבו מי־הירדן למקומם ("the water of the Jordan returned to its place") in Josh 4:18 resembles the narrative of Israel's crossing through the Reed Sea (Exod 14:27) where the similar clause καὶ ἀπεκατέστη τὸ ὕδωρ πρὸς ἡμέραν ἐπὶ χώρας ("the water returned to its place towards the day") appears in Hebrew וישב הים לפנות בקר לאיתנו ("the water returned to its normal level at daybreak") appears.[52]

4:20. The LXX has the third person singular verb ἔλαβεν (לקח, "he took"), but the MT has the third person plural לקחו ("they took").

4:21. a. ויאמר אל־בני ישׂראל. LXX[BA] and some recensions do not represent this clause. Boling and Wright argue that "LXX shows a sizable haplography here: לאמר [ל ויאמר אל־בני ישׂראל]בגלג."[53] However, even if this form appears in 3:6; 4:1b, 15, 21, לאמר after ויאמר is uncommon. Rather, this seems to be MT plus, which shows a conscious editorial expansion of the Hebrew text. A later scribe interpolated this phrase to introduce the direct discourse and to re-emphasize the identity of the speaker and the addressees. In this hypothetical verse, more divergences appear between MT and LXX. Both share the plural "your sons" (οἱ υἱοὶ ὑμῶν), but differ over whom "your sons" will ask: LXX has "you" (pl.), while MT has them ask "their fathers tomorrow."[54] S. Sipilä insists that מחר and את־אבותם are pluses, caused by MT corruptions.[55]

4:22. הזה is an MT plus of "small elucidation"[56] to define "Jordan."

4:24. ὅπως. The Hebrew cognate of this word is למען. The term ὅπως leads purpose clauses twice in Joshua beyond this verse (11:20; 23:7). The second למען in this verse is translated by ἵνα, perhaps simply for variety.[57]

יראתם. The suffix in the MT must be devocalized with the third person plural suffix ("they"), according to the context. MT lacks ὑμεῖς (אתם), which could have been omitted in error by haplography from the *Vorlage* (יראתם אתם).

52. Van der Meer, *Formation and Reformulation*, 401–2.
53. Boling and Wright, *Joshua*, 158.
54. Auld, *Joshua: Jesus, Son of Nauē*, 119.
55. Sipilä, "The Septuagint Version of Joshua 3–4," 69.
56. Tov, "The Growth of the Book of Joshua," 391.
57. Auld, *Joshua: Jesus, Son of Nauē*, 120.

3.2.3. *Conclusion of Text-Critical Study*

Through the text-critical analysis, we can see that there are quite a lot of differences between the MT and the LXX in Josh 3–4. However, these differences do not seem to be caused by errors in copying or misunderstandings of the text or exegetical and theological improvements from the MT to the LXX, as has traditionally been supposed. Rather, LXX Josh 3–4 appears to be based on a Hebrew *Vorlage* different from the textual tradition underlying MT Josh 3–4. Furthermore, the generally shorter Greek is an earlier and better witness than the MT to that common original from which both have diverged:

1. 3:5 and 6 show the literalness and faithfulness of the LXX in rendering the Hebrew *Vorlage*.
2. There are some verses which show the possibility of scribal error on the MT side: dittography (3:8, 9), haplography (4:24).
3. There appear to be more elements of improvement, development and theologizing in the MT than in the LXX: 3:9, 10, 12; 4:5, 8, 13.
4. There is some evidence showing exegetical variations and adjustments by the scribe or copyist of the MT: 3:15, 17; 4:2, 3, 11.
5. In particular, there are a larger number of pluses in the MT than in the LXX (See the table below).

Table 2

MT Pluses	*Verse*	*LXX Pluses*
הוא וכל־בני ישראל	3:1	
ואתם	3:3	ἡμῶν καὶ
	3:5	εἰς αὔριον
לאמר	3:6	Κυρίου
		οἱ ἱερεῖς
		Κυρίου
כי	3:7	υἱῶν
		οὕτως
		καὶ
	3:8	καὶ
ויאמר יהושע	3:10	
לפניכם	3:11	
ועתה	3:12	
איש־אחד		
כפות	3:13	
מלמעלה		
ו---		
נד אחד		

ויהי	3:14	
		οἱ ἱερεῖς
		διαθήκης
כל	3:15	διαθήκης Κυρίου
		τοῦ Ιορδάνου
		πυρῶν
		σφόδρα
מאדם	3:16	κατέβη
		ἕως
הכן	3:17	οἱ υἱοὶ
יהי	4:1	
לכם		
שנים עשר	4:2	
איש־אחד		
לאמר		καὶ
לכם מזה	4:3	
ממצב רגלי הכהנים		καὶ τούτους
ו---		
איש־אחד	4:4	
יהושע		ἔμπροσθέν μου
		ἐκεῖθεν
ארון	4:5	ἀράτω
אלהיכם		δώδεκα
בני		
	4:6	κείμενον διὰ παντός
בירדן		σὺ
נכרתו מי הירדן	4:7	λέγων
		πάσης τῆς γῆς
	4:8	κυρίος
		ἄλλους
בתוך	4:9	Κυρίου
תוך	4:10	τῆς διαθήκης
ככל אשר־צוה משה את־יהושע		
העם	4:11	τῆς διαθήκης
כ	4:13	
עם	4:14	
	4:16	τῆς διαθήκης
		Κυρίου

תוך	4:18	
כפות		
הכהנים		
ויאמר אל־בני ישׂראל	4:21	ὑμᾶς
מחר		
את־אבותם		
ו---	4:22	
הזה		
	4:23	κύριος ὁ θεὸς ἡμῶν
	4:24	ὑμεῖς

As this table shows, the MT contains many more pluses than the LXX. One important point among the features about this complex narrative that we come to notice through this text criticism is that the MT pluses, which seem to be the final layer of this narrative,[58] make conspicuous the possibility of the priority of the LXX.

3.3. *Conclusion*

As we saw above, there are a lot of differences between the MT and the LXX in Josh 3–4. In addition, we have come to know that these differences were not caused by error, misunderstanding or exegetical and theological improvement of the LXX scribe or copyist. Rather, the text-critical study of Josh 3–4 shows that the shorter Greek is an earlier and better witness than the MT. The large number of pluses in MT Josh 3–4 is one of the strongest pieces of evidence which supports this argument.

However, Polzin, one of the best synchronic readers, commits a critical mistake in completely disregarding the LXX. In addition, if we read more closely this complicated narrative with the help of text-critical analysis, we realize that the LXX provides us with a much easier understanding. As we saw above, if we read the LXX, we do not need to apply Polzin's complex literary theory to the two different stone stories in the middle and on the other side of the Jordan. Thus, one of the most difficult stories in this narrative can be better understood.

58. One of the most complex analyses ever of these chapters was made by Langlamet, who divided them into nine subdivisions. A. G. Auld noted that his final three layers were all made up of pluses in MT and these "supplements" would be a form of redaction. For this, see Auld, *Joshua, Moses and the Land*, 43–44, 91. We shall analyze these pluses more closely in Chapter 6.

Chapter 4

Reading Joshua 3–4 as Part of the Developing Ark Narrative

4.1. *Introduction*

The purpose of this chapter is to investigate the literary layers of Josh 3–4 in the wider context of the Old Testament. This chapter aims to explore the literary history of Josh 3–4 in the context of the other ark narratives, in particular Num 10:33–36; Josh 6; 1 Sam 4:1b–7:2; 2 Sam 6//1 Chr 13–16, and 1 Kgs 7:51–8:11//2 Chr 5, in which the ark leads the people of Israel into the Promised Land and comes to rest in the Jerusalem Temple. I will argue here that one should pay attention to recent arguments that suggest new ways of reading the literary history of the Old Testament. I will examine the relevance of Auld's theory, according to which the shared material in Samuel–Kings and Chronicles is the root work of the whole tree of Genesis–Kings. Even though Auld persuasively maintains that the shared materials of Samuel–Kings and Chronicles are the root work of the story of Israel before the monarchy, he has never tried to show how recognition of this root work might affect our understanding of the formation of the literary layers in the other Former Prophets and Pentateuch texts. Thus, I will try to examine how the ark texts are connected with each other. Since the research on 1 Sam 4:1b–7:2; 2 Sam 6//1 Chr 13–16, and 1 Kgs 7:51–8:11//2 Chr 5, which concern the ark's movements in the Promised Land, deals with not only synoptic texts, but also non-synoptic texts, it can provide us with new insights. For this research, I will first briefly survey all the texts of the Old Testament in which the ark is mentioned. Second, I will focus his exploration on the texts in which the ark leads Israel and moves into some promised place, similar to Josh 3–4. Third, I analyze some major words and phrases in these texts as part of the preliminary study. Finally, I will examine the literary history and the formation of relationship among these texts.

4.2. *The Ark in the Old Testament*

The word ארן/ארון appears extensively throughout the Old Testament. While in Gen 50:26 it is employed as a "coffin" for Joseph's bones, and in 2 Kgs 12:9 (10), 10 (11) and 2 Chr 24:8, 10, 11 as a "chest" for financial contributions, it generally refers to "the ark" as a religious focal point. Exodus 25:10–22 explains the origin and model of the ark, while Exod 37:1–9 refers to the real process of Bezalel's manufacturing of it. Besides these texts, "the ark" appears several times in the book of Exodus (Exod 26:33, 34; 30:6, 26; 31:7; 35:12; 39:35; 40:3, 5, 20, 21). In the book of Leviticus, ארן is used just once (Lev 6:2). In the book of Numbers, except for in Num 10:33–36, in which the ark leads Israel in the wilderness itinerary, the word appears in Num 3:31; 4:5; 7:89; 14:44. Deuteronomy 10:1–9 also elucidates the making and origin of the ark. Deuteronomy 10:5 says that the "two tablets of Moses" were deposited in the ark and Deut 31:26 reports that "the law book of Moses" was preserved beside the ark. In Josh 3–4, the ark, which is the symbol of God's presence, plays a leading role in Israel's crossing of the Jordan and its journey into the Promised Land. Joshua 6 shows that the ark led the people of Israel in the conquest of Jericho. Additionally, the ark appears in Josh 7:6 and 8:33. In contrast to the other books of the Former Prophets, in the book of Judges the ark does not play an important role and appears just once in 20:27. In the story of Israel's war with the Philistines in 1 Sam 4:1b–7:2, the ark alone brings victory to Israel after an unexpected initial defeat. In this narrative, the ark moves from Shiloh to Ebenezer (1 Sam 4:4), from Ebenezer to Ashdod (1 Sam 5:1), from Ashdod to Ekron (5:10), from Ekron to Beth-shemesh (6:12), and then from Beth-shemesh to the house of Abinadab on the hill (Kiriath-jearim) (1 Sam 7:1). Besides these, the ark appears in 3:3 and 14:18 in the book of 1 Samuel. Second Samuel 6 recounts the process of the ark's movement from Kiriath-jearim through the house of Obed-edom to Jerusalem. In addition, the ark is referred to in 2 Sam 7:2; 11:11; 15:24, 25, 29. First Kings 7:51–8:11 describes the process of the ark's movement from the city of David to the Temple in Jerusalem, in which the ark is settled. Besides this, it also appears in 1 Kgs 2:26; 3:15; 6:19; 8:21. First Chronicles 13–16 also describes the course of the ark's movement from Kiriath-jearim to David's city, in which material parallel to 2 Sam 6 is included. Other than this, "the ark" is employed in 1 Chr 6:31; 17:1; 22:19; 28:2, 18. Second Chronicles 5 describes the ark's movement from David's city to the Temple in Jerusalem in a similar way to 1 Kgs 7:51–8:11. Besides this, the ark appears in 1:4; 6:11, 41; 8:11; 35:3 in the book of 2 Chronicles. The ark appears also in Pss 78 and 132. Jeremiah 3:16, which mentions the loss of the ark, is the last record of the ark in the canonical order of the Old Testament.

4.3. *Preliminary Analysis: The Literary History of Joshua 3–4 in the Context of the Parallel Ark Narratives*

As we saw above, the ark appears quite a number of times from Genesis to Jeremiah in the canonical order of the Old Testament. Due to limitations of space it will not be possible to deal with all of these ark texts: thus, our focus will be on the ark narratives that display marked similarities to Josh 3–4, an account in which the ark is leading or accompanying the people of Israel. These texts are Num 10:33–36; Josh 3–4; Josh 6; 1 Sam 4:1b–7:2; 2 Sam 6//1 Chr 13–16; 1 Kgs 7:51–8:11//2 Chr 5. For convenience, I will refer to them as the Parallel Ark Narratives.

Before we read the literary history of Josh 3–4 with the help of similar ark narratives, we will investigate whether the texts could best be read in canonical or in historical order by analyzing some major words and phrases in these stories. In this study we will have to consider text-critical issues, for MT and LXX^{B} show a number of differences in these texts. Moreover, we will have to consider challenges raised by 4QSam^{a}, which plays an important role in the research of text-critical issues.[1]

4.3.1. *Designations for the Ark in the Parallel Ark Narratives*

If we tabulate the epithets of the ark in these texts, the results are presented in Table 3 (overleaf).

Numbers 10:33–36 has only two epithets: (ה)ארון ברית יהוה (10:33), הארון (10:35). I initially excluded Num 10:33–36 for the sake of convenience in dealing with the table: it is too short a text for us to find any general rule,[2] although details are mentioned where relevant.

1. For this, see P. K. McCarter, *I Samuel* (AB 8; New York: Doubleday, 1980), 5–11; R. W. Klein, *1 Samuel* (WBC 10; Waco: Word, 1983), xxv–xxviii; G. N. Knoppers, *I Chronicles 1–9* (AB 12A; New York: Doubleday, 2003), 52–65; idem, *I Chronicles 10–29* (AB 12B; New York: Doubleday, 2004), 578–661; see especially F. M. Cross et al., *Discoveries in the Judean Desert XVII: Qumran Cave 4 XII 1–2 Samuel* (Oxford: Clarendon, 2005).

2. In the same manner, the distributions of terms in Num 10:33–36 are omitted in the tables on other words below.

Table 3

Name	*Solomon's Ark* *1 Kgs7:51–8:11//2 Chr 5:1–14*				*David's Ark* *2 Sam 6//1 Chr 13–16*[3]				
	Kgs + or variants		*Synoptic*	*Chr + or variants*	*2 Sam 6 + or variants*			*Synoptic*	*Chr + or variants*
	B	MT			B	Q	MT		
הארון[4]	1 Kgs 8:6		1 Kgs 8:3, 5, 7a, 7b, 9//2 Chr 5:4, 6, 8a, 8b, 10	2 Chr 5:5, 9	2 Sam 6:3b, 4, 7, 13, 16	2 Sam 6:7, 9a	2 Sam 6:4b	B, 4QS[a] 6:7// 1 Chr 13:10	1 Chr 13:9, 10, 13; 15:23, 24b, 27; 16:37b
ארון אלהים[5]									
ארון האלהים[6]					2 Sam 6:6, 12a	2 Sam 6:6, 12a, 12b	2 Sam 6:3, 4a, 6, 7, 12a, 12b	2 Sam 6:2// 1 Chr 13:6	1 Chr 13:5b, 7, 12, 14; 15:1, 2a, 15, 24a; 16:1
ארון אלהיכם									
ארון אלהינו									1 Chr 13:3
ארון יהוה[7]		1 Kgs 8:4			2 Sam 6:3a, 9, 11, 12b, 15, 17	2 Sam 6:3, 4 (2×), 9b, 11, 13, 15, 16, 17	2 Sam 6:9, 10, 11, 13, 15, 16, 17		1 Chr 15:2b, 3; 16:4
ארון אלהי ישראל									
ארון יהוה אלהי ישראל									1 Chr 15:12, 14

3. Since there are significant differences between 2 Sam 6 and 1 Chr 13–16, we should perhaps make a separate comparison of 2 Sam 6:1–11 with 1 Chr 13, and of 2 Sam 6:14b–20a with parts of 1 Chr 15–16, which are equivalent texts to each other. However, it was difficult to make space for this in the tables in this chapter, so the author dealt with these sections together, mentioning details when required.

4. Cf. 2 Sam 11:11; Josh 8:33a. **ארון** in 2 Chr 16:41; Ps 132:8.

5. Cf. 1 Sam 3:3.

6. Cf. 2 Chr 1:4; 1 Sam 14:18a, 18b; 2 Sam 7:2; 15:24ab, 25, 29.

7. Cf. 1 Chr 8:11; Josh 7:6.

Name	*1 Sam 4:1b–7:2*[8]			*Josh 3–4*		*Josh 6*	
	B	Q	MT	B	MT	B	MT
הארון	1 Sam 4:4b; 6:1, 8; 7:2	1 Sam 5:10aβ[9]; 6:1	1 Sam 6:13; 7:2		3:15aα, 15aβ; 4:10		6:4, 9
ארון אלהים	1 Sam 4:11	1 Sam 4:11	1 Sam 4:11				
ארון האלהים	1 Sam 4:13, 17, 18, 19, 21; 5:1, 8b, 10a, 10bα, 11	1 Sam 5:11b; 6:11	1 Sam 4:13, 17, 18, 21, 22; 5:1, 2, 10a, 10bα				
ארון אלהיכם	1 Sam 4:3						
ארון אלהינו							
ארון יהוה	1 Sam 4:4a, 5, 6, 22; 5:2, 3; 6:2, 11, 13, 15, 19, 20, 21	1 Sam 4:4; 6:2, 8, 18, 20, 21	1 Sam 4:6; 5:4; 6:1, 2, 8, 11, 15, 18, 19, 21; 7:1a, 1b		4:11		6:6b, 7, 11, 12, 13 (2×)
ארון אלהי ישׂראל	1 Sam 5:7, 8a, 8c, 10bβ, 12	1 Sam 5:8 (3×), 10aα, 10b, 11a	5:7, 8 (3×), 10bβ; 6:3				
ארון יהוה אלהי ישׂראל							

8. Since 1 Sam 6:1–7:2 does not seem to belong to the same layer of 1 Sam 4–5, we should treat 1 Sam 4–5 separately from 1 Sam 6. For this, see A. G. Auld, *Samuel at the Threshold: Selected Works of Graeme Auld* (SOTSMS; Burlington: Ashgate, 2004), 145–47. However, because of the difficulty in dealing with the tables, this author put them together into one section in this chapter.

9. ארון.

Name	*Solomon's Ark* *1 Kgs 7:51–8:11//2 Chr 5:1–14*				*David's Ark* *2 Sam 6//1 Chr 13–16*				
	Kgs + or variants		*Synoptic*	*Chr + or variants*	*2 Sam 6 + or variants*			*Synoptic*	*Chr + or variants*
	B	MT			B	Q	MT		
(ה)ארון ברית[10] יהוה		1 Kgs 8:6[11]	1 Kgs 8:1//2 Chr 5:2	2 Chr 5:7	2 Sam 6:10	2 Sam 6:10			1 Chr 15:25, 26, 28, 29; 16:37
ארון ברית יהוה צבאות									
ארון ברית[12] האלהים									1 Chr 16:6
ארון יהוה אלהיכם									
ארון ברית־יהוה אלהיכם									
ארון ברית־יהוה אלהינו									
ארון ברית יהוה אלהי ישראל									
(ה)ארון הברית									
ארון יהוה אדון כל־הארץ									
ארון (ה)ברית אדון כל־הארץ									
ארון העדות[13]									
ארון הברית עדות יהוה									

10. Cf. 1 Kgs 6:19; Jer 3:16; Josh 8:33a.
11. B represents הארון here.
12. Judg 20:27; 2 Sam 15:24aα.
13. Cf. Exod 25:22; 26:33, 34; 30:6, 26, 36; 31:7; 39:35; 40:3, 5, 21; Num 4:5; 7:89.

Name	*1 Sam 4:1b–7:2*			*Josh 3–4*		*Josh 6*	
	B	Q	MT	B	MT	B	MT
(ה)ארון ברית יהוה	1 Sam 5:4, 18; 7:1a, 1b	1 Sam 4:3; 7:1	1 Sam 4:3, 5	3:6a, 6b, 15aβ, 17a; 4:9, 11	3:17; 4:7, 18	6:8, 9, 12, 13	6:8
ארון ברית יהוה צבאות			1 Sam 4:4a				
ארון ברית האלהים			1 Sam 4:4b			6:11	
ארון יהוה אלהיכם					4:5		
ארון ברית־יהוה אלהיכם					3:3		
ארון ברית־יהוה אלהינו				3:3			
ארון ברית יהוה אלהי ישׂראל	1 Sam 6:3	1 Sam 6:3					
(ה)ארון הברית				3:8, 14, 15aα; 4:10	3:6 (2×), 8, 14; 4:9		6:6a
ארון יהוה אדון כל־הארץ					3:13		
ארון (ה)ברית אדון כל־הארץ				3:11, 13; 4:7	3:11		
ארון העדות					4:16		
ארון הברית עדות יהוה				4:16			

Table 3 presents the twenty epithets used for the ark in the texts relating its movement. These epithets could be divided into four different kinds: simple (ה)ארון, ארון combined with the divine epithet אלהים, ארון bonded with יהוה, ארון with יהוה and אלהים together.

The epithets that appear most frequently in these texts are (1) (ה)ארון, (2) ארון ברית יהוה, (3) ארון יהוה, and (4) ארון האלהים. ארון appears in all the texts from Num 10:33–36 to 1 Kgs 7:51–8:11//2 Chr 5 except for in LXX^B Josh 3–4, LXX^B Josh 6. ארון ברית יהוה is also employed in all the texts except MT 2 Sam 6 and ארון יהוה except in Num 10:33–36, LXX^B 1 Kgs 7:51–8:11, and 2 Chr 5. However, even though ארון האלהים occurs quite often, its use is concentrated in 1 Sam 4:1b–7:2, 2 Sam 6// 1 Chr 13–16. These four epithets seem to form the basic framework of the texts from Num 10:33–36 to 1 Kgs 7:51–8:11//2 Chr 5. Among these four epithets, הארון is used as a synoptic[14] expression in 1 Kgs 8:3//2 Chr 5:4; 1 Kgs 8:5//2 Chr 5:6; 1 Kgs 8:7a//2 Chr 5:8a; 1 Kgs 8:7b//2 Chr 5:8b; and 1 Kgs 8:9//2 Chr 5:10; ארון האלהים in 2 Sam 6:2//1 Chr 13:6; and ארון ברית יהוה in 1 Kgs 8:1//2 Chr 5:2.[15] Regarding the designations ארון יהוה and ארון האלהים, we notice that the latter is used in the synoptic text of 2 Sam 6:2//1 Chr 13:6, but the former, which is one of the most frequently used epithets, is never used in the synoptic texts of 2 Sam 6//1 Chr 13–16 and 1 Kgs 7:51–8:11//2 Chr 5:1–14. Furthermore, ארון האלהים mainly appears in the first half of 2 Sam 6 and in 1 Chr 13, but הארון (ברית) יהוה mainly in 1 Chr 15–16, which is considered secondary by scholars.[16] In the ark story of 1 Sam 4:1b–7:2, the same trend appears. ארון האלהים mainly occurs in 1 Sam 4:1b–5, but ארון יהוה occurs in 1 Sam 6, which seems to have been added later. Thus, it is impossible to decide whether that ארון יהוה is later than ארון האלהים.[17] We will discuss this further in the study on the divine epithets in these texts.

The unique epithets appearing in one text only are ארון אלהים in 1 Sam 4:11, ארון אלהי ישראל in 1 Sam 5 (vv. 7, 8), ארון אלהינו in 1 Chr 13:3, and ארון יהוה אלהי ישראל in 1 Chr 15 (vv. 12, 14). The text in which the

14. In the present study I have treated only those epithets as synoptic expressions, which are found in exactly the same form in Samuel–Kings and Chronicles.

15. Here synoptic epithet means the expression which Samuel–Kings (MT, B, 4QSam^a) and Chronicles share.

16. H. G. M. Williamson, *1 and 2 Chronicles* (NCBC; Grand Rapids: Eerdmans; London: Marshall, Morgan & Scott, 1982), 119–32; S. Japhet, *I and II Chronicles: A Commentary* (OTL; Louisville: Westminster John Knox, 1993), 272–324; S. L. McKenzie, *1–2 Chronicles* (Nashville: Abingdon, 2004), 131–53.

17. A. G. Auld, "What Was the Main Source of the Books of Chronicles?," in *Samuel at the Threshold*, 145.

most peculiar epithets are used, that is, epithets not found elsewhere in other texts, is Josh 3–4. For example, ארון ברית־יהוה אלהים (3:3), ארון יהוה (3:13), ארון יהוה אדון כל־הארץ (3:11), הברית אדון כל־הארץ אלהים (4:5), and ארון העדות (4:16) are employed only in this text. Of course, although almost all the phrases except ארון כל־הארץ in 3:11, 13 appear in other texts, Josh 3–4 produces its own characteristic epithets using various phrases that are used in other texts. Apart from these, all the other epithets are used more than twice in the ark texts.

Another point arising from the above table is that the epithets of the ark in Num 10:33–36 (הארון and ארון ברית יהוה) are employed in all the ark narratives of Chronicles and the Former Prophets in which the ark's movement is described. Some scholars maintain that ארון ברית יהוה is a "Deuteronomistic expression."[18] That this epithet is used in Num 10:33 attracts our interest. It is possible that Num 10:33–36 was influenced by the Former Prophets and Chronicles, which provide general information about the ark and its epithets. Another possibility is that the epithets in Num 10:33–36 affected and shaped the development of a number of epithets in the Former Prophets and Chronicles. It does not seem to be plausible that ארון ברית יהוה in Num 10:33 could be the source of all the "covenant" passages in Deuteronomy and the Former Prophets, but we do not have to choose between these possibilities, for another instance of the table presents us with an opposing argument. The epithet ארון העדות, often regarded as the Priestly epithet,[19] is used in the text of Joshua, which many scholars regard as Deuteronomistic. Some scholars attempt to explain this as a P insertion in Joshua, but the problem is more complex. Even though the word העדות appears frequently in Kings and Chronicles (1 Kgs 2:3; 2 Kgs 11:12; 17:15; 23:3; 1 Chr 29:19; 2 Chr 23:11; 24:6; 34:31), and is used especially in relationship with the tabernacle in Chronicles (24:6), the word is never combined there with the term "ark" (ארון). Here again, we must consider different possibilities. First, an author or editor of Josh 3–4, who tended to produce his own peculiar epithets for the ark, coined this expression and the ark texts in Exodus and Numbers introduced this epithet. Second, as scholars generally say, ארון העדות in Josh 4:16 is a later insertion, influenced by the ark texts in Exodus and Numbers. In both these cases, it should still be considered that Samuel–Kings and Chronicles did not know this epithet for the ark (ארון העדות). Again, it does not seem to be credible that "the ark of testimony" in Josh 4:16 could be the source of all the

18. For this, see C. L. Seow, "Ark of the Covenant," *ABD* 1:387.
19. Ibid.

"testimony" passages in Exodus–Numbers. Rather, since the epithet, "the ark of testimony" (ארון העדות) appears mainly in the book of Exodus (Exod 25:22; 26:33, 34; 30:6, 26, 36; 31:7; 39:35; 40:3, 5, 21), and only in Josh 4:16 in the Former Prophets, a later editor of Josh 3–4 seems to have inserted the expression into Josh 4:16 to link the book of Joshua with Exodus.[20]

However, since the entire distribution of the epithets of the ark presents us with similar difficulties, any attempt to select just one possibility among these still appears to be impetuous. When we consider their distribution, it does not seem to be easy to find any strategy which could tell us conclusively that there is one prior text from which the others were developed. However, if we move from 1 Kgs 7:51–8:11 to Josh 3–4 in Table 3, we find that the number of the epithets of the ark increases and the gross distribution area of the epithets of the ark widens toward the end. Thus, we can infer one possible conclusion: the epithets of the ark increased and developed from 1 Kgs 7:51–8:11//2 Chr 5, which is the description of the ark in the Temple, to Num 10:33–36. Of course, the opposite reasoning should not be excluded, but the likelihood that a significant number of epithets in Chronicles and Former Prophets were developed from just two epithets in Num 10:33–36 seems to be low.

4.3.2. *The Verbs Describing the Movements of the Ark in the Parallel Ark Narratives*

A tabulation of the verbs that refer to the movements of the ark is offered in Table 4.[21]

The distribution of the verbs used to describe the movement of the ark is similar to that of the epithets of the ark.

The verb which appears most frequently and evenly in all the ark texts, excluding Num 10:33–36, is נשׂא. Besides this word, the next most frequently used verbs in these texts are העלה and בוא, which are used in all the ark narratives in Samuel–Kings and Chronicles. First Samuel 4:1b–7:2 has the most related verbs to the ark among these texts, and Num 10:33–36 and Josh 3–4, 6 use some special words, words which are related to their context.

20. For more on this, see section 6.3.2.14.

21. In Num 10:33–36, נסע (Num 10:33, 35) and נוח (Num 10:36) occur in relationship with the movement of the ark. Of these two verbs, נוח (Num 10:36) also appears in 1 Sam 6:18.

Table 4

Name		*Solomon's Ark* *1 Kgs7:51–8:11//2 Chr 5:1–14*				*David's Ark* *2 Sam 6//1 Chr 13–16*				
		Kgs + or variants		*Synoptic*	*Chr + or variants*	*2 Sam 6 + or variants*			*Synoptic*	*Chr + or variants*
		B	MT			B	Q	MT		
העלה[22]			1 Kgs 8:4	1 Kgs 8:1// 2 Chr 5:2	2 Chr 5:5	2 Sam 6:12b	2 Sam 6:12b	2 Sam 6:12b	2 Sam 6:2, 15// 1 Chr 13:6; 15:28	1 Chr 15:3, 12, 14, 25
נשׂא				1 Kgs 8:3// 2 Chr 5:4				2 Sam 6:3aβ[23], 4[24]	2 Sam 6:13// 15:26	1 Chr 15:2, 15, 27
בוא	Hiphil			1 Kgs 8:6// 2 Chr 5:7					2 Sam 6:17aα// 1 Chr 16:1	
	Qal								2 Sam 6:9, 16// 1 Chr 13:12; 15:29	1 Chr 13:5
לקשׁ										
סבב[25]										1 Chr 13:3
ישׁב									2 Sam 6:11//1 Chr 13:14	

22. This verb is used always as Hiphil form except in B, 4QSam[a] (1 Sam 6:20), where it is used as Qal.
23. This verb is lacking in B, 4QSam[a] 2 Sam 6:3aβ and 1 Chr 13:7.
24. B, 4QSam[a] (2 Sam 6:4) and Chronicles do not represent this verb.
25. This verb is used mainly in Hiphil form except Qal in 1 Sam 5:8aγ. It means "bring over," "carry about," or "return," but in Josh 6:11 "go round."

Name		1 Sam 4:1b–7:2			Josh 3–4		Josh 6	
		B	Q	MT	B	MT	B	MT
העלה		1 Sam 6:20, 21bβ; 7:1aβ	1 Sam 6:20,[26] 21bβ; 7:1aβ	1 Sam 6:21bβ; 7:1aβ				
נשׂא		1 Sam 4:4	1 Sam 4:4	1 Sam 4:4	3:3aβ, 6a, 6b, 8, 13, 14, 15aα, 15aβ, 17a; 4:9, 10, 16, 18	3:3aβ, 6a, 6b, 8, 13, 14, 15aα, 15aβ, 17a; 4:9, 10, 16, 18	6:12	6:6, 12
בוא	Hiphil		1 Sam 5:1, 2aβ		1 Sam 5:1, 2aβ			
	Qal	1 Chr 13:5	1 Sam 4:3, 5, 6; 5:10bα, 12; 7:1aγ	1 Sam 5:10bα,11b[27]; 7:1aγ	1 Sam 4:3, 5, 6; 5:10bα; 7:1aγ			
לקשׁ		1 Sam 4:3, 11, 17, 19, 22; 5:1, 2aα; 6:8aα	1 Sam 4:11; 6:8aα	1 Sam 4:3, 11, 17, 19, 21, 22; 5:1, 2aα; 6:8aα				
סבב		1 Sam 5:8aγ, 8b, 9, 10bβ	1 Sam 5:8aγ, 8b, 9, 10bβ[28]	1 Sam 5:8aγ, 8b, 9, 10bβ			6:11	6:11
ישׁב		1 Sam 5:7		1 Sam 5:7; 7:2				

26. B, 4QSam^a (1 Sam 6:20) represents ארון יהוה as the subject of this verb, but MT does not.

27. 4QSam^a (1 Sam 5:11b), B (1 Sam 5:12) have בוא, but MT does not. R. W. Klein says that MT lost the overlined letters (כבוא ארון אלוהי ישׂראל שמה) in 4QSam^a by homoioteleuton. For this, see Klein, *1 Samuel*, 48; McCarter, *1 Samuel*, 121.

28. B, 4QSam^a (1 Sam 5:10) attest הסבותם, but MT has הסבו here.

Name	Solomon's Ark 1 Kgs7:51–8:11//2 Chr 5:1–14				David's Ark 2 Sam 6//1 Chr 13–16				
	Kgs + or variants		*Synoptic*	*Chr + or variants*	*2 Sam 6 + or variants*			*Synoptic*	*Chr + or variants*
	B	MT			B	Q	MT		
יצג								2 Sam 6:17aβ//1 Chr 16:1	
שׁוב									
שׁלשׁ									
נקף									
נתן									
רכב								2 Sam 6:3aα[29] //1 Chr 13:7aα	
ראה									
אחז								2 Sam 6:6//1 Chr 13:9[30]	1 Chr 13:9
סור								2 Sam 6:10a//1 Chr 13:13	
נטה								2 Sam 6:10b//1 Chr 13:13	1 Chr 13:13
שׂים									
נושׁ									
Hiphil of ירד									
שׁמר									
הלך									
עבר									
עשׂה									
cf. היה									

29. B has singular form here, while MT, 4QSam[a], and Chronicles have plural form here.
30. B, 4QSam[a], 2 Sam 6:6, and 1 Chr 13:9 have the infinitive form of אחז, but MT has waw consecutive imperfect form of it here.

Name	*1 Sam 4:1b–7:2*			*Josh 3–4*		*Josh 6*	
	B	Q	MT	B	MT	B	MT
יצג	1 Sam 5:2b		1 Sam 5:2b				
שוב	1 Sam 5:11; 6:3, 21bα	1 Sam 6:21bα	1 Sam 5:11; 6:3, 21bα				
שלש	1 Sam 5:10a, 11aγ; 6:3	1 Sam 5:10a; 11aγ	1 Sam 5:10a, 11aγ; 6:3				
נקף						6:11	6:11
נתן	6:8aβ	6:8aβ	6:8aβ				
רכב							
ראה	1 Sam 6:13, 19		1 Sam 6:13, 19	3:3aα	3:3aα		
אחז							
סור							
נטה							
שים	1 Sam 6:11, 15aγ	1 Sam 6:11	1 Sam 6:11, 15aγ				
נוש	1 Sam 6:18	1 Sam 6:18	1 Sam 6:18				
Hiphil of ירד	1 Sam 6:15aα	not extant	1 Sam 6:15aα				
שמר	1 Sam 7:1b		1 Sam 7:1b				
הלך						6:8	6:8
עבר				3:11; 4:11	3:11; 4:11		
עשה	1 Sam 5:8aβ; 6:2	1 Sam 5:8aβ; 6:2	1 Sam 5:8aβ; 6:2				
cf. היה	1 Sam 6:1; 7:2	1 Sam 6:1	1 Sam 6:1				

Looking at the verbs used in the synoptic texts, many verses have exactly the same verb in each equivalent verse:

עלה	2 Sam 6:2 (B, 4QSam[a], MT)//1 Chr 13:6; 2 Sam 6:15 (B, 4QSam[a], MT)// 1 Chr 15:28; 1 Kgs 8:1//2 Chr 5:2;
נשׂא	2 Sam 6:13//1 Chr 15:26; 1 Kgs 8:3//2 Chr 5:4
בוא	2 Sam 6:9//1 Chr 13:12; 2 Sam 6:16//1 Chr 15:29; 2 Sam 6:17aα// 1 Chr 16:1; 1 Kgs 8:6//2 Chr 5:7
ישׁב	2 Sam 6:11//1 Chr 13:14; 2 Sam 6:17aβ//1 Chr 16:1
רכב	2 Sam 6:3aα//1 Chr 13:7aα
אחז	2 Sam 6:6//1 Chr 13:9
סור	2 Sam 6:10a//1 Chr 13:13
נטה	2 Sam 6:10b//1 Chr 13:13.

If we consider the distribution of these words in Table 4, we could postulate two possibilities regarding the formation of these texts. One possibility is that Num 10:33–36 was written first and 2 Chr 5 last, that is, equivalent to the canonical order. Yet, since the verbs used in Num 10:33–36 seldom affect the ones in Chronicles and the Former Prophets, this position could not be firmly supported. Only the non-synoptic text, 1 Sam 6:18, shares one word, נוח, with Num 10:36. The other possibility is that the verbs in 1 Kgs 7:51–8:11//2 Chr 5, which report the ark's movement into the Temple, are the earliest expressions and form the basic framework for the use of these words. If we interpret Table 4 according to this latter position, נשׂא, עלה, and בוא, in 1 Kgs 7:51–8:11// 2 Chr 5 are the initial verbs in these ark texts, to which other verbs are added and from which the other various expressions are developed. First Samuel 4:1b–7:2 shows the most varied and developed range of verbs among the texts in the Former Prophets. Joshua 3–4 and 6 add some additional verbs, ones which supplement a unique meaning in connection with their own situation, to the basic word נשׂא: "to cross" (עבר) in Josh 3–4; "to encircle" (סבב, נקף) and "to follow" (הלך אחרי) in Josh 6. Numbers 10:36 employs נוח, which is used in 1 Sam 6:18 (a non-synoptic text); Num 10:33 and 35 have a term, נסע, which never occurs in Chronicles and the Former Prophets.

Even though the former possibility does not seem to be that persuasive, we should not exclude it.

One other thing we have to consider here is that where B and 4QSam[a] agree with each other, they quite often agree with Chronicles but go against MT Samuel.[31] Scholars have maintained that 4QSam[a] is the *Vorlage* of B. With this fact in mind we could consider one more possibility: that in synoptic contexts Chronicles seems to be earlier than MT Samuel.

31. For this, see nn. 23–28, 30.

4.3.3. *Levites and Priests in the Parallel Ark Narratives*

The use of the words הכהנים and הלוים as the carriers of the ark piques our interest in these texts. The distribution of these words is presented in Table 5.[32]

According to Table 5, הכהנים is used frequently in almost all the texts, with the exception of Num 10:33–36, 1 Sam 4:1b–7:2 (B, 4QSam[a], MT), and 2 Sam 6 (B, 4QSam[a], MT). הלוים appears mainly in Chronicles and once in 1 Sam 6:15 (4QSam[a] is not extant), and the combined form with הכהנים appears five times (Josh 3:3; 1 Kgs 8:4; 1 Chr 13:2; 15:14; 2 Chr 5:5—two of these are MT pluses: 1 Kgs 8:4 and 1 Chr 13:2).

Among the texts of 1 Sam 4:1b–7:2, 2 Sam 6//1 Chr 13–16, and 1 Kgs 7:51–8:11//2 Chr 5, in Chronicles (ה)כהנים appears eleven times (except LXX[B] plus in 1 Chr 13:2) and הלוים 15 times. In Samuel–Kings (ה)כהנים is used five times (including one MT plus in 1 Kgs 8:4) and הלוים just twice as a component in הכהנים והלוים, which is also an MT plus. Thus, from the table above, we can deduce that even though the word הלוים often occurs in Chronicles, the frequency of its use in Samuel–Kings is relatively low. If we observe the frequency in the use of these two words in the Old Testament, the reason for this becomes obvious. הכהנים occurs 732 times in the Old Testament: 114 times in Samuel–Kings and 109 times in Chronicles. (ה)לוי(ם) appears 292 times: 100 times in Chronicles, but just four times in Samuel–Kings, one of which is an MT plus (1 Kgs 8:4) and all of the remaining three are non-synoptic.[33] Thus, הלוים occurs relatively often in Chronicles, but rarely in Samuel–Kings. We cannot conclude from this that Samuel–Kings was written first and Chronicles later, or that the author or editor of Samuel–Kings was related to a group of priests, while that of Chronicles was linked with the Levites as well as the priests.[34] However, we can safely conclude that: (1) Samuel–Kings shows interest mainly in the priests, and (2) Chronicles takes an interest in the Levites as well as in the priests. This would be an intriguing area for further research.

32. These terms are not found in Num 10:33–36.

33. לוי in 1 Kgs 12:31; לוים in 1 Sam 6:15; 2 Sam 15:24; 1 Kgs 8:4.

34. For this, see A. C. Welch, "The Chronicler and the Levites," in *The Work of the Chronicler: Its Purpose and Its Date* (London: Oxford University Press, 1939), 55–80; A. Cody, *A History of Old Testament Priesthood* (Rome: Pontifical Biblical Institute, 1969), 183; G. N. Knoppers, "Hierodules, Priest, or Janitors? The Levites in Chronicles and the History of the Israelite Priesthood," *JBL* 118 (1999): 49–72; K. Min, *The Levitical Authorship of Ezra–Nehemiah* (JSOTSup 409; London: T&T Clark, 2004), 65–70.

Table 5

Name	*Solomon's Ark* *1 Kgs 7:51–8:11//2 Chr 5:1–14*				*David's Ark* *2 Sam 6//1 Chr 13–16*				
	Josh 3–4		Josh 6	Josh 3–4	Josh 6			Josh 3–4	Josh 6
	B	MT			B	Q	MT		
הכהנים[35]	1 Kgs 8:3	1 Kgs 8:3	1 Kgs 8:6, 10, 11// 2 Chr 5:7, 11, 14	2 Chr 5:12 (כהנים)					1 Chr 13:2 (LXX) 15:11, 24; 16:6, 39
הלוים				2 Chr 5:4, 12					1 Chr 15:2, 4, 11, 12, 15, 16, 17, 22, 26, 27; 16:4
הכהנים הלוים				2 Chr 5:5					
הכהנים והלוים		1 Kgs 8:4							1 Chr 13:2 (והלוים MT Plus); 15:14
כהנינו והלוים									
בני אהרן[36]									1 Chr 15:4

35. Cf. Num 10:8.
36. Cf. Num 10:8.

Name	*1 Sam 4:1b–7:2*			*Josh 3–4*		*Josh 6*	
	B	Q	MT	B	MT	B	MT
הכהנים				3:6, 8, 13, 14, 15aα, 15aβ, 17; 4:9, 10, 16, 17, 18	3:6, 8, 13, 14, 15aβ, 17; 4:3, 9, 10, 16, 17, 18	6, 8, 9, 12, 13a, 13b, 16	4, 6, 8, 9, 12, 13a, 16
הלוים	1 Sam 6:15	Not Extant[37]	1 Sam 6:15				
הכהנים הלוים					3:3		
הכהנים והלוים							
כהנינו והלוים				3:3			
בני אהרן							

37. 1 Sam 6:15 is not attested at all in 4QSam[a].

In these ark texts, הכהנים is used in the synoptic texts of 1 Kgs 8:6, 10, 11//2 Chr 5:7, 11, 14; however, הלוים is never used in any synoptic accounts. הלוים, used in 1 Sam 6:15, does not seem to be the primary expression in Samuel–Kings. Rather, Chronicles supplies a lot of information on the priests and the Levites, and appears to influence הלוים in 1 Sam 6:15. In 1 Sam 6:15 the ark's movement is expressed by the Hiphil forms of ירד, עלה, and בוא (see Table 4). The pairing of הלוים with the Hiphil form of ירד in 1 Sam 6:15 seems to show the influence of Chronicles.

The compound form of הכהנים (ו)הלוים appears three times in the Chronicles' ark text, including the MT plus of the word, הלוים, in 1 Chr 13:2, but it does not appear in Samuel–Kings. Even though הכהנים והלוים is used once in 1 Kgs 8:4, it is an MT plus. This form is also used in Josh 3:3 (MT: הכהנים הלוים, LXX: הכהנינו והלוים). It is not easy to decide on the relationship between the expressions in Josh 3:3 and those in Chronicles. However, we can say that Chronicles provides a lot of important information about the priests and Levites, and that the ark texts in Chronicles and Josh 3–4 share the compound word הכהנים (ו)הלוים.

4.3.4. *Divine Epithets in the Parallel Ark Narratives*[38]

The word יהוה occurs in all these ark texts; אלהים does not appear in Num 10:33–36, Josh 6 and 1 Kgs 7:51–8:11. In Josh 3–4, all of the four divine epithets exist.

Here, we will have to pay attention to the two divine epithets יהוה and אלהים. יהוה is synoptic in both 2 Sam 6 (including 5:11–25)//1 Chr 13–16 and 1 Kgs 7:51–8:11//2 Chr 5:1–14; אלהים appears only in 2 Sam 6 (including 5:11–25)//1 Chr 13–16. Rose holds that the use of the epithet יהוה gradually decreases in relation to the development of the Israelite religion. According to him, since other gods no longer existed in the Israelite faith, the necessity for the יהוה epithet, which originally distinguished Israel's God from alien gods, diminished. Rose insists that the use of יהוה lessens in post-exilic biblical texts. In particular, it never occurs in Esther, Song of Solomon, Ecclesiastes.[39] Rothstein, Hänel and von Rad also contend that the transition of the divine epithet from Samuel to Chronicles, that is, from יהוה to אלהים, is evidence of a transcendentalizing of the divine name, which shows that Yahweh has gradually become estranged from the human world.

38. Juxtaposed epithets are each counted as a divided word.
39. M. Rose, "Name of God in the OT," *ABD* 4:1002, 1010.

Table 6

Name	*Solomon's Ark* 1 Kgs7:51–8:11//2 Chr 5:1–14				*David's Ark* 2 Sam 6//1 Chr 13–16				
	Kgs + or variants		*Synoptic*	*Chr + or variants*	*2 Sam 6 + or variants*			*Synoptic*	*Chr + or variants*
	B	MT			B	Q	MT		
יהוה[40]	1 Kgs 7:51b; 8:1a,	1 Kgs 7:51b; 8:4, 10, 11bβ	1 Kgs 7:51a; 8:1b, 6, 9, 11bα// 2 Chr 5:1a, 2b, 7, 10, 14bα	2 Chr 13 (3×)	2 Sam 5:19a, 20, 23 (2×), 24, 25; 6:2bβ, 3, 5, 7b, 9a, 9b, 10, 11a, 12 (3×), 14, 16b, 17 (2×)	2 Sam 5:19a; 6:2bβ, 3, 4 (2×), 5, 9a, 9b, 10, 11a, 12aα, 13, 14, 16a, 16b, 17 (2×)	2 Sam 5:19a, 20, 23, 24; 6:1, 2aα, 2bβ, 5, 7aβ, 8, 9a, 9b, 10, 11a; 13, 14, 16a, 16b, 17 (2×), 21 (3×), 25	2 Sam 6:7aα, 7b, 8, 11b; 5:12, 19b; 6:15, 18//1 Chr 13:10aα, 11, 14b; 14:2, 10b; 15:28; 16:2	13:2, 6bα; 14:17; 15:2, 3, 12, 13, 14, 15, 25, 26, 29a; 16:4 (2×), 7, 8, 10, 11, 14, 23, 25, 26, 28 (2×), 29 (2×), 31, 33, 34, 36 (2×), 37, 39, 40 (2×), 41
אלהים[41]				2 Chr 1b, 14bβ	2 Sam 6:6, 7aβ	2 Sam 6:6, 7aβ, 12aβ, 12b	2 Sam 6:3, 4, 6, 7aβ, 12aβ, 12b	2 Sam 6:2bα, 7b //1 Chr 13:6bα, 10b	13:2, 3, 5b, 7, 8, 12a, 2b, 14a; 14:10a, 11, 12, 14 (2×), 15, 16; 15:1, 2 (2×), 12, 13, 14, 15, 24, 26; 16:1 (2×), 4, 6, 14, 25, 26, 35, 36, 42
אדון									
אל									

40. Num 10:33–36 represents only יהוה (10:33 [2×], 34, 35, 36).
41. This includes the construct form, prefixed definite article and suffixed forms such as אלהיכם, אלהינו, etc.

Name	*1 Sam 4:1b–7:2*			*Josh 3–4*		*Josh 6*	
	B	Q	MT	B	MT	B	MT
יהוה	1 Sam 4:3aβ, 4, 5, 6, 8a, 22; 5:2, 3 (2×), 4, 6, 9; 6:2, 3, 5, 11, 13, 14, 15 (2×), 17, 18, 19 (2×), 20 (2×), 21; 7:1 (2×), 2	1 Sam 4:3, 4; 5:9, 11; 6:2, 3, 5, 8, 17, 18, 20 (2×), 21; 7:1	1 Sam 4:3aβ, 3bα, 4, 5, 6; 5:3, 4, 6, 9; 6:1, 2, 8, 11, 14, 15 (2×), 17, 18, 19 (2×), 20, 21; 7:1 (2×), 2	3:3, 5, 6 (2×), 7, 9, 15, 17a; 4:1, 5, 8 (2×), 9, 10, 11, 13, 14, 15, 16, 18, 23 (3×), 24 (2×)	3:3, 5, 7, 9, 13, 17; 4:1, 5, 7, 8, 10, 11, 13, 14, 15, 18, 23 (2×), 24 (2×)	6:2, 7, 8 (2×), 9, 12, 13 (2×), 16, 17, 19 (2×), 24, 26, 27	6:2, 6, 7, 8 (2×), 11, 12, 13 (2×), 16, 17, 19 (2×), 24, 26, 27
אלהים	1 Sam 4:3bα, 7, 8b (2×), 11, 13, 17, 18, 19, 21; 5:1, 7 (2×), 8 (3×), 10 (3×), 11, 12; 6:3, 5	1 Sam 4:11; 5:8 (4×), 10 (3×), 11 (2×); 6:3, 5, 11	4:4, 7, 8 (2×), 11, 13, 17, 18, 19, 21, 22; 5:1, 2, 7 (2×), 8 (3×), 10 (3×), 11 (2×); 6:3, 5 (2×), 20	3:3, 914; 4:23 (3×), 24	3:3, 9; 4:5, 23 (2×), 24	6:11	
ארון				3:11, 13; 4:7	3:11,		
אל				3:10	3:10		

However, if we look at Table 6, we find that these arguments are somewhat overstated. We can see that יהוה occurs frequently in the ark stories of Chronicles (50 times) as well as in Samuel–Kings (55 times). And it occurs quite often in both synoptic texts of the Solomon and David ark stories. Furthermore, as Japhet argues, יהוה appears 559 times in Chronicles, which is more than the 473 times in Samuel and the 534 times in Kings. In addition, in many contexts יהוה and אלהים clearly have the same meaning.[42]

Thus, it would be difficult for us to conclude regarding the divine epithets יהוה and אלהים that the earlier יהוה in Samuel–Kings was replaced with אלהים in Chronicles. Rather, in the study on the epithets of the ark (see section 4.3.2) we see that (ארון ה)אלהים appears to be prior to יהוה (ארון). The distribution of יהוה and אלהים in Table 6 seems to support this: אלהים occurs evenly in 1 Chr 13–16, but in 1 Sam 4:1b–7:2 it is used mainly in chs. 4–5,[43] which scholars argue is the primary layer.[44] Conversely, יהוה appears chiefly in 1 Chr 15–16, which seem to be a reworked version of 1 Chr 13. Also, in 1 Sam 4:1b–7:2 יהוה is used mostly in 1 Sam 6, which is regarded as a secondary layer by scholars.[45] Thus, it is at least feasible that אלהים is rather earlier than יהוה, and that the latter gradually became preferred by the authors or editors of these ark texts to emphasize and distinguish the Israelite God Yahweh from other gods.

4.3.5. כל־ישׂראל *and* כל־העם *in the Parallel Ark Narratives*

Research on the occurrence of the phrases כל־ישׂראל and כל־העם will also provide useful information for our study because these phrases have already been studied as important concepts in the book of Chronicles.

42. Williamson, *1 and 2 Chronicles*.

43. For this, see Auld, "What Was the Main Source of the Books of Chronicles?"

44. R. Kittel, *Geschichte des Volkes Israel*, vol. 2 (2d ed.; Gotha: Friedrich Andreas Perthes, 1909), 408 (6th ed.; Stuttgart: Kohlhammer, 1925), 297; L. Rost, *Die Überlieferung von der Thronnachfolge Davids* (BWANT 3/6; Stuttgart: Kohlhammer, 1926), 119–22; A. F. Campbell, *The Ark Narrative (1 Sam 4–6; 2 Sam 6): A Form-Critical and Traditio-Historical Study* (SBLDS 16; Missoula: Scholars Press, 1975), 7, 21–22; A. G. Auld, "What If the Chronicler Did Use the Deuteronomistic History?," in *Samuel at the Threshold*, 141–50 (145–47); Cf. Klein, *1 Samuel*, 36–61; cf. A. F. Campbell, *1 Samuel* (FOTL 7; Grand Rapids: Eerdmans, 2003), 60–84.

45. Kittel, *Geschichte des Volkes Israel*, vol. 2, 2d ed., 408; 6th ed., 297; Rost, *Die Überlieferung von der Thronnachfolge Davids*, 119–22; Campbell, *The Ark Narrative*, 7, 21–22; Auld, "What if the Chronicler Did Use the Deuteronomistic History?," 145–47; cf. Klein, *1 Samuel*, 55; cf. Campbell, *1 Samuel*, 76–84.

Table 7

Name	*Solomon's Ark* 1 Kgs7:51–8:11//2 Chr 5:1–14				*David's Ark* 2 Sam 6//1 Chr 13–16				
	Kgs + or variants		*Synoptic*	*Chr + or variants*	*2 Sam 6 + or variants*			*Synoptic*	*Chr + or variants*
	B	MT			B	Q	MT		
כל־ישראל	1 Kgs 8:5						2 Sam 6:1[46]		1 Chr 13:5, 6, 8; 14:8; 15:3, 28
כל-x[47]-ישראל	1 Kgs 8:1	1 Kgs 8:2, 5	1 Kgs 8:3// 2 Chr 5:4	2 Chr 5:3, 6	2 Sam 6:1, 15	2 Sam 6:15[48]	2 Sam 6:5, 15, 19		1 Chr 13:2 (2×); 16:3
ישראל					2 Sam 5:17, 21a	2 Sam 5:17	2 Sam 5:17; 6:21a	2 Sam 5:12a// 1 Chr 14:2a	1 Chr 16:40
x־ישראל[49]		1 Kgs 8:1aα, 1aβ	1 Kgs 8:9// 2 Chr 5:10	2 Chr 5:2aα, 2aβ	2 Sam 6:5, 20	2 Sam 6:5[50]	2 Sam 6:20	2 Sam 5:12b// 1 Chr 14:2b	1 Chr 15:12, 14, 25; 16:4, 13, 17, 36
כל־העם					2 Sam 6:2, 19a	2 Sam 6:2	2 Sam 6:2, 19a	2 Sam 6:19b// 1 Chr 16:43	1 Chr 13:4; 16:36
(ה)עם					2 Sam 6:21a		2 Sam 6:21a	2 Sam 6:18; 5:12b//1 Chr 16:2; 14:2b	1 Chr 16:8, 20
כל־עמי־הארץ									
(ה)עמים									1 Chr 16:24, 26, 28

46. Even though 2 Sam 6:1 has כל בחור בישראל, since בחור is verbal form (Qal, passive participle of בחר), I regarded this as a transformation of כל־ישראל.

47. x: noun in this table.

48. B, 4QSam[a], and MT 2 Sam 6:15 have כל בית בישראל, but 1 Chr 15:28 has כל בישראל. כל בית בישראל seems to be a synoptic expression here.

49. In Num 10:33–36, only אלפי ישראל (x-ישראל) appears once in v. 36.

50. B and 4QSam[a] Sam 6:5 use בני בישראל, but MT 2 Sam 6:15 has כל בית בישראל and 1 Chr 13:8 כל בישראל. Here בני בישראל appears to be a synoptic expression.

Name	*1 Sam 4:1b–7:2*			*Josh 3–4*		*Josh 6*	
	B	Q	MT	B	MT	B	MT
כל־ישראל	1 Sam 4:5		1 Sam 4:1, 5		3:7, 17; 4:14		
כל־x־ישראל	1 Sam 7:2		1 Sam 7:2	3:7, 17b	3:1		
ישראל	1 Sam 4:1a, 1b, 2a, 10b, 18	1 Sam 4:10b	1 Sam 4:1, 2 (2×), 10 (2×), 17, 18, 21, 22	4:22	4:22	6:25	
x־ישראל	1 Sam 4:2b, 3, 10a, 17, 22; 5:7, 8 (2×), 10b, 11, 12; 6:3	1 Sam 4:10a; 5:8 (3×), 10a, 10b, 11; 6:3	1 Sam 4:3; 5:7, 8 (3×), 10b, 11; 6:3, 5	3:9, 12; 4:4, 5, 7, 8 (2×), 12, 14	3:9, 12; 4:4, 5, 7, 8 (2×), 12, 21	6:16, 18, 23, 27	6:1, 18, 23, 25
כל־העם			1 Sam 4:11a	3:17b	4:11a	6:5a, 5b, 20bβ, 20bδ	6:5a
(ה)עם	1 Sam 4:4, 17, 10b; 6:19 (2×)	1 Sam 4:4; 5:10b	1 Sam 4:3, 4, 17; 5:10, 11; 6:19 (3×)	3:3, 5, 6 (2×), 14 (2×), 16; 4:2, 10 (2×), 19	3:3, 5, 6 (2×), 14 (2×), 16; 4:2, 10 (2×), 11b, 19	6:7, 10, 20a	6:5b, 7, 8, 10, 16, 20 (4×)
כל־עמי־הארץ				4:24	4:24		
(ה)עמים							

Japhet understood כל־ישׂראל in Chronicles not only as an ethnic concept, but also as a geographical concept. According to her, the concept of the Israelite people in Chronicles is not limited exclusively to the traditional twelve tribes, but includes all the inhabitants of Israel, including the sojourners.[51] Japhet seems to appreciate the sense of כל־ישׂראל in Chronicles correctly. However, according to Auld, this does not mean that all the expressions of כל־ישׂראל in Samuel–Kings are "original" or "earlier," and that those in Chronicles are secondary.[52] In the table above, although כל־ישׂראל appears several times in 1 Chr 13–16, it also appears in MT 1 Sam 4:1, LXX^{B} and MT 1 Sam 4:5, MT 2 Sam 6:1, LXX^{B} 1 Kgs 8:5. In addition, this expression is used in non-synoptic texts. We note that 2 Sam 11:1; 1 Kgs 5:27; 8:62, and 12:18 have כל־ישׂראל, but in the corresponding texts, 1 Chr 20:1; 2 Chr 2:16; 7:4; 10:18, it does not occur.

Besides this, the construct form of כל־x־ישׂראל is synoptic in 1 Kgs 8:3//2 Chr 5:4 and occurs as often in almost all of the ark movement narratives except for Num 10:33–36 and Josh 6. ישׂראל + noun construct form is also a synoptic expression in both the David and Solomon ark stories. This expression occurs most frequently in these ark texts. ישׂראל is synoptic as well.

כל־העם is used in the synoptic text of 2 Sam 6:19b//1 Chr 16:43 and in some other verses. (ה)עם is also a synoptic expression in 2 Sam 5:12b//1 Chr 14:2b and 2 Sam 6:18//1 Chr 16:2. First Kings 8:62, 63 has כל־ישׂראל, and its corresponding text, 2 Chr 7:4, 5 reads כל־העם. Therefore, with regard to this expression one cannot say that Samuel–Kings is prior to Chronicles. In this case, the freshness of כל־העם in Chronicles could be understood as a *lectio difficilior*.[53]

4.3.6. *Additional Evidence*

4.3.6.1. *War Motif.* Among the ark narratives, 1 Kgs 7:51–8:11//2 Chr 5 do not include a military theme. Yet, in all the other texts, the ark stories appear to evolve in a context related to war. Second Samuel 5:11–6:23// 1 Chr 13–16 and 1 Sam 4:1b–7:2 are related to the war against the

51. Japhet, *I and II Chronicles*, 46–47; idem, *The Ideology of the Book of Chronicles and Its Place in Biblical Thought* (2d ed.; BEATAJ 9; Frankfurt am Main: Lang, 1997), 270–78.

52. Auld, "What if the Chronicler Did Use the Deuteronomistic History?," 148–49, takes a similar view.

53. R. C. Rezetko, "Source and Revision in the Narratives of David's Transfer of the Ark: Text, Language and Story in 2 Samuel 6 and 1 Chronicles 13, 15–16" (Ph.D. diss., University of Edinburgh, 2004), 316. For a full explanation of this, see 301–34.

Philistines, and Josh 3–4, 6 to the Canaanite conquest. Numbers 10:33–36 also seems to be connected with war, with which Israel is confronted in the wilderness.[54]

In these texts of the ark's transportation, two words meaning "armed" are used: חמשים (Josh 4:12; 1 Sam 6:19[55]) and חלוץ (Josh 4:13; 6:7, 9, 13). In Josh 6:7, 9, and 13, only חלוץ is used; in 1 Sam 6:19 only חמשים occurs; in Josh 4:12–13, however, both terms are employed.

חנה (מחנה), which is related to battle camp, occurs frequently in these ark texts: Num 9:17, 18, 20, 22, 23; 10:2, 5, 6, 14, 18, 22, 25, 31, 34; Josh 3:2; 4:19; 6:11, 14, 18, 23; 1 Sam 4:1, 3, 5, 6, 7, 9; 1 Chr 14:15, 16.

In Num 9:15–10:36 varied war language is used; and especially in Num 10:13–28 each tribe has its own standard and systematic military formation when it marches. The military march formula in Numbers seems to be the most developed and systematized description of war among the ark narratives.

4.3.6.2. *The Placement of 2 Samuel 5:11–25 and 1 Chronicles 14.*[56] The placement of the synoptic text about the alliance with King Hiram of Tyre, of David's sons born in Jerusalem, and of the battle against the Philistines is different in Samuel and Chronicles. These events occur before the story of David's transportation of the ark into his city in 2 Sam 6, but are placed in the context of its movement into Jerusalem in 1 Chr 13–16. First Chronicles 15:1–24 and 16:4–42 include much non-synoptic, special material. Because of these variants, scholars have traditionally given priority to the disposition of 2 Samuel and held that Chronicles reproduced its arrangement and amplified 2 Sam 6 through its own special material.[57] Japhet holds that the Chronicler moved the material into its present context from the original arrangement of 2 Samuel, "in which the transfer of the ark to Jerusalem is the first act of David as king."[58] Agreeing with Japhet's position, McKenzie contends that the

54. M. Noth, *Das vierte Buch Moses, Numeri* (ATD 7; Göttingen: Vandenhoeck & Ruprecht, 1966), 71–72.

55. In 1 Sam 6:19, it could mean the number "50," but the consonants are the same as in Josh 4:12. There is a textual point, to which we have to pay attention here. In the MT, LXX, and other witnesses, this word was added.

56. 1 Chr 14 is included in this study because it is in the context of the ark's movement in 1 Chr 13–16. 2 Sam 5:11–25, which is not an ark narrative, is referred to here when it is relevant to the discussion.

57. C. T. Begg, "The Ark in Chronicles," in *The Chronicler as Theologian: Essays in Honor of Ralph W. Klein* (ed. M. P. Graham, S. L. McKenzie and G. N. Knoppers; London: T&T Clark International, 2003), 133–45.

58. Japhet, *I & II Chronicles*, 272.

Chronicler changed the location of 2 Sam 5:11–25 and 6:1–11.[59] In addition, he points out the problem of the arrangement in Chronicles: namely, there being no interval between the events in 1 Chr 12 and those in 1 Chr 13; the inevitability of encountering the Philistines while David was bringing the ark to Jerusalem; and the impossibility of the three-month interval between the first and second attempts to bring the ark into Jerusalem in 1 Chr 14.[60]

However, as Japhet herself says,

> From a purely literary point of view there is actually no break between ch. 12 and ch. 13, no concluding formula at the end of ch. 12, and no new introduction for ch. 13. No passage of time is indicated; those "who remain (הנשארים) in all the territories of Israel" (13.2) are identifiable with "the rest (שרית) of Israel" of 12.38.

According to Samuel, David first built his house, then his descendants flourished in Jerusalem; and, after he defeated the Philistines, he finally placed the ark into his temple in Jerusalem. In Chronicles, David wishes to bring the ark to Jerusalem because Israel did not turn to it during the reign of Saul. However, in the course of its transportation Uzzah touched the ark, God struck down Uzzah, and the ark stayed in the house of Obed-edom the Gittite. While the ark was in the house of Obed-edom, David suppressed the Philistines and built in Jerusalem. Finally, David brought the ark, the symbol of the presence of God, to Jerusalem. It is not easy to decide which arrangement is earlier and original. Rather, it might be safer to think that Samuel and Chronicles arrange the shared material in 2 Sam 5:11–25//1 Chr 14 (BTH)[61] according to their own purposes. Moreover, each text has its own special material: in 2 Sam 6 the debate between Michal and David in vv. 20–23 is described, while 1 Chr 13–16 explains the role of the priests and the Levites in 15:1–24 and 16:4–42. Even though 1 Chr 13–16 has a considerable amount of special material, since 2 Sam 6 also contains its own special material we could not say which one is prior simply by considering the quantity of special material in the text.

59. McKenzie, *1–2 Chronicles*, 133.

60. Ibid., 133–34.

61. BTH = the Book of the Two Houses. According to Auld ("The Former Prophets," 67), the synoptic narratives in Samuel–Kings and Chronicles tell "the story of the house (dynasty) of David in Jerusalem and of the house (temple) that Solomon built there for Yahweh from the beginnings at the death of Saul until the uprooting and removal of both by the Babylonians." And "[t]his 'Book of Two Houses' was then extended, supplemented, and reinterpreted independently and in very different ways in Samuel–Kings and in Chronicles."

4.3.6.3. *The Transportation of the Ark and the Playing of Musical Instruments*. One of the frequently appearing themes in texts recounting the transportation of the ark is the playing of musical instruments. In 2 Chr 5, the role of the Levites in playing musical instruments is mentioned (vv. 12, 13), while in 1 Kgs 7:51–8:11, which is equivalent to this text, there is no reference to this. The text providing the most detailed list of musical instruments and their performance is 1 Chr 13–16 (13:8; 15:16, 19, 20, 21, 24, 28; 16:5, 6, 42). However, in 2 Sam 6, which is synoptic with 1 Chr 13–16,[62] music is referred to just once, in v. 5. In 1 Chr 13–16 the role of the Levites in transporting the ark is described. Their role in the musical activities is explained in detail and in 15:24 the names of seven priests who blew trumpets are listed. Joshua 6 also provides a relatively detailed reference to the music in relation to the transportation of the ark: Josh 6:4, 5, 8, 13, 16, 20. In Josh 6, the number seven is stressed, especially in vv. 4, 8, 13: there are seven priests who blew the trumpets in front of the ark. In Num 10:2–10, the ways of blowing trumpets (חצצרות) and marching are described in detail. In sum, the most detailed information about musical instruments is found in Chronicles, then in Josh 6 and Num 10:2–10. There is little reference to music and instruments in Samuel–Kings.

It is also interesting to inquire into the names of these musical instruments in the ark texts. Table 8 tabulates the instruments' distribution within the texts.

According to Table 8, נבלים, כנרות, תפים are synoptic expressions, found in both 2 Sam 6:5 and 1 Chr 13:8; these texts appear to be the source of names in other non-synoptic passages. Here again, B, 4QSam[a] 2 Sam 6:5 and 1 Chr 13:8 use שירים, but MT 2 Sam 6:5 uses ברושים. The antecedent words are עז in B, 4QSam[a] 2 Sam 6:5; in 1 Chr 13:8 it is עז, but עץ in MT 2 Sam 6:5.

Moreover, שופר in 2 Sam 6:15//1 Chr 15:28aαβ also appears in Josh 6 twelve times (vv. 4 [2×], 5, 6, 8 [2×], 13 [3×], 16, 20 [2×]).[63]

Thus, if we synthesize our analysis on the themes of playing musical instruments and on their names, the possible conclusions include: (1) synoptic 2 Sam 6:5//1 Chr 13:8 is the source of other non-synoptic expressions in 1 Chr 13–16, 2 Chr 5; (2) שופר in 2 Sam 6:15//1 Chr 15:28aαβ is the source for Josh 6; (3) B, 4QSam[a] 2 Sam 6:5 also support the priority of 1 Chr 13:8 to MT 2 Sam 6:5.

62. "Synoptic" is used here in its conventional sense.

63. 1 Chr 15:28aγb is not part of the source material: it is Chronicles' plus (part of an expansion of the second half of 2 Sam 6).

Table 8

Name	*Solomon's Ark* 1 Kgs7:51–8:11//2 Chr 5:1–14				*David's Ark* 2 Sam 6//1 Chr 13–16				
	Kgs + or variants		*Synoptic*	*Chr + or variants*	*2 Sam 6 + or variants*			*Synoptic*	*Chr + or variants*
	B	MT			B	Q	MT		
המשררים				2 Chr 5:12, 13					15:16
מצלתים				2 Chr 5:12, 13					13:8; 15:16, 19, 28; 16:5, 42
נבלים				2 Chr 5:12				2 Sam 6:5//1 Chr 13:8	13:15:16, 20, 28; 16:5
כנרות				2 Chr 5:12				2 Sam 6:5//1 Chr 13:8	13:15:16, 21, 28; 16:5
חצצרות[64]				2 Chr 5:12, 13					13:8; 15:24, 28; 16:6, 42
מחצצרים				2 Chr 5:13					15:24
כלי השיר				2 Chr 5:13					
שירים					2 Sam 6:5	2 Sam 6:5[65]			13:8
חללים					2 Sam 6:5	2 Sam 6:5			
תפים								2 Sam 6:5//1 Chr 13:8	
שופר(ות)								2 Sam 6:15//1 Chr 15:28aαβ,	
מנענעים						2 Sam 6:5	2 Sam 6:5		
צלצלים					2 Sam 6:5		2 Sam 6:5		
קרן									

64. Cf. Num 10:2, 8, 9, 10.
65. B, 4QSam[a] 2 Sam 6:5, 1 Chr 13:8 have שירים, but MT 2 Sam 6:5 has ברושים.

Name	*1 Sam 4:1b–7:2*			*Josh 3–4*		*Josh 6*	
	B	Q	MT	B	MT	B	MT
המשררים							
מצלתים							
נבלים							
כנרות							
חצצרות							
מחצצרים							
כלי השיר							
שירים							
חללים							
תפים							
שופר(ות)						6:4 (2×), 5, 6, 8 (2×), 13 (3×), 16, 20 (2×)	6:4 (2×), 5, 6, 8 (2×), 13 (3×), 16, 20 (2×)
מנענעים							
צלצלים							
קרן							6:5

4.3.6.4. תרועה / רוע *in Numbers 10:5, 6, 7, 9, Joshua 6:5, 10, 16, 20, 1 Samuel 4:5, 6, 2 Samuel 6:15//1 Chronicles 15:28aαβ.* תרועה and the verbal form רוע are used frequently in these ark narratives. Nelson contends that תרועה, meaning "battle cry," is "a motif of the divine war tradition (1 Sam 4:5; 17:20, 52; etc.)."[66] According to Kang, the battle cry plays an important role in the emergence of the Jericho conquest story.[67] In Josh 6, the nominal form appears in vv. 5, 20 and the verbal form in vv. 5, 10, 16, and 20. In Num 10, the nominal form appears in vv. 5 and 6; the verbal form appears in vv. 7 and 9. תרועה, which is used in 2 Sam 6:15//1 Chr 15:28aαβ, appears also in Num 10, Josh 6, and 1 Sam 4.

In Josh 6, "to shout" is one of the major expressions: in Josh 6:10, the people of Israel are commanded to keep quiet for six days to make the battle cry of the seventh day more dramatic: לא תריעו ולא־תשמיעו את־קולכם ולא־יצא מפיכם דבר ("You shall not shout or let your voice be heard, nor shall you utter a word"). In Josh 6:16, 20, Israel breaks its silence, makes a loud war cry, and the narrative of the Jericho conquest reaches its climax. In Num 10, the ways of using or not using "war cry" in marching and in battle are described in a more systematic and concrete manner.

Thus, it is possible to conclude that תרועה in 2 Sam 6:15//1 Chr 15:28aαβ is the source of the similar expression in Num 10, Josh 6, and 1 Sam 4.

4.3.6.5. *The Problem of Geographical Names Between Kiriath-Jearim and Baale-judah.* In 2 Sam 6 and 1 Chr 13–16 the ark is carried to Jerusalem. However, the names of those places whence David brings the ark into his city are not consistent: Kiriath-jearim or Baale-judah in 1 Chr 13 and Baale-judah in 2 Sam 6. According to 1 Sam 6:21–7:2, when the ark, which had been captured by the Philistines, was returned, the inhabitants of Kiriath-jearim took it to the house of Abinadab. In 2 Sam 6:2, David and 30,000 chosen men carried the ark to Baale-judah. There is no explanation of the geographical discontinuity. However, according to 1 Chr 13:6, the two place names denote the same geographical area: "And David and all Israel went up to 'Baalah, that is, to Kiriath-jearim…'" Traditionally, scholars have thought that 1 Chr 13:6 was inserted to solve

66. Nelson, *Joshua*, 93. For more of this, see G. von Rad, *Holy War in Ancient Israel* (Grand Rapids: Eerdmans, 1991), 41–51.

67. S. M. Kang, *Divine War in the Old Testament and in the Ancient Near East* (BZAW 177: Berlin: de Gruyter, 1989).

the discontinuity.[68] However, we cannot simply accept this, because Joshua repeats the claim that Baalah is Kiriath-jearim in 1 Chr 13: בעלה היא קרית יערים (Josh 15:9), קרית בעל היא קרית יערים (Josh 15:60). 4QSam[a] 2 Sam 6:2 also represents a similar expression to 1 Chr 13:6: בעלה היא קרית יערים. We should entertain two possibilities once again: (1) the reading of MT in Samuel is *lectio difficilior* and is earlier than Chronicles and Joshua; (2) the understanding in 1 Chr 13 is prior to that in 1 Sam 4:1b–7:2 and 2 Sam 6 (MT), and Josh 15 and 4QSam[a] 2 Sam 6:2 support its authority and priority.

4.3.6.6. עד היום הזה *(2 Samuel 6:8//1 Chronicles 13:11; 1 Kings 8:8// 2 Chronicles 5:9; Joshua 4:9; 6:25; 1 Samuel 5:5; 6:18).* The phrase עד היום הזה occurs 96 times in the Old Testament.[69] The distribution of this expression is as follows: Genesis (5×), Exodus (1×), Leviticus (1×), Numbers (1×), Deuteronomy (8×), Joshua (19×), Judges (7×), Samuel (13×), Kings (16×), Chronicles (10×), Ezra (2×), Nehemiah (1×), Isaiah (2×), Jeremiah (6×), Ezekiel (2×). It appears most frequently in Joshua, and in Chronicles, Samuel–Kings, and Judges.

The phrase עד היום הזה occurs in almost all the texts in which the ark is carried to some place of promise: 2 Sam 6:8//1 Chr 13:11; 1 Kgs 8:8// 2 Chr 5:9; Josh 4:9; 6:25; 1 Sam 5:5; 6:18. The exception is Num 10:33–36.[70] It is quite interesting that in almost all the narratives dealing with the carrying of the ark in Chronicles and the Former Prophets, the expression עד היום הזה, which attests to aetiological concerns, appears.

68. For this, see, McCarter, *I Samuel*, 137; idem, *II Samuel* (AB 9; New York: Doubleday, 1984), 162–63; Klein, *1 Samuel*, 60; idem, *II Samuel* (WBC 11; Texas: Word, 1989), 99; S. J. Pisano, *Additions or Omissions in the Books of Samuel: The Significant Pluses and Minuses in the Masoretic, LXX and Qumran Texts* (OBO 57; Freiburg, Switzerland: Universitätsverlag, 1984), 101–4; Knoppers, *I Chronicles 10–29*, 586; A. F. Campbell, *2 Samuel* (FOTL 8; Grand Rapids: Eerdmans, 2005), 65.

69. Gen 26:33; 31:48; 32:33; 47:26; 48:15; Exod 10:6; Lev 23:14; Num 22:30; Deut 2:22; 3:14 (2×); 9:7 (2×); 10:8; 11:4; 29:3; 34:6; Josh 4:9; 5:9 (2×); 6:25; 7:26 (2×); 8:28, 29 (2×); 9:27; 10:27; 13:13; 14:14; 15:63; 16:10; 22:3, 17; 23:8, 9; Judg 1:21, 26; 6:24; 10:4; 15:19; 18:12; 19:30; 1 Sam 5:5; 6:18; 12:2, 5 (×2); 27:6; 29:3, 6, 8; 30:25; 2 Sam 4:3; 6:8; 7:6; 18:18; 1 Kgs 8:8; 9:13, 21; 10:12; 12:19; 2 Kgs 2:22; 7:9; 8:22; 14:7; 16:6; 17:23 (2×), 34, 41; 19:3; 20:17; 1 Chr 4:41, 43; 5:26; 13:11; 17:5; 2 Chr 5:9; 8:8; 10:19; 21:10; Ezra 9:7 (2×); Neh 9:32; Isa 37:3; 39:6; Jer 7:25 (2×); 32:20 (2×); 35:14; 44:10; Ezek 2:3; 20:29.

70. This expression appears just once in Num 22:30.

4.3.6.7. יד יהוה *(Joshua 4:24; 1 Samuel 5:6, 9)*. This phrase appears 39 times in the Hebrew Bible: Exod 9:3; 16:3; Deut 2:15; Josh 4:24; 22:31; Judg 2:15; Ruth 1:13; 1 Sam 5:6, 9; 7:13; 12:15; 2 Sam 24:14; 1 Kgs 18:46; 2 Kgs 3:15; 1 Chr 21:13; 28:19; 2 Chr 29:25; Ezra 7:6, 28; Job 12:9; Pss 75:9; Prov 21:1; Isa 19:16; 25:10; 40:2; 41:20; 51:17; 59:1; 62:3; 66:14; Jer 25:17; 51:7; Ezek 1:3; 3:14, 22; 8:1 (יד אדני יהוה); 33:22; 37:1; 40:1. Of these, only 1 Sam 5:6, 9 and Josh 4:24 are related to the movements of the ark.

In 1 Sam 4:1b–7:2, the Philistines marvel at the power of God's hand. In 1 Sam 4:8, in order to describe Yahweh's hand, which struck the Egyptians, the Philistines use the expression "from the hand of the mighty gods" (מיד האלהים האדירים). The phrase יד האלהים is rare in the Old Testament. It is only attested in 1 Sam 5:11; 2 Chr 30:12; and Eccl 2:24; 9:1. In 1 Sam 5:4, the hands of Dagon, Philistine's god, were lying severed on the ground, meaning that he could do nothing to protect his people from the God of Israel; in contrast, "the hand of Yahweh" appears figuratively as the symbol of Yahweh's power, fighting alone in the land of the Philistines and leading his people to victory (5:6, 7, 9, 11; 6:3, 5, 9). In addition, in Josh 4:24, the hand of Yahweh is described not as the symbol of power, which is a comparable object with the gods of the Gentiles, but as the absolute symbol of power, which all the people of the lands know and revere. Here, it should be noted that Josh 4:24 shares the expression יד יהוה with 1 Sam 4:1b–7:2, a non-synoptic text, and shows a theologically developed element.

4.3.6.8. (כ)מתמול שלשים *(Joshua 3:4; 4:18)*; אתמול שלשים *(1 Samuel 4:8)*. אתמול שלשים occurs in 1 Sam 4:8; 10:11; 14:21; 19:7; 2 Sam 5:2; 1 Chr 11:2. Joshua 3–4 has similar expressions: מתמול שלשים (Josh 3:4), כתמול שלשים (Josh 4:18). מתמול שלשים is also used in Exod 21:36; Deut 4:42; 19:6, and Josh 20:5; כתמול שלשים appears also in Gen 31:2; Exod 5:7, 14; Josh 4:18; 1 Sam 21:6; 2 Kgs 13:5.

4.3.6.9. התקדשו *and* יתקדשו *(Joshua 3:5; 1 Chronicles 15:12, 14; 2 Chronicles 5:11)*. The words התקדשו *and* יתקדשו are also linked with the movements of the ark. They appear in Josh 3:5; 1 Chr 15:12, and 2 Chr 5:11: Hithpael, imperative, plural in Josh 3:5 and 1 Chr 15:12 and 3rd person, plural, imperfect in 1 Chr 15:14, Hithpael, perfect, 3rd person, plural in 2 Chr 5:11. It is important to note that התקדשו is a non-synoptic expression, which does not appear in 2 Sam 6 and 1 Kgs 8, although it does in 1 Chr 15 and 2 Chr 5. In 1 Chr 15:11, 14, the Levites and priests sanctify themselves, but in 2 Chr 5:11 only the priests do. Moreover, in Josh 3:5 all the people of Israel are ordered to sanctify themselves. Thus, the expression in Josh 3:5 seems to be more generalized and developed. Therefore, Josh 3:5 is related to the non-synoptic expression התקדשו in Chronicles.

4.3.6.10. נפלאתיו *(Joshua 3:5; 1 Chronicles 16:9, 12, 24).* פלא is mainly used in the Niphal form, and occasionally in the Hiphil form, and three times in the Piel form in the Old Testament (Lev 22:21; Num 15:3, 8).

The Niphal form of פלא appears in Gen 18:14; Exod 3:20; 34:10; Deut 17:8; 30:11; Josh 3:5; Judg 6:13; 2 Sam 1:26; 13:2; 1 Chr 16:9, 12, 24; Neh 9:17; Job 5:9; 9:10; 37:5; 14; 42:3; Pss 9:1(2); 26:7; 40:5(6); 71:17; 72:18; 75:1(2); 78:4, 11, 32; 86:10; 96:3; 98:1; 105:2, 5; 106:7, 22; 107:8, 15, 21, 24, 31; 111:4; 118:23; 119:18, 27; 131:1; 136:4; 139:14; 145:5; Prov 30:18; Jer 21:2; 32:17, 27; Dan 8:24; 11:36; Mic 7:15; Zech 8:6 (2×). Of these, in Josh 3:5 and 1 Chr 16:9, 12, 24, which describe the ark's movements, פלא is always in the participle form.

4.3.6.11. וישכמו *(Joshua 6:15; 1 Samuel 5:3, 4) and* וישכם *(Joshua 3:1; 6:12).* שכם is used 64 times in the Old Testament, and only in the Hiphil form. שכם occurs 28 times in singular form, 22 times in plural form, and 14 times in infinitive form. If we tabulate the subjects of השכם from Genesis to Chronicles, in which שכם occurs frequently, the result is as follows:

Table 9

Genesis	Sg.	Abraham (19:27; 21:14; 22:3), Abimelech (20:8), Jacob (28:18), Laban (31:55 [32:1])
	Pl.	Two angels (19:20), Isaac and Abimelech (26:31)
Exodus	Sg.	Moses (8:16; 9:13; 24:4; 34:4)
	Pl.	Israel (32:6)
Joshua	Sg.	Josh (3:1; 6:12; 7:16; 8:10)
	Pl.	Israel (6:15; 8:14)
Judges	Sg.	Gideon (6:38), Jerubbaal(Gideon) (7:1), Abimelech (9:33), a Levite (19:8)
	Pl.	The men of the city (6:28), a Levite and his concubine (19:5), a Levite and his concubine and servant (19:9)
Samuel	Sg.	Samuel (1 Sam 15:12), David (1 Sam 17:20; 29:10), Absalom (2 Sam 15:2)
	Pl.	Elkanah and Hannah (1 Sam 1:19), the people of Ashdod (1 Sam 5:3, 4), Samuel and Saul (1 Sam 9:26), David and his men (1 Sam 29:10, 11)
Kings	Sg.	The servant of the man of God (2 Kgs 6:15)
	Pl.	The Moabites (2 Kgs 3:22), "they" (2 Kgs 19:35)
Chronicles	Sg.	Hezekian (2 Chr 29:20)
	Pl.	The Inhabitants of Judan and Jerusalem (2 Chr 20:20)

As we can see in Table 9, שׁכם is used to highlight the diligence of the subject. Especially in Genesis, Exodus, and Joshua it is used to stress the leadership role of Abraham, Moses, and Joshua.

In the ark texts, שׁכם usually appears as a *waw* consecutive, Hiphil, imperfect form. In Josh 6:15 and 1 Sam 5:3, 4 it appears in the plural form; in Josh 3:1 and 6:12 in singular form. In Josh 3:1 and 6:12 the subject of שׁכם is Joshua; in Josh 6:15 it is the Israelites; in 1 Sam 5:3, 4 it is the people of Ashdod.

4.3.6.12. קְצִיר־חִטִּים *(LXX Joshua 3:15; 1 Samuel 6:13)*. קְצִיר־חִטִּים occurs in Gen 30:14; Exod 34:22; LXX Josh 3:15; Judg 15:1; 1 Sam 6:13; 12:17. In MT Josh 3:15 כל ימי קציר is attested, rather than קְצִיר־חִטִּים in LXX Josh 3:15. As we saw in Chapter 3, it seems that the Hebrew *Vorlage* of LXX Josh 3:15 had קְצִיר־חִטִּים as in 1 Sam 6:13, and the MT changed the phrase into כל ימי קציר to stress and generalize this expression.

4.3.6.13. מִלְמַעְלָה *(Joshua 3:13, 16; 1 Kings 8:7//2 Chronicles 5:8)*. מִלְמַעְלָה appears in Gen 6:16; 7:20; Exod 25:21; 26:14; 36:19; 39:31; 40:19, 20; Num 4:6; 25; Josh 3:13, 16; Judg 8:13; 1 Kgs 7:11, 25; 8:7; 2 Chr 4:4; 5:8; Jer 31:37; Ezek 1:11, 22, 26; 10:19; 11:22; 37:8.

In 1 Kgs 7:25 and 2 Chr 4:4, which are synoptic, מִלְמַעְלָה is used to describe the position of the cast sea which stood on twelve oxen in Solomon's temple. In 1 Kgs 8:7 and 2 Chr 5:8, which are also synoptic, this word is used to delineate the wings of the cherubim, which spread out above the ark and its poles. In Josh 3:13, 16, it is employed to describe the waters, which are flowing down from above toward the procession of the people crossing the Jordan following the ark. In Exodus (Exod 25:21; 26:14; 36:19; 39:31; 40:19, 20), it depicts the shape of divine vessels related to the Tabernacle: the propitiatory seat on the ark (25:21; 40:20), the fine leather or tent covering the tabernacle (26:14; 36:19; 40:19), and the violet cord on the high priest's turban (39:31). In these Exodus texts, the word מִלְמַעְלָה is put to use in various and developed ways. Even though it is used differently in Joshua, the fact that it is used at all may suggest further influence from BTH. The use of the word in the texts of Exod 25–40 seems to reflect that in both synoptic texts (1 Kgs 7:25//2 Chr 4:4; 1 Kgs 8:7//2 Chr 5:8).

4.3.6.14. מָחָר *(Joshua 3:5; 4:6, 21)*; מָחֳרָת *(1 Samuel 5:3, 4)*. מָחָר occurs frequently in the Old Testament. In 1 Sam 5:3, 4 it means "tomorrow or the next day," but in Josh 3–4 it acquires an extended meaning: not only "the next day" (Josh 3:5), but also "in the future or in the time to come" (Josh 4:6, 21).

4.3.6.15. מהר *(Joshua 4:10; 1 Samuel 4:14).* מהר is mainly used in the Piel form in the Old Testament and rarely in the Qal form; the Piel form is used exclusively in the ark texts. In Josh 4:10, it means that the people crossed the Jordan quickly and in 1 Sam 4:14 it means that the messenger was in a hurry.

4.3.6.16. אוצר יהוה *(Joshua 6:19);* אוצר בית־יהוה *(Joshua 6:24);*[71] באצרות בית יהוה *(1 Kings 7:51)//*באצרות בית האלהים *(2 Chronicles 5:1).* אוצר appears frequently in the Old Testament: Deut 28:12; 32:34; Josh 6:19, 24; 1 Kgs 7:51; 14:26; 15:18; 2 Kgs 12:18 (19); 14:14; 16:8; 18:15; 20:13, 15; 24:13; 1 Chr 9:26; 26:20, 22, 24, 26; 27:25, 27, 28; 28:12; 29:8; 2 Chr 5:1; 8:15; 11:11; 12:9; 16:2; 25:24; 32:27; 36:18; Ezra 2:69; Neh 7:70, 71, 10:38 (39); 12:44; 13:12, 13; Job 38:22; Pss 33:7; 135:7; Prov 8:21; 10:2; 15:16; 21:6, 20; Isa 2:7; 30:6; 33:6; 39:2, 4; 45:3; Jer 10:13; 15:13; 17:3; 20:5; 38:11; 48:7; 49:4; 50:25, 37; 51:13, 16; Ezek 28:4; Dan 1:2; Hos 13:15; Joel 1:17; Mic 6:10; Mal 3:10.

In 1 Kgs 7:51 and 2 Chr 5:1, which are synoptic texts, once Solomon had finished building the house of Yahweh he stored the silver, the gold, and all the vessels in "the treasuries of the house of God." In Josh 6:19, Joshua commands the people to take all the silver and gold, and all the bronze and iron vessels to "the treasury of Yahweh"; in Josh 6:24, the people of Israel put these into "the treasury of the house of Yahweh." However, the phrase "the treasury of the house of Yahweh" in the context of the battle of Jericho (Josh 6:24) seems to be out of place because it is anachronistic. It might be that 1 Kgs 7:51//2 Chr 5:1 influenced this passage. We will discuss this a little further in the study on the literary history of Josh 6 below.

4.3.6.17. הענן *in 1 Kings 8:10b//2 Chronicles 5:13b; 1 Kings 8:11// 2 Chronicles 5:14; Numbers 10:34 (cf. 9:15–23; 10:11–12).* The "cloud" and "glory," which are symbols of Yahweh's presence, appear in the main hall of the house of Yahweh in 1 Kgs 8:10b//2 Chr 5:13b and 1 Kgs 8:11//2 Chr 5:14. The cloud stopped the priests from continuing the service. Japhet holds that here the use of הענן recalls the divine visitation in Exod 40:34–35 and the "pillar of cloud" in Num 12:5 and Deut 31:15.[72] In Exod 40, the cloud and glory are used separately.

> The cloud, [on the one hand,] dwells on the tabernacle from without, is visible to the whole people and with its arising signals the time to break

71. בית is an MT plus in Josh 6:24.
72. Japhet, *I & II Chronicles*, 581.

> camp and resume the journey. The glory, on the other hand, fills the tabernacle from within, and even Moses himself cannot then enter it (cf. Exod 40. 35 et al.; also Ezek 10.4).[73]

However, we cannot exclude the possibility that the descriptions of the cloud and glory in Exod 40 and Num 9:15–23; 10:11–12 are more developed, thus these texts were influenced by the synoptic text 1 Kgs 8:10b//2 Chr 5:13b and 1 Kgs 8:11//2 Chr 5:14. Although in 1 Kgs 8:10b//2 Chr 5:13b and 1 Kgs 8:11//2 Chr 5:14 (BTH), “cloud” and “glory” are used as synonyms, in Exod 40, as Japhet herself mentions, the distinction between them is explained clearly. In Num 9:15–23 and 10:11–12, 34, the cloud is a signal to the people about when to camp or when to leave: when it lifts from the Tabernacle it is time to leave, but when it rests on it the people are to remain in camp. This detailed description of the role of the cloud points to a more developed and systematized text.

As we can see from this general analysis of the additional evidence (see section 4.3.6), only some of the word studies directly suggest influence from the synoptic material to Joshua.

4.3.7. *Summary*

The analysis above demonstrates that the narratives about the movements and whereabouts of the ark share a number of words, phrases, and major themes: the epithets of the ark, the verbs used to describe the movement of the ark, the priests and the Levites as the carriers of the ark, the divine epithets, all Israel and all the people, the names of musical instruments, motifs of war, etc.

ארון האלהים, ארון יהוה, (ה)ארון ברית יהוה, הארון are basic epithets for the ark which appear in Num 10:33–36 to 2 Chr 5. We can see from Table 3 that other epithets, added to those basic names in 2 Sam 6//1 Chr 13–16 and 1 Kgs 7:51–8:11//2 Chr 5, the epithets of the ark in the Former Prophets appear to have gradually increased. Of course, we cannot exclude the opposite possibility that the two epithets in Num 10:33–36, (ה)ארון ברית יהוה, הארון, gave rise to the development of other epithets in the Former Prophets. However, if we look into the verbs used for the carrying of the ark, the probability of the latter seems to be rather small. Indeed, Table 4 suggests that these verbs also seem to have been developed from נשׂא in 2 Sam 6//1 Chr 13–16; 1 Kgs 7:51–8:11//2 Chr 5 into various words in the Former Prophets, while the verbs in Num 10:33–36 do not seem to exert any influence on the verbs used in the ark texts in Chronicles and the Former Prophets. Other words and expressions,

73. Ibid.

including the names of musical instruments, also seem to support the new way of reading the literary history of these texts suggested by Auld, namely, that the shared materials by Samuel–Kings and Chronicles are earlier than the story of Israel before the monarchy.

It was also found that Joshua and non-synoptic texts in Chronicles share some expressions: for example, those non-synoptic ark texts in Chronicles and Josh 3–4 share the compound word הכהנים (ו)הלוים. There seem to be some later special materials, which are also shared by non-synoptic texts in Samuel–Kings and Chronicles, and Joshua. The analysis of additional points also supports this position: יד יהוה (Josh 4:24; 1 Sam 5:6, 9);[74] אתמול שלשים (1 Sam 4:8) and (כ)מתמול שלשים (Josh 3:4; 4:18);[75] נפלאתיו (Josh 3:5; 1 Chr 16:9, 12, 24);[76] וישכמו (Josh 6:15; 1 Sam 5:3, 4) and וישכם (Josh 3:1; 6:12);[77] מחרת (1 Sam 5:3, 4); מחר (Josh 3:5; 4:6, 21);[78] מהר (Josh 4:10; 1 Sam 4:14),[79] etc.

This study also revealed that where B, 4QSam[a] agree with each other, they quite often agree with Chronicles but not with MT Samuel.[80] Therefore, this writer could guess that in terms of the synoptic texts, Chronicles seems to have been written before Samuel was revised into MT Samuel. However, this does not mean that the non-synoptic elements of Chronicles are earlier than pre-MT Samuel.

Bearing in mind these points, I intend to read these ark texts and provide a possible literary history of each text. Of course, we cannot still definitively claim that we should read these texts in historical, and not canonical, order. Yet, mainstream research so far on these texts has not considered this challenge and has focused solely on exploration in the context of the canonical order. Thus, this study will consider the challenges caused by the preliminary analysis above, and will attempt to suggest possible examples to read these texts in literary-historical order.

4.4. *The Literary-Historical Reading of Joshua 3–4 in the Context of the Parallel Ark Narratives*

In this section, considering the challenges raised by the preliminary analysis in section 4.3, we will investigate the literary history of Josh 3–4 in the context of ark texts, that is, texts in which the ark moves to the

74. See section 4.3.6.7.
75. See section 4.3.6.8.
76. See section 4.3.6.10.
77. See section 4.3.6.11.
78. See section 4.3.6.14.
79. See section 4.3.6.15.
80. See nn. 24–28, 30.

land of promise, in literary-historical order. First, we will consider the recent trends in the discussion of the relationship between Samuel–Kings and Chronicles, which was also raised in section 4.3.

4.4.1. *Ark Stories in the Books of Samuel–Kings and Chronicles (1 Samuel 4:1b–7:2, 2 Samuel 6//1 Chronicles 13–16, 1 Kings 7:51–8:11//2 Chronicles 5)*

The presentation of the divided kingdom in Chronicles and Kings exhibits a number of common characteristics that resulted in these books being viewed as reliable witnesses to Israel's past. These books came to be understood as having been based on prior material known to the writers of both versions.[81] Eichhorn, a representative of the research history of Chronicles in the pre-critical period, held that the accounts in 1 and 2 Kings, on the one hand, and 2 Chronicles, on the other, derive from a common source, and that Ezra[82] often utilized other sources, besides taking excerpts from materials of the common source with extensive histories of Israel and Judah.[83]

However, since de Wette maintained that the Chronicler used Samuel and Kings as a source in the first volume of his *Beiträge*,[84] views on the relationship between Samuel–Kings and Chronicles have changed radically. Mainstream scholarship since de Wette has maintained that much of the literature of the Old Testament had already been written by the time of the composition of Chronicles.[85] This modern scholarship ascribes the deviation of Chronicles from Samuel–Kings to the Chronicler's theological interests and differences.[86] Yet, this conventional modern scholarship has been challenged by evidence from the Dead Sea

81. L. Kucova, "Common Source Theory and Composition of the Story of the Divided Monarchy in Kings with Special Emphasis on the Account of Josiah's Reform" (Ph.D. diss., University of Edinburgh, 2005), 1.

82. Ezra is the author of Chronicles in the understanding of pre-critical era.

83. See J. G. Eichhorn, *Einleitung in das Alte Testament* (2d ed.; 3 vols.; Leipzig: Weidmanns, Erben & Reich, 1787), 606–56.

84. W. M. L. de Wette, *Kritischer Verzug über die Glaubwürdigkeit der Bücher der Chronik mit Hinsicht auf die Geschichte der Mosaischen Bücher und Gesetzgebung. Ein Nachtrag zu den Vaterschen Untersuchungen über den Pentateuch* in the first volume of *Beiträge zur Einleitung in das Alten Testament* (2 vols.; Halle: Schimmelpfenning, 1806).

85. Knoppers, *I Chronicles 10–29*, 66.

86. K. Peltonen, *History Debated: The Historical Reliability of Chronicles in Pre-Critical and Critical Research* (2 vols.; Publications of the Finnish Exegetical Society 64; Göttingen: Vandenhoeck & Ruprecht, 1996).

Scrolls discovered in the Judean Desert between 1947 and 1956.[87] Werner Lemke in his book *Synoptic Studies in the Chronicler's History* (1963), with the help of 4QSam[a][88] and the Greek witnesses,[89] has shown that not every deviation in Chronicles from Samuel and Kings derives from the Chronicler's *Tendenz*; but some differences had already been part of Chronicler's *Vorlage*.[90] According to him, it can no longer be held that the differences of the respective Masoretic texts of Samuel–Kings and Chronicles are in every case due to the tendentious interests of the Chronicler.[91]

Macy also made a significant contribution to the studies of the relationship between the biblical books of Samuel–Kings and Chronicles.[92] On the basis of a close examination of the standard formulaic notices, which Kings and Chronicles regularly employ at the beginning and the end of the narratives of each king's reign, Macy concluded that both the Chronicler and the Deuteronomist (or the author/editor of Kings) depended on an earlier common source or sources which they utilized, each according to the aims and purposes of his own work.[93] Macy called

87. See F. M. Cross, "The History of the Biblical Text in the Light of Discoveries in the Judaean Desert," *HTR* 57 (1964): 294; J. R. Porter, "Old Testament Historiography," in *Tradition and Interpretation: Essays by Members of the Society for Old Testament Study* (ed. G. W. Anderson; Oxford: Clarendon, 1979), 155–56; G. F. Hasel, "Books of Chronicles," in *The International Standard Bible Encyclopedia*. Vol. 1, *A–D* (ed. G. W. Bromiley; Grand Rapids: Eerdmans, 1979), 667; H. G. M. Williamson, "Introduction," in *The Chronicler's History* (trans. H. G. M. Williamson with an introduction; JSOTSup 50; Sheffield: Sheffield Academic, 1987), originally published as the second part of *Überlieferungsgeschichtliche Studien: Die sammelnden und bearbeiten Geschichtswerke im Alten Testament* (Halle: Niemeyer, 1943).

88. W. E. Lemke, "Synoptic Studies in the Chronicler's History" (Ph.D. diss., Harvard University, 1963).

89. Ibid., 240; idem, "The Synoptic Problem in the Chronicler's History," *HTR* 58 (1965): 362–63.

90. See P. R. Ackroyd, "History and Theology in the Writings of the Chronicler," *CTM* 38 (1967): 501–15 (507–8) for the significance of this conclusion when approaching the question of the Chronicler's theology.

91. This conclusion is nowadays generally accepted in studies and commentaries on Chronicles. See, for example, the 2004 commentary on 1 Chronicles by Knoppers.

92. H. R. Macy, "The Sources of the Books of Chronicles: A Reassessment" (Ph.D. diss., Harvard University, 1975).

93. See also R. C. Rezetko, "Dating Biblical Hebrew: Evidence from Samuel–Kings and Chronicles," in *Biblical Hebrew: Studies in Chronology and Typology* (ed. I. Young; JSOTSup 369; London: T&T Clark International, 2003), 215 n. 2,

this primary source "Deuteronomistic" or stemming from the "Deuteronomistic school," which is dependent upon the occurrence of the evaluative phrase "to do right/evil in the eyes of Yahweh" in the formulaic notices.

McKenzie also contributed to the study of the relationship between Chronicles and Samuel–Kings.[94] Pursuing F. M. Cross's (1973) double redaction of the Deuteronomistic History, McKenzie suggested that only the first edition (Dtr 1 in the terminology of Cross) of the Deuteronomistic History was available to the Chronicler. In other words, he contended that the principal source used by the Chronicler was an earlier edition of Samuel–Kings, which ended with the death of Josiah.[95]

who mentions others before Auld consenting to the idea of a common source employed by the author(s) of Samuel–Kings and Chronicles.

94. S. L. McKenzie, *The Chronicler's Use of the Deuteronomistic History* (HSM 33; Atlanta: Scholars Press, 1985).

95. McKenzie has somewhat changed his views since his 1985 monograph, in which he utilized Cross's single Dtr 1 for the Josianic and Dtr 2 for a later exilic editor of the Deuteronomistic History. In his book, *The Trouble with Kings: The Composition of the Book of Kings in the Deuteronomistic History* (VTSup 42; Leiden: Brill), though still espousing the view of a primary Deuteronomistic work composed in Josianic times, he considered this history to be written by a single author/editor that was only lightly updated by several post-Deuteronomistic additions. Still later, he completely abandoned a pre-exilic date for the History. He now considers the Deuteronomistic History to be an exilic work written by a single historian, thus favouring the position of Noth; see S. L. McKenzie, "Cette royauté qui fait problème," in *Israël construit son histoire: L'historiographie deutéronomiste à la lumière des recherches récentes* (ed. A. de Pury, T. Römer and J.-D. Macchi; Le Monde de la Bible 34; Geneva: Labor et Fides, 1996), 267–95 (translated as "The Trouble with Kingship," in de Pury, Römer and Macchi, eds., *Israel Constructs Its History: Deuteronomistic Historiography in Recent Research* [JSOTSup 306; Sheffield: Sheffield Academic, 2000], 286–314); idem, "Mizpah of Benjamin and the Date of the Deuteronomistic History," in *"Lasset uns Brücken bauen...": Collected Communications to the XVth Congress of the International Organization for the Study of the Old Testament, Cambridge 1995* (ed. K. Schunck and M. Augustin; BEATAJ 42; Frankfurt am Main: Lang, 1998), 149–55; idem, "Postscript: The Laws of Physics and Pan-Deuteronomism," in Schearing and McKenzie, eds., *Those Elusive Deuteronomists*, 262–71; idem, "The Divided Kingdom in the Deuteronomistic History and in Scholarship On It," in *The Future of the Deuteronomistic History* (ed. T. Römer; BETL 147; Leuven: Leuven University Press, 2000), 135–45. McKenzie regards the Deuteronomistic History as being enlarged by post-Deuteronomistic additions—although these were made according to him in no systematic way. Thus he may be close to Van Seters' view of the Deuteronomist as a creative historian (for this, see Van Seters, *In Search of History*; cf. S. L. McKenzie, "The Book of Kings in the Deuteronomistic History," in *The History of Israel's*

In a more radical way than the three Harvard theses of Lemke (1963), Macy (1975), and McKenzie (1985), Auld challenged mainstream scholarship relating to the composition of the books of the Hebrew Bible from Deuteronomy to Kings and Chronicles.[96] According to him, Samuel–Kings and Chronicles are based on common source material from which they each developed in their distinctive ways. As a result of a number of responses and criticisms,[97] Auld made some modifications to his original proposal,[98] and further developed the main tenets of *Kings Without Privilege*.[99] The shared material by Samuel–Kings and Chronicles he now calls the "Book of Two Houses" (BTH), which is "the story of the royal and the divine house in Jerusalem from the death of Saul until the uprooting and removal of both 'houses' by the Babylonians."[100] For Auld, BTH is "the root work of the whole tree of Genesis–Kings."[101]

However, it is not my objective to deal with all the recent issues concerning Samuel–Kings and Chronicles. Instead, the focus will be on those that are essential for the reading of the literary history of Josh 3–4. We will consider here the findings of the preliminary study (section 4.3) and investigate the general points and the question of priority between Samuel–Kings and Chronicles.

Traditions: The Heritage of Martin Noth [ed. S. L. McKenzie and M. P. Graham; JSOTSup 182; Sheffield: Sheffield Academic, 1994], 300–302), whose work was supplemented with several additions by later writers.

96. Auld, *Kings Without Privilege*.

97. For the challenges Auld has encountered, see H. G. M. Williamson, "A Response to A. Graeme Auld," *JSOT* 27 (1983): 33–39; idem, Review of A. G. Auld, *Kings Without Privilege*, *VT* 46 (1996): 553–55; G. N. Knoppers, Review of A. G. Auld, *Kings Without Privilege: David and Moses in the Story of the Bible's Kings*, *ATJ* 27 (1995): 118–21; R. J. Coggins, Review of *Kings Without Privilege* by A.G. Auld," *Theology* 98 (1995), 383; W. Johnstone, Review of A. G. Auld, *Kings Without Privilege*, *SJT* 50 (1997): 256–58; S. L. McKenzie, "The Chronicler as Redactor," in *The Chronicler as Author: Studies in Text and Texture* (ed. M. P. Graham and S. L. McKenzie; JSOTSup 263; Sheffield: Sheffield Academic, 1999), 70–90; Z. Talshir, "Textual and Literary Criticism of the Bible in Post-Modern Times: The Untimely Demise of Classical Biblical Philology," *Henoch* 21 (1999): 249–51; idem, "The Reign of Solomon in the Making: Pseudo-connections Between 3 Kingdoms and Chronicles," *VT* 50 (2000): 248 n. 31; Knoppers, *I Chronicles 1–9*, 67.

98. See, e.g., his response to McKenzie in Auld, "What Was the Main Source of the Books of Chronicles?"

99. See the essays collected in Auld, *Samuel at the Threshold*.

100. Auld, "The Former Prophets," 67.

101. Ibid., 53–68; idem, "The Deuteronomist Between History and Theology," 353–67; idem, *I & II Samuel*, 1–17.

4.4.1.1. *The Ark's Arrival to the Temple in Jerusalem (1 Kings 7:51–8:11//2 Chronicles 5).* Regarding these synoptic texts, modern scholars have generally argued that Chronicles was written with the help of the materials found in 1 Kgs 7:51–8:11.[102] Japhet insists that "the Chronicler adopts the material from I Kings with only a few omissions, and these are compensated for by the few additions so that the overall scope remains the same."[103] McKenzie also holds that the Chronicler omits (1 Kgs 8:2//2 Chr 5:3), substitutes (1 Kgs 8:3//2 Chr 5:4), and adds (2 Chr 5:11–13) some expressions to compose 2 Chr 5:1–6:2 for his own purpose.[104] If we tabulate these two texts, compare the differences between them, and reflect on the consequences of the preliminary analysis above, the situation could be changed somewhat.

Table 10

	1 Kgs 7:51–8:11	*2 Chr 5:1–14*	
7:51	ותשלם כל־המלאכה אשר עשה המלך* שלמה בית יהוה ויבא שלמה את־קדשי דוד אביו את־הכסף ואת־הזהב ואת־__־הכלים נתן באצרות בית יהוה	ותשלם כל־המלאכה אשר־ עשה___שלמה *לבית יהוה ויבא שלמה את־קדשי דוד אביו *ואת־הכסף ואת־הזהב ואת־כל*־הכלים נתן באצרות בית האלהים	5:1
8:1	אז יקהל שלמה את־זקני ישראל את־כל־ראשי המטות נשיאי האבות לבני ישראל אל־המלך שלמה* ירושלם להעלות את־ארון ברית־יהוה מעיר דוד היא ציון	אז יקהל שלמה את־זקני ישראל *ואת־כל־ראשי המטות נשיאי האבות לבני ישראל אל־_____ ירושלם להעלות את־ארון ברית־יהוה מעיר דוד היא ציון	5:2
8:2	ויקהלו אל־המלך שלמה* כל־איש ישראל בירח האתנים* בחג הוא החדש השביעי	ויקהלו אל־המלך ___ כל־איש ישראל _______ בחג הוא החדש השביעי	5:3
8:3	ויבאו כל זקני ישראל וישאו הכהנים את־הארון	ויבאו כל זקני ישראל וישאו הלוים את־הארון	5:4

102. For this see, B. O. Long, *1 Kings with an Introduction to Historical Literature* (FOTL 9; Grand Rapids: Eerdmans, 1984); S. J. DeVries, *1 Kings* (WBC 12; Waco: Word, 1985); idem, *1 and 2 Chronicles* (FOTL 11; Grand Rapids: Eerdmans, 1989); Japhet, *I & II Chronicles*; Begg, "The Ark in Chronicles"; McKenzie, *1–2 Chronicles*.

103. Japhet, *I & II Chronicles*, 573.

104. McKenzie, *1–2 Chronicles*, 244–45.

8:4	ויעלו את־ארון יהוה* ואת־אהל מועד ואת־כל־כלי הקדש אשר באהל ויעלו אתם הכהנים והלוים	ויעלו את־הארון ___ ואת־אהל מועד ואת־כל־כלי הקדש אשר באהל העלו אתם הכהנים הלוים	5:5
8:5	והמלך שלמה וכל־עדת ישראל הנועדים עליו אתו* לפני הארון מזבחים צאן ובקר אשר לא־יספרו ולא ימנו מרב	והמלך שלמה וכל־עדת ישראל הנועדים עליו ___ לפני הארון מזבחים צאן ובקר אשר לא־יספרו ולא ימנו מרב	5:6
8:6	ויבאו הכהנים את־ארון ברית־ יהוה אל־מקומו אל־דביר הבית אל־קדש הקדשים אל־תחת כנפי הכרובים	ויביאו הכהנים את־ארון ברית־ יהוה אל־מקומו אל־דביר הבית אל־קדש הקדשים אל־תחת כנפי הכרובים	5:7
8:7	כי הכרובים פרשים כנפים אל־מקום הארון ויסכו הכרבים על־הארון ועל־בדיו מלמעלה	ויהיו הכרובים פרשים כנפים על־מקום הארון ויכסו הכרבים על־הארון ועל־בדיו מלמעלה	5:8
8:8	ויארכו הבדים ויראו ראשי הבדים מן־הקדש על־פני הדביר ולא יראו החוצה ויהיו שם עד היום הזה	ויאריכו הבדים ויראו ראשי הבדים מן־הארון על־פני הדביר ולא יראו החוצה ויהי שם עד היום הזה	5:9
8:9	אין בארון רק שני לחות האבנים* אשר הנח שם* משה בחרב אשר כרת יהוה עם־בני ישראל בצאתם מארץ* מצרים	אין בארון רק שני הלחות ___ אשר־נתן ___ משה בחרב אשר כרת יהוה עם־בני ישראל בצאתם מ___ מצרים	5:10
8:10a	ויהי בצאת הכהנים מן־הקדש	ויהי בצאת הכהנים מן־הקדש כי כל־הכהנים הנמצאים התקדשו אין לשמור למחלקות*	5:11
		והלוים המשררים לכלם לאסף להימן לידתון ולבניהם ולאחיהם מלבשים בוץ במצלתים ובנבלים וכנרות עמדים מזרח למזבבח ועמהם כהנים למאה ועשרים מחצצרים בחצצרות	5:12*
		ויהי כאחד למחצצרים ולמשררים להשמיע קול־אחד להלל ולהדות ליהוה וכהרים קול בחצצרות ובמצלתים ובכלי השיר ובהלל ליהוה כי טוב כי לעולם חסדו	5:13a*
8:10a	והענן מלא את־בית יהוה	והבית מלא ענן בית יהוה	5:13b

8:11	ולא־יכלו הכהנים לעמד לשרת מפני הענן כי־מלא כבוד־יהוה את־בית יהוה	ולא־יכלו הכהנים לעמוד לשרת מפני הענן כי־מלא כבוד־יהוה את־בית האלהים	5:14

* = Plus

In 1 Kgs 7:51–8:11 there are nine small pluses, while there are four small pluses in 2 Chr 5, along with one big plus in 2 Chr 5:11b–13. Japhet holds that the non-synoptic text in 2 Chr 5:11b–13 is the Chronicler's own insertion, "elaborating on the ceremonial aspects of the installation of the ark."[105]

One interesting point worth noting is that the description of the Levites, priests, and musical instruments in 2 Chr 5:11b–13 also appears in 1 Chr 13:8; 15:16, 19, 20, 21, 24, 28; 16:5, 6, 42 (and Num 10:2, 8, 9, 10). McKenzie claims that these peculiar texts in Chronicles originated from some "non-canonical source" which the Chronicler used, as opposed to the canonical Samuel–Kings.[106] As we have seen in section 4.3.6.3, those expressions also appear in 2 Sam 6:5, 15, and the synoptic report (2 Sam 6:5//1 Chr 13:8 and 2 Sam 6:15//1 Chr 15:28aαβ) is the source of this list. One could argue that the problem is that he considers only the influence which Samuel–Kings exerts on Chronicles. Nevertheless, he appears to consider the existence of some later special material such as 2 Chr 5:11b–13.

Therefore, if we take into account the above findings in Table 10, it does not seem possible to conclude simply that 1 Kgs 7:51–8:11 is prior to 2 Chr 5. Rather, if we consider the challenges raised by B, 4QSam[a] 2 Sam 6:5 in section 4.3.6.3, 1 Chr 13:8 seems to be earlier than MT 2 Sam 6:5.

4.4.1.2. *The Ark Is Carried to Jerusalem (2 Samuel 6//1 Chronicles 13–16)*. Mainstream scholarship has generally argued that 1 Chr 13–16 took its main material from 2 Sam 6.[107] Japhet holds that the Chronicler mixed various sources and produced a new literary structure. According to her, "Some of these elements have been taken from biblical sources, mainly II Samuel; some have probably been drawn from non-biblical sources, while some he penned himself."[108]

105. Japhet, *I & II Chronicles*, 574.

106. McKenzie, *1–2 Chronicles*, 40–43.

107. For this, see Long, *1 Kings with an Introduction to Historical Literature*; DeVries, *1 Kings*; idem, *1 and 2 Chronicles*; S. Japhet, *I & II Chronicles*; Begg, "The Ark in Chronicles"; McKenzie, *1–2 Chronicles*.

108. Japhet, *I & II Chronicles*, 272.

Table 11

	2 Sam 6	*1 Chr 13–16*	
		1 ויועץ דויד עם־שׂרי האלפים והמאות לכל־נגיד 2 ויאמר דויד לכל קהל ישׂראל אם־עליכם טוב ומן־יהוה אלהינו נפרצה נשׁלחה על־אחינו הנשׁארים בכל ארצות ישׂראל ועמהם הכהנים והלוים בערי מגרשׁיהם ויקבצו אלינו 3 ונסבה את־ארון אלהינו אלינו כי־לֹא דרשׁנהו בימי שׁאול 4 ויאמרו כל־הקהל לעשׂות כן כי־ישׁר הדבר בעיני כל־העם	*13:1–4
6:1	ויסף עוד דוד את־כל־בחור בישׂראל שׁלשׁים אלף	ויקהל דויד את־כל־ישׂראל מן־שׁיחור מצרים ועד־לבוא חמת	13:5a
6:2	ויקם וילך דוד וכל ־העם אשׁר אתו מבעלי יהודה להעלות משׁם את ארון האלהים אשׁר־נקרא שׁם שׁם יהוה צבאות ישׁב הכרבים עליו	להביא את ־ארון האלהים מקרית יערים	13:5b
		ויעל דויד וכל־ישׂראל בעלתה אל־קרית יערים אשׁר ליהודה להעלות משׁם את ארון האלהים יהוה יושׁב הכרובים אשׁר־נקרא שׁם	*13:6

6:3	וירכבו את־ארון האלהים אל־עגלה חדשה *וישאהו מבית אבינדב *אשר בגבעה ועזא ואחיו *בני אבינדב נהגים את־העגלה *חדשה	וירכיבו את־ארון האלהים על־עגלה חדשה ____ מבית אבינדב ______ ועזא ואחיו ______ נהגים בעגלה ___	13:7
*6:4	וישאהו מבית אבינדב אשר בגבעה עם ארון האלהים ואחיו הלך לפני הארון		
6:5	ודוד וכל־*בית ישראל משחקים לפני יהוה בכל עצי ברושים ובכנרות ובנבלים ובתפים ובמנענעים ובצלצצים	ודויד וכל־__ ישראל משחקים לפני האלהים בכל עז *ובשירים ובכנרות ובנבלים ובתפים ובמצלתים ובחצצרות	13:8
6:6	ויבאו עד־גרן נכון וישלח עזא ______ אל־ארון האלהים ויאחז בו* כי שמטו הבקר	ויבאו עד־גרן כידן וישלח עזא את־ידו לאחז* את־הארון ________ כי שמטו הבקר	13:9
6:7	ויחר־אף יהוה בעזה ויכהו שם האלהים על־השל וימת שם עם ארון האלהים	ויחר־אף יהוה בעזא ויכהו על אשר־שלח ידו על־הארון וימת שם לפני אלהים	13:10
6:8	ויחר לדוד על אשר פרץ יהוה פרץ בעזה ויקרא למקום ההוא פרץ עזה עד היום הזה	ויחר לדויד כי־ פרץ יהוה פרץ בעזא ויקרא למקום ההוא פרץ עזה עד היום הזה	13:11
6:9	וירא דוד את־יהוה ביום ההוא ויאמר איך יבוא אלי __ ארון יהוה	ויירא דויד את־האלהים ביום ההוא לאמר היך אביא אלי *את ארון האלהים	13:12

13:13	ולא־הסיר דויד את־הארון אליו אל־עיר דוד ויטהו אל־בית עבד־אדום הגתי	ולא־אבה דוד *להסיר אליו את־ארון יהוה על־עיר דוד ויטהו דוד בית עבד־אדום הגתי	6:10
13:14	וישב ארון האלהים עם* בית עבד אדם בביתו שלשה חדשים ויברך יהוה את־בית*עבד־אדם ואת־כל־אשר־לו	וישב ארון יהוה _בית עבד אדם הגתי שלשה חדשים ויברך יהוה את־__ עבד אדם ואת־כל־ביתו	6:11
14:1	וישלח חירם מלך־צר מלאכים אל־דויד ועצי ארזים וחרשי קיר וחרשי עצים לבנות לו בית	וישלח חורם מלך־צר מלאכים אל־דויד ועצי ארזים וחרשי עץ וחרשי אבן קיר ויבנו־בית לדוד	5:11
14:2	וידע דויד כי־הכינו יהוה למלך על־ישראל כי־נשאת למעלה* מלכותו בעבור עמו ישראל	וידע דוד כי־הכינו יהוה למלך על־ישראל ו*כי ־נשא ___ ממלכתו בעבור עמו ישראל	5:12
14:3	ויקח דויד עוד ____ נשים בירושלם ________ ויולד דויד עוד בנים ובנות	ויקח דוד עוד פלגשים ו*נשים מירושלם אהרי באו מחברון* ויולדו עוד לדוד בנים ובנות	5:13
14:4	ואלה שמות הילודים אשר היו־לו בירושלם שמוע ושובב נתן ושלמה	ואלה שמות הילדים ____ לו בירושלם שמוע ושובב ו* נתן ושלמה	5:14
14:5	ויבחר ואלישוע *ואלפלט	ויבחר ואלישוע ונפג ויפיע	5:15
14:6	*ונגה ונפג ויפיע		
14:7	ואלישמע ובעלידע ואליפלט	ואלישמע ואלידע ואליפלט	5:16
14:8	וישמעו פלשתים כי־נמשח _ דויד למלך על־*כל־ישראל ויעלו כל־פלשתים לבקש את־דויד וישמע דויד ויצא לפניהם	וישמעו פלשתים כי־משחו *את־דויד למלך על־_־ישראל ויעלו כל־פלשתים לבקש את־דוד וישמע דוד וירד אל־המצודה	5:17

5:18	ופלשתים באו וינטשו בעמק רפאים	ופלשתים באו ויפשטו בעמק רפאים	14:9
5:19	וישאל דויד ביהוה לאמר האעלה אל־פלשתים התתנם בידי ויאמר __ יהוה *אל־דוד עלה כי־נתן *אתן את־הפלשתים בידך	וישאל דויד באלהים לאמר האעלה על־פלשתיים ונתתם בידי ויאמר *לו יהוה ____ עלה ונתתים ___________ בידך	14:10
5:20	ויבא *דוד בבעל־פרצים ויכם שם דוד ויאמר __ פרץ יהוה את־איבי לפני כפרץ מים על־כן קרא שם־המקום ההוא בעל פרצים	ויעלו __ בבעל־פרצים ויכם שם דויד ויאמר דויד פרץ האלהים את־אויבי בידי כפרץ מים על־כן קראו שם־המקום ההוא בעל פרצים	14:11
5:21	ויעזבו־שם את־עצביהם וישאם דוד ואנשיו	ויעזבו־שם את־אלהיהם ויאמר דויד וישרפו באש	14:12
5:22	ויספו עוד פלשתים *לעלות וינטשו בעמק *רפאים	ויסיפו עוד פלשתים ____ ויפשטו בעמק ____	14:13
5:23	וישאל __ דוד ביהוה ויאמר _____ לא תעלה הסב אל־אחריהם ובאת להם ממול בכאים	וישאל *עוד דויד באלהים ויאמר *לו האלהים לא תעלה אחריהם הסב מעליהם ובאת להם ממול הבכאים	14:14
5:24	ויהי בשמעך את־קול צעדה בראשי הבכאים אז תחרץ _____ כי *אז יצא יהוה לפניך להכות במחנה פלשתים	ויהי כשמעך את־קול הצעדה בראשי הבכאים אז תצא *במלחמה כי־__יצא האלהים לפניך להכות את־מחנה פלשתים	14:15
5:25	ויעש דוד *כן כאשר צוהו יהוה ויך את־___ פלשתים מגבע עד־באך* גזר	ויעש דויד __ כאשר צוהו האלהים ויכו את־*מחנה פלשתים מגבעון ו*עד־ __ גזרה	14:16

		ויצא שם־דויד בכל־הארצות ויהוה נתן את־פחדו על־כל־הגוים	*14:17
		1 ויעש־לו בתים בעיר דויד ויכן מקום לארון האלהים ויט־לו אהל 2 אז אמר דויד לא לשׂאת את־ארון האלהים כי אם־הלוים כִי־בם~ בחר יהוה לשׂאת את־ארון יהוה ולשרתו עד־עולם 3 ויקהל דויד את־כל־ישׂראל אל־ירושלם להעלות את־ארון יהוה אל־מקומו אשר־הכין לו 4 ויאסף דויד את־בני אהרן ואת־הלוים 5 לבני קהת אוריאל השׂר ואחיו מאה ועשׂרים 6 לבני מררי עשׂיה השׂר ואחיו מאתים ועשׂרים 7 לבני גרשום יואל השׂר ואחיו מאה ושלשים 8 לבני אליצפן שמעיה השׂר ואחיו מאתים 9 לבני חברון אליאל השׂר ואחיו שמונים 10 לבני עזיאל עמינדב השׂר ואחיו מאה ושנים עשׂר 11 ויקרא דויד לצדוק ולאביתר הכהנים וללוים לאוריאל עשׂיה ויואל שמעיה ואליאל ועמינדב 12 ויאמר להם אתם ראשי האבות ללוים התקדשו אתם ואחיכם והעליתם את ארון יהוה אלהי ישׂראל	*15:1–24

אל־הכינותי לו
13 כי למבראשונה לא אתם פרץ יהוה אלהינו
בנו כי־לא דרשנהו כמשפט
14 ויתקדשו הכהנים והלוים להעלות
את־ארון יהוה אלהי ישראל
15 וישאו בני־הלוים את ארון האלהים
כאשר צוה משה כדבר יהוה
בכתפם במטות עליהם
16 ויאמר דויד לשרי הלוים
להעמיד את־אחיהם המשררים
בכלי־שיר נבלים וכנרות
ומצלתים משמיעים להרים־בקול לשמחה
17 ויעמיד הלוים את הימן
בן־יואל ומן־אחיו אסף
בן־ברכיהו ומן־בני מררי
אחיהם איתן בן־קושיהו
18 ועמהם אחיהם המשנים
זכריהו בן ויעזיאל ושמירמות
ויחיאל ועני אליאב ובניהו
ומעשיהו ומתתיהו ואליפלהו
ומקניהו ועבד אדם ויעיאל השערים
19 והמשררים הימן אסף
ואיתן במצלתים נחשת להשמיע
20 וזכריה ועזיאל ושמירמות
ויחיאל ועני ואליאב ומעשיהו
ובניהו בנבלים על־עלמות
21 ומתתיהו ואליפלהו ומקניהו

	ועבד אדם ויעיאל ועזיזהו בכנרות על־השמינית לנצח 22 וכנניהו שר־הלוים במשא יסר במשא כי מבין הוא 23 וברכיה ואלקנה שערים לארון 24 ושבניהו ויושפט ונתנאל ר ועמשי וזכריהו ובניהו ואליעז הכהנים מחצצרים בחצצרות לפני ארון האלהים ועבד אדם ויחיה שערים לארון		
15:25		12a* ויגד למלך דוד לאמר ברך יהוה את־בית עבד אדם ואת־כל־אשר־לו בעבור ארון האלהים	6:12
	ויהי דויד וזקני ישראל ושרי האלפים ההלכים להעלות את־ארון ברית־יהוה מן־בית עבד־אדם בשמחה	12b וילך דוד ויעל את־ארון האלהים מבית עבד אדם עיר דוד בשמחה	
15:26	ויהי בעזר האלהים את־הלוים נשאי ארון ברית־יהוה ויזבחו שבעה־פרים ושבעה אילים	ויהי כי צעדו נשאי ארון־יהוה ששה צעדים ויזבח שור ומריא	6:13
15:27	ודויד מכרבל במעיל בוץ וכל־הלוים הנשאים את־הארון והמשררים וכנניה השר המשא המשררים ועל־דויד אפוד בד	ודוד מכרכר בכל־עז לפני יהוה ודוד חגור אפוד בד	6:14
15:28	__ וכל־_ישראל מעלים את־ארון *ברית־יהוה בתרועה ובקול שופר *ובחצצרות ובמצלתים משמעים בנבלים וכנרות	*ודוד וכל־*בית ישראל מעלים את־ארון יהוה בתרועה ובקול שופר __________	6:15

6:16	והיה ארון__ יהוה בא __ עיר דוד ומיכל בת־שאול נשקפה בעד החלון ותרא את־המלך דוד מפזז ומכרכר לפני יהוה ותבז לו בלבה	ויהי ארון *ברית יהוה בא *עד־עיר דויד ומיכל בת־שאול נשקפה בעד החלון ותרא את־המלך דויד מרקד ומשחק ותבז לו בלבה	15:29
6:17	ויבאו את־ארון יהוה ויצגו אתו *במקומו בתוך האהל אשר נטה־לו דוד ויעל *דוד עלות לפני יהוה ושלמים	ויביאו את־ארון האלהים ויציגו אתו _____ בתוך האהל אשר נטה־לו דויד ויקריבו __ עלות ושלמים לפני האלהים	16:1
6:18	ויכל דוד מהעלות העולה והשלמים ויברך את־העם בשם יהוה *צבאות	ויכל דויד מהעלות העלה והשלמים ויברך את־העם בשם יהוה _____	16:2
6:19a	ויחלק לכל־העם לכל־המון ישראל למאיש ועד־אשה לאיש חלת לחם אחת ואשפר אחד ואשישה אחת וילך	ויחלק לכל־איש ישראל מאיש ועד־אשה לאיש ככר־לחם ואשפר ואשישה	16:3
		4 ויתן לפני ארון יהוה מן־הלוים משרתים ולהזכיר ולהודות ולהלל ליהוה אלהי ישראל 5 אסף הראש ומשנהו זכריה יעיאל ושמירמות ויחיאל ומתתיה ואליאב ובניהו ועבד אדם ויעיאל בכלי נבלים ובכנרות ואסף במצלתים משמיע	16:4–42

		6 ובניהו ויחזיאל הכהנים בחצצרות תמיד לפני ארון ברית־האלהים 7 ביום ההוא אז נתן דויד בראש להדות ליהוה ביד־אסף ואחיו 8 הודו ליהוה קראו בשמו הודיעו בעמים עלילתיו 9 שירו לו זמרו־לו שיחו בכל־נפלאתיו 10 התהללו בשם קדשו ישמח לב מבקשי יהוה 11 דרשו יהוה ועזו בקשו פניו תמיד 12 זכרו נפלאתיו אשר עשה מפתיו ומשפטי־פיהו 13 זרע ישראל עבדו בני יעקב בחיריו 14 הוא יהוה אלהינו בכל־הארץ משפטיו 15 זכרו לעולם בריתו דבר צוה לאלף דור 16 אשר כרת את־אברהם ושבועתו ליצחק 17 ויעמידה ליעקב לחק לישראל ברית עולם 18 לאמר לך אתן ארץ־כנען חבל נחלתכם 19 בהיותכם מתי מספר כמעט וגרים בה 20 ויתהלכו מגוי אל־גוי וממלכה אל־עם אחר 21 לא־הניח לאיש לעשקם ויוכח עליהם מלכים 22 אל־תגעו במשיחי ובנביאי אל־תרעו 23 שירו ליהוה כל־הארץ בשרו מיום־אל־יום ישועתו	

24 ספרו בגוים את־כבודו
בכל־העמים נפלאתיו
25 כי גדול יהוה ומהלל מאד
ונורא הוא על־כל־אלהים
26 כי כל־אלהי העמים אלילים
ויהוה שמים עשה
27 הוד והדר לפניו עז וחדוה במקמו
28 הבו ליהוה משפחות
עמים הבו ליהוה כבוד ועז
29 הבו ליהוה כבוד שמו שאו מנחה
ובאו לפניו השתחוו ליהוה בהדרת־קדש
30 חילו מלפניו כל־הארץ
אל־תכון תבל בל־תמוט
31 ישמחו השמים ותגל הארץ
ויאמרו בגוים יהוה מלך
32 ירעם הים ומלואו יעלץ
השדה וכל־אשר־בו
33 אז ירננו עצי היער מלפני יהוה
כי־בא לשפוט את־הארץ
34 הודו ליהוה כי טוב כי לעולם חסדו
35 ואמרו הושיענו אלהי ישענו
וקבצנו והצילנו מן־הגוים
להדות לשם קדשך להשתבח בתהלתך

		[36] ברוך יהוה אלהי ישׂראל מן־העולם ועד העלם ויאמרו כל־העם אמן והלל ליהוה [37] ויעזב־שם לפני ארון ברית־יהוה לאסף ולאחיו לשׁרת לפני הארון תמיד לדבר־יום ביומו [38] ועבד אדם ואחיהם ששׁים ושׁמונה ועבד אדם בן־ידיתון וחסה לשׁערים [39] ואת צדוק הכהן ואחיו הכהנים לפני משׁכן יהוה בבמה אשׁר בגבעון [40] להעלות עלות ליהוה על־מזבח העלה תמיד לבקר ולערב ולכל־הכתוב בתורת יהוה אשׁר צוה על־ישׂראל [41] ועמהם הימן וידותון ושׁאר הברורים אשׁר נקבו בשׁמות להדות ליהוה כי לעולם חסדו [42] ועמהם הימן וידותון חצצרות ומצלתים למשׁמיעים וכלי שׁיר האלהים ובני ידותון לשׁער	
6:19b–20a	[19b] וילך כל־העם אישׁ לביתו [20a] וישׁב דוד לברך את־ביתו	__ וילכו כל־העם אישׁ לביתו ויסב דויד לברך את־ביתו	16:43

*6:20b–23	20b ותצא מיכל בת־שאול לקראת דוד ותאמר מה־נכבד היום מלך ישראל אשר נגלה היום לעיני אמהות עבדיו כהגלות נגלות אחד הרקים 21 ויאמר דוד אל־מיכל לפני יהוה אשר בחר־בי מאביך ומכל־ביתו לצות אתי נגיד על־עם יהוה על־ישראל ושחקתי לפני יהוה 22 ונקלתי עוד מזאת והייתי שפל בעיני ועם־האמהות אשר אמרת עמם אכבדה 23 ולמיכל בת־שאול לא־היה לה ילד עד יום מותה		

* = Plus

McKenzie argues that the Chronicler divided 2 Sam 6 into three parts (6:1–11, 12b–19a, 19b–20), and used them as the framework of 1 Chr 13–16.[109] In addition, the passages in Chronicles that are non-synoptic could be divided into three categories: the Chronicler's own compositions (1 Chr 13:1–4; 14:17); sources that are from material no longer extant (1 Chr 15:1–24; 16:4–7, 37–42); portions of three Psalms pieced together, Pss 105:1–15; 96:1–13; 106:1, 47–48 (1 Chr 16:8–22, 23–33, 34–36).[110]

Yet, if we compare and analyze the materials in 2 Sam 6 and 1 Chr 13–16, the situation may prove to be different from this.

Table 11 shows that there are a lot of pluses in both 2 Sam 6 and 1 Chr 13–16. Although there are two large segments of special material in 1 Chr 15:1–24 and 16:4–42, there is also one in 2 Sam 6:20b–23. As we saw in section 4.3, the verbs used to move the ark in B and 4QSam[a] 2 Sam 6 agree with those in 1 Chr 13–16, but not with those in MT 2 Sam 6. Thus, we can say that these textual observations support the priority of the alternative text of 2 Sam 6 over 2 Sam 6 (MT). That alternative text is also prior to 1 Chr 13–16.

We also have to consider the long non-synoptic material about the Levites carrying the ark while the people worshipped God with music and singing (1 Chr 15:1–24; 16:4–42). As we have seen in section 4.3.6.3, especially in Table 8, those materials in 1 Chr 15:1–24 and 16:4–42 are influenced by the materials on musical instruments and praise in 2 Sam 6:5//1 Chr 13:8 (BTH). In addition, 2 Sam 6:15//1 Chr 15:28aαβ share vocabulary with Josh 6. Thus, Auld's position on the textual development should be sustained.[111]

4.4.1.3. *The Ark Is Carried to Kiriath-jearim (1 Samuel 4:1b–7:2)*. The point that needs consideration before we deal with the ark narrative in 1 Sam 4:1b–7:2 is the question of its relationship with 2 Sam 6. Since Rost included 2 Sam 6 with the "ark narrative," which begins in 1 Sam 4:1b–7:2, through a cautious and circumspect analysis of their vocabulary and style,[112] a number of scholars have followed his argument. In reality, while there are many thematic, structural, and terminological links between the two ark stories, there are also considerable differences, such as the place and personal names and the absence of the Levites from

109. McKenzie, *1–2 Chronicles*, 133.

110. Ibid., 133–34.

111. A. G. Auld, "Solomon at Gibeon," in *Samuel at the Threshold*, 105.

112. Rost, *Die Überlieferung von der Thronnachfolge Davids*; Campbell, *The Ark Narrative*, 6–8; idem, *1 Samuel*, 300.

2 Sam 6.[113] Thus, many scholars now support the position that the stories form distinct literary layers rather than an independent source.[114]

Here, we have to consider some recent challenges that explore the priority of 2 Sam 6 over 1 Sam 4:1b–7:2. Even though almost all mainstream scholars have argued that the former was composed in response to the latter, there have been others who consider the possibility that the latter presupposes the former.[115] As we see in Tables 3 and 4, among the ark narratives in Samuel–Kings and Chronicles, 1 Sam 4:1b–7:2 shows the most varied and developed use of epithets for the ark. The same can also be said for the verbs used to describe the movement of the ark. This narrative is also one of the most theologically important in Samuel–Kings as a whole: the story of the capture and return of the ark symbolizes how Yahweh's power is not diminished by Israel's defeat or the plunder of its shrine.[116] Furthermore, it implies that just as Yahweh overcame the Philistine oppressors and journeyed to Jerusalem in triumph, so too would the people of the exile be freed from their Babylonian captors and return to Jerusalem.[117] Nevertheless, we should not miss the point

113. Rezetko, "Source and Revision," 16, 450–53. For more of this, see J. Blenkinsopp, *The Role of Gibeon and the Gibeonites in the Political and Religious History of Early Israel* (Society for Old Testament Study Monograph Series 2; Cambridge: Cambridge University Press, 1972), 71–74; M. J. Steussy, *David: Biblical Portraits of Power* (Studies on Personalities of the Old Testament; Columbia: University of South Carolina Press, 1999), 59; Campbell, *The Ark Narrative*, 6–54; idem, *1 Samuel*, 300–309.

114. Rezetko, "Source and Revision," 16; J. Van Seters, *In Search of History*, 346–53; Polzin, *Moses and the Deuteronomist*, 18–71; J. P. Fokkelman, *Narrative Art and Poetry in the Books of Samuel: A Full Interpretation Based on Stylistic and Structural Analyses*. Vol. 1, *King David (II Sam. 9–20 & I Kings 1–2)* (SSN 20; Assen: Van Gorcum, 1993), 1–316.

115. Rezetko, "Source and Revision," 16. For further study on this point, see F. Schicklberger, *Die Ladeerzählungen des ersten Samuelbuches: eine literaturwissenschaftliche und theologiegeschichtliche Untersuchung* (Würzburg: Echter, 1973), 144–48; Polzin, *Samuel and the Deuteronomist*, 68; A. G. Auld, "1 and 2 Samuel," in *Eerdmans Commentary on the Bible* (ed. J. D. G. Dunn and J. W. Rogerson; Cambridge: Eerdmans, 2003), 233.

116. A. G. Auld, "Re-reading Samuel (Historically): '*Etwas mehr Nichtwissen*,'" in *Samuel at the Threshold*, 153.

117. Rezetko, "Source and Revision," 16–17. For more of this, see H. Timm, "Die Ladeerzählung (1 Sam 4–6, 2 Sam 6) und das Kerygma des deuteronomistischen Geschichtswerks," *EvT* 26 (1966): 509–26; P. R. Ackroyd, *The First Book of Samuel* (CBC; Cambridge: Cambridge University Press, 1971), 52, 63; G. W. Ahlström, "The Travel of the Ark: A Religio-Political Composition," *JNES* 43 (1984): 143–44; K. A. D. Smelik, "The Ark Narrative Reconsidered," in *New*

that the principal topic of this narrative is God rather than the ark itself. Scholars understood that the return of the ark hints at the reinstatement of the Davidic kingship.[118] However, in 1 Sam 4:1b–7:2 the autonomy of the deity is stressed in an extraordinary way: even though the Israelites bring the ark to the battlefield, God allows himself to be captured; he pours out his wrath on both the Philistines and the people of Beth-shemesh and miraculously guides the milch cows, before returning on his own.[119] As the ark returned alone without any human leadership in 1 Sam 4:1b–7:2, so God will lead history autonomously and bring about Israel's return from the exile with his own power.

The narrative in 1 Sam 4:1b–7:2 demonstrates the difference between Samuel–Kings and Chronicles most clearly in that Chronicles pays attention to the affirmative aspect of the Davidic royal kingship and takes a close interest in its recovery,[120] whereas Samuel–Kings points out the limitations of the Davidic kingship and emphasizes the recovery of God's kingship. First Samuel 4:1b–7:2 conclusively reflects the theological feature of Samuel–Kings, material which is a special feature of Samuel–Kings.

One more point we have to bear in mind here is that the language used to describe the Levites' role in worship in 1 Sam 6:15 is rather unusual in the entire context of Samuel–Kings. As we saw in section 4.3.3, the word, "Levite[s]" appears mainly in Chronicles, but rarely (only four times) in Samuel–Kings, particularly in non-synoptic texts. In the ark texts of Samuel–Kings, הלוים occurs only once (1 Sam 6:15), except for its appearance in the MT plus, הכהנים והלוים, in 1 Kgs 8:4.

4.4.2. *The Literary History of Joshua 3–4*

According to our analysis so far, Josh 3–4 seems to rely on the shared texts of the ark's movements in Samuel–Kings and Chronicles. Among those eighteen epithets of the ark, nine epithets appear in Josh 3–4, which shows that this text uses the most varied and developed form of the epithets of the ark among all the ark texts.[121] Of the synoptic epithets, there are instances of הארון and הארון ברית יהוה.

Avenues in the Study of the Old Testament (ed. A. S. Van der Woude; Leiden: Brill, 1989), 140–44; Auld, "Re-reading Samuel (Historically)," 153.

118. Rezetko, "Source and Revision," 17; Polzin, *Samuel and the Deuteronomist*, 71; Auld, "Re-reading Samuel (Historically)," 153.

119. Rezetko, "Source and Revision," 17.

120. McKenzie, *1–2 Chronicles*, 17–58.

121. For this, see Table 3.

Furthermore, Josh 3–4 shares some materials with late non-synoptic texts in Samuel–Kings and Chronicles. As we saw in section 4.3.6.12, קציר־חטים in the Hebrew *Vorlage* of LXX Josh 3:15 also appears in 1 Sam 6:13, while in MT Josh 3:15 it is generalized into כל ימי קציר. In these texts on the movement of the ark, two different words for "armed" (חמשים and חלוץ) appear. First Samuel 6:19 uses only חמשים, while Josh 6:7, 9, and 13 use חלוץ; Josh 4:12–13 uses both terms. There are several other instances, as we have seen in section 4.3.

Thus, we will read the literary history of Josh 3–4 in Chapter 6 more closely, while considering the results of the present chapter together with those of Chapter 3 (text-critical analysis), and after we consider the relevance of reading this narrative in the context of water-crossing story in Chapter 5 once again.

4.4.3. *The Literary History of Joshua 6: The Ark in the Conquest Story of Jericho (Joshua 6:1–27)*

Although there have been some archaeological approaches to the investigation of the descriptions in Josh 6,[122] scholars have concentrated mainly on diachronic research based on the textual study of this narrative.[123] However, in most cases, the value of such research is limited in no attention is paid to the challenges of the LXX, only to the presumed literary history of the MT.[124]

MT Joshua 6 is approximately 30 percent longer than LXX Josh 6.[125] There are a number of pluses in MT, in particular the long plus of

122. See K. M. Kenyon, *Digging Up Jericho* (London: Benn, 1957), 256–63.

123. For this, see J. Wellhausen, *Die Composition des Hexateuchs und der historischen Bücher des Alten Testaments* (3d ed.; Berlin: Reimer, 1899), 121–22; Dus, "Die Analyse zweier Ladeerzählungen des Josuabuches (Jos 3–4 und 6)," 108; Noth, *Das Buch Josua* (1953), 21–22, 40–43; J. A. Wilcoxin, "Narrative Structure and Cult Legend: A Study of Joshua 1–6," in *Transitions in Biblical Scholarship* (ed. J. C. Rylaarsdam; Chicago: University of Chicago Press, 1968), 50, 53; E. Otto, *Das Mazzotfest in Gilgal* (BWANT 107; Stuttgart: Kohlhammer, 1973), 80; Butler, *Joshua*, 63–72; Peckham, "The Composition of Joshua 3–4," 427; J. van Seters, "Joshua's Campaign of Canaan and Near Eastern Historiography," *SJOT* 4, no. 2 (1990): 5; Fritz, *Das Buch Josua*, 65–76; Nelson, *Joshua*, 83–95. For more of this, see Chapter 1, above.

124. Of those scholars listed in n. 123, we should note that Butler and Nelson do pay close attention to the challenges of the LXX. Nelson especially takes the testimony of B in Joshua more seriously than any other.

125. Especially in Josh 6:1–20, the LXX lacks at least 92 words out of a total of approximately 350 words. For this, see L. Mazor, "A Nomistic Re-Working of the Jericho Conquest Narrative Reflected in LXX to Joshua 6:1–20," *Textus* 18 (1995): 47–62; Van der Meer, *Formation and Reformulation*, 72–73.

MT Josh 6:3b–4, which appears to show that the large number of pluses in MT constitute the final layer of this text, having been inserted to solve the inexplicabilities in the shorter Greek text. It is difficult for us to distinguish "whether 'encircling' the city meant 'going round' or 'being around' it."[126] The Greek could be understood as reporting that the Israelites formed a stationary circle around Jericho. Thus, according to Nelson, the MT plus in v. 3b is added to clarify "that the encirclement of Jericho is not to be understood as a static siege, but as a parade around the city."[127] In addition, Nelson holds that v. 4 in MT is based on vv. 8 and 13. It is possible that the MT editor added v. 4 to highlight the fact that the priests will blow the horn only on the seventh day by using vv. 8 and 13. In doing so, he/she seems to have attempted to reconcile the inconsistencies between the request for total silence by the people in v. 10 and the repeated blowing of the trumpets in vv. 8, 9, and 13.

Another point to consider here that results from the investigations in section 4.3 is the validity of reading this text (Josh 6) with the help of the ark texts in Samuel–Kings and Chronicles. The preliminary analysis carried out in section 4.3 revealed that the epithets of the ark and the verbs used to describe the movement of the ark, as well as some other shared expressions and themes, point to the possibility that Josh 6 relies on the synoptic texts of the ark's movement in Samuel–Kings and Chronicles.[128]

One of the frequently repeated themes related to the movement of the ark in Josh 6 is the playing of music, which occurs in vv. 4, 5, 8, 13, 16, 20. As we have already pointed out, the text of Josh 6 was influenced by 2 Sam 6:15//1 Chr 15:28aαβ.[129] Joshua 6 uses the name of a musical instrument, שׁופר(ות), and "war cry" (תרועה), both of which appear in 2 Sam 6:15//1 Chr 15:28aαβ.

Furthermore, Josh 6 shares a biblical outlook with non-synoptic text in Chronicles. Seven named priests who blow trumpets are listed in 1 Chr 15:24, though the number "seven" is not made explicit in this text. In Josh 6, by contrast, the number "seven" is repeated and emphasized. In Josh 6:4, 8, 13, references to the "seven" priests who blow the trumpets before the ark are repeated and may indicate that this text was related to 1 Chr 15:24.

126. Auld, *Joshua: Jesus, Son of Nauē*, 134.
127. Nelson, *Joshua*, 86.
128. For this, see sections 4.3.1, 4.3.2, and 4.3.3.
129. Of these, 1 Chr 13:8, 28 are synoptic with 2 Sam 6:5, 15.

"War cry" (תרועה), which is "a motif of the divine war tradition (1 Sam 4:5; 17:20, 52; etc.),"[130] plays an important role in this conquest story.[131] As we have seen above, this vocabulary item is one of the major words that dominate the flow of this narrative. תרועה was used in the synoptic text 2 Sam 6:15//1 Chr 15:28aαβ, and in the non-synoptic text 1 Sam 4:5. In these ark texts, תרועה is used in the contexts of "raising sounds to make others hear." In Josh 6, the war cry was used almost in the same way as in Chronicles and Samuel, though perhaps more dramatically. In Josh 6:10, the people of Israel are ordered to keep quiet for six days to make the warcry of the seventh day more terrifying. Joshua 6:10 seems to be a redactional layer inserted into the basic layer (the latter influenced by Samuel and Chronicles) in order to heighten the dramatic effect of the Jericho conquest story.

The word שכם ("to rise early in the morning") occurs six times in Joshua,[132] and is used twice in this narrative (6:12, 15): once in relation to Joshua (v. 12), and once in relation to the whole people (v. 15).[133] As we saw in section 4.3.6.11, this word also occurs in 1 Sam 5:3, which belongs to later non-synoptic material.

Nelson maintains that the phrase "put all silver and gold, and vessels of bronze and iron into 'the treasury of Yahweh'" (Josh 6:19, 24) is either anachronistic or proleptic.[134] Here, MT inserts בית between אוצר and יהוה in Josh 6:24. Likewise, MT interpolates "house" in Josh 9:23, and "sanctuary" in 24:26.[135] Joshua 6:19, 24 appear to recall the synoptic text, 1 Kgs 7:51//2 Chr 5:1. Recollecting the phrase באצרות בית יהוה in these texts, MT may insert בית in Josh 6:24.

The curse upon "anyone who builds Jericho again" (6:26) is one of two curses by Joshua: the other is on the Gibeonites (9:23).[136] According to Dietrich, this verse belongs to the "DtrP layer,"[137] which prepares for the Hiel story in 1 Kgs 16:34.[138] Even though his hypothesis is based on a

130. Nelson, *Joshua*, 93. See also von Rad, *Holy War in Ancient Israel*, 41–51.

131. Kang, *Divine War in the Old Testament and in the Ancient Near East.*

132. Josh 3:1; 6:12, 15; 7:16; 8:10, 14.

133. Auld, *Joshua: Jesus, Son of Nauē*, 137.

134. Nelson, *Joshua*, 95.

135. Auld, *Joshua: Jesus, Son of Nauē*, 138.

136. Ibid., 139.

137. DtrP: a prophetic Deuteronomistic layer, which is a redactional layer, reconstructed basically on the basis of the book of Kings, but compatible with the DH and DtrN stages. See Van der Meer, *Formation and Reformulation*, 149.

138. W. Dietrich, *Prophetie und Geschichte: Eine redaktionsgeschichtliche Untersuchung zum deuteronomistischen Geschichtswerk* (FRLANT 108; Göttingen: Vandenhoeck & Ruprecht, 1972), 110–12.

"flexible" identity,[139] he seems to catch the relationship between Josh 6:26 and 1 Kgs 16:34. Joshua 6:26 also appears to consider 1 Kgs 16:34. Tov sensibly holds that the latter is earlier than the former.[140]

Therefore, we can divide the literary layers of Josh 6 as follows:

1. Basic layer, which is influenced by the synoptic source materials (BTH) of the ark's movement in Samuel–Kings and Chronicles: Josh 6:1–3a, 5–6aα, 7, 8aβb, 9, 11, 13, 14, 16, 18–20, 21, 24, 27.
2. Late-biblical outlook shared by Josh 6 and non-synoptic special materials in Samuel–Kings and Chronicles: Josh 6:4 (שבעה), 8 (שבעה), 12, 13 (שבעה), 15a, 16 (השביעית), 26.
3. Redactional insertion: Josh 6:10, 17, 22–23, 25.
4. MT pluses: Josh 6:1 (מפני בני ישׂראל), 3 (תעשׂה ששׁת ימים), 4 (ושׁבעה כהנים ישׂאו שׁבעה שׁופרות היובלים לפני הארון וביום השׁביעי תסבו את־העיר שׁבע פעמים והכהנים יתקעו בשׁופרות), 5 (בשׁמעכם את־קול השׁופר), 6aβb (שׂאו את־ארון הברית ושׁבעה כהנים ישׂאו שׁבעה שׁופרות יובלים לפני ארון יהוה), 8aα (ויהי כאמר יהושׁע אל־העם), 10 (ולא־יצא מפיכם דבר), 13 (הלך ארון), 15 (רק ביום ההוא סבבו את־העיר שׁבע פעמים, כמשׁפט הזה), 17 (כי החבאתה את־המלאכים אשׁר שׁלחנו) 20 (וירע העם), 24 (בית), 26 (את־יריחו, לפני יהוה).

4.4.4. *The Movement of the Ark in the Wilderness (Numbers 10:33–36)*
Concerning Num 10:33–36, Noth regards v. 33 as J and contends that the expression "the covenant" in the epithet "the ark of the covenant of Yahweh" is *ein späterer deuteronomistischer Zusatz*.[141] In addition, the description of the pillar of cloud in v. 34 is a later insertion to explain that the ark in v. 33 plays a different role from that of the pillar of cloud, which told Israel when to camp and when to move on in P material. According to Noth, vv. 35–36 also belongs to J and is linked to v. 33.[142]

According to Seebass, vv. 29–32 belongs to J, vv. 33–34 to post-Dtr and vv. 35–36 to post-Priestly Redaction.[143]

139. For this, see Auld, Review of M. N. Van der Meer, *Formulation and Reformulation*, *JSJ* 36 (2005): 133–35. According to Auld, R. Smend Jr. himself argued that these many Deuteronomistic figures are flexible.

140. Auld, *Joshua: Jesus, Son of Nauē*, 139; Tov, *The Greek and Hebrew Bible*, 159.

141. Noth, *Das vierte Buch Moses, Numeri*, 70.

142. Ibid., 71–72.

143. H. Seebass, *Numeri* (BKAT 4/1ff.; Lieferung 1; Neukirchen–Vluyn: Neukirchener Verlag, 1993), 1–19.

For Coats, recognizing a literary history made up of J, P, and redactional elements is not a meaningful way to study Num 10:33–36.[144] According to him, this text should be considered in the context of Num 10:11–36, which is a unit. He holds that "the structure of this text is determined by a conceptual unity, to which the composition of the text's heterogeneous elements has remained subordinate."[145]

However, some other scholars have considered the relationship between the Pentateuch and Former Prophets from a different direction. Wellhausen contends that the priestly description of the ark in the Pentateuch is younger than the portrait drawn in Samuel, and Rost supports him by arguing that the ark narrative was a tenth-century B.C.E. document which functioned as the ἱερὸς λόγος of the Jerusalem sanctuary.[146] Von Rad also denies the origin of the ark narrative in the wilderness and focuses on connecting the ark with rituals of worship, linking it to the sanctuaries in Shiloh and Jerusalem.[147] Campbell similarly holds that the ark narrative originated from a priestly circle during the period of David and Solomon.[148] Of course, they see that the ark texts in the Pentateuch reflect those in the Former Prophets, but they do not appear to recognize the relationship between the formation of Chronicles, Former Prophets, and the Pentateuch closely.

The epithet ארון ברית יהוה in Num 10:33 is a basic expression which appears in all the texts on the carrying of the ark. This verse seems to be a non-Priestly addition, affected by the ark texts in the Former Prophets.

The expression "the cloud of Yahweh" in Num 10:34 also seems to recall the phrase "a cloud filled the house of Yahweh" in the synoptic text 1 Kgs 8:11//2 Chr 5, which is also non-Priestly.

The departure and the return of the ark in vv. 35–36 do not appear to be connected with the itinerary of the ark, but to the battle with the enemy.[149] The texts in which the ark and war are related, are 2 Sam 5:11–6:23//1 Chr 13–16 and 1 Sam 4:1b–7:2 (Philistines) and Josh 3–4,

144. W. Coats, *Numbers* (FOTL 4; Grand Rapids: Eerdmans, 2005), 149–70.

145. Ibid., 152.

146. L. Rost, *The Succession to the Throne of David* (trans. M. D. Rutter and D. M. Gunn; Historic Texts and Interpreters in Biblical Scholarship 1; Sheffield: Almond, 1982), 6–34.

147. G. von Rad, *Studies in Deuteronomy* (London: SCM, 1953), 127; idem, *Deuteronomy* (OTL; London: SCM, 1966), 79–80; idem, *Old Testament Theology*. Vol. 1, *The Theology of Israel's Historical Traditions* (trans. D. M. G. Stalker; New York: Harper & Row, 1962), 234–41.

148. Campbell, *The Ark Narrative*, 221.

149. Noth, *Das vierte Buch Moses, Numeri*, 71–72.

6 (Jericho). Verses 35–36 also appear to be influenced by a war story related with the movements of the ark; these verses are also non-Priestly.[150]

4.5. *Conclusion*

Through the analysis of words and expressions in the ark narratives we can argue for a possible development of texts from the materials shared between Samuel–Kings and Chronicles. In particular, הארון, ארון ברית יהוה, ארון יהוה, and ארון האלהים are the basic designations of the ark, which appear in all the texts from Num 10:33–36 to 1 Kgs 7:51–8:11//2 Chr 5. Other designations were added to these four expressions, which are the basic epithets of the ark dwelling in the Temple of Jerusalem, the texts on the path of the ark in Chronicles and the Former Prophets seem to have formed, by which the two epithets in Num 10:33–36 also appear to be influenced. Scholars such as Wellhausen, Rost, von Rad, and Campbell also hold that the expressions dealing with the movement of the ark in the Pentateuch rely on those in the Former Prophets. The verbs which appear in the texts describing the ark's movement also support this possibility. Among the verbs, נשׂא is the basic expression that occurs in all the narratives, Num 10:33–36 excluded. In the ark texts of Samuel–Kings and Chronicles, עלה and בוא are also used as the basic verbs, to which other expressions are added, and the epithets have been developed into various expressions. The two verbs used in Num 10:33–36 (נסע, נוח—only נוח in v. 36 is used in the non-synoptic text of 1 Sam 6:18) do not exert any influence on the verbs used in Chronicles and the Former Prophets. In addition, the priests and the Levites as the carriers of the ark, the divine epithets, all Israel and all the people, the names of musical instruments, the expressions describing the ritual, the war theme, and so on, all support the possibility of reading the literary history of these ark texts in an inverted way, as Auld suggested: the basic story of the monarchy (BTH) is earlier than the story of Israel before the monarchy.

Furthermore, Joshua, and the non-synoptic texts in Samuel–Kings and Chronicles share some biblical perspectives and expressions: (1) Joshua and Chronicles share a late-biblical outlook (seven named priests who blow trumpets in 1 Chr 15:24, "seven" priests, who blow the trumpets before the ark in Josh 6); (2) Josh 3:3 shares the compound word הכהנים (ו)הלוים with 1 Chr 15:14 and 2 Chr 5:5; (3) 1 Sam 6:15 shares

150. The systematized contents related with the march in Num 9:15–10:32 seem to be later than 10:33–36, which belongs to P.

the expression related to the Levites and rituals with late special materials in Chronicles. There are some other late non-synoptic materials that are also shared by the similar texts in Joshua.

The analysis of 2 Sam 6//1 Chr 13–16, 1 Kgs 7:51–8:11//2 Chr 5, shows that it is not possible simply to argue that Chronicles was written later than Samuel–Kings. Although there are long non-synoptic materials in 1 Chr 15:1–24; 16:4–42, and 2 Chr 5:11b–13, there are many more small pluses in 2 Sam 6 and 1 Kgs 7:51–8:11 including a long plus in 2 Sam 6:20b–23. B and 4QSam^{a} also support the possible priority of Chronicles to MT Samuel: (1) the verbs used to describe the movement of the ark in B and 4QSam^{a} 2 Sam 6 agree with those in 1 Chr 13–16, but not with those in MT 2 Sam 6; (2) B and 4QSam^{a} 2 Sam 6:5; 1 Chr 13:8 use שירים, but MT 2 Sam 6:5 uses ברושים and B and 4QSam^{a} 2 Sam 6:5, 1 Chr 13:8 represent עז, while MT 2 Sam 6:5 represents עץ.

In the light of all this, we can read the literary history of Josh 3–4 with the help of similar ark texts in 1 Sam 4:1b–7:2, 2 Sam 6//1 Chr 13–16, 1 Kgs 7:51–8:11//2 Chr 5. Joshua 3–4 is influenced by the synoptic texts of the ark's movement in Chronicles and Samuel–Kings.

There are similar water crossings in Exod 13:17–14:31 and 2 Kgs 2. How do they affect the formation of Josh 3–4? The next chapter will investigate the relevance of reading Josh 3–4 in the context of Moses' and Elijah–Elisha's water-crossing story.

Chapter 5

Reading Joshua 3–4 in the Context of Exodus 13:17–14:31 and 2 Kings 2

5.1. *Introduction*

The purpose of this chapter is to explore the relevance of reading Josh 3–4 in the wider context of Exod 13:17–14:31 and 2 Kgs 2, which are the water-crossing stories of Moses and Elijah–Elisha.

I noted that the shared materials in the ark texts of Samuel–Kings and Chronicles affect those in the Pentateuch and Former Prophets in Chapter 4. This chapter will examine how the "special Kings material"[1] such as Elijah–Elisha's crossing of the Jordan (2 Kgs 2) is linked to other similar texts in the Pentateuch (Exod 13:17–14:31) and in the Former Prophets (Josh 3–4).

In order to find enough connections to justify putting them in any order at all, I will examine some shared words, major themes and motifs in these texts. Then, I will examine how the literary layers in Exod 13:17–14:31, Josh 3–4, and 2 Kgs 2 are connected with each other.

5.2. *Preliminary Analysis of the Study of the Literary History of Exodus 13:17–14:31, Joshua 3–4, and 2 Kings 2*

Before we read the literary history of Josh 3–4 with the help of Exod 13:17–14:31 and 2 Kgs 2, we will analyze some common words, phrases, and major themes in these texts.

5.2.1. *Shared Words*

5.2.1.1. *Words That Are Used in the Same Way in All Three Passages.*

5.2.1.1.1. חרבה *(Exodus 14:21; Joshua 3:17; 4:18; 2 Kings 2:8).* חרבה is common to all three narratives (Exod 14:21; Josh 3:17; 4:18; 2 Kgs 2:8), referring to "dry ground."

1. Auld, *Joshua Retold*, 107.

5.2.1.2. *Words That Are Used in All Three Passages, But Are Used Differently.*

5.2.1.2.1. רום *(Exodus 14:8, 16; Joshua 4:5; 2 Kings 2:13)*. Forms of רום appear in all three narratives, once each as a verb in the Hiphil form (הרים), and adjectivally in Exod 14:8. It is used in Qal, participle form in Exod 14:8 and the phrase ביד רמה contains a rather different meaning ("boldly") from the others (Exod 14:16; Josh 4:5; 2 Kgs 2:13).

הרים is not common in Exodus or Kings; and it is used in Joshua only in 4:5.

The term הרים is used in Exod 14:16, when Moses was commanded to "lift up" his staff to divide the waters of the sea. It also appears in Exod 7:20, where Moses lifts up his rod and strikes the water (of the Nile), and changes it into blood in the sight of Pharaoh. In Josh 4:5, it was used to describe the action of twelve appointed men who "lift high" a stone. In 2 Kgs 2:13, it occurs in the situation where Elisha "lifts up" his master's mantle. Although הרים is used in each narrative, there is variation in its use. In Josh 4:5, what they "lift high" is not the medium by which the waters are parted (as in Exod 14:16 and 2 Kgs 2:13), but the stones by which they remember the event. Perhaps a pattern is being both suggested and deliberately altered. Thus, with only the fact that רום appears in all three texts, it does not seem possible to find a definite relationship between these texts.

5.2.1.2.2. חמשים *(Exodus 13:18; Joshua 4:12; 2 Kings 2:16)*. Exodus 13:18, Josh 4:12, and 2 Kgs 2:16 all include the consonants חמשים, but each text understands this differently: "in [military] formation" in MT or "the fifth generation" in LXX Exod 13:18; "in [military] formation" in Josh 4:12 and "50" in 2 Kgs 2:16. MT Exodus 13:18 reads חמשים as "in [military] formation" like Josh 4:12, but LXX Exod 13:18 recognizes a numerical meaning, just as in 2 Kgs 2:16.[2] The possible significance of this consonantal cluster comes from the fact that it does occur in all three stories, but is not common elsewhere in these three books. However, because of the semantic variation, it may be more difficult to establish a historical order of the texts just by the appearance of the same consonants.

5.2.1.3. *Words That Appear Only in Exodus and Joshua.*

5.2.1.3.1. יבשה *(Exodus 14:16, 22, 29; Joshua 4:22, 23)*. The other expression for "on dry ground," יבשה, occurs in Exod 14:16, 22, 29; Josh 4:22, 23, but 2 Kgs 2 does not represent this word.

2. For more of this, see B. S. Childs, *Exodus* (OTL; London: SCM, 1974), 218; D. U. Rottzoll, *Abraham Ibn Esras Langer Kommentar zum Buch Exodus 1* (Berlin: de Gruyter, 2000), 373–74.

5.2.1.3.2. שׁוב *(Exodus 14:26, 27, 28; Joshua 4:18)*. In Moses' Reed Sea-crossing story, שׁוב was used repeatedly in Exod 14:26, 27, 28 to describe the return of the waters and the drowning of every member of the Egyptian army. In Josh 4:18, it was used to explain the return of the waters of the Jordan to their original place. However, there is no special reference to the water returning to its original place in 2 Kgs 2.

5.2.1.3.3. ים סוף *(Exodus 13:18; Joshua 4:23)*. Exodus 13:18 and Josh 4:23 share ים סוף. Second Kings 2 does not represent the name ים סוף.

5.2.1.4. *Words That Appear Only in Exodus and Kings.*

5.2.1.4.1. רוח *(Exodus 14:21; 2 Kings 2:9, 15, 16)*. The word רוח ("breath," "wind," "spirit," etc.) is used in Exod 14:21 and 2 Kgs 2:9, 15, 16. In Exod 14:21, God causes a strong easterly "wind" (ברוח) to blow all night. It is apparent that this wind has no divine nature.[3] It is God's tool to drive the waters of the sea back. Moreover, even though it is used in only two contexts of shared material by Samuel–Kings and Chronicles (1 Kgs 10:5//2 Chr 9:4; 1 Kgs 22:21, 22, 23, 24//2 Chr 18:20, 21, 22, 23), רוח is an important element in the succession narrative of Elijah–Elisha. It appears three times in this narrative (2 Kgs 2:9, 15, 16).[4] It refers to "the spirit of the prophet" in 2 Kgs 2:9, 15, and "the spirit of Yahweh" (רוח יהוה) in 2 Kgs 2:16. Therefore, the רוח in 2 Kgs 2 had a divine nature, but in Exod 14:21 it refers to wind in general. Joshua 3–4 does not represent this word at all. Therefore, the word רוח does not help us to find a link between the narratives.

5.2.1.5. *Words That Appear Only in Joshua and Kings.*

5.2.1.5.1. עבר *(Joshua 3:1, 2; 4:10, 11, 12; 2 Kings 2:8)*. Joshua 3–4 and 2 Kgs 2 represent עבר, but Exod 13:17–14:31 does not use the word. It is rather extraordinary that the word עבר does not appear in the Reed Sea-crossing story.

3. The similar use of רוח can be found in Gen 1:2 in the phrase "wind of God (רוח אלהים) was hovering over the face of the waters" and in Num 11:31, "and a wind went out from the Lord" (ורוח נסע מאת יהוה). For the formation relationship of Genesis, Exodus, and Numbers, see A. G. Auld, "Leviticus at the Heart of the Pentateuch," and "Leviticus: After Exodus and Before Numbers," in *Samuel at the Threshold*.

4. Auld, "Samuel, Numbers, and the Yahwist-Question," 241. Auld holds that "[t]he spirit which Isaiah says Yahweh will put on the king of Assyria (II Kgs 19,7//Isa 37,7) to make him return home will be a theme borrowed from I Kings 22."

5.2.2. *Shared Themes*

5.2.2.1. *Succession Narratives.* The theme of succession is common to Josh 3–4 and 2 Kgs 2. In Josh 3–4, the succession of Moses' leadership to Joshua is emphasized by the following verses: in Josh 3:7, God promises to Joshua that that day he will begin to increase him in the eyes of all Israel, that they may know that, as he was with Moses, so he will be with Joshua. In 4:10, MT inserts the phrase ככל אשר־צוה משה את־יהושע ("according to all that Moses had commanded Joshua") to stress the succession. In 4:14, we read that Yahweh increased Joshua in the sight of all Israel because of the Jordan-crossing event, and they stood in awe of him—as they had stood in awe of Moses, all the days of his life. Joshua's leadership succession is also accepted by the priests who faithfully obeyed his command (Josh 3:6; 4:16–18).

In 2 Kgs 2:9, Elisha asks his master to let him inherit a double share of his spirit. Some argue that here Elisha wished to be recognized and equipped as the true successor of Elijah.[5] Deuteronomy 12:17 explains that to receive the double portion was the share of the eldest son in Hebrew law. In 2 Kgs 2:14, when Elisha struck the water with the mantle of Elijah, the waters parted. In 2:15, recognizing that the spirit of Elijah rested upon Elisha, the sons of prophets "prostrated themselves" (וישתחוו) before him. In 2:19–25, two further episodes demonstrate Elisha's authority and show the succession of the spirit and leadership of Elijah to Elisha.

Thus, we can see that Josh 3–4 and 2 Kgs 2 contain a story of succession, but we cannot find any shared words supporting this common theme. However, Exod 13:17–14:31 lacks the theme of succession.

5.2.2.2. *War Motif.* In Exod 13:17–14:31, strong military terminology and motifs appear often: "in [military] formation" (חמשים, MT Exod 13:18), "fight" (לחם, Exod 14:14, 25), "all Pharaoh's army" (כל חיל פרעה, Exod 14:4, 9, 17, 28), "chariot" (רכב, 14:6, 7, 17, 18, 23, 28), "horseman" (פרש, 14:9, 17, 18, 23, 25, 26, 28), "horses" (סוס, 14:9, 23), "chariot wheels" (אפן מרכבתיו, 14:25), and "army or camp" (מחנה, 14:20, 24).

5. J. Gray, *I & II Kings: A Commentary* (2d ed.; OTL; London: SCM, 1970), 475; T. R. Hobbs, *2 Kings* (WBC 13; Waco: Word, 1985), 21; E. Würthwein, *Die Bücher der Könige 1.Kön. 17–2.Kön. 25* (ATD 11/2; Göttingen: Vandenhoeck & Ruprecht, 1984), 275; B. O. Long, *2 Kings* (FOTL 10; Grand Rapids: Eerdmans, 1991), 22, 26–27.

In Josh 3–4, there are also some military connotations. Joshua 3:2 includes the word מחנה ("camp") and Josh 3:10 the phrase "[Yahweh will] certainly drive out" (והורש יוריש) the Canaanites, the Hittites, the Hivites, the Perizzites, the Girgashites, the Amorites, and the Jebusites. In 3:16 and 4:13 those expressions seem to connect the event of crossing the Jordan with the conquest of Jericho: "and the people passed over opposite Jericho" (והעם עברו נגד יריחו), "(about) forty thousand ready for battle passed over before Yahweh for battle to the Plains of Jericho" ([כ]ארבעים אלף חלוצי הצבא עברו לפני יהוה למלחמה אל ערבות יריחו).[6] In 4:12 and 13 more concrete military expressions are used. In 4:12 the word חמשים ("in [military] formation") appears. Verse 13 includes exact military phrases "forty thousand ready for battle" (ארבעים אלף חלוצי[7] הצבא) and "for battle" (למלחמה).

In 2 Kgs 2:11 the terms "a chariot of fire" (רכב אש) and "horses of fire" (וסוסי אש) are used. In this verse, the words are not closely related to war, but simply used to distinguish between the two actors. In 2 Kgs 2:12, the titles "the chariots of Israel" (רכב ישראל) and "its horsemen" (ופרשיו) appear. The LXX and Vulgate use the singular form ופרשו in this verse. Some argue that these titles are applied to Elisha, who was more involved in external politics than Elijah, and that the present story of Elijah's translation is really secondary to the tradition of his bequeathing a double portion of the prophetic spirit to Elisha.[8] However, Hobbs holds that this attempt to show a literary dependency of Elijah's titles on Elisha's story (2 Kgs 13:14) is not successful.[9] In any case, the expressions referring to war in this verse are not closely linked to a war context, but are simply used to emphasize Elijah. In 2 Kgs 2:16, the phrase "50 valiant people" (חמשים אנשים בני־חיל) appears. בני־חיל is ambiguous in the narrative of 2 Kgs 2. Some argue that it means "men of substance" able, and expected, to maintain themselves, or "substitutes in readiness for war"[10] or "sons of power", which can refer to soldiers, although not exclusively so.[11] However, according to Long, בני־חיל

6. Only MT has "about" here.

7. For the use of this word (חלוצי), see also Rottzoll, *Abraham Ibn Esras Langer Kommentar*, 373–74. This will be discussed further in the next chapter.

8. Gray, *I & II Kings*, 472; J. C. Williams, "The Prophetic 'Father,'" *JBL* 85 (1966): 346; A. Rofé, "The Classification of the Prophetical Stories," *JBL* 89 (1970): 436; Würthwein, *Die Bücher der Könige 1.Kön. 17–2.Kön. 25*, 275; cf. M. A. Beek, "The Meaning of the Expression 'The Chariots and the Horsemen of Israel,'" *OTS* 17 (1971): 1–10; Long, *2 Kings*, 27.

9. Hobbs, *2 Kings*, 21–22.

10. Gray, *I & II Kings*, 476.

11. Hobbs, *2 Kings*, 22.

should be understood as "loyal and upstanding" men, ones worthy of another's trust.[12] Thus, בני־חיל does not seem to be directly related to war, but is more likely to refer to strong men who are capable of searching the area for days to find Elijah.[13]

If we survey the shared expressions again briefly, the following words may be included: חמשים (MT Exod 13:18; Josh 4:12), רכב (Exod 14:6, 7, 17, 18, 23, 28; 2 Kgs 2:12), פרש (Exod 14:9, 17, 18, 23, 25, 26, 28; 2 Kgs 2:12), מחנה (Exod 14:20, 24; Josh 3:2), חיל (Exod 14:4, 9, 17, 28; 2 Kgs 2:16), לחם in Exod 14:14, 25, and מלחמה in Josh 4:13. First, Exod 13:17–14:31 makes use of the expressions used in both Josh 3–4 and 2 Kgs 2. Regarding the frequency and variety of these words, Exod 13:17–14:31 seems to be the most developed story. Coats holds that water-crossing stories are mainly related with the conquest tradition, and the motifs of war and the crossing of in Exod 13:17–14:31 are later than those in Josh 3–4.[14] However, it is not easy to decide. Second, we can see that there is no single word that can be found in all these three narratives regarding the war motif. Furthermore, as we have seen above, it is difficult to assign a military context to these expressions in the case of 2 Kgs 2.

5.2.2.3. *The Route to the Water*. In Exod 13:17–22, the people of Israel set out from Succoth and camped at Etham[15] (13:20). In Exod 14:1–4, a

12. Long, *2 Kings*, 28. For similar expressions of this, see בני־חיל (2 Sam 2:7; 13:28), איש חיל (1 Kgs 1:42), בן־חיל (1 Kgs 1:52), כל־בני־חיל (Deut 3:18), אנשי־חיל (Gen 47:6; Exod 18:21, 25).

13. J. Van Seters argues that "crossing water" has an idiomatic meaning referring to military campaigns that can be traced back to Near Eastern inscriptions, particularly in Assyrian annals and the letters to the god. According to him, they may also stress at the onset of a campaign the overcoming of special physical obstacles, such as a flooding river or a difficult mountain range. For this, see Van Seters, *In Search of History*, 60–68, 330. Yet, as we see here, even though these texts include some words that could be related to war, 2 Kgs 2 does not have any direct military connotations. Thus, it would be more plausible to read them in the context of other water-crossing stories in the Old Testament, which are about entering and leaving a land: leaving Egypt (Exod 13:17–14:31), the Israelites' entering Canaan (Josh 3–4), Elijah's ascension to Heaven (2 Kgs 2).

14. G. W. Coats, "The Song of the Sea," *CBQ* 31 (1969): 1–17; idem, "The Ark of the Covenant in Joshua: A Probe into the History of a Tradition," *HAR* 9 (1985): 137–57.

15. Symmachus, Aquila and Theodotion represent אתן, which appears in 14:27. After אתם, the Samaritan Pentateuch and most likely the *Vorlagen* of Syriac and Targum add אשר. MT seems to be original. For this, see W. H. C. Propp, *Exodus 1–18: A New Translation with Introduction and Commentary* (AB 2; New York: Doubleday, 1998), 465.

somewhat different place-name, Pi-hahiroth, a place situated between Migdol and the sea and in front of Baalzephon, appears. The use of different proper names in these two texts (Exod 13:17–22 and 14:1–4) seems to be the result of the distinct histories of the literary layers. However, given that the topographical locations of so many of the named biblical places are no longer known, it is not easy to explain the differences between the MT and LXX.[16]

In Josh 3–4 Joshua and his people go from the Jordan to Gilgal, from where Elijah and Elisha leave (2 Kgs 2).[17] The route taken by Elijah and Elisha before crossing the Jordan is Gilgal–Bethel–Jericho–Jordan River.

What we see here is that Josh 3–4, and 2 Kgs 2 both mention the place names Jordan and Gilgal, and the crossing takes place at the same location, though in opposite directions.

On the other hand, Exod 13:17–14:31 is about the crossing of the Reed Sea; therefore, that story cannot be compared to the other two in terms of the place names.

5.2.2.4. *Water:* הים *(Exodus 14:2, 9, 16, 21, 22, 23, 26, 27, 28, 29, 30),* מי הירדן *(Joshua 3:8, 13; 4:7, 18, 23),* המים הירדים *(Joshua 3:13, 16),* הירדן *(2 Kings 2:6, 7, 13),* המים *(2 Kings 2:8, 14)*. If we pay attention to the expressions for "water," in Exod 13:17–14:31, הים ("the sea") is most frequently used (14:2, 9, 16, 21, 22, 23, 26, 27, 28, 29, 30). In Josh 3–4 the words הירדן and המים appear in the construct form: מי הירדן (Josh 3:8, 13; 4:7, 18, 23), המים הירדים (Josh 3:13, 16). However, in 2 Kgs 2 the words הירדן and המים appear separately. הירדן is used three times (2 Kgs 2:6, 7, 13), but in the scene itself, where the miracle of dividing the water takes place (2 Kgs 2:8, 14), the word המים is used. Here again, it is not easy to find common points in using words related with "water."

5.2.2.5. *The Shape of the Divided Water*. Exodus 14:21 describes in some detail the divided waters: "Yahweh drove the sea back by a strong east wind all night" (ויולך יהוה את־הים ברוח קדים עזה כל־הלילה); "and turned the sea into dry land" (וישׂם את־הים לחרבה); "and the waters were divided" (ויבקעו המים). In Josh 3–4, the division and the stopping of the waters are also described extensively. In Josh 3:13, Joshua predicts that the waters of the Jordan flowing from above "shall be cut off" (יכרתון),

16. For this, see M. Noth, *Das zweite Buch Mose: Exodus* (ATD 5; Göttingen: Vandenhoeck & Ruprecht, 1973), 86–87; Propp, *Exodus 1–18*, 465–66. Cf. Rottzoll, *Abraham Ibn Esras Langer Kommentar*, 379.

17. A. G. Auld, *Joshua, Judges, and Ruth* (The Daily Study Bible Series; Louisville: Westminster John Knox, 1984), 23.

and "shall stand in one heap" (ויעמדו נד אחד). Then, in 3:16, the prediction comes true; the waters flowing from above "stood" (יעמדו) still, were "rising up" (קמו) in one heap, and "were wholly cut off" (נכרתו־־־תמו). Yet, to describe the shape of the divided water, 2 Kgs 2 (vv. 8, 14) uses only one word, חצה, in Niphal, which means "to be parted."

In Exod 14 the divided waters formed a wall (והמים להם חמה מימינם ומשׂמאלם, Exod 14:22, 29). In Josh 3–4, the waters stood still and rose up in "one heap" (נד־אחד, Josh 3:16). Origen holds that Joshua's miracle is greater than Moses': the waters were gathered in one heap, rather than forming two walls.[18] In 2 Kgs 2:8, 14, the water is described as being parted "to the one side and to the other" (הנה והנה).

Here, we can see that some key elements used in Exod 13:17–14:31, such as נטה, נבקעו, and מימינם ומשׂמאלם, do not appear in Josh 3–4 and 2 Kgs 2. Yet, there are some similar motifs and expressions, such as נוח (Josh 3:13), נטבלו (Josh 3:15), and הכה (2 Kgs 2:8, 14), instead of נטה (Exod 14:21); יעמדו, קמו, נכרתו־־־תמו (Josh 3:16) and נחצה (2 Kgs 2:8, 14) instead of נבקעו (Exod 14:21); נד־אחד־־־הרחק (Josh 3:16) and הנה והנה (2 Kgs 2:8, 14) instead of מימינם ומשׂמאלם (Exod 14:22). Here, one can argue that the clusters of words in the earlier text influenced the later texts. Furthermore, even though the later texts are affected by the earlier text, it does not mean that the former should use exactly the same words as the latter. Rather, it is possible that the writers of the later texts used fresh and creative expressions to highlight their authenticity or skill. However, if one wants to establish a line of development, or even a linkage of these water-dividing stories, it is necessary to identify a convincing number of shared yet distinctive words within the accounts. How can one imagine development from one to another when so many distinctive elements fail to be used? It does not seem to be enough simply to say that different words have been employed.

5.2.2.6. *The Media Used to Perform a Miracle: Moses' Staff, (the Feet of the Priests Carrying) the Ark, and Elijah's Mantle.* In all of these three narratives, some kind of medium is used to perform a miracle. In Exod 14, Moses lifts up his staff to divide the sea. In Josh 3–4, the feet of the priests carrying the ark work as the medium of miracle. Elijah used his rolled up mantle to part the waters of the Jordan.

If we consider their relationship with each other, we can see that Moses' rod and Elijah's mantle are associated with Yahweh as the symbol of his power, authorizing Moses and Elijah to be human carriers

18. Auld, *Joshua: Jesus, Son of Nauē*, 109.

of God's symbol and agents of miracle. The ark in general is associated with Yahweh as the symbol of his presence and power. Yet, unlike Moses' rod and Elijah's mantle, it is not closely associated with Joshua, but with the priests. Although the rod and mantle belonged to Moses and Elijah, the ark in no sense belonged to Joshua. The ark is much more associated with Moses or David than with Joshua in the sense that Moses had made it and David carried it into Jerusalem.

5.2.2.7. *The Pillar of Cloud and Fire, and the Ark: The Symbols of Yahweh's Presence.* In Exod 13:21–22, the pillar of cloud and fire, which is also the symbol of Yahweh's presence, shows Israel the way to the Reed Sea. In Exod 14:19, the messenger of God and the pillar of cloud were behind the Israelites. In 14:20, the pillar of cloud and fire becomes a barrier protecting the Israelites in an image of terrifying splendor.

The interpretation of v. 20—ויבא בין מחנה מצרים ובין מחנה ישראל ויהי הענן והחשך ויאר את־הלילה ולא־קרב זה אל־זה כל־הלילה—has proved to be extremely difficult. There have been three major approaches to this problem. One approach follows the MT and tries to explain this verse along the lines of the Targum: the same cloud produced darkness to the Egyptians and light to the Israelites. Another approach seeks a different root meaning of the verb יאר using the comparative philological method. A third approach tries to reconstruct a verbal form from the noun "darkness" or make some use of the LXX ἦλθεν.[19] LXX has a quite different text: καὶ ἐγένετο σκότος καὶ γνόφος καὶ διῆλθεν ἡ νύξ ("and there was darkness and blackness, and the night passed"). If its meaning is that at night the pillar did not light up as a pillar of fire but remained dark, the gap between the two camps was veiled with mysterious and total darkness so that no one could—or in view of the miraculous nature of the phenomenon dared to—penetrate.[20] In this sense, the understanding of LXX seems to be relevant. In Exod 14:24—ויהי באשמרת הבקר וישקף יהוה אל־מחנה מצרים בעמוד אש וענן ויהם את מחנה מצרים—Yahweh himself looked down upon the camp of the Egyptians from within the pillar of fire and cloud and caused them to panic. These are the same two pillars that led the Israelites in their wilderness journey.[21]

19. Childs, *Exodus*, 218.

20. Noth, *Das zweite Buch Mose*, 91.

21. J. Van Seters, *The Life of Moses: The Yahwist as Historian in Exodus–Numbers* (Louisville: Westminster John Knox, 1994), 138.

In Josh 3–4, the ark, being the symbol of God's presence, leads Israel's crossing of the Jordan. As we have seen in Chapter 4, the ark carried by the priests dominates the narratives of Josh 3:1–4:19.

In 2 Kgs 2, Elisha simply follows his master Elijah, there is no symbol of the guiding presence of God.

Although Van Seters argues that the pillar of cloud and fire in Exod 13:17–14:31 has the similar function to the ark in Josh 3–4,[22] we cannot find any strong connections between these three narratives relating to the symbol of God's guiding presence.

5.2.3. *Summary of the Preliminary Analysis*

The preliminary analysis revealed that these three stories share some words, but only חרבה appears in all of these three narratives (Exod 14:21; Josh 3:17; 4:18; 2 Kgs 2:8) and refers to the same meaning in all three passages.

However, in almost all other cases, most of the shared words are used in different ways: חמשים—"in [military] formation" in MT Exod 13:18 and Josh 4:12, but "50" in LXX Exod 13:18 and 2 Kgs 2:16; רום—"boldly" (ביד רמה) in Exod 14:8, "lift up" in Exod 14:16, "raise high" in Josh 4:5, and "pick up" in 2 Kgs 2:13; רוח—"wind" in general sense in Exod 14:21, "the spirit of Yahweh or prophet" in 2 Kgs 2:9, 15, 16; רכב, פרש, חיל—used in a military context in Exod 14, but with no military connotations in 2 Kgs 2.

Some of these terms are absent from some of the water-crossing stories: שוב in 2 Kgs 2, עבר in Exod 13:17–14:31. There are other key expressions related to the division of waters in Exod 13:17–14:31, such as נטה, נבקעו, and מימינם ומשמאלם, that do not occur in Josh 3–4 and 2 Kgs 2. Even although one can find some similar words, these do not enable us to establish a line of development, or even a linkage of these water-dividing stories.

There are also some thematic similarities and shared motifs in these three stories.

Joshua 3–4 and 2 Kgs 2 have the similar theme of succession, namely, Moses–Joshua and Elijah–Elisha, but there are no shared words related to this theme. Exodus 13:17–14:31 does not contain this story of succession.

Exodus 13:17–14:31 and Josh 3–4 represent strong military terminology and connotations, but it is not easy to find them in 2 Kgs 2.

22. Ibid., 144.

Exodus 13:17–14:31, Josh 3–4, and 2 Kgs 2 have similar accounts of travelling from one place to another. Joshua 3–4 and 2 Kgs 2 have common place names, such as Jordan and Gilgal, but Exod 13:17–14:31 represents rather different names.

In all three narratives some different word and expressions are used to describe the divided waters. For the water itself, Exod 13:17–14:31 uses הים, Josh 3–4 the construct forms מי הירדן and המים הירדים, and 2 Kgs 2 הירדן and המים separately. To describe the shape of divided waters, Exod 14:21 uses the phrases ויולך יהוה את־הים ברוח קדים עזה כל־הלילה, וישׂם את־הים לחרבה, and ויבקעו המים, Josh 3:13 has יכרתון and ויעמדו, Josh 3:16 employs יעמדו, קמו, and נכרתו־־־תמו, while 2 Kgs 2 offers just one word, חצה (2 Kgs 2:8, 14). To describe piled-up waters, Exod 14 employs the phrase והמים להם חמה מימינם ומשׂמאלם (Exod 14:22, 29), while Josh 3–4 uses נד־אחד (Josh 3:16).

Concerning the media used to perform a miracle (Moses' staff, the feet of the priests carrying the ark, and Elijah's mantle) and the symbols of Yahweh's presence (the pillar of cloud and fire, and the ark), each narrative uses different expressions and it is not easy to find any clue to explain their connection.

We can see here that Exod 13:17–14:31, Josh 3–4, and 2 Kgs 2 have some similar themes and motifs. Yet, in the use of detailed words and phrases to describe them, these three water stories demonstrate significant differences. In almost all of the cases they use different words.

5.3. *Conclusion*

The aim of this chapter was to explore the relevance of reading Josh 3–4 in the wider context of Exod 13:17–14:31 and 2 Kgs 2, which are the water-crossing stories of Moses and Elijah-Elisha. In particular, we noted how non-shared material such as Elijah–Elisha's crossing of the Jordan (2 Kgs 2) is linked to other texts in the Pentateuch (Exod 13:17–14:31) and in the Former Prophets (Josh 3–4).

However, the analysis of words, themes, and motifs in these three narratives led us to make unexpected findings. There appears to be only one word, חרבה, that is used in exactly the same way across all three passages, although this is not so surprising given that חרבה, which means "dry ground," appears in stories dealing with the division of waters and the crossing through it. There are two more words, הרים and חמשׁים, which occur in all three passages, though with different meanings. In Exod 14:16 and 2 Kgs 2:13 הרים is used to express the motion of raising high the medium by which the waters are divided, while in Josh 4:5 the term is used in connection with the setting up of twelve stones on the other side of the Jordan. The consonantal cluster חמשים also occurs in all three passages, and it is notable that the cluster is not common elsewhere in these three books. Furthermore, the varied vocalization and interpretation of these consonants makes it more difficult to find the appropriate link between them. Almost all the other shared words are also used in different ways. Moreover, most of the expressions used to describe the shared themes and motifs are different in each narrative. We can find only some superficial connection between these texts.

Therefore, even if we found some shared words and themes in these three stories, it would not be easy to establish a line of development or a historical order of the texts. Rather, it would be better to read the literary history of Josh 3–4 in the context of other ark narratives, as suggested in Chapter 4.

Chapter 6

THE LITERARY HISTORY OF JOSHUA 3–4

6.1. *Introduction*

The purpose of this chapter is to reconstruct the literary history of Josh 3–4 in the light of the results of our study up until now. This kind of diachronic historical-critical analysis should (with Polzin) be based on the complex narrative, as being "necessary for an *adequate* scholarly understanding of what it means."[1] Even though Polzin states that his competent literary reading is "*preliminary*"[2] and calls for a historical-critical analysis, he does not present any consequent diachronic study of Josh 3–4. Polzin's synchronic reading is certainly not the only way to understand this complex text and leaves many text-critical issues unanswered. How, for example, would Polzin explain the large number of MT pluses, about which he said nothing in his synchronic study? This chapter aims to address these issues by studying the literary history of Josh 3–4, this being one of the most complex literary composites in the book of Joshua.

However, to reconstruct the literary history of Josh 3–4, we will have to complete the textual history first. Through text-critical analysis, we have come to understand the limitations of Polzin's literary reading on Josh 3–4. By considering only the final shape of MT Josh 3–4, his study overlooks several differences between the MT and the LXX in Josh 3–4. Text-critical analysis led us to conclude that these differences were not caused by scribal error or exegetical variation from the LXX side. Rather, the Greek text of Josh 3–4 appears to be more faithful to the Hebrew *Vorlage* of the LXX and earlier than the MT. Thus, we will consider both the Hebrew *Vorlage* of the LXX and the MT in order to examine the complex literary history of Josh 3–4.

1. Polzin, *Moses and the Deuteronomist*, 3.
2. Ibid., 5.

Therefore, we will first make a comparison between the OG[3] *Vorlage* and the MT Josh 3–4. In the areas where they disagree, which of the two seems to be primary—or is neither primary?

Second, we will reconstruct the literary history of Josh 3–4 based on our findings.

Finally, we will critique Polzin's literary reading of this narrative, especially on his lack of attention to its literary history.

6.2. *The Textual History of Joshua 3–4: Comparison Between the OG* Vorlage *and the MT*

Before we examine the literary history of Josh 3–4, it is necessary to decide which text we should read, as we have found a lot of differences between the LXX and the MT, and have discovered in Chapter 3 that these reflect differences between the OG *Vorlage* and the MT Josh 3–4. First, we will analyze the pluses in the OG *Vorlage* and MT Josh 3–4. Subsequently, we will investigate the other disagreements between the OG *Vorlage* and MT. If we study those differences more closely, we may come to understand the textual history better, and can decide whether we should read the literary history of Josh 3–4 based on the MT, or the Hebrew *Vorlage* of the LXX, or a possible reconstruction of an "original" text common to the MT and the LXX *Vorlage*.

6.2.1. *The Pluses in the MT and the OG* Vorlage *Joshua 3–4*

If we look at Table 1 in Chapter 3 (section 3.2.1), which shows the LXX, the retroversion of the LXX, and the MT, we find a considerable number of pluses in the MT and the OG *Vorlage* Josh 3–4 and many more pluses in the MT than in the Hebrew *Vorlage* of LXX:

> MT pluses: 3:1 (הוא וכל־בני ישראל), 3 (ואתם), 6 (לאמר), 7 (כי), 10 (ויאמר יהושע), 11 (לפניכם), 12 (ועתה, איש־אחד), 13 (כפות, מלמעלה, נד אחד, ו---), 14 (ויהי), 15 (כל), 16 (מאדם), 17 (הכן); 4:1 (יהי), 2 (לכם, שנים עשר, איש־אחד), 3 (לאמר, לכמ מזה, ממצב רגלי הכהנים, בירדן, ו---), 4 (איש־אחד), 5 (יהושע, ארון, אלהיכם, בני), 7 (בירדן, נכרתו מי הירדן), 9 (בתוך), 10 (תוך, ככל אשר־צוה משה את־יהושע), 11 (העם), 13 (כ), 14 (עם), 18 (הכהנים, כפות, תוך), 21 (ויאמר אל־בני ישראל, מחר, את־אבותם), 22 (הזה, ו---).

3. OG: I mean what Margolis calls OG. Here OG = LXX^{B} except when noted.

Pluses in OG *Vorlage*: 3:3 (ו--- ---ינו), 5 (למחר), 6 (הכהנים, יהוה, יהוה), 7 (גם, כן, בני), 8 (ו---), 15 (הירדן, ברית יהוה, הברית, הכהנים, הטים), 16 (עד, ירד, מאד), 17 (בני); 4:3 (ואותם, ו---), 5 (משם, לפני, שנים עשׂר, לנשה), 6 (תמיד), 7 (כל הארץ, לאמר, אתה), 8 (יהוה), 9 (יהוה, אחרות), 10 (הברית), 11 (ברית), 16 (יהוה, ברית), 19 (בני ישׂראל), 21 (אליכם), 23 (יהוה אלהינו), 24 (אתם).

Some pluses in the above list are specific to this text, while others are very common in the Old Testament. We can better understand both pluses and the textual history of Josh 3–4 by focusing on the more unusual words and expressions.

6.2.1.1. *The Pluses in* MT *Joshua 3–4*.

6.2.1.1.1. הוא וכל־בני ישׂראל, *"he and all the sons of Israel" (3:1)*. In the first verse of this narrative, only MT represents הוא וכל־בני ישׂראל. Syriac attests only בני ישׂראל ("the sons of Israel").[4] "All Israel" is the usual expression in the Hebrew Bible.[5] Joshua 1:2 has a similar MT plus (לבני ישׂראל). According to Van der Meer, לבני ישׂראל after להם in the MT is merely redundant and superfluous, but not unique.[6] He insists that this is possible Classical Hebrew, in which there exists a construction containing a double indirect object with the same preposition as in ויתן להם משה לבני גדו לבני ראובן ולחצי שבט מנשה (Num 32:33). In addition, he says that the absence of לבני ישׂראל is the result of a shortening of a superfluous Hebrew expression by the Greek translator. However, even if we admit the redundancy in the Hebrew expression, in Josh 1:2 וכל־העם identifying להם had already appeared in the preceding clause. Therefore, לבני ישׂראל might be an MT plus, inserted by an editor to elucidate a shorter text.[7] Similarly, an MT editor interpolated הוא וכל־בני ישׂראל in Josh 3:1. In the entire Old Testament, this rather unusual expression appears only once, this being in Num 27:21. This is a plus in the MT, which seems to be interpolated to manage the awkward shift of subject from the singular "he got up early" to the plural "they went…"

6.2.1.1.2. לאמר *(3:6)*, ויאמר אל־בני ישׂראל *(4:21)*. The LXX does not represent לאמר in Josh 3:6. Similarly, ויאמר אל־בני ישׂראל is absent in LXX Josh 4:21. Boling holds that this is a mechanical copying error: a sizable haplography (בגלג[ל ויאמר אל־בני ישׂרא]ל לאמר) in the LXX.[8]

4. Boling and Wright, *Joshua*, 156.
5. Holmes, *Joshua, the Hebrew and Greek Texts*, 22.
6. Van der Meer, *Formation and Reformulation*, 196.
7. E. Tov, "The Growth of the Book of Joshua in the Light of the Evidence of the LXX Translation," in *The Greek and Hebrew Bible*, 391.
8. Boling and Wright, *Joshua*, 183.

However, even if this form appears in 4:1b, 15, לאמר after ויאמר is still uncommon. Therefore, this might rather be a conscious editorial expansion of the Hebrew text. Both לאמר in 3:6 and ויאמר אל־בני ישראל in 4:21 are redactional interpolations to introduce the direct discourse and to re-emphasize the identity of speaker and addressees.

6.2.1.1.3. כי *(3:7)*. Only MT contains the plus כי in 3:7. Sipilä insists that ὅτι was omitted because of the following καθότι.[9] This is the only case in the book of Joshua where כי initiating an object clause has no "visible counterpart" in the LXX *Vorlage*; it is, therefore, an uncertain case to judge.

6.2.1.1.4. ויאמר יהושע *(3:10)*. MT Josh 3:10 has the plus ויאמר יהושע. The MT repeats the phrase "and Joshua said," which appeared already in 3:9. As in 3:6 and 4:21, this plus was inserted by an editor to introduce the direct discourse and emphasize the speaker Joshua. In 4:5 and 4:10 as well, MT inserted יהושע to emphasize and legitimize the role of Joshua.

6.2.1.1.5. לפניכם *(3:11)*. The LXX does not represent לפניכם. Except for this MT plus, לפניכם appears only once in Josh 24:12.

6.2.1.1.6. כפות *(3:13; 4:18)*. כפות is absent in LXX Josh 3:13 and 4:18.[10] In the book of Joshua, כף appears once in 1:3, and כפות twice (3:13; 4:18). Even though כף in 1:3 is rendered by ἴχνει, כפות in the other two verses are MT pluses. This appears to be redactional interpolation by an MT editor to describe the miracle more vividly and concretely.

6.2.1.1.7. מלמעלה ו--- נד אחד *(3:13)*. MT is much longer at the end of 3:13, and represents the plus מלמעלה ו--- נד אחד. מלמעלה and אחד are quite common, but נד is quite a rare word in the Old Testament, appearing only in Exod 15:8; Josh 3:13, 16; Pss 33:7; 78:13, and Isa 17:11. Even though מלמעלה --- נד אחד appears once more in this narrative (Josh 3:16), this expression cannot be found again in the Hebrew Bible. An editor seems to have inserted this phrase from 3:16 to make the two clauses correspond.

6.2.1.1.8. הכן *(3:17)*. MT Josh 3:17 contains the plus הכן. הכן is a quite uncommon form in the Old Testament. These three consonants are vocalized and used in different ways: in Gen 43:16; Num 23:1, 29; 1 Chr 29:18; Ps 119:133; Prov 24:27; Jer 46:14 as in Ezek 38:7 as a Hiphil imperative form, in Ezek 38:7 also as a Niphal imperative; in Nah 2:6 as Hophal *waw* consecutive perfect; and in Josh 3:17 as a Hiphil infinitive absolute.

9. Sipilä, *Between Literalness and Freedom*, 185.

10. כפות appears in Num 7:84, 86; Josh 3:13; 4:18; 1 Sam 5:4; 1 Kgs 5:17; 2 Kgs 9:15; 2 Chr 24:14; Song 5:5; Isa 60:14; Ezek 43:7; Dan 10:10; Mal 3:21, etc.

6.2.1.1.9. לכם *(4:2, 3)*. The LXX has no corresponding *dativus ethicus* in 4:2, 3. Margolis holds that לכם was not expressed in LXX Josh 4:2, because "implied in παραλαβών." In 4:3 as well, he suggests that it is not expressed in Greek because it is "implied in the middle [voice]."[11] However, Tov lists לכם in 4:2, 3 as an MT plus. He describes it as a small elucidation interpolated by MT editor.[12] We should also judge this to be an uncertain case.

6.2.1.1.10. איש־אחד *(4:2)*. It is surprising that the MT ends each of 3:12; 4:2, 4 with the same words, as does B, but only MT Josh 3:12; 4:2, 4 represent one more איש־אחד. The uncommon repetitive expression, איש־אחד איש־אחד, appears only once in Num 13:2 except for these MT pluses in the entire Old Testament. An MT editor seems to have interpolated this phrase in order to make the same repetitive emphatic expression in all of these three verses.

6.2.1.1.11. ממצב רגלי הכהנים *(4:3)*. This long phrase ממצב רגלי הכהנים is absent in OG *Vorlage* of Josh 4:3. Boling holds that the LXX lost this phrase by haplography from the LXX *Vorlage*, having been framed by words which begin and end with the same letter ה: הירדן and הכין.[13] However, his idea that a mechanical copying error caused this variant is highly implausible, as behind his assumption lies the prejudice that this kind of problem happened because of mistakes on the LXX side. The word מצב used in this sense also appears in Josh 4:9; Isa 29:3.[14] Furthermore, this form ממצב, appears only once in Isa 22:19 (ממצבך), other than this MT plus in Josh 4:3. This MT plus probably originated through an editor, who tries to emphasize the middle of the Jordan.

6.2.1.1.12. יהושע *(4:5)*. OG *Vorlage* does not represent יהושע in Josh 4:5. The repetition of יהושע is rather awkward, because this subject leads v. 4 as well. This is a redactional interpolation from the MT side to remove ambiguity in this verse.

6.2.1.1.13. ארון *(4:5)*. LXX Josh 4:5 does not contain ארון. The MT seems to have inserted this word in order to correct theological problems in this verse.[15] An MT scribe tried to solve the clumsiness of this verse, in which Yahweh himself stands in the middle of the Jordan.[16] In addition,

11. Auld, *Joshua: Jesus, Son of Nauē*, 111.
12. Tov, "The Growth of the Book of Joshua," 391.
13. Boling and Wright, *Joshua*, 157.
14. Even though מצב appears several times in the book of Samuel (1 Sam 13:23; 14:1, 4, 6, 11, 15; 2 Sam 23:14), it has a different meaning, "garrison," in these verses.
15. Tov, "The Growth of the Book of Joshua," 394.
16. Sipilä, "The Septuagint Version of Joshua 3–4," 69.

the redundancy of לפני was awkward to him. To sort out all these problems, he removed one לפני, and interpolated ארון between לפני and יהוה. In several places of the OG *Vorlage*, the expression "in front of the Lord" appears. This idea, which implies direct contact with God, has been changed by the interpolation of the words "the ark of": 6:7, 13; 7:6.[17]

6.2.1.1.14. אלהיכם *(4:5)*. OG *Vorlage* does not have אלהיכם in Josh 4:5. The MT appears to insert this word for the purpose of theological correction as ארון above.[18] By adding these words, the MT tries to remove the anthropomorphic feature in OG *Vorlage* of Yahweh standing in the middle of the Jordan and clearly explain it as God of Israel (אלהיכם).

6.2.1.1.15. תוך *(4:9, 10, 18)*. Only MT represents בתוך or מתוך in Josh 4:9, 10, 18. Den Hertog explains the phrase ἐν αὐτῷ τῷ Ιορδάνῃ as being one of many cases where Greek has left תוך untranslated, but without mentioning αὐτῷ. The other תוך pluses are in MT Josh 7:21, 23; 12:2; 13:16. Auld holds that it may be better to explain αὐτῷ as at least a "shadow" of תוך. In 4:10 as well, "in the midst of" (בתוך) is rendered simply as "ב" (ἐν).[19] This may be another uncertain case.

6.2.1.1.16. ככל אשר־צוה משה את־יהושע *(4:10)*. MT Josh 4:10 includes the long plus ככל אשר־צוה משה את־יהושע. Van der Meer maintains that the Greek translator stylistically shortened this verse for the sake of a smooth, intelligible and elegant Greek text.[20] According to him, if there had been some specific additional instructions which a later editor sought to incorporate into the MT text, this plus could have been regarded as a redactional interpolation.[21] However, no extra instructions could be found. There are no specific instructions from Moses to Joshua with respect to the crossing of the Jordan recorded in the Pentateuch. This makes it very difficult to suppose that a later editor deliberately interpolated this phrase.[22] However, as he himself explains the clumsiness of this plus, we cannot find any equivalent instructions from Moses to Joshua with regard to the crossing of the Jordan. Rather, this plus seems to be due to the influence of Deuteronomy.[23] In Deut 3:28, we find that God commands Moses to command Joshua. It may be possible to assume that a later editor inserted this phrase to show the fulfillment of God's

17. Tov, "The Growth of the Book of Joshua," 394.
18. Ibid.
19. Auld, *Joshua: Jesus, Son of Nauē*, 115–16.
20. Van der Meer, *Formation and Reformulation*, 189.
21. Ibid., 182.
22. Ibid., 183.
23. Tov, "The Growth of the Book of Joshua," 394.

command, as given in Deut 3:28. In addition, these phrases could be related to the attempt to underline the transition from Moses to Joshua, which could be found in Josh 3:7 and 4:14.

6.2.1.1.17. את־אבותם ,מחר *(4:21)*. MT Josh 4:21 contains the pluses את־אבותם ,מחר. In this case as well, since the OG *Vorlage* is closer to the general form of the formula,[24] these pluses are due to proto-Masoretic additions. It is likely that an MT scribe put מחר to match this verse with the general form in Deut 6:20 and Josh 4:6. את־אבותם also makes the syntax of this verse a bit awkward. The subject of this verse is בניכם, so the cognate object would be אתכם, not את־אבותם. This plus (את־אבותם) seems to have been inserted by an MT redactor, who misread the syntax of this verse.

6.2.1.1.18. הזה *(4:22)*. The OG *Vorlage* does not represent the plus הזה in Josh 4:22. Van der Meer argues that the pronoun is removed in the LXX *Vorlage* to improve the style of the redundant Hebrew text.[25] However, the phrase הירדן הזה is quite uncommon in the Old Testament. הירדן הזה appears only in Gen 32:11; Deut 3:27; 31:2; Josh 1:2, 11; 4:22. Furthermore, these demonstrative elements in Josh 1:2 and 4:22 are MT pluses. The plus is a small elucidation introduced by a later editor of the book.[26] An MT scribe inserted the word into this verse to stress the Jordan and the miracle of its stopping.

6.2.1.2. *The Pluses in the OG* Vorlage *Joshua 3–4*.

6.2.1.2.1. ---ינו ו--- *(3:3)*. LXX Josh 3:3 represents the plus ἡμῶν καὶ. The Hebrew *Vorlage* of the LXX may have had כהנינו והלוים. The division between the priests and Levites, inserting a conjunction (ו) between the two words is later than that of Deuteronomy, which emphasizes only one Levitical priesthood.[27] However, the OG *Vorlage* also seems to understand them as a single group: "the ark, and (carrying it) our priests and the Levites." One difficult problem we have to solve in these pluses is 'our priests'. "Our priests" appears only four times in the MT in Ezra 9:7 and in Neh 9:32, 34; 10:1. Vulgate's *et sacerdotes stirpis leviticae* supports the MT. On the other side, Targum and Syriac underscore the LXX distinction here and in 9:2.[28]

24. Sipilä, "The Septuagint Version of Joshua 3–4," 69.
25. Van der Meer, *Formation and Reformulation*, 195.
26. Tov, "The Growth of the Book of Joshua," 332.
27. Butler, *Joshua*, 39.
28. Auld, *Joshua: Jesus, Son of Nauē*, 103.

6.2.1.2.2. למחר *(3:5)*. The OG *Vorlage* contains the plus למחר in Josh 3:5. Numbers 11:18 bears a similarity to this verse, where the rare התקדשו is also used and where Moses specifies למחר. The close connection between the Hebrew *Vorlage* of the LXX and Numbers seems to explain the literalness of the Greek rendering.[29]

6.2.1.2.3. חטים *(3:15)*. MT Joshua 3:15 does not attest the Hebrew word חטים. The word pair קציר חטים occurs quite often in the Bible (Gen 30:14; Exod 34:22; Judg 15:1; Ruth 2:23; 1 Sam 6:13; 12:17). The paraphrase of this passage in 4QApJosh[b] also agrees with the OG *Vorlage* in specifying this harvest time as the period of the wheat harvest.[30] MT might have smoothed and generalized the specified reading of the Hebrew *Vorlage* of LXX Josh 3:15. However, as it is an LXX plus, supralinear in 4QJosh[b], it would also be possible to think that the shorter MT is more original. Therefore, we should judge this as being another uncertain case.

6.2.1.3. *Conclusion on the Pluses in the OG* Vorlage *and MT Joshua 3–4*. Through the close examination of the pluses in both the OG *Vorlage* and MT, we learned that there are a larger number of pluses in the MT than in the OG *Vorlage*, and that those MT pluses are quite rare and unusual in the Hebrew Bible. Furthermore, this large number of pluses in MT seems to have been interpolated later to solve some clumsiness in a verse (often syntactic), or redactionally inserted with some theological or exegetical purpose. However, the pluses in the OG *Vorlage* are quite common in the Old Testament and appear to belong to the original text of Josh 3–4. Thus, we can entertain the possibility that the pluses in the Hebrew *Vorlage* of LXX are original and primary, while those in the MT are secondary and are possibly later interpolations. However, we cannot confirm this possibility yet as there are some uncertain cases that cannot be judged, and there are still a number of questions to be answered.

6.2.2. *Other Divergences Between the OG* Vorlage *and MT in Joshua 3–4*
In the previous section (6.2.1), we examined the pluses in the two texts. In this section, we will identify and analyze the various other divergences between the OG *Vorlage* and the MT. We have already discussed many issues regarding the differences between the OG *Vorlage* and the MT in Josh 3–4 in Chapter 3 on text-critical analysis. In this section, we will focus mainly on those issues that were not examined closely in Chapter 3.

29. Ibid., 104.
30. Bieberstein, *Joshua–Jordan–Jericho*, 152–54.

The OG *Vorlage* of 3:1 has ויסע, in comparison to MT's ויסעו. The syntax of the Hebrew *Vorlage* is a bit awkward, where only Joshua "set out" from Shittim and all the people went to the Jordan. The MT smoothes the *lectio difficilior* contained in the OG *Vorlage* by changing the singular ויסע into the plural ויסעו. Furthermore, a later editor interpolated the plus הוא וכל־בני ישׂראל to clarify the syntax of this verse.

At 3:3 the MT has אלהיכם, but the Hebrew *Vorlage* of LXX has the inclusive אלהינו. This occurs quite often in this narrative (3:3, 4, 5, 9, 10; 4:23, 24). In the OG *Vorlage* Joshua includes himself among the people, but in the MT Joshua excludes himself from the people. The MT shows theological development, distinguishing Joshua from other people to authorize the leadership.

The MT version of 3:4 attests במדה ("by the measure") but the OG *Vorlage* תעמדו. Even although במדה appears in Lev 19:35 and 2 Chr 3:3, its use in this verse is rather unusual.[31] One could postulate a possible copying error by an MT scribe. However, it would be safer to assume a theological variation from the MT side. The command to keep a measurement of exactly two thousand cubits distance seems to show ritual enactment and cultic development. There are many scholars who regard this narrative as cultic. Soggin relates this event with liturgical preparation for the Passover in Exodus.[32] Wilcoxin also understands all the narrative of Josh 1–6 in the context of the cult legend of the Passover.[33] According to him, the whole narrative of Josh 1–6 consists of two seven-day periods. First, the series of events constituted by the crossing from its preparation in Josh 1 to its sequel of the Passover observance in Josh 5 occupies a seven-day period.[34] Second, the capture of Jericho (ch. 6) also occupies a period of seven days. He links the seven days of the circumambulations of Jericho with ritual events. Soggin believes that this event would have exactly corresponded to the seven days of the spring Festival of Unleavened Bread, which follows immediately upon the first event, Passover.[35] Furthermore, by paying attention to the two additions made by an editor in Josh 5:11, 12, Auld also noted the MT's effort to make this text correspond to the correct ritual date of the Passover in Lev 23:5–6.[36] In 3:4, an MT editor pays attention to the keeping of exact distance from the ark by changing תעמדו into במדה ("by the measure"). In the regulations on the towns for the Levites in Num 35:4 as well, the

31. Auld, *Joshua: Jesus, Son of Nauē*, 104.
32. Soggin, *Joshua*, 55–56.
33. Wilcoxen, "Narrative Structure and Cult Legend," 43–70.
34. Ibid., 60–61.
35. Ibid., 61–63.
36. Auld, *Joshua Retold*, 12.

concrete distance of one thousand cubits is emphasized. The ark could be explained as the symbol of divine presence. In Exod 33:17–23, Israel is warned to keep its distance from the danger of the divine holiness. Reviewing the past incident of Uzzah in 2 Sam 6:1–11//1 Chr 13:5–14, an MT editor seems to have tried to enact the safe and exact ritual distance from the ark, about two thousands cubits by the measure in 3:4.

At 3:8, the Hebrew *Vorlage* of LXX has ועתה but MT has ואתה. The two terms sound alike, so a scribal mistake could have been made in dictation from one to the other. However, it could also have been possible that the MT changed ועתה into ואתה to emphasize the subject and to authorize the leadership of Joshua as observed in other parts of this narrative.

The MT at 3:9 represents דברי יהוה but the OG *Vorlage* דבר יהוה. In the Hebrew Bible, both expressions appear quite often. As Soggin suggests, we can assume possible dittography of the *yod* in the MT; the early abbreviation for יהוה was later confused with the suffix.[37] However, it would not be plausible to guess a copying error in the other direction. In some other parts of the book of Joshua, supporting the OG *Vorlage*, יהוה accompanies the singular form דבר: דבר יהוה (8:27), את־הדבר
אשר־דבר יהוה (14:6), דבר יהוה את־הדבר (14:10), and הדבר הטוב
אשר־דבר יהוה (21:45).

As we have seen in Chapter 3, the presence of the article before ברית in the MT's version of 3:11 and its absence in the LXX are quite difficult to explain. Soggin contends that the Syriac insertion of יהוה after ברית as in v. 13 is more probable.[38] However, Langlamet correctly points out his grammatical problem with the article before the *nomen regens*.[39] *Zāqēp parvum* on הברית in the MT makes two short phrases in apposition: "the ark of the covenant, the lord of all the earth." The lack of the article in many Greek witnesses is all the more striking. Auld suggests that "lord" here is not the divine name, but a common Hebrew noun.[40] If "lord" is a common noun and part of a chain of nouns in genitive relationship, then it and also "covenant" should have the Greek article. Den Hertog comments that the presence of a redundant article in the corresponding phrase in the MT may let the absence of a normal article in B appear original.[41] The problem in the MT might be caused by a copyist's interpolation of the definite article, who thought the absence of it in the Hebrew *Vorlage* of LXX was unusual.

37. Soggin, *Joshua*, 48.
38. Ibid.
39. Langlamet, *Gilgal et les récits de la traversée du Jourdain*, 46–47.
40. Auld, *Joshua: Jesus, Son of Nauē*, 107.
41. Ibid.

The beginning of v. 14 in the OG *Vorlage* is a little different from that of the MT: that is, ויסע in LXX *Vorlage* but ויהי בנסע in MT. The opening formulaic "and it came to be" is generally resumed by a finite verb in Biblical Hebrew. Joshua 4:18 starts in a similar way with ויהי בעלות and represents finite verb נתקו; but MT Josh 3:14–15 is more complex: the main finite verb does not appear until v. 15. The same phrase ויהי בנסע appears in Num 10:35 but the finite verb ויאמר follows later in the verse. Probably, MT Josh 3:14 adapted the opening of this verse clumsily.[42]

The MT version of 3:16 has the geographical name מאדם but the OG *Vorlage* simply attests מאד, "extremely." The Hebrew *Vorlage* of LXX has קרית יערים but MT reads צרתן. However, the geographical description in the OG *Vorlage* seems to be more difficult. Because Kiriath-jearim is fairly distant from the Jordan, it is hardly possible for the Jordan water to stand, rising up in a single heap far from a city that is beside Kiriath-jearim. Theodotion, Aquila, and Symmachus also support the MT's צרתן. Furthermore, both textual traditions attest two different verbs in v. 16: עמדו in the LXX *Vorlage* but עברו in the MT. However, if we read this narrative more closely, all the people finish crossing the Jordan toward the city of Jericho in 4:13. Thus, in 3:16 עמדו נגד יריחו ("had stood opposite Jericho") would be better. An MT editor might have changed this word into עברו to solve the inconsistency that all the people had already completed crossing the Jordan in 3:17 and 4:1.

At 3:17 the MT represents הגוי but B *Laos*, which is the standing equivalent for the Hebrew עם.[43] The Hebrew word הגוי in the MT is rather exceptional for העם in the OG *Vorlage* because the regular term to express "the people [Israel]" throughout the Hebrew Bible is העם. However, in 3:17 and 4:1, 11 MT reads הגוי, "which is normally used for one of the other nations of the earth. [OG *Vorlage*] is more straightforward: it has understood 'all the people' as being equivalent to the preceding 'all the sons of Israel.' Jewish tradition has understood 'all the *goy*' as referring to those members of other nations who were associated here with Israel."[44] Some would say the word, הגוי, is used to make all the nations participate in this miracle of God's people, so it is original. However, its use here in the MT is unusual in the Hebrew Bible.

The MT at 4:6–7 represents the plural form כי־ישאלון בניכם and ואמרתם להם, but the OG *Vorlage* singular כי־ישאל בנך and ואתה אמרת לבנך. Exodus 13:14–15 and Deut 6:20–21, which have the same question

42. Ibid., 108.
43. Ibid., 110.
44. Ibid.

and answer form as in Josh 4:6–7, support the LXX *Vorlage*. For more on this, see below on the literary history of Josh 4:6–7.

At 4:8 the Hebrew *Vorlage* of LXX has כאשר צוה יהוה יהושע but the MT reads כאשר צוה יהושע. Similarly, the MT attributes an instruction to Joshua, but the OG *Vorlage* to Yahweh in 9:3. In 4:5 and 5:15 as well, "Joshua" is a plus in the MT. The MT tries to magnify Joshua to compare his leadership to that of Moses. The MT seems to be later than the OG *Vorlage*.

Staying with 4:8, the MT attests למספר שבטי בני־ישראל but the OG *Vorlage* בתם בני־ישראל לעבר. As in 3:12, the MT has more theologized term שבטי. The MT tries to connect the number twelve with the number of tribes, which shows that the MT is later than the Hebrew *Vorlage* of LXX.

In the OG *Vorlage* of 4:10 we find the wording "till Joshua fulfilled all that Yahweh commanded to tell the people" (עד תם יהושע כל־הדבר אשר־צוה יהוה לדבר אל־העם), while in the MT this becomes "till everything was completed that Yahweh commanded Joshua to tell the people" (עד תם כל־הדבר אשר־צוה יהוה את־יהושע לדבר אל־העם). The MT also represents ככל אשר־צוה משה את יהושע, which is lacking in the OG ("according to everything which Moses commanded Joshua"). Barthélemy seems to be right in that there were two distinct literary treatments in the MT and the LXX—and these were not just small differences. Moatti-Fine also supports his detailed diagnosis, that the LXX had omitted what appeared contradictory, while the MT had wanted to underline the transmission from Moses to Joshua. She finds some harmonizing variations in vv. 4, 5, 9, 10.[45] However, it seems to be difficult to decide from which text those variations happened.

The MT at 4:11 represents לפני העם but the OG *Vorlage* לפניהם. Here, the syntax of the MT is awkward, because in v. 11a, all the people completed the crossing of the Jordan, but in 11b, the priests are crossing the river before the people. Joshua 4:11 again supports the priority of the OG *Vorlage*.

At 4:18 the OG *Vorlage* contains ויתנו but the MT נתקו. Since כפות is an MT plus, ויתנו רגלים in the OG *Vorlage* would be more correct syntax.

The Hebrew *Vorlage* of the LXX version of 4:20 has the third person singular verb לקח, while the MT has the third person plural לקחו. The OG *Vorlage* suggests that Joshua is the subject of the action that had taken twelve stones from the Jordan, but in the MT, the subject is "twelve men from each tribe." Even though twelve esteemed men chosen from each tribe have taken those stones in 4:1–8, the Hebrew *Vorlage* of LXX may use the singular verb לקח to emphasize the role of Joshua as the

45. Ibid., 116.

commander in charge of all the action. The MT seems to have adjusted the singular of the OG *Vorlage* to the plural, given the syntax of 4:1–8.

The OG *Vorlage* of 4:24 contains כל־מעשה, while the MT כל־הימים. כל־הימים occurs here only in the book of Joshua. One can find the similar expression כל־ימי חייו in Josh 4:14 and 24:31. A's reading, χρόνῳ, is also the straightforward rendering of ימים.[46] However, כל־מעשה appears also in B's reading of Josh 24:29 (Heb. 31). There seems to be some relationship between 4:14 and 4:24.[47] It is possible that the MT adjusted בכל־מעשה in the OG *Vorlage* to כל־הימים in Josh 4:24, reading כל־ימי חייו in 4:14. בכל־מעשה as in the OG *Vorlage* Josh 4:24 also occurs in Deut 2:7; 14:29; 16:15; 24:19; 30:9; 2 Kgs 22:17; 2 Chr 31:21; Esth 10:2.

Through the analysis of those instances where the OG *Vorlage* and the MT disagree (outwith the pluses in both texts), we can also find some important features regarding the textual history of Josh 3–4.

First, the OG *Vorlage* contains rather common and usual expressions, which can be supported by other parts of the Old Testament, while, on the other hand, the MT attests rare and unusual variations in the Hebrew Bible (3:9, 14, 17; 4:6–7, 18, 24). Second, the MT shows theological development and improvement: the OG *Vorlage* has the inclusive "our," but the MT "your" (3:3, 4, 5, 9, 10; 4:23, 24), which reflects the MT's theological development, distinguishing Joshua from other people to authorize his leadership; the MT contains variations which show ritual enactment and cultic development (3:4); the MT also uses more developed and theologized terms than the OG *Vorlage* (3:12; 4:8); in addition, the MT tries to compare Joshua's leadership to that of Moses and to emphasize the transmission from Moses to Joshua (4:8, 10); finally, the MT changes the expression in the OG *Vorlage* to highlight the fulfillment of God's promise (4:14). Third, the OG *Vorlage* has some more difficult readings, and the MT smoothes these over by exegetically and redactionally changing them (3:1; 4:20). Fourth, the OG *Vorlage* sometimes shows a better understanding of the context of this narrative than the MT (3:16; 4:11, 18). Fifth, even though it is not so plausible to assume scribal error from one to another, there are some verses which could be better explained by copying error from the MT side: 3:3, 9, 11; 4:22, 24.

Therefore, one could argue that almost all of these features in the cases in which the OG *Vorlage* and the MT disagree (except for the pluses in both texts of Josh 3–4), seem to support the priority of the OG *Vorlage*. Furthermore, the OG *Vorlage* appears to be the better text for reading the literary history of Josh 3–4.

46. Ibid., 120.
47. Ibid.

6.2.3. *Conclusion: Differences Between the OG* Vorlage *and the* MT *Joshua 3–4*

Through a comparison of the OG *Vorlage* and MT Josh 3–4, we found many differences, notably many more pluses in the MT than in the OG *Vorlage*. A close examination of these differences brings to light some interesting aspects of both the Hebrew *Vorlage* of the LXX and the MT.

A great number of pluses and variants in the MT Josh 3–4 are rather rare and unusual in the Hebrew Bible. Furthermore, we considered the possibility that these divergences in the MT were inserted later with theological and exegetical intention: these being redactionally interpolated to solve some syntactical clumsiness in a verse. However, almost all the pluses and variants in the OG *Vorlage* are quite common in Old Testament Hebrew. Thus, we can conclude that the divergences in the Hebrew *Vorlage* of LXX are primary and original to the text of Josh 3–4, while those in the MT are secondary and were inserted later.

However, some critics might argue that the text with more unusual expressions shows the writer's or editor's originality and should be primary, and that a later scribe had simplified these. We can answer this by saying that there are some expressions or styles that a writer or editor usually uses, and if an expression or style of any part is different, then it is not impossible to think there may have been some variation by another hand.

However, this study will keep an open mind yet regarding the textual history and reconstruct the literary history of Josh 3–4 based on both texts, as there are only a few cases that could be judged as being uncertain, as in, for example, sections 6.2.1.1.3, 6.2.1.1.9, 6.2.1.1.15, and 6.2.1.2.3, etc.

6.3. *Literary-Critical Analysis of Joshua 3–4*

6.3.1. *Introduction*

Scholars have made many attempts to explain the many repetitions, inconsistencies, and mislocations in this text: for example, the period problem of "three days" between 1:11 and 3:2; the sudden and awkward command to select twelve men from each tribe in v. 12; two different stories of the erection of twelve stones in the middle of the Jordan (4:9) and on the other side of the Jordan (4:1–8, 20); the repetition of the cultic question and answer between children and parents (4:6–7, 21–24), etc.[48] However, the criteria for their diachronic readings are considerably

48. For more of this, see P. M. A. Pitkänen, *Joshua* (AOTC 6; Nottingham: Apollos, 2010), 129–30.

divergent: almost all of them have too many literary strata, and their results are too fragmentary. Furthermore, almost all of their investigations are focused only on the MT text, notwithstanding, as we saw in our text-critical analysis above, that the Hebrew *Vorlage* of LXX seems to be the better and prior text. This study will, therefore, reconstruct the literary history of Josh 3–4 based on both the OG *Vorlage* and MT, compare these, and see carefully where these take us.

Through the literary-critical analysis to the retroversion of the LXX *Vorlage* and the MT, I intend to explore the various layers of materials in this highly complex narrative.[49] Then, I provisionally name the possible layers in the retroversion of the LXX *Vorlage* a, b, c, d...and in MT α, β, γ, δ..., not using the familiar Deuteronomistic theory, to which almost all diachronic researchers are indebted.[50] In particular, I will try to read the literary history of Josh 3–4 with the help of those conclusions reached in Chapters 4 and 5. I will consider the findings of previous chapters, namely, that the shared material in Samuel–Kings and Chronicles (BTH) influenced those texts in the Pentateuch and Former prophets.

Initially, we will try to observe how far the material that began in 3:1 could be continued without break, and then will try to read each new section, as far as is possible, without severance. At the conclusion of the literary-critical analysis, we will examine the result of our research as archaeologists or geologists do when they find evidence of different strata: this will involve the characters in each layer of text, the episodes in each layer; and then, the changes to those episodes, as the different layers are combined. Then, we will investigate the distribution of major words in each layer to observe whether our research comes to a satisfactory result. Furthermore, we will try to compare the result of our research on the literary history of Josh 3–4 based on the retroversion of the LXX *Vorlage* and the MT, and examine what emerges from these results.

49. However, for those parts where the LXX and the MT are different, other than the MT and the LXX pluses, with regard to the results of our text-critical analysis, this research followed the LXX *Vorlage*.

50. The concept of the so-called Deuteronomistic or Deuteronomic history has recently been persuasively challenged by many scholars. For further information on this, see A. G. Auld, "The Former Prophets," in McKenzie and Graham, eds., *The Hebrew Bible*, 53–68; idem, "The Deuteronomist Between History and Theology," 353–67; idem, "The Deuteronomist and the Former Prophets," 116–26; idem, "Samuel, Numbers, and the Yahwist-Question," 233–46; de Pury, Römer, and Macchi, eds., *Israel Constructs Its History*.

6.3.2. *Literary-Critical Analysis of Joshua 3–4 Based on the Retroversion of the LXX* Vorlage

6.3.2.1. *Departure from Shittim (3:1).*

וישכם יהושע בבקר ויסע מהשטים ויבאו עד־הירדן וילנו שם טרם יעברו׃

As observed in the textual study, the syntax of this verse is somewhat clumsy. The change of the subject from third person singular into plural makes one suspect the integrity of this material from the beginning. Some may object that the change of number from singular into plural is quite usual in Old Testament Hebrew, when the sentence is begun by third person singular verb. However, it is not clear who the subject of the plural form of וילנו is in this verse.

Verse 1 is held by many to interrupt the context of crossing the Jordan related with the conquest war, which continues from ch. 1 to 3:2–3.[51] The lodging for one night after three days of spying in ch. 2 cuts off the stream of time ("three days") from 1:11 to 3:2.

The first scribe of B also treated this verse as a separate paragraph, this coming after one of the longest paragraphs.[52] This verse seems to be one of final editors' insertions to mark "the beginning of the long-awaited realization of the divine promise"[53] and to emphasize the leadership role of Joshua. This redactional layer will be called "d" for the moment.

The phrase "And Joshua rose at morning"[54] (וישכם יהושע בבקר) is a stereotypical formula[55] and also appears in 7:16; 8:10 in the book of Joshua.[56] The verb (וישכם) is used in similar ark stories (1 Sam 5:3, 4; Josh 6:12; 15) as a *waw* consecutive imperfect form.

The pattern, ויסע---וילנו, in v. 1 is similar to the itinerary concern of the so-called P in the Pentateuch.[57] A similar expression appears several times from Exodus to Numbers, especially in the texts between Israel's departure from Egypt and its arrival in the Moabite wilderness; Exod 12:37 (ויסעו); 13:20 (ויסעו---ויחנו); 14:2 (ויחנו); 15:22 (ויסעו); 16:1 (ויסעו); 17:1 (ויסעו---ויחנו); 19:2 (ויסעו---ויחנו); Num 10:12 (ויסעו); 20:22 (ויסעו); 21:10–13 (ויסעו---ויחנו); 22:1 (ויסעו---ויחנו). However, nowhere in these

51. Butler, *Joshua*, 44; Van Seters, *In Search of History*, 325.

52. Auld, *Joshua: Jesus, Son of Nauē*, 102.

53. Ibid.

54. Ibid. However, Boling maintains that השכם does not mean simply "to rise," but "to act persistently, diligently." For this, see Boling and Wright, *Joshua*, 158.

55. Fritz, *Das Buch Josua*, 46; Auld, *Joshua: Jesus, Son of Nauē*, 102.

56. M. H. Woudstra, *The Book of Joshua* (NICOT; Grand Rapids: Eerdmans, 1981), 79.

57. G. W. Coats, "The Wilderness Itinerary," *CBQ* 34 (1972): 135–52; Cross, *Canaanite Myth and Hebrew Epic*, 308.

texts does וילנו appear, as in Josh 3:1. The root לון also appears in 4:3; 6:11; 8:9; 9:18 in the book of Joshua. It is difficult to explain the relationship between the expressions of Exodus and Numbers and that of Josh 3:1. Thus, it appears to be a little dangerous to say that this instance is the same as the itinerary concern in the Pentateuch.

The geographical designation "*Shittim*" (see also 2:1) is "identified with tell el-khammān, or tell el kefrēn, both of which are approximately 11–12 km east of the Jordan and 1–2 km apart. שטים means 'acacias'"[58] and actually the ark is made of שטים ("acacias") in Exod 25:10.[59] It is quite interesting that the place name, שטים, appears in a text where the ark is mentioned.[60]

6.3.2.2. *Preparation for Crossing the Jordan (3:2–4).*

3:2 ויהי מקצה שלשת ימים ויעברו השטרים בקרב המחנה:
3:3 ויצוו את־העם לאמר כראותכם את ארון ברית־יהוה אלהינו
וכהנינו והלוים נשאים אתו תסעו ממקומכם והלכתם אחריו
3:4 אך רחוק יהיה בינינו ובינו כאלפים אמה תעמדו אל־תקרבו אליו
למען אשר־תדעו את־הדרך אשר תלכו־בה כי לא עברתם
בדרך מתמול שלשום:

This section is connected to Joshua's command given to "the officers" of the people to "pass through the camp," and to order the people to prepare provisions, referring to the passing over of the Jordan and entrance into the land within "three days" in 1:10–11. The term "three days," of course, emerges in 2:16, 22 as well, and Van Seters holds that ch. 2 is of a different material from the conquest story, which continues from ch. 1 to ch. 6, because the conquest story of Jericho in ch. 6 does not use any information from the spy story in ch. 2.[61] However, Rahab and her household's survival story in the community of Israel in both Josh 2 and 6 are quite closely connected and it seems hardly possible to read Rahab's story in the two chapters as being different stories.

In v. 3, we meet the ark for the first time. There has been no indication of it in previous chapters.[62] From this point, the ark, the symbol of Yahweh's presence, dominates the whole account related to the crossing

58. Soggin, *Joshua*, 40.

59. In Exod 25:5, 10, 13, 23, 28; 26:15, 26, 32, 37; 27:1, 6; 30:1, 5; 35:7, 24; 36:20, 31, 36; 37:1, 4, 10, 15, 25; 38:1, 6; Deut 10:3; Isa 41:19. In these it is used as *Shittim* tree, as well.

60. In Num 25:1; 33:49; Josh 2:1; Joel 4:18 (3:18); it is used as place name, as well, in Mic 6:5.

61. Van Seters, *In Search of History*, 325.

62. Boling and Wright, *Joshua*, 159.

of the Jordan (3:4, 6, 8, 11, 13–14, 17; 4:7, 9, 11, 16, 18). Accordingly, Yahweh also enters the Promised Land with his people, carrying the ark.[63]

Some scholars maintain that the materials related to the ark were inserted later.[64] However, as we have seen in Chapter 4, some others considered that the ark texts in the Pentateuch reflect those in the Former Prophets,[65] and our analysis of the texts of the transportation of the ark supports the reading of Josh 3–4 in the context of the ark narratives backwards,[66] and that those verses related with the ark in Josh 3–4 are the basic layer of this narrative.

According to Exodus (chs. 25–31; 35–40), the ark first had its advent in connection with the tabernacle. Then, it led Israel into wilderness journeys and wars (Num 10:33–36; 14:44).[67] Deuteronomy describes the ark as the sacred container of two tablets (10:1–5), beside which the Deuteronomic law would be laid (31:26).

The many titles of the ark in Josh 3–4 represent a sample of the many titles given to the ark throughout the Hebrew Scripture, which is at its most varied and developed in the Former Prophets. ארון ברית־יהוה אלהיכם in this verse is one of the variations of the basic epithet (ארון ברית־יהוה) used in these ark transportation stories in the Old Testament. ארון ברית־יהוה is used in Deut 10:8; 31:9, 25, 26; Josh 3:3; 4:7, 18; 6:8; 8:33; 1 Sam 4:3, 4, 5; 1 Kgs 6:19; 8:1, 6; 1 Chr 15:25, 26, 28, 29; 16:37; 17:1; 22:19; 28:18; 2 Chr 5:2, 7; Jer 3:16). Of these, 1 Kgs 8:1//2 Chr 5:2 and 1 Kgs 8:6//2 Chr 5:7 are synoptic (BTH). With the Pentateuch (excluding Deuteronomy), the expression only occurs in Num 10:33 and 14:44, seemingly being influenced by the epithet in the synoptic texts of Samuel–Kings and Chronicles, as we have seen in Chapter 4. The

63. Woudstra, *The Book of Joshua*, 79–80.

64. For this, see G. H. Davies, "The Ark of the Covenant," *ASTI* 5 (1967): 30–47; J. Morgenstern, "The Ark, the Ephod and the 'Tent of Meeting,'" *HUCA* 17 (1942–43): 153–266; G. von Rad, "The Tent and the Ark," in *The Problem of the Hexateuch and Other Essays* (New York: McGraw–Hill, 1966), 103–24. Cf. Fritz, who also regarded almost all the ark materials in this narrative as later insertions: 4:7 (part of second joint piece); 3:11, 13, 14b, 17; 4:9 (RedD); 4:15–17 (post-priestly insertion); 3:4, 6, 8; 4:11b (later redactional insertion). For him, only 4:18 among the ark materials in this Jordan-crossing story belongs to the basic layer. For this, see Fritz, *Das Buch Josua*, 46–56.

65. Rost, *The Succession to the Throne of David*, 6–34; von Rad, *Studies in Deuteronomy*, 127; Campbell, *The Ark Narrative*, 221.

66. For Auld as well, 1 Kgs 8 underlies Josh 3–4. For this, see Auld, *Samuel at the Threshold*, 193.

67. Butler, *Joshua*, 44–45.

similar expression וכהנינו והלוים is found also in LXX Josh 9:6 (for this, see the text-critical analysis in Chapter 3).[68] If we look closely into the grammar of this verse in the MT, "the Levitical priests bearing the ark," we see that it stresses the ark, and the priests are in a secondary position.[69] Verses 2–3 belong to the basic layer (a) which is influenced by those synoptic texts in Samuel–Kings and Chronicles (BTH), and related to the conquest story, which continues from ch. 1.[70]

אך in v. 4 appears only once in this book. Gibson insists that the conjunction אך is used in exclusive syntax.[71] Nelson holds that "[t]he disjunctive and emphatic syntax of v. 4a interrupts the connection between v. 3 and the rest of v. 4 and introduces an extraneous (probably Priestly) concern about the ark's perilous holiness."[72] The similar conjunction רק was used as an interpolation mark in Josh 13:14.[73] However, no one could say that אך and רק are always used in the same way. In addition, רק in Josh 13:14 was used in narrative, but אך in this verse was used in speech. In this verse, we see that the narrators indicate the ark, which appeared in v. 3, as the third person singular pronominal suffix "it" (אליו, ובינו). This part is a continuation of the speech by the officers, which emphasizes the distance between the ark and the people. The demand for a respectful distance seems to recall the incident of Uzzah in 2 Sam 6:1–11//1 Chr 13:5–14 (BTH). The similar expression of מתמול שלשום in v. 4 also appears in the similar story of the ark being carried to the battle camp to lead the people in 1 Sam 4:8 (אתמול שלשים). Verse 4 is also connected with basic layer (vv. 2–3), which is influenced by the synoptic ark texts in Samuel–Kings and Chronicles.

6.3.2.3. *Instructions from Joshua (3:5–6).*

3:5 ויאמר יהושע אל־העם התקדשו למחר כי מחר יעשה יהוה בקרבכם נפלאות
3:6 ויאמר יהושע אל־הכהנים שאו את־ארון ברית יהוה ועברו לפני העם וישאו
הכהנים את־ארון ברית יהוה וילכו לפני העם:

68. הכהנים והלוים in LXX Josh 9:6 and הכהנים הלוים in MT Josh 8:33.

69. Butler, *Joshua*, 45.

70. Gray, *Joshua, Judges and Ruth*, 60.

71. J. C. L. Gibson, *Davidson's Introductory Hebrew Grammar Syntax* (Edinburgh: T. &. T. Clark, 1994), 175–76.

72. Nelson, *Joshua*, 60. Gray also argues that the reference to the exact distance of two thousand cubits from the ark, found similarly in Num 35:5 (P), in which the gap of the boundaries between Levitical lands and the actual settlements is underscored, seems to be a P addition. See Gray, *Joshua, Judges and Ruth*, 60.

73. Auld, *Joshua Retold*, 21.

Although the demand "sanctify yourselves" represents cultic tradition,[74] holiness was also a requirement in the ideology of divine war (Deut 23:15 [14]; 1 Sam 21:5).[75] מחר ("tomorrow") seems to be part of a routine formula of sanctification (Josh 7:13; Num 11:18).[76] Even though Van Seters argues that 3:5 is a P addition of cultic tradition, I do not find any good reason to separate this verse, which has התקדשו, from v. 6, which has הכהנים, when we read B, which marks 3:5–6 as a paragraph.[77] התקדשו(י) occurs in 1 Chr 15:12, 14; 2 Chr 5:11 and נפלאות also in 1 Chr 16:9, 12, 24, all of which belong to similar ark-moving stories. As we have seen in Chapter 4, those three terms (שׂאו, ארון ברית יהוה, העם) in v. 6 are synoptic expressions, which are employed in almost all the ark-moving stories in the Former Prophets and Chronicles. These verses are a continuation of basic layer, "a," which is influenced by the shared materials in Samuel–Kings and Chronicles.

6.3.2.4. *Yahweh Addresses Joshua and Joshua Prepares His People (3:7–11).*

3:7 ויאמר יהוה אל־יהושע היום הזה אחל גדלך בעיני כל־בני ישׂראל
אשר ידעון כאשר הייתי עם־משה כן אהיה גם עמך׃
3:8 ועתה תצוה את־הכהנים נשׂאי ארון־הברית לאמר כבאכם
עד־קצה מי הירדן ובירדן תעמדו׃
3:9 ויאמר יהושע אל־בני ישׂראל גשו הנה ושמעו את־דבר יהוה אלהינו׃
3:10 בזאת תדעון כי אל חי בקרבכם והורש יוריש מפנינו את־הכנעני
ואת־החתי ואת־הפרזי ואת־החוי ואת־האמרי ואת־הגרגשי ואת־היבוסי׃
3:11 הנה ארון ברית אדון כל־הארץ עבר בירדן׃

In sequence, Yahweh's exaltation of Joshua continues (v. 7), which is linked with 1:5, 17–18 and 4:14. The syntax of v. 8 is disjunctive, but appears to be a pause for further detail. Verse 8 is connected with v. 7, which emphasizes the leadership role of Joshua (ועתה תצוה, "and now you shall command") and the flow of the content from the exaltation in v. 7 to the story of the conquest of the land in vv. 9–10 continues through v. 8. Verses 7–8 also use the basic expressions in the ark transportation narratives in the Former Prophets and Chronicles (נשׂאי, כל־בני ישׂראל) and the variation, ארון־הברית, of the basic expression, ארון־ברית יהוה. This is the section in which Joshua delivers Yahweh's word (דבר יהוה) to his people, which ends in v. 13.[78] If we look at the LXX and the

74. Soggin, *Joshua*, 47–48.
75. Nelson, *Joshua*, 61.
76. Ibid.
77. Auld, *Joshua: Jesus, Son of Nauē*, 104.
78. Butler, *Joshua*, 39.

Vulgate, we see that the "Word" (see the text-critical study) in v. 9 is emphasized, which is typical of Deuteronomy.[79] As mentioned before, the meaning of בזאת ("by this") is ambiguous. However, in this narrative we can see that the basic layer (a) understands the event of "crossing the Jordan" in connection with that of "the conquest war." Therefore, we can understand this section as God's promise that Israel will learn the fact that "the conquest of the Promised Land" in v. 10b will come true through "the wonder of crossing the Jordan" in v. 11. This could be more easily explained if we think that הנה ("behold") in v. 11 leads the apodosis. A similar example appears in Exod 7:17 (כה אמר יהוה בזאת תדע כי אני יהוה: הנה אנכי מכה במטה אשר־בידי על־המים אשר ביאר ונהפכו לדם:) in which the authority of Yahweh is also emphasized. Therefore, we can say בזאת refers to the event of crossing the Jordan in v. 11.

אל חי בקרבכם ("living God is among you") is an expression which confirms the fulfillment of the promise. The title "living God" (אל חי) in v. 10 has a confessional ring to it and is also used in 1 Sam 17:26; Pss 42:3, 9 (2, 8); 84:3 (2); Hos 2:1 (1:10, חי יהוה).[80] According to Soggin, it is used to represent God, who controls "nature" and "history," in contrast with the gods of Canaan who died and rose again periodically in a seasonal cycle. The expression "the living God" linked with the emphatic verb form "he will surely drive out" (והורש יוריש) shows that the promise will be realized without fail.[81]

The list of indigenous inhabitants here is in a standard form, which contains seven names (Gen 15:19; Exod 3:8, 17; Deut 7:1; 20:17; etc.).[82] However, in Josh 9:1 only six names are present—the Girgashites are omitted. These short lists also appear in Exod 12:8; 13:5; 23:23; 24:11; 33:2; 34:11; Josh 11:3; Judg 3:5; 1 Kgs 9:20.[83] These lists of aboriginal people in the Pentateuch seem to be influenced by those in the conquests and settlement stories in the Former Prophets. "The Canaanite" is often used as a collective noun for all inhabitants of the Canaan,[84] but here it means the people living "by the sea" (Josh 5:1; Num 13:29; cf. 11:3).[85] The Greeks referred to "the Canaanites" as "Phoenicians," the latter being a name related to the purple dye produced from the murex shellfish and exported to all parts of the Mediterranean.[86] In 5:1 as well, the LXX

79. Soggin, *Joshua*, 57.
80. Nelson, *Joshua*, 61.
81. Soggin, *Joshua*, 58.
82. Ibid.
83. Fritz, *Das Buch Josua*, 50.
84. Ibid.
85. Woudstra, *The Book of Joshua*, 84.
86. Boling and Wright, *Joshua*, 165.

reads "the Canaanite" as Φοινίκες. However, here in 3:10, the LXX shows variety, reading "the Canaanite" as το Χαναναῖον.

Regarding the title "the Lord of all the earth" (in v. 11 with v. 13), some scholars have suggested a non-Israelite origin.[87] However, it is not easy to decide whether this is to be understood narrowly as suzerain of the land of Canaan or universally as ruler of the entire earth. On the one hand, it could be interpreted as "the land of Canaan," as in Deut 11:25; 19:8; Josh 6:27; 10:40; 11:16, 23. On the other hand, it could contain the universal meaning "earth," as in Deut 10:14; Josh 2:11. The latter meaning occurs also in Ps 97:5; Mic 4:13; Zech 4:14; 6:5. As Nelson contends, either meaning could make the same point: the God who is crossing the Jordan with Israel has both the power and the right to endow them with the land.[88]

6.3.2.5. *Choose Twelve Men (3:12).*

3:12 קחו לכם שני עשר איש מבני ישראל איש־אחד לשבט׃

Nelson maintains that this isolated command creates suspense and anticipates more story than the miraculous crossing.[89] The sudden appearance of the command to take twelve men from the tribes of Israel makes the flow of the passage a bit awkward.[90] This verse is later redactional "Zusatz, der mit 4,1–8 eine geschlossen Einheit darstellt, durch eine Bemerkung über die Auswahl der Träger vorzubereiten."[91] However, if we compare 3:12 and 4:2, we can see that 3:12 is a different layer from 4:1–8:

3:12 קחו לכם שני עשר איש מבני ישראל איש־אחד לשבט׃

4:2 קחו מן־העם אנשים איש־אחד משבט׃

As we can see, 3:12 offers some additional words (לכם, שני עשר) and seems later than 4:2. This verse (3:12) appears to be a redactional addition inserted to this part by an editor who knew the story of 4:1–8 in order to connect the contents of chs. 3 and 4. This verse also belongs to "d" layer. This insertion breaks the context between 3:11 and 13.[92]

87. Nelson, *Joshua*, 61. For this, see Langlamet, *Gilgal et les récits de la traversée du Jourdain*, 112–15.

88. Nelson, *Joshua*, 61.

89. Ibid.

90. Saydon, "The Crossing of the Jordan," 199.

91. Fritz, *Josua*, 55.

92. Ibid.

6.3.2.6. *Descent and Passing Over on "Dry Ground" (3:13–17).*

3:13 והיה כנוח רגלי הכהנים נשׂאי ארון הברית אדון כל־הארץ במי הירדן
מי הירדן יכרתון המים הירדים יעמדו :
3:14 ויסע העם מאהליהם לעבר את־הירדן והכהנים נשׂאי את־ארון
הברית לפני העם:
3:15 וכבוא הכהנים נשׂאי ארון הברית עד־הירדן ורגלי הכהנים נשׂאי ארון
ברית יהוה נטבלו בקצה מי הירדן והירדן מלא על־כל־גדותיו כימי
קציר חטים:
3:16 ויעמדו המים הירדים מלמעלה קמו נד־אחד הרחק מאד מאד
העיר אשר מצד קרית
יערים והירד ירד על ים הערבה ים־המלח עד־תם נכרת והעם עמדו
נגד יריחו:
3:17 ויעמדו הכהנים נשׂאי ארון ברית־יהוה בחרבה בתוך הירדן
וכל־בני ישׂראל עברים בחרבה עד אשר־תמו כל־העם לעבר את־הירדן:

The focus of interest in v. 13, as in v. 11, is also on the ark. "The Lord of all the earth" is modifying "the ark." The words נשׂא and ארון הברית אדון כל־הארץ connect this verse with the similar basic expression in the ark narratives of Samuel–Kings and Chronicles. This part is a continuation of the basic "a" layer. When the soles of the feet of the priests who bear the ark of the Lord of all the earth rest in the waters, the miracle that the Jordan is cut off shall happen. Thus, the prominence of the ark shall be revealed.[93] We can find a chiasm between vv. 13 and 16: "cut off" and "stand still," then "stood still" and "was cut off."[94]

The statement that "the people set out from their tents and the priests bearing the ark of the covenant were before the people" in v. 14 is connected with the story in which the officers go through the camp and command the people that when they see the Levitical priests bearing the ark, they should set out from their place (vv. 2–3). And now, Joshua's address in vv. 9–13 begins to be carried out. The concrete reference to the cutting off of the water in vv. 15 and 16 is linked with Joshua's prophecy in v. 13 that "when the feet of the priests rest in the waters, the waters of the Jordan shall stand." The intention behind the addition of v. 15b (והירדן מלא על־כל־גדותיו כימי קציר חטים) appears to have been to make the miracle dramatic.[95] קציר חטים is also used in the same ark story in 1 Sam 6:13. All of these verses are a continuation of "a," which continues the story of the people's passing over opposite Jericho in v. 16b.

93. Woudstra, *The Book of Joshua*, 86.

94. Nelson, *Joshua*, 61.

95. Gray, *Joshua, Judges and Ruth*, 62. However, we know that even during harvest time the waters of the Jordan do not make passage impossible. See Auld, *Joshua, Judges and Ruth*, 23.

Some hold that v. 16aβ (מאד העיר אשר מצד קרית יערים) is a P insertion.[96] However, we cannot find any persuasive reason to separate this phrase from the other part of this verse. The reference of the geographical name is an attempt to describe the miracle more accurately, but it is not easy for us to come to any conclusion about the names of the places.[97] This part is the specific content of "By this" in v. 10, describing the miracle of the Jordan in detail. In these verses with v. 13, complex Hebrew sentence structures go on to add tension as the climax of this event.[98] Judging from the explanation of Israel's crossing over opposite Jericho in v. 16b, the "a" layer connects this wonder with the conquest of Jericho rather than with anything else.[99]

Verse 17 shows the concern about priests standing in the middle of the Jordan and about Israel's passing over on "dry ground" (בחרבה). This verse is connected to the report over the crossing in v. 16. Verse 17 is a summary of two simultaneous actions, standing and crossing,[100] and explicates the event concretely in that the priests stood on "dry ground" and the people passed over on "dry ground." The Hebrew word for "dry ground" (בחרבה) in this verse is different from that used in 4:20–24 (יבשה). As we have seen in Chapter 5, בחרבה is used in Exod 13:17–14:31, and 2 Kgs 2. This verse is also the continuation of basic "a" layer. כל־בני ישׂראל, נשׂאי הארון ברית־יהוה link this verse with the basic layer of this narrative.

6.3.2.7. *Carrying Twelve Stones Over to the Other Side of the Jordan (4:1–8).*

4:1 ויהי כאשר־תמו כל־העם לעבור את־הירדן ויאמר יהוה אל־יהושע לאמר:
4:2 קח לך אנשים מן־העם איש־אחד משבט:
4:3 צוהאותם ושאו מתוך הירדן הכין שׁתים־עשׂרה אבנים והעברתם
אותם עמכם ואותם
הנחתם אותם במלון אשר־תלינו בו הלילה:
4:4 ויקרא יהושע אל־שׁנים העשׂר איש אשר הכין מבני ישׂראל איש־אחד משבט:

96. Some scholars hold that this part, which is explanatory, is a P addition. For this view, see B. S. Childs, "Deuteronomic Formulae of the Exodus Traditions," *Hebräische Wortforschung: Festschrift zum 80. Geburtstag von Walter Baumgartner* (ed. B. Hartmann et al.; VTSup 16; Leiden: Brill, 1967): 30–39; idem, "A Traditio-Historical Character of the Reed Sea Tradition," *VT* 20 (1970): 406–18; Coats, "The Song of the Sea," 1–17.

97. Butler, *Joshua*, 48; Auld, *Joshua: Jesus, Son of Nauē*, 109–10.

98. Butler, *Joshua*, 48.

99. Ibid.

100. Nelson, *Joshua*, 61.

4:5 ויאמר להם עברו לפני לפני יהוה אל־תוך הירדן והרימו משם איש אבן אחת
לשאת על־שכמו למספר שנים עשר שבטי ישראל:
4:6 למען תהיה זאת אות בקרבכם תמיד כי־ישאלך בנך מחר
לאמר מה האבנים האלה לכם:
4:7 ואתה אמרת לבנך לאמר אשר נכרת מי הירדן מפני ארון ברית־אדון
כל־הארץ בעברו
והיו האבנים האלה לזכרון לבני ישראל עד־עולם:
4:8 ויעשו־כן בני־ישראל כאשר צוה יהוה אל־יהושע וישאו שתי־עשרה אבנים
מתוך הירדן
כאשר דבר יהוה אל־יהושע בתם בני־ישראל לעבר ויעברום עמם
אל־המלון וינחום שם:

Two parallel stories of twelve stones at the brink of and in the middle of the Jordan dominate all of ch. 4.[101] This section is about the stones at the riverbank. Verse 1a sums up the event of crossing the Jordan and introduces a different story.[102] Verse 1ff. belongs to "b" layer, which continues to v. 8. This part emphasizes the twelve stones being set up at the brink of the river for the twelve tribes. The number *twelve* occurs four times in these verses.[103] However, the place named Gilgal is not referred to as yet, but only the expression "where you lodge" (v. 3). Thus, Soggin's attempt to connect this part with amphictyony and the Gilgal sanctuary seems to be somewhat rash.[104] The account of stones being set up at Gilgal appears in v. 20 for the first time. According to Auld, the narrative of the altar on the mountain Ebal in LXX Josh 9:3–8 is later than the Greek Deut 27:5–6.[105] Not to speak of δευτερονόμιον in LXX Josh 9:5, this narrative of Gerizim and Ebal seems to know (Greek) Deut 27. Ulrich holds that Joshua's first altar in the Promised Land was built immediately after Israel's crossing of the Jordan.[106] This is also attested to in Josephus' *Jewish Antiquities* 20, which links the building of the altar not to the commands given by God to Joshua during the crossing of the people, but to the instructions by Moses in Deut 27.[107] This story of the twelve stones set up on the other side of the Jordan seems to reflect Moses' order in Deut 27:1–6. The verbal form "he had appointed" (הכין) in v. 4 is not easy to understand (see text-critical analysis). Joshua calls the twelve men appointed already and transmits the divine command in vv. 4–5.

101. Soggin, *Joshua*, 64; Fritz, *Josua*, 45.
102. Woudstra, *The Book of Joshua*, 90; Fritz, *Josua*, 53; Nelson, *Joshua*, 68.
103. Boling and Wright, *Joshua*, 172.
104. Soggin, *Joshua*, 65.
105. Auld, *Joshua: Jesus, Son of Nauē*, 152.
106. E. Ulrich, "4QJosh[a]," in *Qumran Cave 4.IX: Deuteronomy, Joshua, Judges, Kings* (ed. E. Ulrich et al.; DJD 14; Oxford: Clarendon, 1995), 145–46.
107. For this, see Van der Meer, *Formation and Reformulation*, 489.

Verse 6–7 are composed in the form of question and answer between parents and children, in which parents teach their children the meaning of Yahweh's presence in Israel's history.

A similar expression to Josh 4:6–7 also appears in Deut 6:20–21:

Deut 6:20	כי ישאלך בנך מחר לאמר מה העדת והחקים והמשפטים אשר צוה יהוה אלהינו אתכם
6:21	ואמרת לבנך עבדים היינו לפרעה במצרים ויוציאנו יהוה ממצרים ביד חזקה

The retroversion of the LXX *Vorlage* in Josh 4:6–7, which has the singular form of בנך, has more similarity with Deut 6:20–21 than the MT. The structure of each verse in both Josh 4:6–7 and Deut 6:20–21 is almost identical. However, Josh 4:6–7 has a much longer and developed form: Josh 4:6 has the additional phrase למען תהיה זאת אות בקרבכם תמיד before כי ישאל, while in Deut 6:20 the verse starts with only כי ישאלך. Deuteronomy 6:21 tells only *what* parents should tell their son; Josh 4:7 also tells *why*, with the additional phrase והיו האבנים האלה לזכרון לבני ישראל עד־עולם, which explains the purpose of their speech. Thus, Josh 4:6–7 seem to be later than and influenced by Deut 6:20.

However, a similar non-Priestly text in Exod 13:8–10 appears to be influenced by the expression in Josh 4:6–7.[108]

Exod 13:8	והגדת לבנך ביום ההוא לאמר בעבור זה עשה יהוה לי בצאתי ממצרים׃
13:9	והיה לך לאות על־ידך ולזכרון בין עיניך למען תהיה תורת יהוה בפיך כי ביד חזקה הוצאך יהוה ממצרים׃
13:10	ושמרת את־החקה הזאת למועדה מימים ימימה׃ ס

Even though in Josh 4:6–7 twelve memorial stones are a sign, in Exod 13:8–9 the ritual serves as a sign for their hand, as a reminder for their forehead, so that תורת יהוה may be on their lips. Exod 13:8–9 shows a more concretized and developed ritual form. Furthermore, החקה in Exod 13:10 shows the more firmly established ritual, which is mainly used in the book of Leviticus (3:17; 7:36; 10:9; 16:29, 31, 34; 17:7; 18:3, 4, 5, 26, 30; 19:19, 37; 20:8, 22, 23; 23:14, 21, 31, 41; 24:3; 25:18; 26:3, 15, 43). Thus, we could surmise that this non-Priestly text is later than Josh 4:6–7.

How about similar Priestly texts in Exod 12:26–27 and 13:14–15?

Exod 12:26	והיה כי־יאמרו אליכם בניכם מה העבדה הזאת לכם׃
12:27	ואמרתם זבח־פסח הוא ליהוה אשר פסח על־בתי בני־ישראל במצרים בנגפו את־מצרים ואת־בתינו הציל ויקד העם וישתחוו׃

108. For this, see Gertz et al., eds., *Abschied vom Jahwisten*.

Exod 13:14 והיה כי־ישאלך בנך מחר לאמר מה־זאת ואמרת אליו
בחזק יד הוציאנו יהוה ממצרים מבית עבדים׃
13:15 ויהי כי־הקשה פרעה לשלחנו ויהרג יהוה כל־בכור
בארץ מצרים מבכר אדם ועד־בכור בהמה על־כן אני זבח
ליהוה כל־פטר רחם הזכרים וכל־בכור בני אפדה׃

The words "service" (העבדה) and "sacrifice of Passover" (זבח־פסח) in Exod 12:26 and "sacrifice" (זבח) of the "first-born" (בכור) in Exod 12:27 are more ritualized and are later expressions than that of Josh 4:6–7. Furthermore, בחזק יד הוציאנו יהוה ("by strength of hand Yahweh brought us out") in Exod 13:14 seems to read a similar expression את־יד יהוה כי חזקה in Josh 4:24. Thus, this Priestly text shows the most developed aspects among these texts.

Therefore, we can guess that this form of question and answer has developed in the order of Deut 6:20–21 > Josh 4:6–7 > non-Priestly Exod 13:8–10 > Priestly texts in Exod 12:26–27; 13:14–15.

We can also find similar expressions, which stress "sign" (אות) and "eternal memorial" (לזכרון עד־עולם), also appearing in Priestly covenant texts of Genesis and Exodus in the Pentateuch. In Noah's covenant (Gen 9:8–17), "the rainbow" (הקשת) is emphasized as "a sign" (אות) of "everlasting covenant" (ברית עולם) "to remember" (לזכר) between God and every living creature. In Abraham's covenant (Gen 17:1–21), "the circumcision" (המולה) and "Isaac" (יצחק) are underscored as "a sign" (אות) of everlasting covenant (ברית עולם) between God and his people. In the Sinai covenant (Exod 31:12–17), "the Sabbath" (השבת) is also pointed up as "an eternal sign" (אות לעלם) of "perpetual covenant" (ברית עולם) "to keep" (לשמר). It is not easy for us to come to any conclusion about the relationship among these. However, we could say that the stones as a sign of covenant in Josh 4:6–7 are the more concrete expression and that "the rainbow," "the circumcision," and "the Sabbath" in the Pentateuch are the more religious, abstract, and spiritually developed concept. Furthermore, it is quite interesting that in those "covenant" texts in the book of Genesis the Niphal form of כרת was used as in Josh 4:7, but in quite another sense—the cutting off all flesh by the waters of a flood in Gen 9:11 and any uncircumcised male from his people in Gen 17:14. Here again, the expression מי הירדן in Josh 4:7 is more concrete, and the word הברית and the cutting off all flesh by the waters of a flood and any uncircumcised male from his people in Gen 17:14 are more religiously developed concepts. It might be possible to say that Josh 4:6–7 is earlier than those covenant texts in the book of Genesis.

Thus, rather than viewing vv. 6–7 as a later insertion, it would be safer to say that this purposive clause, led by למען, which corresponds to the

Greek ινα, is the continuation of Joshua's speech, begun in v. 5. Therefore, it would be relevant to think that this verse depends on vv. 1–5 (b), which seems to be influenced by Deuteronomy. This also appears to be in accord with this writer's intention to read each stratum as far as he can without discontinuation. And then, the people of Israel take twelve stones from the middle of the river and carry them over to the place where they lodge and lay them down as Joshua ordered in v. 8 (b). Here we can suggest that Josh 4:1–8 is later than the similar story in Deuteronomy, but earlier than those in Genesis and Exodus.

6.3.2.8. *Erecting Memorial Stones in the Middle of the Jordan (4:9).*

ושתים עשׂרה אבנים אחרות הקים יהושע בו בירדן תחת מצב רגלי
הכהנים נשׂאי ארון ברית יהוה ויהיו שׁם עד היום הזה:

The sudden appearance of the account that Joshua set up twelve stones in the middle of the Jordan seems to make a clumsy connection with v. 8. As we have seen in Chapter 3, it does not seem probable that the original story featured two different sets of twelve stones. The words, שׁתים עשׂרה אבנים אחרות ("twelve other stones") make this verse stand out clearly and seems to show that it is divided from 4:1–8. This verse belongs to "c" layer, which knows 4:1–8 ("b" layer).

6.3.2.9. *The Priests Standing in the Middle of the Jordan (4:10a).*

הכהנים נשׂאי ארון הברית עמדו בירדן עד אשר כלה יהושע
ו את־כל־אשר־צוה יהוה לדבר אל־העם

In this part, the priests who bore the ark were standing in the middle of the Jordan until the command of Yahweh to set up twelve stones on the other side of the Jordan, given Joshua in 4:1b, was completed, this being a continuation of "b." The Hebrew phrase והכהנים נשׂאי ארון הברית עמדו בירדן in this verse is similar to ויעמדו הכהנים נשׂאי הארון ברית־יהוה בחרבה בתוך הירדן in 3:17, but is slightly different. As we have seen above, 3:17 ("a" layer) is earlier than this.

6.3.2.10. *Peoples' Passing Over in Haste (4:10b–11a).*

4:10b וימהר העם ויעברו:
4:11a ויהי כאשר־תם כל־העם לעבור

Verse 10b ("The people passed over in haste") again makes the sequence of the story harsh, because in v. 1a, the people had already completed passing over the Jordan. This verse appears to be linked with the account that "the people passed over opposite Jericho" (3:16b), which belongs to "a." Verse 11a is also the continuation of "a" layer.[109]

6.3.2.11. *The Crossing Over of the Ark and the Stones (4:11b).*

ויעבר ארון ברית־יהוה והאבנים לפניהם:

Once again, a different story appears. In v. 11a the people finished crossing the Jordan, but in v. 11b the ark is crossing and והאבנים (οἱ λίθοι) are before the people. The MT has והכהנים instead of והאבנים (οἱ λίθοι) in the LXX *Vorlage*. However, instructions to the priests are given in v. 17. This verse requires something more to be understood properly.[110] Cooke tries to settle this problem by translating לפני ("before") into "in the presence of." However, when לפני is used with "verbs of motion," it means "before, at the head of," not "in the presence of."[111] As we have seen in Chapter 3, this is the MT's adjustment והאבנים to והכהנים, recollecting the command to the priests in 3:6 too literally.[112] The complexity of this verse is also related to the cohesion of materials. Verse 11b is connected with v. 10a ("b" layer). This is the sequence of the story in which the ark and the stones, which had been taken from the middle of the Jordan by the command of Yahweh (10a), passed over the Jordan for the completion of the task (11b).

6.3.2.12. *Eastern Tribes Crossing the Jordan (4:12–13).*

4:12 ויעברו בני־ראובן ובני־גד וחצי שבט המנשה חמשים לפני
בני ישראל כאשר דבר אליהם משה:
4:13 ארבעים אלף חלוצי הצבא עברו לפני יהוה למלחמה אל עיר יריחו: ס

The special reference to the sons of Reuben, of Gad and of the half-tribe of Manasseh seems to emphasize that all the tribes took part in the passing over and the conquest war. This is a flashback report of what Moses commanded in Deut 3:18 and which Joshua reiterated (Josh 1:12–15).[113] חמשים (v. 13) occurs in Josh 1:14; 4:12; MT Exod 13:18. The content of v. 13 repeats that of v. 12, but the vocabulary is different. "Armed" (חלוצי), "for battle" (למלחמה) (v. 13) also shows the interest in the war, which connects this event with the conquest of the land. חלוצי appears in Deut 3:18, which also connects this part to the eastern tribes

109. Van Seters, *In Search of History*, 325–26.
110. Soggin, *Joshua*, 63.
111. Saydon, "The Crossing of the Jordan, Josue 3 and 4," 204.
112. Auld, *Joshua: Jesus, Son of Nauē*, 116.
113. Soggin, *Joshua*, 65; Nelson, *Joshua*, 70.

in Deuteronomy.[114] This section (vv. 12–13) belongs to the "b" layer, which is influenced by the book of Deuteronomy.

6.3.2.13. *The Exaltation of Joshua (4:14).*

ביום ההוא גדל יהוה את־יהושע בעיני כל־עם ישראל ויראו אתו
כאשר יראו את־משה כל־ימי חייו:

The exaltation of Joshua as a leader like Moses then follows. The basic "a" layer regards the completion of the passing over as the accomplishment of Yahweh's promise of the exaltation of Joshua. Here, the promise, the exaltation of Moses' successor, is realized, as given in 3:7, and in 1:16–18.

6.3.2.14. *The Ark of the Covenant of the Testimony of Yahweh (4:15–16).*

4:15 ויאמר יהוה אל־יהושע לאמר:
4:16 צוה את־הכהנים נשאי ארון ברית עדות יהוה ויעלו מן־הירדן:

Unlike the conclusion of "b" (vv. 12–14), the ark and the priests are stressed. Different material ("e") continues. "The ark of the covenant of the testimony of Yahweh" (ארון ברית עדות יהוה) in v. 16 is an extraordinary epithet. The MT's simpler ארון העדות appears to be the older text. B's complexity may have been caused by the later inclusion within the text of an explanation that "the ark of the testimony" was none other than "the ark of the covenant of Yahweh."[115] ארון העדות is used mostly in Exodus but twice also in Numbers[116] (Exod 25:16, 21; cf. 25:22; 26:33, 34; 30:6, 26; 31:7; 39:35; 40:3, 5, 21; Num 4:5; 7:89).[117] As we saw in Chapter 4, vv. 15–16 is a later insertion to connect this part with Exodus and belongs to final layer of this narrative ("e").

6.3.2.15. *Ascent and Arrival at Gilgal (4:17–19).*

4:17 ויצו יהושע את־הכהנים לאמר עלו מן־הירדן:
4:18 ויהי בעלות הכהנים נשאי ארון ברית־יהוה מן־הירדן ויתנו רגליהם
על החרבה וישבו מי־הירדן למקומם וילכו כתמול־שלשום על־כל־גדותיו:
4:19 והעם עלו מן־הירדן בעשור לחדש הראשון ויחנו בני־ישראל בגלגל
בקצה מזרח יריחו:

114. Nelson, *Joshua*, 70. For the use of this word (חלוצי), see also Rottzoll, *Abraham Ibn Esras Langer*, 373–74.

115. Auld, *Joshua: Jesus, Son of Nauē*, 118.

116. Seow, "Ark of the Covenant," *ABD* 1:387; Butler, *Joshua*, 50.

117. Butler, *Joshua*, 45.

Joshua commands the priests to "come up out of the Jordan." The same word as "the dry ground" (החרבה) appears in 3:17, but is different from יבשה in 4:20–24. The similar expression of "the priests' feet were separated unto the dry ground" (נתקו רגלי הכהנים אל החרבה) in v. 18 is also used in 3:15a ("a" layer). The expressions in this part (נשאי, ארון ברית־יהוה) are connected with the basic layer ("a") of this narrative and those expressions in similar ark stories. The water stopped in 3:16 "returns" (שׁוב) to its place here in 4:18. This section (vv. 17–19) belongs to the basic "a" layer. Soggin holds that the 10th of Nisan was an important day of spring festival in Gilgal, when a celebration of the Exodus was held as a present reality.[118] However, the attempt to link this text with the feast in Gilgal in relation to 5:9–12 is a little problematic. The phrase "the sons of Israel camped in Gilgal" (ויחנו בני־ישראל בגלגל) in 5:10 is an MT plus. ממחרת הפסח in v. 11 is also an MT plus. Auld holds that "[t]his text was economically altered through two neat additions to correspond to the 'Priestly' calendar of Passover in Lev 23:5–6, where Passover belongs to the fifteenth day of the month. [It] has a strengthening function to underline that it was on the *following* day that unleavened bread was eaten."[119] Thus, it appears to be somewhat hasty to connect Israel's arrival at Gilgal after crossing the Jordan with the feast in Gilgal, as some scholars have tried to do. Rather, this part might be the basic layer that connects the Jordan miracle with the place name "Gilgal." In 9:6; 10:6–7; 14:6, Gilgal plays an important role as the headquarters for Israel.[120]

6.3.2.16. *Stones at Gilgal and the Confession (4:20–24).*

4:20 ואת שתים עשׂרה האבנים האלה אשר לקח מן־הירדן הקים יהושע בגלגל:
4:21 לאמר אשר ישׁאלון בניכם אליכם לאמר מה האבנים האלה:
4:22 והודעתם את־בניכם כי ביבשה עבר ישׂראל את־הירדן
4:23 אשר־הוביש יהוה אלהינו את־מי הירדן מפניהם עד־עברו כאשר עשׂה יהוה
אלהינו לים־סוף אשר־הוביש יהוה אלהינו מפנינו עד־עברנו:
4:24 למען דעת כל־עמי הארץ את־יד יהוה כי חזקה היא למען יראתם אתם
את־יהוה אלהינו בכל־מעשה:

118. Soggin, *Joshua*, 66.

119. Auld, *Joshua Retold*, 12–13. However, Van der Meer has argued that the whole context (shorter LXX, and not just the MT pluses) is related to Lev 23. For this, see Van der Meer, *Formation and Reformulation*, 249–415, as well as A. G. Auld, Review of M. N. Van der Meer, *Formulation and Reformulation*, *JSJ* 36 (2005): 133–35.

120. Nelson, *Joshua: A Commentary*, 70.

Now the theme returns to the story of the twelve stones at Gilgal.[121] The cultic teaching form is repeated. The vocabulary and style are quite different from those in the basic and second layer, but similar to that of Rahab's confession in 2:10, which is related to the Reed Sea event. There is no more interest in the ark and the cutting-off of the water in this section. The liturgical teaching about the appearance of the dry ground makes this event more dramatic, and then the confession follows.[122]

As we have seen in section 6.2.2, the OG *Vorlage* has לקח instead of לקחו in the MT, stressing the leading role of Joshua, although the twelve chosen men have taken those stones in 4:1–8. This part is not linked with 4:1–8 ("b" layer). Verses 22 and 23 also represent the concept of "dry ground," but do so by using a different Hebrew word (ביבשה) from החרבה in the basic "a" layer (3:17; 4:18). Thus, this part is not connected with the basic "a" layer. ים־סוף in 4:23 is linked to the Reed Sea story in Exod 14. This part is the final layer ("e") in this narrative to link Josh 3–4 with similar water crossing events in Exod 13:17–14:31. We have already faced a similar problem in Chapter 4 with the epithet of "the ark of testimony" (ארון העדות) in Josh 4:16.[123] We saw that a later editor of Josh 3–4 seems to have inserted the expression in Josh 4:16 in order to connect the book of Joshua with the Exodus. In the very same manner, a later editor inserted the references to the Reed Sea crossing into this Jordan crossing story. Thus, Josh 4:15–16, 20–24 seem to be later than Exod 13:17–14:31. Verse 24 is also connected with the Israelite awe to Yahweh due to the miracle at the Reed Sea in Exod 14:31. The purpose of the event, which dried up the waters of the Jordan, is to show that Yahweh's hand is mighty and that the God of Israel rules over all the earth. However, the nations do not take part in this cult. Therefore, the ultimate purpose of this event is for the Israelites, so that they will be in awe of Yahweh and worship him.[124]

6.3.2.17. *The Examination of the Result of Literary-Critical Analysis Based on the Hebrew* Vorlage *of LXX Joshua 3–4*. Through literary-critical analysis, we can see that Josh 3–4 is composed of five layers of different materials. First, the basic layer of this narrative is "a": 3:2–11, 13–17; 4:10b–11a, 14, 17–19. Second, the first addition to these chapters

121. Woudstra, *The Book of Joshua*, 95.
122. Butler, *Joshua*, 51.
123. MT Josh 4:16 represents ארון העדות, but B ארון ברית עדות יהוה.
124. Butler, *Joshua*, 51.

is "b": 4:1–8, 10a, 11b, 12–13. Third, "c": 4:9. Fourth, "d": 3:1, 12. Fifth, the final redactional insertion to this narrative is "e": 4:15–16, 20–24.

At this point it is necessary for us to question whether our research so far has proceeded correctly and has come to a satisfactory outcome. To test the result of our research, we will reconstruct each stratum in the retroversion of LXX *Vorlage* on to a table and examine the following aspects: (1) the character each layer has; (2) the separate episodes each layer has; (3) what kind of changes appear to those episodes; (4) how many separate episodes should be detected; (5) which episodes are missed and which new episodes appear at each stage when we reconstruct the text according to the process of combining each layer (a, a + b, a + b + c…etc.). In the same way as archaeologists find geological strata and remains, then, we will investigate the distribution of major words in each layer to observe whether our research comes to a satisfactory result.

In Table 12, layer "a" shows the episodes of "passing over the Jordan on dry ground to Jericho and arrival at Gilgal by means of the ark, related to the conquest story," "the emphasis on the holiness of the ark and cultic sanctification," "the exaltation of Joshua and his succession to Moses," "the priests coming out of the Jordan," and "the return of the waters of the Jordan into their place."

Layer "b" records the episodes of "Joshua's calling twelve men already appointed," "Carrying twelve stones over to the place, where they will lodge," and "two and a half tribes armed for battle passing over to Jericho."

Layer "c" has "twelve other stones in the middle of the Jordan."

Layer "d" offers "Joshua's diligence and departure from Shittim," and "the prefiguration of command to choose twelve men for twelve tribes."

Layer "e" contains the episode of "the command to Joshua to tell the priests who bore the ark of the covenant of the testimony of Yahweh to come up from the water," and "setting up twelve stones for the twelve tribes at Gilgal."

At each stage of amalgamation, we can see that the number of episodes in each layer conforms to the number of episodes we expected and no new episode appears. We can confirm that this result is in accord with our conclusion.

Table 12

	a Layer	b Layer	c Layer	d Layer	e Layer
	3:2–11, 13–17; 4:10b–11a, 14, 17–19	4:1–8, 10a, 11b, 12–13	4:9	3:1, 12	4:15–16, 20–24
EPISODES	• Passing over the Jordan on dry ground to Jericho and arrival at Gilgal by means of the ark, related to the conquest story • The emphasis on the holiness of the ark and cultic sanctification • The emphasis on passing over on dry ground • The exaltation of Joshua and his succession to Moses • The priests coming out of the Jordan • The return of the waters of the Jordan to their place	• *Joshua's calling twelve men already appointed* • *Carrying twelve stones over to the place, where they will lodge* • *Two and a half tribes armed for battle passing over to Jericho*	• Twelve other stones in the middle of the Jordan	• **Joshua's diligence and departure from Shittim** • **The prefiguration of the command to choose twelve men for twelve tribes**	• The command to Joshua to tell the priests who bore the ark of the covenant of the testimony of Yahweh to come up from the water • Setting up twelve stones for the twelve tribes at the brink of the Jordan (Gilgal)
AMALGAMATION OF ALL THE LAYERS	a + b: 3:2–11, 13–17; 4:1–8, 10–14, 17–19				
	• Passing over the Jordan on dry ground to Jericho and arrival at Gilgal by means of the ark, related to the conquest story • The emphasis on the holiness of the ark and cultic sanctification • The emphasis on passing over on dry ground • The exaltation of Joshua and his succession to Moses • *Joshua's calling twelve men already appointed* • *Carrying twelve stones over to the place, where they will lodge* • *Two and a half tribes armed for battle passing over to Jericho* • The priests coming out of the Jordan • The return of the waters of the Jordan to their place				

<table>
<tr><td rowspan="4">AMALGAMATION OF ALL THE LAYERS</td><td>a + b + c: 3:2–11, 13–17; 4:1–14, 17–19</td><td></td><td></td></tr>
<tr><td>• Passing over the Jordan on dry ground to Jericho and arrival at Gilgal by means of the ark, related to the conquest story
• The emphasis on the holiness of the ark and cultic sanctification
• The emphasis on passing over on dry ground
• The exaltation of Joshua and his succession to Moses
• Joshua's calling twelve men already appointed
• Carrying twelve stones over to the place, where they will lodge
• <u>Twelve other stones in the middle of the Jordan</u>
• Two and a half tribes armed for battle passing over to Jericho
• The priests coming out of the Jordan
• The return of the waters of the Jordan to their place</td><td></td><td></td></tr>
<tr><td colspan="2">a + b + c + d: 3:1–17; 4:1–14, 17–19</td><td rowspan="2"></td></tr>
<tr><td colspan="2">• <u>Joshua's diligence and departure from Shittim</u>
• Passing over the Jordan on dry ground to Jericho and arrival to Gilgal by means of the ark, related to the conquest story
• The emphasis on the holiness of the ark and cultic sanctification
• <u>The prefiguration of command to choose twelve men for twelve tribes</u>
• The emphasis on passing over on dry ground
• The exaltation of Joshua and his succession to Moses
• Joshua's calling twelve men already appointed
• Carrying twelve stones over to the place where they will lodge
• <u>Twelve other stones in the middle of the Jordan</u>
• Two and a half tribes armed for battle passing over to Jericho
• The priests coming out of the Jordan
• The return of the waters of the Jordan to their place</td></tr>
</table>

	a + b + c + d + e: 3:1–17; 4:1–24
AMALGAMATION OF ALL THE LAYERS	• **Joshua's diligence and departure from Shittim** • Passing over the Jordan on dry ground to Jericho and arrival to Gilgal by means of the ark, related to the conquest story • The emphasis on the holiness of the ark and cultic sanctification • **The prefiguration of command to choose twelve men for twelve tribes** • The emphasis on passing over on dry ground • The exaltation of Joshua and his succession to Moses • *Joshua's calling twelve men already appointed* • *Carrying twelve stones over to the place where they will lodge* • Twelve other stones in the middle of the Jordan -• *Two and a half tribes armed for battle passing over to Jericho* • The command to Joshua to tell the priests who bore the ark of the covenant of the testimony of Yahweh to come up from the water • The priests coming out of the Jordan • The return of the waters of the Jordan to their place • Setting up twelve stones for the twelve tribes at Gilgal

Here, once again, it is necessary for us to examine the result of our research through the investigation of the major words in each layer. When the distribution of major words is tabulated, it will be possible for us to distinguish the features of the layers in this narrative more clearly.

Table 13

	a	b	c	d	e	Total
the ark	10	3	1	0	1	15
Israel	6	6	0	1	1	14
the people	10	3	0	0	1	14
the priests	10	1	1	0	1	13
cross over (עבר)	8	8	0	1	3	20
the Jordan	14	6	1	1	4	26

As we see in Table 13, "the passing over (20) the Jordan (26) with the ark (15) by the priests (13) and the Israelite people (14 + 14 = 28)" is the theme of the whole narrative. We can see that these words have a relatively even distribution in "a" layer, so "a" is basic layer of this narrative. The "b" layer, which is about "Israel's crossing over the Jordan to carry twelve stones over to the place, where they will lodge," also shows a regular distribution of words, although there is less interest in "the priests," "the ark," and "the people." Thus, we could say "a" and "b" are major layers of this narrative, but "b" is later. Added to these basic layers is the "c" layer, in which "the ark," "the priests," and "the Jordan" are emphasized (by "setting up the twelve stones in the middle of the Jordan"). The "d" layer shows interest in "crossing the Jordan" and "Israel" (by selecting twelve men for each tribe). Finally, the "e" layer, which knows all the important expressions in this narrative, was redactionally added. We can see that the analytical result of the word distribution supports our research.

6.3.2.18. *Conclusion: Literary-Critical Analysis of Joshua 3–4 Based on the Retroversion of the* LXX Vorlage. Through the literary-critical analysis, we found five layers of different materials in Josh 3–4.

First, the basic layer (a), influenced by similar synoptic ark texts in Samuel–Kings and Chronicles (i.e. 2 Sam 6//1 Chr 13–16, 1 Kgs 7:51–8:11//2 Chr 5), is that which connects the passing-over of the Jordan on dry ground to Gilgal and the exaltation of Joshua and his succession to Moses: Josh 3:2–11, 13–17; 4:10b–11a, 14, 17–19.

Another basic layer of this narrative, and the first addition to this narrative, is "b," which shows interest in carrying twelve stones over to the other side of the Jordan, and two and a half tribes passing over the

Jordan according to Moses' command: Josh 4:1–8, 10a, 11b, 12–13. This second layer appears to be influenced by Deuteronomy (Deut 3:18; 6:20–21; 27:1–6).

Third comes "c," the second additional layer, which is concerned with the aetiology of the twelve stones in the middle of the Jordan: Josh 4:9.

Fourth, we have the third insertion ("d") which emphasizes Joshua's diligence and the beginning of the realization of the Jordan crossing, and which links ch. 3 to 4: Josh 3:1, 12.

These four layers compose the primary story of this narrative.

Fifth, to those four layers, a final fourth redactional layer ("e") is added to connect this story with the ark narratives and Reed Sea story in Exodus: Josh 4:15–16, 20–24.

One point we should bear in mind here is that the form of question and answer seems to be developed in the order of Deut 6:20–21 > Josh 4:6–7 > non-Priestly Exod 13:8–10 > Priestly Exod 12:26–27; 13:14–15.

6.3.3. *Literary-Critical Analysis of Joshua 3–4 Based on the Final Shape of the* MT

6.3.3.1. *Preparation for Crossing the Jordan (3:1–4).*

3:1 וַיַּשְׁכֵּם יְהוֹשֻׁעַ בַּבֹּקֶר וַיִּסְעוּ מֵהַשִּׁטִּים וַיָּבֹאוּ
עַד־הַיַּרְדֵּן הוּא וְכָל־בְּנֵי יִשְׂרָאֵל וַיָּלִנוּ שָׁם טֶרֶם יַעֲבֹרוּ׃
3:2 וַיְהִי מִקְצֵה שְׁלֹשֶׁת יָמִים וַיַּעַבְרוּ הַשֹּׁטְרִים בְּקֶרֶב הַמַּחֲנֶה׃
3:3 וַיְצַוּוּ אֶת־הָעָם לֵאמֹר כִּרְאוֹתְכֶם אֵת אֲרוֹן בְּרִית־יְהוָה
אֱלֹהֵיכֶם וְהַכֹּהֲנִים הַלְוִיִּם נֹשְׂאִים אֹתוֹ וְאַתֶּם תִּסְעוּ
מִמְּקוֹמְכֶם וַהֲלַכְתֶּם אַחֲרָיו׃
3:4 אַךְ רָחוֹק יִהְיֶה בֵּינֵיכֶם וּבֵינָו כְּאַלְפַּיִם אַמָּה
בַּמִּדָּה אַל־תִּקְרְבוּ אֵלָיו לְמַעַן אֲשֶׁר־תֵּדְעוּ אֶת־הַדֶּרֶךְ אֲשֶׁר
תֵּלְכוּ־בָהּ כִּי לֹא עֲבַרְתֶּם בַּדֶּרֶךְ מִתְּמוֹל שִׁלְשׁוֹם׃ ס

As we saw above, the phrase "rose at morning" is the stereotypical rendering of a common Hebrew formula,[125] which also appears in 6:12, 15; 7:16; 8:10.[126] The change of the subject from third person singular to plural makes the syntax of this verse a bit clumsy. An MT redactor seems to have tried to solve this awkwardness by inserting הוא וכל־בני ישראל. By the insertion of this phrase, the ambiguity of the subject of this verse disappears and the phrase כל־בני ישראל, which is a synoptic expression in 2 Sam 6//1 Chr 13–16 and 1 Kgs 7:51–8:11//2 Chr 5, connects this verse with the basic layer of the narrative. As we saw above, there are a number of pluses in MT like this, which seems to be the final redactional layer of this narrative. These pluses in the MT will be termed the "δ" layer.

125. Fritz, *Das Buch Josua*, 46; Auld, *Joshua: Jesus, Son of Nauē*, 102.
126. Woudstra, *The Book of Joshua*, 79.

The references to “three days” and “the officers” “passing through the camp,” and the order given to the people (vv. 2–4) are connected to Joshua’s command in 1:10–11. This section is the continuation of the basic layer of this narrative, which is related to the conquest story that continues from ch. 1.[127] This basic layer will be called “α” for the moment. The term “officers” also appears at some important points of Josh 8:33; 23:2, and 24:1. The respectful distance in v. 4 belongs to the basic layer, which is influenced by the accident of Uzzah in 2 Sam 6// 1 Chr 13.

6.3.3.2. *“Sanctify yourselves” (3:5–6).*

3:5 וַיֹּאמֶר יְהוֹשֻׁעַ אֶל־הָעָם הִתְקַדָּשׁוּ כִּי מָחָר יַעֲשֶׂה יְהוָה
בְּקִרְבְּכֶם נִפְלָאוֹת׃
3:6 וַיֹּאמֶר יְהוֹשֻׁעַ אֶל־הַכֹּהֲנִים לֵאמֹר שְׂאוּ אֶת־אֲרוֹן הַבְּרִית
וְעִבְרוּ לִפְנֵי הָעָם וַיִּשְׂאוּ אֶת־אֲרוֹן הַבְּרִית וַיֵּלְכוּ לִפְנֵי הָעָם׃ ס

מחר (“tomorrow”), a routine formula of sanctification, seems to be connected with the single night chronology of v. 1,[128] which belongs to the “α” layer. “The priests” in v. 6 also appears to be connected with the demand of “sanctification in cultic tradition”[129] in v. 5. The MT marks vv. 5–6 as a paragraph, as does LXX^{B}. This section is the continuation of the “α” layer.

6.3.3.3. *Yahweh Addresses Joshua and Joshua Prepares His People (3:7–11).*

3:7 וַיֹּאמֶר יְהוָה אֶל־יְהוֹשֻׁעַ הַיּוֹם הַזֶּה אָחֵל גַּדֶּלְךָ בְּעֵינֵי
כָּל־יִשְׂרָאֵל אֲשֶׁר יֵדְעוּן כִּי כַּאֲשֶׁר הָיִיתִי עִם־מֹשֶׁה אֶהְיֶה עִמָּךְ׃
3:8 וְאַתָּה תְּצַוֶּה אֶת־הַכֹּהֲנִים נֹשְׂאֵי אֲרוֹן־הַבְּרִית לֵאמֹר כְּבֹאֲכֶם
עַד־קְצֵה מֵי הַיַּרְדֵּן בַּיַּרְדֵּן תַּעֲמֹדוּ׃ פ
3:9 וַיֹּאמֶר יְהוֹשֻׁעַ אֶל־בְּנֵי יִשְׂרָאֵל גֹּשׁוּ הֵנָּה וְשִׁמְעוּ אֶת־דִּבְרֵי
יְהוָה אֱלֹהֵיכֶם׃
3:10 וַיֹּאמֶר יְהוֹשֻׁעַ בְּזֹאת תֵּדְעוּן כִּי אֵל חַי בְּקִרְבְּכֶם וְהוֹרֵשׁ
יוֹרִישׁ מִפְּנֵיכֶם אֶת־הַכְּנַעֲנִי וְאֶת־הַחִתִּי וְאֶת־הַחִוִּי וְאֶת־הַפְּרִזִּי
וְאֶת־הַגִּרְגָּשִׁי וְהָאֱמֹרִי וְהַיְבוּסִי׃
3:11 הִנֵּה אֲרוֹן הַבְּרִית אֲדוֹן כָּל־הָאָרֶץ עֹבֵר לִפְנֵיכֶם בַּיַּרְדֵּן׃

Verses 7–8 are a continuation of the basic layer (“α”). Yahweh’s promise regarding the exaltation of Joshua in Josh 1 is being carried out in 3:7, which is linked with 1:5, 17–18 and 4:10, 14.

127. Gray, *Joshua, Judges and Ruth*, 60.
128. Nelson, *Joshua*, 61.
129. Soggin, *Joshua*, 47–48.

In v. 8 the leadership role of Joshua (ואתה תצוה, "and you yourself shall command") is also stressed, and v. 8 connects the content of exaltation in v. 7 with the story of the conquest of the land.

In vv. 9–11 Joshua delivers Yahweh's words (דברי יהוה) to his people, which ends in v. 13.[130] Here, we can also see that the basic layer ("α") understands the event of "crossing the Jordan" in connection with that of "the conquest war."

6.3.3.4. *Choose Twelve Men (3:12).*

3:12 וְעַתָּה קְחוּ לָכֶם שְׁנֵי עָשָׂר אִישׁ מִשִּׁבְטֵי יִשְׂרָאֵל אִישׁ־אֶחָד
אִישׁ־אֶחָד לַשָּׁבֶט׃

The sudden appearance of the command to take twelve men from the tribes of Israel makes the context a bit clumsy.[131] This verse (3:12) seems to be a redactional addition inserted by an editor, who knew the story of 4:1–8 and who did so to connect the contents of Chapters 3 and 4.

3:12 קחו לכם שני עשר איש מבני ישראל איש־אחד (איש־אחד) לשבט׃
4:2 קחו (לכם) מן־העם (שנים עשר) אנשים איש־אחד (איש־אחד) משבט׃

As we have seen above, LXX Josh 3:12 and 4:2 show a quite different style, although MT Josh 3:12 and 4:2 show a rather similar structure. An MT editor seems to have put some pluses into both verses to sort out the differences between them. With the help of pluses in each verse, 3:12 belongs to the same layer as 4:1–8 ("β").

6.3.3.5. *Descent and Passing Over on "Dry Ground" (בחרבה) (3:13–17).*

3:13 וְהָיָה כְּנוֹחַ כַּפּוֹת רַגְלֵי הַכֹּהֲנִים נֹשְׂאֵי אֲרוֹן יְהוָה אֲדוֹן
כָּל־הָאָרֶץ בְּמֵי הַיַּרְדֵּן מֵי הַיַּרְדֵּן יִכָּרֵתוּן הַמַּיִם הַיֹּרְדִים
מִלְמָעְלָה וְיַעַמְדוּ נֵד אֶחָד׃
3:14 וַיְהִי בִּנְסֹעַ הָעָם מֵאָהֳלֵיהֶם לַעֲבֹר אֶת־הַיַּרְדֵּן וְהַכֹּהֲנִים
נֹשְׂאֵי הָאָרוֹן הַבְּרִית לִפְנֵי הָעָם׃
3:15 וּכְבוֹא נֹשְׂאֵי הָאָרוֹן עַד־הַיַּרְדֵּן וְרַגְלֵי הַכֹּהֲנִים נֹשְׂאֵי הָאָרוֹן
נִטְבְּלוּ בִּקְצֵה הַמָּיִם וְהַיַּרְדֵּן מָלֵא עַל־כָּל־גְּדוֹתָיו כֹּל יְמֵי קָצִיר׃
3:16 וַיַּעַמְדוּ הַמַּיִם הַיֹּרְדִים מִלְמַעְלָה קָמוּ נֵד־אֶחָד הַרְחֵק
מְאֹד מֵאָדָם הָעִיר אֲשֶׁר מִצַּד צָרְתָן וְהַיֹּרְדִים עַל
יָם הָעֲרָבָה יָם־הַמֶּלַח תַּמּוּ נִכְרָתוּ וְהָעָם עָבְרוּ נֶגֶד יְרִיחוֹ׃
3:17 וַיַּעַמְדוּ הַכֹּהֲנִים נֹשְׂאֵי הָאָרוֹן בְּרִית־יְהוָה בֶּחָרָבָה בְּתוֹךְ
הַיַּרְדֵּן הָכֵן וְכָל־יִשְׂרָאֵל עֹבְרִים בֶּחָרָבָה עַד אֲשֶׁר־תַּמּוּ
כָּל־הַגּוֹי לַעֲבֹר אֶת־הַיַּרְדֵּן׃

130. Butler, *Joshua*, 39.

131. Saydon, "The Crossing of the Jordan," 199.

Verse 13 has the same phrase "the Lord of all the earth" as in v. 11. The focus of interest in v. 13 is also on the ark, as it is in v. 11. Verse 13 is the continuation of the basic "α" layer.

The people's departure from their tents and the priests' bearing of the ark of the covenant before the people in v. 14 are linked with the officers' command in vv. 2–3. The detailed explanation on the cutting-off of the waters in vv. 15 and 16 is connected with Joshua's prophecy in v. 13 ("when the feet of the priests rest in the waters, the waters of the Jordan shall stand"). All of these verses are a continuation of "α," which continues the story of the people's passing over opposite Jericho in v. 16b. As we see from the explanation of Israel's crossing over opposite Jericho in this verse, the basic layer ("α") seems to connect this wonder with the conquest of Jericho.[132]

Verse 17 shows the same concern for passing over on "dry ground" (בחרבה) as in 4:20–24. However, the Hebrew word for "dry ground" (בחרבה) in this verse is different from that employed in 4:20–24, where יבשה is used. נשא and הארון ברית יהוה also connect this verse with the basic layer of this narrative ("α").

6.3.3.6. *Carrying Twelve Stones Over to the Other Side of the Jordan and Erecting Twelve Memorial Stones in the Middle of the Jordan (4:1–9).*

4:1 וַיְהִי כַּאֲשֶׁר־תַּמּוּ כָל־הַגּוֹי לַעֲבוֹר אֶת־הַיַּרְדֵּן פ
וַיֹּאמֶר יְהוָה אֶל־יְהוֹשֻׁעַ לֵאמֹר׃
4:2 קְחוּ לָכֶם מִן־הָעָם שְׁנֵים עָשָׂר אֲנָשִׁים אִישׁ־אֶחָד אִישׁ־אֶחָד מִשָּׁבֶט׃
4:3 וְצַוּוּ אוֹתָם לֵאמֹר שְׂאוּ־לָכֶם מִזֶּה מִתּוֹךְ הַיַּרְדֵּן מִמַּצַּב
רַגְלֵי הַכֹּהֲנִים הָכִין שְׁתֵּים־עֶשְׂרֵה אֲבָנִים וְהַעֲבַרְתֶּם אוֹתָם
עִמָּכֶם וְהִנַּחְתֶּם אוֹתָם בַּמָּלוֹן אֲשֶׁר־תָּלִינוּ בוֹ הַלָּיְלָה׃ ס
4:4 וַיִּקְרָא יְהוֹשֻׁעַ אֶל־שְׁנֵים הֶעָשָׂר אִישׁ אֲשֶׁר הֵכִין מִבְּנֵי
יִשְׂרָאֵל אִישׁ־אֶחָד אִישׁ־אֶחָד מִשָּׁבֶט׃
4:5 וַיֹּאמֶר לָהֶם יְהוֹשֻׁעַ עִבְרוּ לִפְנֵי אֲרוֹן יְהוָה אֱלֹהֵיכֶם
אֶל־תּוֹךְ הַיַּרְדֵּן וְהָרִימוּ לָכֶם אִישׁ אֶבֶן אַחַת עַל־שִׁכְמוֹ
לְמִסְפַּר שִׁבְטֵי בְנֵי־יִשְׂרָאֵל׃
4:6 לְמַעַן תִּהְיֶה זֹאת אוֹת בְּקִרְבְּכֶם כִּי־יִשְׁאָלוּן בְּנֵיכֶם מָחָר
לֵאמֹר מָה הָאֲבָנִים הָאֵלֶּה לָכֶם׃
4:7 וַאֲמַרְתֶּם לָהֶם אֲשֶׁר נִכְרְתוּ מֵימֵי הַיַּרְדֵּן מִפְּנֵי אֲרוֹן
בְּרִית־יְהוָה בְּעָבְרוֹ בַּיַּרְדֵּן נִכְרְתוּ מֵי הַיַּרְדֵּן וְהָיוּ הָאֲבָנִים
הָאֵלֶּה לְזִכָּרוֹן לִבְנֵי יִשְׂרָאֵל עַד־עוֹלָם׃
4:8 וַיַּעֲשׂוּ־כֵן בְּנֵי־יִשְׂרָאֵל כַּאֲשֶׁר צִוָּה יְהוֹשֻׁעַ וַיִּשְׂאוּ שְׁתֵּי־עֶשְׂרֵה
אֲבָנִים מִתּוֹךְ הַיַּרְדֵּן כַּאֲשֶׁר דִּבֶּר יְהוָה אֶל־יְהוֹשֻׁעַ לְמִסְפַּר
שִׁבְטֵי בְנֵי־יִשְׂרָאֵל וַיַּעֲבִרוּם עִמָּם אֶל־הַמָּלוֹן וַיַּנִּחוּם שָׁם׃
4:9 וּשְׁתֵּים עֶשְׂרֵה אֲבָנִים הֵקִים יְהוֹשֻׁעַ בְּתוֹךְ הַיַּרְדֵּן תַּחַת מַצַּב
רַגְלֵי הַכֹּהֲנִים נֹשְׂאֵי אֲרוֹן הַבְּרִית וַיִּהְיוּ שָׁם עַד הַיּוֹם הַזֶּה׃

132. Butler, *Joshua*, 48.

Verse 1a sums up the event of crossing the Jordan in ch. 3 and introduces a different story.[133] Verses 1–8 comprise another basic layer ("β") of this narrative, which emphasizes the twelve stones being moved to the brink of the river for twelve tribes, but this is later than α. The number "twelve" occurs five times in these verses (one MT plus).[134] As we have seen in 6.3.2.7, this part is later than Deuteronomy and is influenced by it.

The sudden appearance of the account that Joshua set up twelve other stones in the middle of the Jordan in LXX Josh 4:9 makes a clumsy connection with v. 8. However, by removing the word אחרים from LXX Josh 4:9, the MT solves the disconnection with 4:1–8 ("β"). The plus ממצב רגלי הכהנים in 4:3 also seems to be inserted so as to connect 4:9, which has the similar phrase מצב רגלי הכהנים, with 4:1–8. In the MT, 4:9 also belongs to "β." Here the middle of the Jordan, which is related to the location of the ark (3:17; 4:18) and the source of the memorial stones (4:3, 5, 8), is itself highlighted by the placement of stones.[135] The similar expression and phrases that Joshua set up twelve stones at Gilgal appears in 4:20. However, as we have seen in the textual criticism, the phrases ושתים עשׂרה אבנים in v. 9 and ואת שׁתים עשׂרה האבנים האלה in v. 20 ("γ") show us that these two parts originate from different materials.

6.3.3.7. *The Succession of Joshua to Moses (4:10–14).*

4:10 וְהַכֹּהֲנִים נֹשְׂאֵי הָאָרוֹן עֹמְדִים בְּתוֹךְ הַיַּרְדֵּן עַד תֹּם
כָּל־הַדָּבָר אֲשֶׁר־צִוָּה יְהוָה אֶת־יְהוֹשֻׁעַ לְדַבֵּר אֶל־הָעָם כְּכֹל
אֲשֶׁר־צִוָּה מֹשֶׁה אֶת־יְהוֹשֻׁעַ וַיְמַהֲרוּ הָעָם וַיַּעֲבֹרוּ׃
4:11 וַיְהִי כַּאֲשֶׁר־תַּם כָּל־הָעָם לַעֲבוֹר וַיַּעֲבֹר אֲרוֹן־יְהוָה וְהַכֹּהֲנִים לִפְנֵי הָעָם׃
4:12 וַיַּעַבְרוּ בְּנֵי־רְאוּבֵן וּבְנֵי־גָד וַחֲצִי שֵׁבֶט הַמְנַשֶּׁה חֲמֻשִׁים
לִפְנֵי בְּנֵי יִשְׂרָאֵל כַּאֲשֶׁר דִּבֶּר אֲלֵיהֶם מֹשֶׁה׃
4:13 כְּאַרְבָּעִים אֶלֶף חֲלוּצֵי הַצָּבָא עָבְרוּ לִפְנֵי יְהוָה לַמִּלְחָמָה
אֶל עַרְבוֹת יְרִיחוֹ׃ ס
4:14 בַּיּוֹם הַהוּא גִּדַּל יְהוָה אֶת־יְהוֹשֻׁעַ בְּעֵינֵי כָּל־יִשְׂרָאֵל וַיִּרְאוּ
אֹתוֹ כַּאֲשֶׁר יָרְאוּ אֶת־מֹשֶׁה כָּל־יְמֵי חַיָּיו׃ פ

The priests who bore the ark were standing in the middle of the Jordan until everything was fulfilled. This part is linked to the basic "α" layer, which stresses the succession of Joshua to Moses, as in 3:17; 4:14 (cf. 2 Kgs 2). The MT plus (ככל אשר־צוה משה את־יהושע) in 4:10 is connected with the similar expression כאשר דבר אליהם משה in 4:12 and כאשר יראו את־משה כל־ימי חייו in 4:14 and puts vv. 10–14 together. Verses 10–11a repeat the element of 3:16b–17 ("α" layer), but in a different order and

133. Woudstra, *The Book of Joshua*, 90.
134. Boling and Wright, *Joshua*, 172.
135. Nelson, *Joshua*, 69.

with altered grammar in order to "restart" the frozen narrative action of the crossing.[136] MT Joshua 4:11b represents הַכֹּהֲנִים instead of הָאֲבָנִים in the LXX *Vorlage*. As we have seen above, this is an MT adjustment to be faithful to the command to the priests to take up the ark of the covenant, and to pass on before the people in 3:6 ("α"). Verse 11b is also connected with v. 10a ("α"). This is the sequence of the story in which the ark and the priests, who had stood in the middle of the Jordan while Joshua carried out what Yahweh commanded (v. 10a), passed over the Jordan once the task had been completed (v. 11b).

Verses 12–14 are the continuation of "α," which connects this event with the conquest of the land. Here the command given in 1:12–15 is carried out.[137] The special reference to the two and a half tribes seems to emphasize that all the tribes took part in the passing over and in the conquest war. Verse 13 repeats the content of v. 12, although the vocabulary is different. The phrase "passed over to the Plains of Jericho" is directly linked with the conquest story of Jericho in ch. 6. The exaltation of Joshua as a leader like Moses belongs to "α." The "α" layer regards the completion of the passing over as the accomplishment of Yahweh's promise of the exaltation of Joshua, as given in ch. 1.

6.3.3.8. *The Ark of the Testimony (4:15–16).*

4:15 וַיֹּאמֶר יְהוָה אֶל־יְהוֹשֻׁעַ לֵאמֹר׃
4:16 צַוֵּה אֶת־הַכֹּהֲנִים נֹשְׂאֵי אֲרוֹן הָעֵדוּת וְיַעֲלוּ מִן־הַיַּרְדֵּן׃

As we have seen in Chapter 4, this is the only occurrence of ארון העדות in the entire Former Prophets and Chronicles. It appears mainly in Exodus and Numbers. These two verses are later insertion ("γ") to link this ark narrative with those in Exodus.

6.3.3.9. *Ascent and Arrival at Gilgal (4:17–19).*

4:17 וַיְצַו יְהוֹשֻׁעַ אֶת־הַכֹּהֲנִים לֵאמֹר עֲלוּ מִן־הַיַּרְדֵּן׃
4:18 וַיְהִי בַּעֲלוֹת הַכֹּהֲנִים נֹשְׂאֵי אֲרוֹן בְּרִית־יְהוָה
מִתּוֹךְ הַיַּרְדֵּן נִתְּקוּ כַּפּוֹת רַגְלֵי הַכֹּהֲנִים אֶל הֶחָרָבָה וַיָּשֻׁבוּ
מֵי־הַיַּרְדֵּן לִמְקוֹמָם וַיֵּלְכוּ כִתְמוֹל־שִׁלְשׁוֹם עַל־כָּל־גְּדוֹתָיו׃
4:19 וְהָעָם עָלוּ מִן־הַיַּרְדֵּן בֶּעָשׂוֹר לַחֹדֶשׁ הָרִאשׁוֹן וַיַּחֲנוּ בַּגִּלְגָּל
בִּקְצֵה מִזְרַח יְרִיחוֹ׃

136. Ibid.
137. Soggin, *Joshua*, 65.

This part uses the same expressions (ארון ברית־יהוה, נשׂאי) as in the basic layer of this narrative and the ark narratives of Samuel–Kings and Chronicles. This part is the conclusion of the basic layer of this water crossing narrative ("α"): the water that is cut off in 3:16 returns to its place and the people of Israel arrive at Gilgal.

6.3.3.10. *Stones at Gilgal and Confession (4:20–24).*

4:20 וְאֵת שְׁתֵּים עֶשְׂרֵה הָאֲבָנִים הָאֵלֶּה אֲשֶׁר לָקְחוּ מִן־הַיַּרְדֵּן
הֵקִים יְהוֹשֻׁעַ בַּגִּלְגָּל׃
4:21 וַיֹּאמֶר אֶל־בְּנֵי יִשְׂרָאֵל לֵאמֹר אֲשֶׁר יִשְׁאָלוּן בְּנֵיכֶם מָחָר
אֶת־אֲבוֹתָם לֵאמֹר מָה הָאֲבָנִים הָאֵלֶּה׃
4:22 וְהוֹדַעְתֶּם אֶת־בְּנֵיכֶם לֵאמֹר בַּיַּבָּשָׁה עָבַר יִשְׂרָאֵל
אֶת־הַיַּרְדֵּן הַזֶּה׃
4:23 אֲשֶׁר־הוֹבִישׁ יְהוָה אֱלֹהֵיכֶם אֶת־מֵי הַיַּרְדֵּן מִפְּנֵיכֶם
עַד־עָבְרְכֶם כַּאֲשֶׁר עָשָׂה יְהוָה אֱלֹהֵיכֶם לְיַם־סוּף אֲשֶׁר־הוֹבִישׁ
מִפָּנֵינוּ עַד־עָבְרֵנוּ׃
4:24 לְמַעַן דַּעַת כָּל־עַמֵּי הָאָרֶץ אֶת־יַד יְהוָה כִּי חֲזָקָה הִיא
לְמַעַן יְרָאתֶם אֶת־יְהוָה אֱלֹהֵיכֶם כָּל־הַיָּמִים׃ ס

Now the narrative returns to the story of the twelve stones at Gilgal in 4:1–8 ("β"). Although twelve chosen men have taken stones in 4:1–8, the Hebrew *Vorlage* of LXX uses a singular form of the verb לקח to emphasize the role of Joshua in 4:20. The MT seems to have adjusted the singular verb in the OG *Vorlage* to plural in order to connect this part with the syntax of 4:1–8. The MT also tries to connect this section with 4:6 by inserting מָחָר. However, we can still see some disconnection with 4:1–9. Even though the first part of 4:20 uses almost the same expressions as that of 4:9, the former displays a different style from the latter. In addition, this section does not show any interest in the ark and the cutting-off of the water. Instead, this part uses a different word, ביבשה, compared to החרבה (3:17; 4:18), in the basic "α" layer and represents ים־סוף trying to connect this Jordan crossing with the Reed Sea story in Exod 13:17–14:31. This part is a redactional insertion ("γ") so as to link this story with the Exodus story.

6.3.3.11. *The Examination of the Result of Literary-Critical Analysis Based on the Final Shape of the MT.* Through literary-critical analysis based on the MT, we can see that Josh 3–4 is composed of four layers of different materials. First, the basic layer of this narrative is "α": 3:1–11, 13–17; 4:10–14, 17–19. Second, the first addition to these chapters is "β": 3:12; 4:1–9. Third, "γ": 4:15–16, 20–24. Fourth, the final redactional insertion to this narrative is "δ," which contains MT pluses:

3:1 (הוא וכל־בני ישראל), 3 (ואתם), 6 (לאמר), 7 (כי), 10 (ויאמר יהושע), 11 (לפניכם), 12 (ועתה, איש־אחד), 13 (כפות, מלמעלה, ר---, נד אחד), 14 (ויהי), 15 (כל), 16 (מאדם), 17 (הכן); 4:1 (יהי), 2 (לכם, שנים עשר, איש־אחד), 3 (לאמר, לכמ מזה, הכהנים, ממצב רגלי, ר---), 4 (איש־אחד), 5 (יהושע, ארון, אלהיכם, בני), 7 (בירדן, נכרתו מי הירדן), 9 (בתוך), 10 (תוך, ככל אשר־צוה משה את־יהושע), 11 (העם), 13 (כ), 14 (עם), 18 (תוך, כפות, הכהנים), 21 (ויאמר אל־בני ישראל, מחר, את־אבותם), 22 (הזה, ר---).

Here again it is necessary for us to test the results of our research by putting each stratum of the MT into a table in order to examine each layer and the changes that arise when we reconstruct the text by combining each layer (α, α + β, α + β + γ…etc.). Then we can investigate the distribution of major words in each layer to observe whether our research comes to a satisfactory result, as we did above with the retroversion of LXX *Vorlage*.

In Table 14, "α" layer shows the episodes of "passing over the Jordan on dry ground to Jericho and arrival at Gilgal by means of the ark, related to the conquest story," "the emphasis on the holiness of the ark and cultic sanctification," "the emphasis on passing over on dry ground," "the exaltation of Joshua and his succession to Moses," "two and a half tribes armed for battle passing over to Jericho," and "the priests coming out of the Jordan," and "the return of the waters of the Jordan to their place."

The "β" layer contains the episodes of "the command to choose twelve men for twelve tribes," "carrying twelve stones over to the place, where they will lodge," and "setting up twelve stones in the middle of the Jordan."

The "γ" layer contains the episode of "the command to Joshua to tell the priests who bore the ark of the testimony to come up from the water," and "setting up twelve stones for the twelve tribes at Gilgal."

In the "δ" layer, there are a number of MT pluses. In fact, thanks to the "δ" layer, this narrative becomes simpler and could be read more continuously without severance of context.

At each stage, we can see that the number of episodes in each layer conforms to the number of episodes we expected and no new episode appears once each layer is combined. We can confirm that this result is in accordance with the conclusion that we came to in our literary-critical analysis based on the MT.

Table 14

δ	γ	β	α	
הוּא וְכָל־בְּנֵי יִשְׂרָאֵל			וַיַּשְׁכֵּם יְהוֹשֻׁעַ בַּבֹּקֶר וַיִּסְעוּ מֵהַשִּׁטִּים וַיָּבֹאוּ עַד־הַיַּרְדֵּן הוּא וְכָל־בְּנֵי יִשְׂרָאֵל וַיָּלִנוּ שָׁם טֶרֶם יַעֲבֹרוּ׃	3:1
			וַיְהִי מִקְצֵה שְׁלֹשֶׁת יָמִים וַיַּעַבְרוּ הַשֹּׁטְרִים בְּקֶרֶב הַמַּחֲנֶה׃	3:2
וְאַתֶּם			וַיְצַוּוּ אֶת־הָעָם לֵאמֹר כִּרְאוֹתְכֶם אֵת אֲרוֹן בְּרִית־יְהוָה אֱלֹהֵיכֶם וְהַכֹּהֲנִים הַלְוִיִּם נֹשְׂאִים אֹתוֹ וְאַתֶּם תִּסְעוּ מִמְּקוֹמְכֶם וַהֲלַכְתֶּם אַחֲרָיו׃	3:3
			אַךְ רָחוֹק יִהְיֶה בֵּינֵיכֶם וּבֵינוֹ כְּאַלְפַּיִם אַמָּה בַּמִּדָּה אַל־תִּקְרְבוּ אֵלָיו לְמַעַן אֲשֶׁר־תֵּדְעוּ אֶת־הַדֶּרֶךְ אֲשֶׁר תֵּלְכוּ־בָהּ כִּי לֹא עֲבַרְתֶּם בַּדֶּרֶךְ מִתְּמוֹל שִׁלְשׁוֹם׃ ס	3:4
			וַיֹּאמֶר יְהוֹשֻׁעַ אֶל־הָעָם הִתְקַדָּשׁוּ כִּי מָחָר יַעֲשֶׂה יְהוָה בְּקִרְבְּכֶם נִפְלָאוֹת׃	3:5
לֵאמֹר			וַיֹּאמֶר יְהוֹשֻׁעַ אֶל־הַכֹּהֲנִים לֵאמֹר שְׂאוּ אֶת־אֲרוֹן הַבְּרִית וְעִבְרוּ לִפְנֵי הָעָם וַיִּשְׂאוּ אֶת־אֲרוֹן הַבְּרִית וַיֵּלְכוּ לִפְנֵי הָעָם׃ ס	3:6

3:7	וַיֹּאמֶר יְהוָה אֶל־יְהוֹשֻׁעַ הַיּוֹם הַזֶּה אָחֵל גַּדֶּלְךָ בְּעֵינֵי כָּל־יִשְׂרָאֵל אֲשֶׁר יֵדְעוּן כִּי כַּאֲשֶׁר הָיִיתִי עִם־מֹשֶׁה אֶהְיֶה עִמָּךְ:			כִּי
3:8	וְאַתָּה תְּצַוֶּה אֶת־הַכֹּהֲנִים נֹשְׂאֵי אֲרוֹן־הַבְּרִית לֵאמֹר כְּבֹאֲכֶם עַד־קְצֵה מֵי הַיַּרְדֵּן בַּיַּרְדֵּן תַּעֲמֹדוּ: פ			
3:9	וַיֹּאמֶר יְהוֹשֻׁעַ אֶל־בְּנֵי יִשְׂרָאֵל גֹּשׁוּ הֵנָּה וְשִׁמְעוּ אֶת־דִּבְרֵי יְהוָה אֱלֹהֵיכֶם:			
3:10	וַיֹּאמֶר יְהוֹשֻׁעַ בְּזֹאת תֵּדְעוּן כִּי אֵל חַי בְּקִרְבְּכֶם וְהוֹרֵשׁ יוֹרִישׁ מִפְּנֵיכֶם אֶת־הַכְּנַעֲנִי וְאֶת־הַחִתִּי וְאֶת־הַחִוִּי וְאֶת־הַפְּרִזִּי וְאֶת־הַגִּרְגָּשִׁי וְהָאֱמֹרִי וְהַיְבוּסִי:			וַיֹּאמֶר יְהוֹשֻׁעַ
3:11	הִנֵּה אֲרוֹן הַבְּרִית אֲדוֹן כָּל־הָאָרֶץ עֹבֵר לִפְנֵיכֶם בַּיַּרְדֵּן:			לִפְנֵיכֶם
3:12		וְעַתָּה קְחוּ לָכֶם שְׁנֵי עָשָׂר אִישׁ מִשִּׁבְטֵי יִשְׂרָאֵל אִישׁ־אֶחָד אִישׁ־אֶחָד לַשָּׁבֶט:		וְעַתָּה
3:13	וְהָיָה כְּנוֹחַ כַּפּוֹת רַגְלֵי הַכֹּהֲנִים נֹשְׂאֵי אֲרוֹן יְהוָה אֲדוֹן כָּל־הָאָרֶץ בְּמֵי הַיַּרְדֵּן מֵי הַיַּרְדֵּן יִכָּרֵתוּן הַמַּיִם הַיֹּרְדִים מִלְמָעְלָה וְיַעַמְדוּ נֵד אֶחָד:			מִלְמָעְלָה נֵד אֶחָד:
3:14	וַיְהִי בִּנְסֹעַ הָעָם מֵאָהֳלֵיהֶם לַעֲבֹר אֶת־הַיַּרְדֵּן וְהַכֹּהֲנִים נֹשְׂאֵי הָאָרוֹן הַבְּרִית לִפְנֵי הָעָם:			

3:15	וּכְבוֹא נֹשְׂאֵי הָאָרוֹן עַד־הַיַּרְדֵּן וְרַגְלֵי הַכֹּהֲנִים נֹשְׂאֵי הָאָרוֹן נִטְבְּלוּ בִּקְצֵה הַמָּיִם וְהַיַּרְדֵּן מָלֵא עַל־כָּל־גְּדוֹתָיו כֹּל יְמֵי קָצִיר:			כל
3:16	וַיַּעַמְדוּ הַמַּיִם הַיֹּרְדִים מִלְמַעְלָה קָמוּ נֵד־אֶחָד הַרְחֵק מְאֹד בְאָדָם הָעִיר אֲשֶׁר מִצַּד צָרְתָן וְהַיֹּרְדִים עַל יָם הָעֲרָבָה יָם־הַמֶּלַח תַּמּוּ נִכְרָתוּ וְהָעָם עָבְרוּ נֶגֶד יְרִיחוֹ:			
3:17	וַיַּעַמְדוּ הַכֹּהֲנִים נֹשְׂאֵי הָאָרוֹן בְּרִית־יְהוָה בֶּחָרָבָה בְּתוֹךְ הַיַּרְדֵּן הָכֵן וְכָל־יִשְׂרָאֵל עֹבְרִים בֶּחָרָבָה עַד אֲשֶׁר־תַּמּוּ כָּל־הַגּוֹי לַעֲבֹר אֶת־הַיַּרְדֵּן:			הָכֵן
4:1		וַיְהִי כַּאֲשֶׁר־תַּמּוּ כָל־הַגּוֹי לַעֲבוֹר אֶת־הַיַּרְדֵּן פ וַיֹּאמֶר יְהוָה אֶל־יְהוֹשֻׁעַ לֵאמֹר:		וַיְהִי
4:2		קְחוּ לָכֶם מִן־הָעָם שְׁנֵים עָשָׂר אֲנָשִׁים אִישׁ־אֶחָד אִישׁ־אֶחָד מִשָּׁבֶט:		לָכֶם שְׁנֵים עָשָׂר אִישׁ־אֶחָד
4:3		וְצַוּוּ אוֹתָם לֵאמֹר שְׂאוּ־לָכֶם מִזֶּה מִתּוֹךְ הַיַּרְדֵּן מִמַּצַּב רַגְלֵי הַכֹּהֲנִים הָכִין שְׁתֵּים־עֶשְׂרֵה אֲבָנִים וְהַעֲבַרְתֶּם אוֹתָם עִמָּכֶם וְהִנַּחְתֶּם אוֹתָם בַּמָּלוֹן אֲשֶׁר־תָּלִינוּ בוֹ הַלָּיְלָה: ס		לֵאמֹר לָכֶם מִזֶּה מִמַּצַּב רַגְלֵי הַכֹּהֲנִים

		וַיִּקְרָא יְהוֹשֻׁעַ אֶל־שְׁנֵים הֶעָשָׂר אִישׁ אֲשֶׁר הֵכִין מִבְּנֵי יִשְׂרָאֵל אִישׁ־אֶחָד אִישׁ־אֶחָד מִשָּׁבֶט׃		4:4
יְהוֹשֻׁעַ ארון אלהיכם בְּנֵי		וַיֹּאמֶר לָהֶם יְהוֹשֻׁעַ עִבְרוּ לִפְנֵי אֲרוֹן יְהוָה אֱלֹהֵיכֶם אֶל־תּוֹךְ הַיַּרְדֵּן וְהָרִימוּ לָכֶם אִישׁ אֶבֶן אַחַת עַל־שִׁכְמוֹ לְמִסְפַּר שִׁבְטֵי בְנֵי־יִשְׂרָאֵל׃		4:5
		לְמַעַן תִּהְיֶה זֹאת אוֹת בְּקִרְבְּכֶם כִּי־יִשְׁאָלוּן בְּנֵיכֶם מָחָר לֵאמֹר מָה הָאֲבָנִים הָאֵלֶּה לָכֶם׃		4:6
נִכְרְתוּ מֵי הַיַּרְדֵּן		וַאֲמַרְתֶּם לָהֶם אֲשֶׁר נִכְרְתוּ מֵימֵי הַיַּרְדֵּן מִפְּנֵי אֲרוֹן בְּרִית־יְהוָה בְּעָבְרוֹ בַּיַּרְדֵּן נִכְרְתוּ מֵי הַיַּרְדֵּן וְהָיוּ הָאֲבָנִים הָאֵלֶּה לְזִכָּרוֹן לִבְנֵי יִשְׂרָאֵל עַד־עוֹלָם׃		4:7
		וַיַּעֲשׂוּ־כֵן בְּנֵי־יִשְׂרָאֵל כַּאֲשֶׁר צִוָּה יְהוֹשֻׁעַ וַיִּשְׂאוּ שְׁתֵּי־עֶשְׂרֵה אֲבָנִים מִתּוֹךְ הַיַּרְדֵּן כַּאֲשֶׁר דִּבֶּר יְהוָה אֶל־יְהוֹשֻׁעַ לְמִסְפַּר שִׁבְטֵי בְנֵי־יִשְׂרָאֵל וַיַּעַבְרוּם עִמָּם אֶל־הַמָּלוֹן וַיַּנִּחוּם שָׁם׃		4:8

בְּתוֹךְ		וּשְׁתֵּים עֶשְׂרֵה אֲבָנִים הֵקִים יְהוֹשֻׁעַ בְּתוֹךְ הַיַּרְדֵּן תַּחַת מַצַּב רַגְלֵי הַכֹּהֲנִים נֹשְׂאֵי אֲרוֹן הַבְּרִית וַיִּהְיוּ שָׁם עַד הַיּוֹם הַזֶּה׃		4:9
בְּתוֹךְ כְּכֹל אֲשֶׁר־צִוָּה מֹשֶׁה אֶת־יְהוֹשֻׁעַ			וְהַכֹּהֲנִים נֹשְׂאֵי הָאָרוֹן עֹמְדִים בְּתוֹךְ הַיַּרְדֵּן עַד תֹּם כָּל־הַדָּבָר אֲשֶׁר־צִוָּה יְהוָה אֶת־יְהוֹשֻׁעַ לְדַבֵּר אֶל־הָעָם כְּכֹל אֲשֶׁר־צִוָּה מֹשֶׁה אֶת־יְהוֹשֻׁעַ וַיְמַהֲרוּ הָעָם וַיַּעֲבֹרוּ׃	4:10
			וַיְהִי כַּאֲשֶׁר־תַּם כָּל־הָעָם לַעֲבוֹר וַיַּעֲבֹר אֲרוֹן־יְהוָה וְהַכֹּהֲנִים לִפְנֵי הָעָם׃	4:11
			וַיַּעַבְרוּ בְּנֵי־רְאוּבֵן וּבְנֵי־גָד וַחֲצִי שֵׁבֶט הַמְנַשֶּׁה חֲמֻשִׁים לִפְנֵי בְּנֵי יִשְׂרָאֵל כַּאֲשֶׁר דִּבֶּר אֲלֵיהֶם מֹשֶׁה׃	4:12
כְּ			כְּאַרְבָּעִים אֶלֶף חֲלוּצֵי הַצָּבָא עָבְרוּ לִפְנֵי יְהוָה לַמִּלְחָמָה אֶל עַרְבוֹת יְרִיחוֹ׃ ס	4:13
			בַּיּוֹם הַהוּא גִּדַּל יְהוָה אֶת־יְהוֹשֻׁעַ בְּעֵינֵי כָּל־יִשְׂרָאֵל וַיִּרְאוּ אֹתוֹ כַּאֲשֶׁר יָרְאוּ אֶת־מֹשֶׁה כָּל־יְמֵי חַיָּיו׃ פ	4:14
	וַיֹּאמֶר יְהוָה אֶל־יְהוֹשֻׁעַ לֵאמֹר׃			4:15
	צַוֵּה אֶת־הַכֹּהֲנִים נֹשְׂאֵי אֲרוֹן הָעֵדוּת וְיַעֲלוּ מִן־הַיַּרְדֵּן׃			4:16
			וַיְצַו יְהוֹשֻׁעַ אֶת־הַכֹּהֲנִים לֵאמֹר עֲלוּ מִן־הַיַּרְדֵּן׃	4:17

4:18	וַיְהִי בַּעֲלוֹת הַכֹּהֲנִים נֹשְׂאֵי אֲרוֹן בְּרִית־יְהוָה מִתּוֹךְ הַיַּרְדֵּן נִתְּקוּ כַּפּוֹת רַגְלֵי הַכֹּהֲנִים אֶל הֶחָרָבָה וַיָּשֻׁבוּ מֵי־הַיַּרְדֵּן לִמְקוֹמָם וַיֵּלְכוּ כִתְמוֹל־שִׁלְשׁוֹם עַל־כָּל־גְּדוֹתָיו:			תּוֹךְ כַּפּוֹת
4:19	וְהָעָם עָלוּ מִן־הַיַּרְדֵּן בֶּעָשׂוֹר לַחֹדֶשׁ הָרִאשׁוֹן וַיַּחֲנוּ בַּגִּלְגָּל בִּקְצֵה מִזְרַח יְרִיחוֹ:			
4:20			וְאֵת שְׁתֵּים עֶשְׂרֵה הָאֲבָנִים הָאֵלֶּה אֲשֶׁר לָקְחוּ מִן־הַיַּרְדֵּן הֵקִים יְהוֹשֻׁעַ בַּגִּלְגָּל:	
4:21			וַיֹּאמֶר אֶל־בְּנֵי יִשְׂרָאֵל לֵאמֹר אֲשֶׁר יִשְׁאָלוּן בְּנֵיכֶם מָחָר אֶת־אֲבוֹתָם לֵאמֹר מָה הָאֲבָנִים הָאֵלֶּה:	וַיֹּאמֶר אֶל־בְּנֵי יִשְׂרָאֵל מָחָר אֶת־אֲבוֹתָם
4:22			וְהוֹדַעְתֶּם אֶת־בְּנֵיכֶם לֵאמֹר בַּיַּבָּשָׁה עָבַר יִשְׂרָאֵל אֶת־הַיַּרְדֵּן הַזֶּה:	הַזֶּה:
4:23			אֲשֶׁר־הוֹבִישׁ יְהוָה אֱלֹהֵיכֶם אֶת־מֵי הַיַּרְדֵּן מִפְּנֵיכֶם עַד־עָבְרְכֶם כַּאֲשֶׁר עָשָׂה יְהוָה אֱלֹהֵיכֶם לְיַם־ סוּף אֲשֶׁר־הוֹבִישׁ מִפָּנֵינוּ עַד־עָבְרֵנוּ: ס	
4:24			לְמַעַן דַּעַת כָּל־עַמֵּי הָאָרֶץ אֶת־יַד יְהוָה כִּי חֲזָקָה הִיא לְמַעַן יְרָאתֶם אֶת־יְהוָה אֱלֹהֵיכֶם כָּל־הַיָּמִים: ס	

δ Layer: MT pluses	γ Layer: 4:15–16, 20–24	β Layer: 3:12; 4:1–9	α Layer: 3:1–11, 13–17; 4:10–14, 17–19	THE EPISODES
3:1 (הוא וכל־בני ישׂראל), 3 (ואתם), 6 (לאמר), 7 (כי), 10 (ויאמר יהושע), 11 (לפניכם), 12 (ועתה, איש־אחד), 13 (כפות, מלמעלה, ו---, נד אחד), 14 (ויהי), 15 (כל), 16 (מאדם), 17 (הכן); 4:1 (יהי), 2 (לכם, שנים עשׂר, איש־אחד), 3 (לאמר, לכם מזה, ממצב רגלי הכהנים, ו---), 4 (איש־אחד), 5 (יהושע, ארון, אלהיכם, בני), 7 (נכרתו מי הירדן, בירדן), 9 (בתוך), 10 (תוך, ככל אשר־צוה משה את־יהושע), 11 (העם), 13 (כ), 14 (עם), 18 (הכהנים, כפות, תוך), 21 (ויאמר אל־בני ישׂראל, מחר, את־אבותם), 22 (ו---, הזה)	• The command to Joshua to tell the priests who bore the ark of the testimony to come up from the water • Setting up twelve stones for the twelve tribes at Gilgal	**• The prefiguration of the command to choose twelve men for twelve tribes** **• Joshua's calling twelve men already appointed** **• Carrying twelve stones over to the place, where they will lodge** **• The memorials in the middle of the Jordan**	• Passing over the Jordan on dry ground to Jericho and arrival to Gilgal by means of the ark, related to the conquest story • The emphasis on the holiness of the ark and cultic sanctification • The emphasis on passing over on dry ground • The exaltation of Joshua and his succession to Moses • Two and a half tribes armed for battle passing over to Jericho • The priests coming out of the Jordan • The return of the waters of the Jordan to their place	

<table>
<tr><th>δ Layer: MT pluses</th><th>γ Layer: 4:15–16, 20–24</th><th>β Layer: 3:12; 4:1–9</th><th>α Layer: 3:1–11, 13–17; 4:10–14, 17–19</th><td rowspan="3">THE EPISODES</td></tr>
<tr><td></td><td></td><td colspan="2">α + β + MT pluses inserted into α and β layers [3:1 (הוא וכל־בני ישראל), 3 (ואתם), 6 (לאמר), 7 (כי), 10 (ויאמר יהושע), 11 (לפניכם), 12 (ועתה, איש־אחד), 13 (כפות, מלמעלה, ו---, נד אחד), 14 (ויהי), 15 (כל), 16 (מאדם), 17 (הכן); 4:1 (יהי), 2 (לכם, שנים עשר, איש־אחד), 3 (לאמר, לכם מזה, ממצב רגלי הכהנים, ו---), 4 (איש־אחד), 5 (יהושע, ארון, אלהיכם, בני), 7 (נכרתו מי הירדן, בירדן), 9 (בתוך), 10 (תוך, ככל אשר־צוה משה את־יהושע), 11 (העם), 13 (כ), 14 (עם), 18 (תוך, כפות, הכהנים)]</td></tr>
<tr><td></td><td></td><td colspan="2">• Passing over the Jordan on dry ground to Jericho and arrival to Gilgal by means of the ark, related to the conquest story
• The emphasis on the holiness of the ark and cultic sanctification
• The prefiguration of command to choose twelve men for twelve tribes
• The emphasis on passing over on dry ground
• The exaltation of Joshua and his succession to Moses
• Joshua's calling twelve men already appointed
• Carrying twelve stones over to the place, where they will lodge
• The memorials in the middle of the Jordan
• Two and a half tribes armed for battle passing over to Jericho
• The priests coming out of the Jordan
• The return of the waters of the Jordan to their place</td></tr>
</table>

<table>
<tr><td>δ Layer: MT pluses</td><td>γ Layer: 4:15–16, 20–24</td><td>β Layer: 3:12; 4:1–9</td><td>α Layer: 3:1–11, 13–17; 4:10–14, 17–19</td><td rowspan="3">AMALGAMATION OF LAYERS</td></tr>
<tr><td></td><td colspan="3">α + β + γ + δ: 3:1 (הוא וכל־בני ישראל), 3 (ואתם), 6 (לאמר), 7 (כי), 10 (ויאמר יהושע), 11 (לפניכם), 12 (ועתה, איש־אחד), 13 (כפות, מלמעלה, ו־־־ נד אחד), 14 (ויהי), 15 (כל), 16 (מאדם), 17 (הכן); 4:1 (יהי), 2 (לכם, שנים עשר, איש־אחד), 3 (לאמר, לכם מזה, הכהנים רגלי ממצב, ו־־־), 4 (איש־אחד), 5 (יהושע, ארון, אלהיכם, בני), 7 (בירדן, נכרתו מי הירדן), 9 (בתוך), 10 (תוך, ככל אשר־צוה משה את־יהושע), 11 (העם), 13 (כ), 14 (עם), 18 (תוך, כפות, הכהנים), 21 (ויאמר אל־בני ישראל, מחר, את־אבותם), 22 (ו־־־, הזה).</td></tr>
<tr><td></td><td colspan="3">• Passing over the Jordan on dry ground to Jericho and arrival to Gilgal by means of the ark, related to the conquest story
• The emphasis on the holiness of the ark and cultic sanctification
• The prefiguration of command to choose twelve men for twelve tribes
• The emphasis on passing over on dry ground
• The exaltation of Joshua and his succession to Moses
• Joshua’s calling twelve men already appointed
• Carrying twelve stones over to the place, where they will lodge
• The memorials in the middle of the Jordan
• Two and a half tribes armed for battle passing over to Jericho
<u>• The command to Joshua to tell the priests who bore the ark of the testimony to come up from the water</u>
• The priests coming out of the Jordan
• The return of the waters of the Jordan to their place
<u>• Setting up twelve stones for the twelve tribes at Gilgal</u></td></tr>
</table>

* “δ” layer (MT plus): underlined bold words

Here, once again, we need to examine the results of our literary-critical analysis based on the MT through the investigation of the major words in each layer. When the distribution of major words is tabulated, it will be possible for us to distinguish more clearly the features of the layers in this narrative.

Table 15

	Layer α	Layer β	Layer γ	Layer δ	Total
the ark	11	3	1	1	16
Israel	6	6	2	2	16
the people	11	2	1	0	14
the priests	10	2	1	1	14
cross over (עבר)	12	5	3	0	20
the Jordan	14	7	4	1	26

As we see in Table 15, "the passing over (20) the Jordan (26) with the ark (16) by the priests (14) and the Israelite people (16 + 14 = 30)" is the theme of the whole narrative. We can see these words have a relatively even distribution in the "α" layer, so "α" is the basic layer of this narrative. The "β" layer, which is concerned with the carrying of twelve stones over to the other side of the Jordan and setting up twelve stones in the middle of the Jordan, also shows a regular distribution of words, although there is less interest in "the ark," "the priests," and "the people." Thus, we could say "α" and "β" are major layers of this narrative, but "β" is later. Into these basic layers, the "γ" layer, which shows interest in the ark of testimony and the twelve memorials in Gilgal, was inserted. Then, the "δ" layer, which is an MT plus, was redactionally added.

6.3.3.12. *Conclusion: Literary-Critical Analysis of Joshua 3–4 Based on the Final Shape of the MT.*

Through the literary-critical analysis, we found four layers of different materials in MT Josh 3–4.

First, the basic layer ("α") of this narrative is that which is influenced by the synoptic ark narratives in Samuel–Kings and Chronicles, that is, 2 Sam 6//1 Chr 13–16, 1 Kgs 7:51–8:11//2 Chr 5. This layer connects passing over the Jordan on dry ground to Jericho and the arrival at Gilgal by the ark with the conquest story of the land begun in ch. 1 and continued to ch. 6, as well as the exaltation of Joshua and his succession to Moses: 3:1–11, 13–17; 4:10–14, 17–19.

The first addition to this narrative is "β," which is also a basic layer influenced mainly by Deuteronomy. It shows interest in the twelve stones carried to the other side of the Jordan and set up for the twelve tribes in the middle of the Jordan: 3:12; 4:1–9.

The second addition to this basic layer is "γ," which connects this narrative with the epithet of "the ark of testimony" and Reed Sea story in Exodus: 4:15–16, 20–24.

Then, the final redactional interpolation to this complex text, "δ," is a number of pluses in the MT.

Chapter 7

CONCLUSION

7.1. *The Most Probable Literary History of Joshua 3–4*

This investigation has unearthed two different apparent literary histories, each interesting and valuable in its own right.

There seem to be five layers of different materials in Josh 3–4 based on the LXX *Vorlage*:

First, the basic layer ("a"): 3:2–11, 13–17; 4:10b–11a, 14, 17–19. This has been influenced by the synoptic materials in similar ark narratives in Samuel–Kings and Chronicles, that is, 2 Sam 6//1 Chr 13–16, 1 Kgs 7:51–8:11//2 Chr 5.

Another basic layer of this narrative, and the first addition to this narrative is "b," which shows an interest in carrying twelve stones over to the other side of the Jordan, and two and a half tribes passing over the Jordan according to Moses' command: 4:1–8, 10a, 11b, 12–13. This second layer appears to be influenced by Deuteronomy, and especially by Deut 3:18; 6:20–21; 27:1–6.

Third is the second additional layer ("c"), which is concerned with the aetiology of the twelve stones in the middle of the Jordan: 4:9.

Fourth, the third redactional insertion ("d") to this narrative is 3:1, 12.

These four layers compose the primary story of this narrative.

Fifth, to those four layers, the final redactional layers are added to connect this story with the ark narratives and Reed Sea story in Exodus: 4:15–16, 20–24.

On the other hand, there seem to be only four layers of different materials in the final shape of MT Josh 3–4:

"α" layer: 3:1–11, 13–17; 4:10–14, 17–19.

"β" layer: 3:12; 4:1–9.

"γ" layer: 4:15–16, 20–24.

"δ" layer (pluses in MT): 3:1 (הוא וכל־בני ישׂראל), 3 (ואתם), 6 (לאמר),
7 (כי), 10 (ויאמר יהושע), 11 (לפניכם), 12 (ועתה), 13 (כפות, אחד
מלמעלה ו--- נד), 15 (כל), 17 (הכן); 4:1 (יהי), 2 (לכם, שנים עשׂר, איש־אחד),

3 (ו---, ממצב רגלי הכהנים, לכמ מזה, לאמר), 5 (בני, אלהיכם, ארון, יהושע), 7 (נכרתו מי הירדן), 9 (בתוך), 10 (ככל אשר־צוה משה את־יהושע, בתוך), 13 (כ) 18 (כפות, תוך), 21 (ויאמר אל־בני ישראל), 22 (את־אבותם, מחר, הזה).

Here, we can see that the result of our investigation is rather surprising and even paradoxical. On the one side, we found five levels in the earlier Hebrew *Vorlage* of B and four levels in the later final shape of the MT. It does not seem to be a plausible situation. Yet, some could argue that just as one can identify more than one dimension and see things better with two eyes than with one, by using both the Hebrew *Vorlage* of LXX and the MT one can read the textual and literary history of each text from more than one perspective and with more accuracy. Thus, it seems more appropriate to keep an open mind regarding the textual history and the reconstruction of the literary history of this complex text of Josh 3–4 based both on the Hebrew *Vorlage* of LXX and the MT.

However, as an expert in reading these complex texts, one should be open to all possibilities and be able to question how these chapters really did develop. How can we reconstruct the stage before the MT and the LXX? Did the MT add words to it? Did the LXX *Vorlage* add words to it? Did the MT change words in it? Did the LXX *Vorlage* change words in it? Did all these things happen? Or did other things happen too? The analysis on the consequences of the literary history of the OG *Vorlage* and the MT Josh 3–4 could help to answer these questions. The results above show some differences between them. First, those layers in the OG *Vorlage* are more complex and more frequently disconnected than in the MT. On the other hand, the layers in the MT Josh 3–4 are simpler and could be read much further without severance of context; this seems to have been caused by two main differences between the LXX *Vorlage* and MT: (1) Josh 3:1, 12 belong to the fourth ("d") layer in the LXX *Vorlage*, but 3:1 to the basic layer ("α"), and 3:12 to the second layer ("β") in the MT. (2) The two stories about the twelve stones in the middle of the Jordan and on the other side of the Jordan belong to two different layers ("b," "c") in the OG *Vorlage*, but to the same layer ("β") in the MT. These differences are closely related to those many pluses and variants in the LXX *Vorlage* and the MT.

The comparison between the OG *Vorlage* and MT Josh 3–4 showed us a number of differences between them, especially many more pluses in the MT than in the OG *Vorlage*. As we have seen in 6.2, a lot of pluses and variants in the MT Josh 3–4 are rather rare and unusual in the Hebrew Bible, but almost all the pluses and variants in the OG *Vorlage* are quite common in Old Testament Hebrew. Even though there were some cases we cannot decide upon, these divergences in MT seem to have been inserted later with theological and exegetical intention, having been redactionally interpolated to solve some parallel syntactical clumsiness within a verse. Thus, it might be possible to consider that the divergences in the Hebrew *Vorlage* of the LXX are primary and original to the text of Josh 3–4, but those in the MT are secondary and were inserted later. If we pay attention to those differences between the LXX *Vorlage* and MT in 3:1, 12 and 4:9, we can understand this position more easily.

In the results of the literary-critical analysis, Josh 3:1 is at a different level in LXX *Vorlage* than it is in the MT.

LXX *Vorlage* Josh 3:1	וישכם יהושע בבקר ויסע מהשטים ויבאו עד־הירדן ( ) וילנו שם טרם יעברו:
MT Josh 3:1	וישכם יהושע בבקר ויסעו מהשטים ויבאו עד־הירדן (הוא וכל־בני ישראל) וילנו שם טרם יעברו:

The lodging of one night in Josh 3:1 after three days of spying in ch. 2 cuts off the stream of "three days" from 1:11 to 3:2. The change of the subject from third person singular into plural makes the syntax of this verse clumsier. In addition, it is not clear who is the subject of the plural form of ויבאו---וילנו in LXX *Vorlage* Josh 3:1. These problems seem to be caused by the insertion of this verse by one of the final editors ("d" layer) to stress the diligence of Joshua and the realization of the divine promise on crossing the Jordan. The first scribe of B, who also regarded this verse as a separate and independent paragraph, appears to support this position.

The final editor of the MT seems to have tried to solve this problem by changing ויסע in the OG *Vorlage* into ויסעו and by putting in הוא וכל־בני ישראל. By these variations, the MT editor attempts to solve the awkwardness of the syntax of LXX *Vorlage* 3:1, where only Joshua "set out" from Shittim and ambiguous plural, "people," go to the Jordan. Moreover, the insertion of the phrase הוא וכל־בני ישראל also solves the problem of the dislocation and isolation of this verse. Even though הוא וכל־בני ישראל is a rare expression in the Hebrew Bible, (כל־)בני ישראל is a basic expression which appears in similar synoptic ark texts (1 Kgs 8:3//2 Chr 5:4; 1 Kgs 8:9//2 Chr 5:10). This plus (כל־)בני ישראל connects this verse with the same expression in Josh 3:9, 12 and with the basic layer of this narrative ("α" layer).

The command to take twelve men from the tribes of Israel (3:12) breaks the context between 3:11 and 3:13. This verse is a later insertion. If we compare the LXX *Vorlage* Josh 3:12 and 4:2, we can see that 3:12 is a different layer from 4:1–8.

LXX *Vorlage* Josh 3:12	קחו לכם שׁני עשׂר איש מבני ישראל איש־אחד לשבט:
LXX *Vorlage* Josh 4:2	קחו מן־העם אנשים איש־אחד משבט:

LXX *Vorlage* Josh 3:12 includes additional words (לכם, שׁני עשׂר) and shows a different style from 4:2. This verse (3:12) is a later insertion, which was added to this section by an editor in order to connect the contents of chs. 3 and 4. However, an MT editor who noted this break has tried to connect these two verses.

MT Josh 3:12	קחו לכם שׁני עשׂר איש מבני ישראל איש־אחד (איש־אחד) לשבט:
MT Josh 4:2	קחו (לכם) מן־העם (שׁנים עשׂר) אנשים איש־אחד (איש־אחד) משבט:

Unlike LXX Josh 3:12 and 4:2, MT Josh 3:12 and 4:2 show a rather similar style and structure. An MT editor has interpolated some words into both verses to sort out the differences between them. With the help of pluses in MT, 3:12 belongs to the same layer as 4:1–8 ("β").

The differences between the LXX *Vorlage* and MT Josh 4:9 explain the opposite cases:

LXX *Vorlage* Josh 4:9	ושתים עשׂרה אבנים (אחרות) הקים יהושע בו בירדן תחת מצברגלי הכהנים נשׂאי ארון ברית (יהוה) ויהיו שׁם עד היום הזה:
MT Josh 4:9	ושתים עשׂרה אבנים ( ) הקים יהושע בתוך הירדן תחת מצברגלי הכהנים נשׂאי ארון הברית ( ) ויהיו שׁם עד היום הזה:

As already stated in Chapter 3, it does not seem possible that the original story had two sets of twelve stones. Joshua 4:9 appears to have been inserted later to stress the cutting off of the waters and dry ground in the middle of the Jordan in connection with the twelve-stone story on the other side of the Jordan. In this sense, LXX *Vorlage* Josh 4:9, which represents אחרות, seems to be primary and makes a clear distinction between the twelve stones on the other side of the Jordan and in the middle of the Jordan. As we have seen in section 6.2, even though there are some uncertain cases that cannot be judged, the pluses and variants in the OG *Vorlage* are quite common expressions in the Old Testament and appear to be primary and earlier than those in MT. ἄλλους is used quite often in the Old Testament and also occurs in synoptic texts of Samuel–Kings and Chronicles (1 Kgs 9:6//2 Chr 7:19; 1 Kgs 9:9//2 Chr 7:22; 2 Kgs 22:17//2 Chr 34:25) to warn Israel against forsaking Yahweh and serving other gods. In other biblical texts, it appears mainly in similar situations to warn Israel or prevent Israel against sinning by serving other gods (Exod 20:3; 34:14; Deut 5:7; 6:14; 7:4; 8:19; 11:16, 28; 13:2 [3], 6 [7], 13 [14]; 17:3; 18:20; 28:14, 36, 64; 29:26 [25]; 30:17; 31:18, 20;

Josh 23:16; 24:2, 16; Judg 2:12, 17, 19; 10:13; 1 Sam 8:8; 11:4, 10; 14:9; 19:21; 26:19; 28:8; 2 Kgs 17:7, 35, 37, 38; 2 Chr 28:25; 34:25; Jer 1:16; 7:6, 9, 18; 11:10; 13:10; 16:11, 13; 19:4; 22:9; 25:6; 35:15; 44:3, 5, 8, 15; Hos 3:1; cf. Num 14:24). Thus, this word (ἄλλους) automatically reminds Israel of the first commandment in Exod 20:3 and Deut 5:7: "You shall have no other gods before me." In the book of Joshua too, this word was used in the negative context to warn Israel's guilty against serving other gods: Josh 23:16; 24:2, 16. Thus, the words אבנים אחרות in LXX *Vorlage* Josh 4:9 can remind the Israelite readers of these negative meanings, just as the other altar near the Jordan, set up by the Transjordanian tribes in Josh 22:10–34, did for the people of Israel. Therefore, an MT editor might have eliminated this word (אחרות) exegetically and bestowed the same authority to the stones in the middle of the Jordan as the stones on the other side of the Jordan, in order to read this verse without discontinuity.

The next example, יהוה, supports this position. The LXX *Vorlage* Josh 4:9 represents יהוה, but the MT does not. As we have seen in Chapter 4, the epithet ארון ברית יהוה in LXX *Vorlage* 4:9 is a basic expression which occurs in 1 Kgs 8:1//2 Chr 5:2 (BTH). ארון הברית in MT Josh 4:9 is a variation of the basic expression. In this case, MT seems to have removed יהוה from ארון ברית יהוה, considering the negative meaning of אחרות, sinning against יהוה in LXX *Vorlage* 4:9.

Thus, we can now try to suggest the most probable literary history of Josh 3–4 and name the layers in the context of existing scholarly research.

The basic layer of this narrative was LXX *Vorlage* Josh 3:2–11, 13–17; 4:10b–11a, 14, 17–19, which was influenced by the shared material of Samuel–Kings and Chronicles (BTH).

Into this basic layer, the twelve-stone story on the other side of the Jordan and the two and half tribes story in LXX *Vorlage* Josh 4:1–8, 10a, 11b, 12–13, which is influenced by Deuteronomy, and especially by Deut 3:18; 6:20–21; 27:1–6, is added. This layer could possibly be a Deuteronomic addition to the narrative.

The third layer in this narrative is LXX *Vorlage* Josh 4:9, which emphasizes the dry ground in the middle of the Jordan.

The fourth layer of this narrative is LXX *Vorlage* Josh 3:1, 12 which highlights the diligence of Joshua and the realization of the divine promise to cross the Jordan, and connects Josh 3 with Josh 4.

The fifth layer (LXX *Vorlage* Josh 4:15–16, 20–24) was added to link this narrative with Exodus. This seems to be a probable Priestly addition.

At the final stage, an MT editor tried to solve the clumsiness and disconnection in context by deleting such expressions in LXX *Vorlage* as

אחרות and יהוה in 4:9, by changing such words as ויסע in the OG *Vorlage* into ויסעו, and by adding such words into LXX *Vorlage* as איש־אחד in MT Josh 3:12 and איש־אחד, שנים עשׂר, לכם in MT Josh 4:2. This made the final shape of MT Josh 3–4 much simpler and helped to solve the discontinuity of context and decreased the complexity of this narrative.

7.2. *Polzin, the Textual and Literary History, and* MT *Pluses in Joshua 3–4*

Through the study of the textual history of the OG *Vorlage* and the MT of Josh 3–4, we find some indicators that the former seems to be prior to the latter. However, at least without much firmer evidence, it is more prudent to reconstruct the literary history of Josh 3–4 based on both the OG *Vorlage* and the MT. In addition, with the help of the study of the literary history of this complex narrative based on the Hebrew *Vorlage* of LXX, it is possible to find five layers of different materials in Josh 3–4, and based on the MT, four layers of different materials.

However, by not paying attention to the textual and literary history of both the LXX *Vorlage* and the MT, but by reading only from the final form of the MT, Polzin demonstrates a limited reading and understanding of this complex narrative.

One of the weaknesses of Polzin's understanding is his failure to consider that certain words and phrases are, in fact, MT pluses. These warrant closer attention.

According to Polzin, "the ritual nature" of Josh 3:1–5:1 allows the so-called Deuteronomist to construct a highly intricate and amazingly precise compositional structure. He holds that this narrative is a well-programmed and stylized literary unity on *a cultic procession* that interconnects the various surface points of view of the story to a degree that approaches geometric precision.[1] However, a deeper analysis of the passage and "cultic narrative" is necessary in order to render a proper understanding. Many scholars, including Soggin,[2] tried to connect this narrative with the spring festival in Gilgal by means of linking the phrases "the sons of Israel camped in Gilgal" (ויחנו בני־ישראל בגלגל) in 5:10 and ממחרת הפסח in v. 11. However, these are MT pluses.[3] Thus, his attempt to understand Josh 3–4 in connection with cultic performances only from the perspective of the MT seems problematic.

1. Polzin, *Moses and the Deuteronomist*, 94.
2. Soggin, *Joshua*, 66.
3. Auld, *Joshua Retold*, 12–13.

Maintaining that the chronological discrepancy between 3:2 and 4:19 is not a "crucial problem," and does not play a "key role," Polzin insists that it is not worthwhile to invest hermeneutic energy in this question.[4] However, his point stands at variance to the text. He regards the event of crossing the Jordan as a cultic procession based on the chronological contents in this narrative and pluses in 5:10–11. Problematically, he seeks to read only the final form of the MT of this narrative as a literary unity without noticing the problems behind the text.

According to him, 3:12 and 4:11 are also "literary signals" that create temporal shifts in order to highlight those two events, the setting up of the twelve stones (4:1–8) and the coming up of the priests (4:15–18).[5] However, a closer analysis of the Hebrew text reveals a different picture. Joshua 3:12 seems to be connected with the twelve stones set up on the other side of the Jordan in 4:1–8, especially 4:2. However, if we consider the literary history of Josh 3–4, we can see that 3:12 and 4:2 are from different material. Although 3:12 and 4:2 have an almost identical word order and sentence structure, the words לכם and שנים עשר, in 4:2 appear only in the MT and איש־אחד in a few manuscripts. Thus, even though Polzin, with the help of Russian literary theory, holds that this is a shift in temporal point of view, 3:12 appears to be a redactional addition, using the story of 4:1–8 to connect the contents of chs. 3 and 4. Similarly, an MT editor tried to solve these problems between 3:12 and 4:2 by MT pluses in 4:2. His argument that 4:11 is literary anticipation is also a little problematic. The OG *Vorlage* represents והאבנים instead of והכהנים and לפניהם instead of לפני העם. By following only the MT, Polzin's contention that 4:11 foreshadows 4:15–18, thereby emphasizing the coming up of "the priests," is not plausible.

His attempt to explain the inconsistencies in Josh 3–4 regarding the shift of the narrator's spatial point of view is problematic in that it ignores the textual and literary history of this narrative. According to Polzin, in 3:1–4:14 the narrator "took his narrating position from the point of view of the Israelites entering the land, but then in 4:15–5:1 takes his perspective from the point of view of a non-Israelite watching the progress of this miraculous procession."[6] For this purpose, he especially focuses on the second episode of 4:1–8. Noticing the threefold indication, "from here," "from the middle of the Jordan," and "where the priests' feet stand firm," Polzin asserts that, although it is not clear where Yahweh is while speaking to Joshua in 4:3, Joshua and the twelve men

4. Polzin, *Moses and the Deuteronomist*, 91–92.
5. Ibid., 97.
6. Ibid., 101.

should be together with the priests, where he should command the men to carry the twelve stones to the camp.[7] However, if we look closely at the Hebrew *Vorlage* of the LXX and the MT, here לכם מזה and ממצב רגלי הכהנים are MT pluses. Thus, by following only the MT, his assertion that Joshua is in the middle of the Jordan and with the priests in 4:3 is rendered implausible. He commits a similar error in 4:5. He insists that in 4:5 Joshua is giving orders to the twelve men on the western side of the Jordan, but here יהושע, ארון, אלהיכם are MT pluses and the OG *Vorlage* represents one more לפני. Thus, in the verse where Yahweh gives the order, it is difficult to believe that Polzin understands this verse correctly, thereby casting doubt on his assertions regarding the location of the characters. In addition, a careful reading of 4:10b–11 reveals that until all that Moses commanded was completed, the priests stood firm and the people crossed in a hurry after the completion of them. Although it appears in 4:1–8 that the people are already on the western side of the river, in 4:10b–11a they are in the middle of the Jordan with the priests while the commands are carried out. Furthermore, as we noticed above, the OG *Vorlage* represents והאבנים instead of והכהנים and לפניהם instead of לפני העם. Therefore, his attempt to solve the discrepancies between these two parts from a spatial point of view by reading only from the MT is problematic.

In conclusion, we find that Polzin's attempt to read this narrative only from the final shape of the MT is limited in that he does not pay attention to the textual and literary history of Josh 3–4, at least, in that he does not properly consider a lot of the pluses in the MT.

7. Ibid., 99–100.

BIBLIOGRAPHY

Ackroyd, P. R. *The First Book of Samuel*. CBC. Cambridge: Cambridge University Press, 1967.

———. "History and Theology in the Writings of the Chronicler." *CTM* 38 (1967): 501–15.

Ahlström, G. W. "The Travels of the Ark: A Religio-Political Composition." *JNES* 43 (1984): 141–49.

Auld, A. G. "1 and 2 Samuel." Pages 213–45 in *Eerdmans Commentary on the Bible*. Edited by J. D. G. Dunn and J. W. Rogerson. Grand Rapids: Eerdmans, 2003.

———. *I & II Samuel*. OTL. Louisville: Westminster John Knox, 2011.

———. "The Deuteronomist and the Former Prophets, or What Makes the Former Prophets Deuteronomistic?" Pages 116–26 in Schearing and McKenzie, eds., *Those Elusive Deuteronomists*.

———. "The Deuteronomist Between History and Theology." Pages 353–67 in *Congress Volume: Oslo, 1998*. Edited by A. Lemaire. Leiden: Brill, 2000.

———. "The Former Prophets." Pages 53–68 in McKenzie and Graham, eds., *The Hebrew Bible*.

———. *Joshua: Jesus Son of Nauē in Codex Vaticanus*. Septuagint Commentary Series. Leiden: Brill, 2005.

———. *Joshua, Judges and Ruth*. Daily Study Bible. Edinburgh: St. Andrew's Press, 1984.

———. *Joshua, Moses and the Land: Tetrateuch–Pentateuch–Hexateuch in a Generation of Study Since 1938*. Edinburgh: T. & T. Clark, 1980.

———. *Joshua Retold: Synoptic Perspectives*. Edinburgh: T. & T. Clark, 1998.

———. *Kings Without Privilege: David and Moses in the Story of the Bible's Kings*. Edinburgh: T. & T. Clark, 1994.

———. Review of M. N. Van der Meer, *Formulation and Reformulation*. *JSJ* 36 (2005): 133–35.

———. "Samuel, Numbers, and the Yahwist-Question." Pages 233–46 in Gertz, Schmid and Witte, eds., *Abschied vom Jahwisten*.

———. *Samuel at the Threshold: Selected Works of Graeme Auld*. SOTSMS. Burlington: Ashgate.

———. "Studies in Joshua: Text and Literary Relations." Ph.D. diss., University of Edinburgh, 1976.

———. What if the Chronicler Did Use the Deuteronomistic History?" Pages 141–50 in *Samuel at the Threshold*.

———. "What Was the Main Source of the Books of Chronicles?" Pages 91–99 in Graham and McKenzie, eds., *The Chronicler as Author*.

Beek, M. A. "The Meaning of the Expression 'The Chariots and the Horsemen of Israel.'" *OTS* 17 (1971): 1–10.

Begg, C. T. "The Ark in Chronicles." Pages 133–45 in *The Chronicler as Theologian: Essays in Honor of Ralph W. Klein*. Edited by M. P. Graham et al. London: T&T Clark International, 2003.

Bieberstein, K. *Joshua–Jordan–Jericho. Archäologie, Geschichte und Theologie der Landnahmeerzählungen Josua 1–6*. OBO 143. Freiburg: Universitätsverlag, 1995.

Blenkinsopp, J. *The Role of Gibeon and the Gibeonites in the Political and Religious History of Early Israel*. Society for Old Testament Study Monograph Series 2. Cambridge: Cambridge University Press, 1972.

Boling, R. G., and G. E. Wright. *Joshua*. AB 6. New York: Doubleday, 1982.

Butler, T. C. *Joshua*. WBC 7. Waco: Word, 1983.

Campbell, A. F. *2 Samuel*. FOTL 8. Grand Rapids: Eerdmans, 2005.

———. *The Ark Narrative (1 Sam 4–6; 2 Sam 6): A Form-Critical and Traditio-Historical Study*. Missoula: Scholars Press, 1975.

———. *Samuel*. FOTL 7. Grand Rapids: Eerdmans, 2003.

Childs, B. S. "The Ark of the Covenant in Joshua: A Probe into the History of Tradition." *HAR* 9 (1985): 137–57.

———. "Deuteronomic Formulae of the Exodus Traditions." Pages 30–39 in *Hebräische Wortforschung: Festschrift zum 80. Geburtstag von Walter Baumgartner*. Edited by B. Hartmann et al. VTSup 16. Leiden: Brill, 1967.

———. *Exodus*. OTL. London: SCM, 1974.

———. *Numbers*. FOTL 4. Grand Rapids: Eerdmans, 2005.

———. "The Song of the Sea." *CBQ* 31 (1969): 1–17.

———. "A Traditio-Historical Character of the Reed Sea Tradition." *VT* 20 (1970): 406–18.

———. "The Wilderness Itinerary." *CBQ* 34 (1972): 135–52.

Cody, A. *A History of Old Testament Priesthood*. Rome: Pontifical Biblical Institute, 1969.

Coggins, R. J. Review of A. G. Auld, *Kings Without Privilege*. *Theology* 98 (1995): 383.

Cooke, G. A. *The Book of Joshua*. The Cambridge Bible. Cambridge: Cambridge University Press, 1918.

Cross, F. M. *Canaanite Myth and Hebrew Epic: Essays in the History of the Religion of Israel*. Cambridge, Mass.: Harvard University Press, 1973.

———. "The History of the Biblical Text in the Light of Discoveries in the Judaean Desert." *HTR* 57 (1964): 281–99.

———. "The Priestly Tabernacle." *BAR* 1 (1961): 201–28.

Cross, F. M., D. W. Parry, R. J. Saley, and E. Ulrich. *Discoveries in the Judean Desert XVII: Qumran Cave 4 XII 1–2 Samuel*. Oxford: Clarendon, 2005.

Davies, G. H. "The Ark of the Covenant." *ASTI* 5 (1967): 30–47.

Davis, M. T. Review of R. Polzin, *Samuel and the Deuteronomist*. *Theology Today* 46 (1990): 458–60.

De Pury, A., T. Römer and J.-D. Macchi, eds. *Israel Constructs Its History: Deuteronomistic Historiography in Recent Research*. JSOTSup 306. Sheffield: Sheffield Academic, 2000. Originally published as *Israël construit son histoire: L'historiographie deutéronomiste à la lumière des recherches écentes*. Le Monde de la Bible 34. Geneva: Labor et Fides, 1996.

De Vries, S. J. *1 and 2 Chronicles*. FOTL 11. Grand Rapids: Eerdmans, 1989.
———. *1 Kings*. WBC 12. Waco: Word, 1985.
De Wette, W. M. L. *Beiträge zur Einleitung in das Alten Testament*. 2 vols. Halle: Schimmelpfenning, 1806.
Dietrich, W. *David, Saul und die Propheten*. BWANT 7/2. Stuttgart: Kohlhammer, 1987.
———. *Prophetie und Geschichte: Eine redaktionsgeschichte Untersuchung zum deuteronomistischen Geschichtswerk*. FRLANT 108. Göttingen: Vandenhoeck & Ruprecht, 1972.
Driver, S. R. *An Introduction to the Literature of the Old Testament*. 9th ed. Edinburgh: T. & T. Clark, 1913 (1891).
Dus, J. "Die Analyse zweier Ladeerzählungen des Josuabuches (Jos 3–4 und 6)." *ZAW* 72 (1960): 106–34.
Edelman, D. Review of R. Polzin, *Samuel and the Deuteronomist*. *JNES* 52 (1993): 306–8.
Eichhorn, J. G. *Einleitung in das Alte Testament*. 2d ed. 3 vols. Leipzig: Weidmanns, Erben & Reich, 1787.
Eissfeldt, O. *Hexateuch-Synopse*. Leipzig: Hinrichs, 1922.
Fokkelman, J. P. *Narrative Art and Poetry in the Books of Samuel*, vols. 2 and 4. SSN 20. Assen: Van Gorcum, 1986, 1993.
Fritz, V. *Das Buch Josua*. HAT 1/7. Tübingen: Mohr–Siebeck, 1994.
Gertz, J. C., K. Schmid and M. Witte, eds. *Abschied vom Jahwisten*. BZAW 315. Berlin: de Gruyter, 2002.
Gibson, J. C. L. *Davidson's Introductory Hebrew Grammar: Syntax*. Edinburgh: T. & T. Clark, 1994.
Gray, J. *I & II Kings: A Commentary*. 2d ed. OTL. London: SCM, 1970.
———. *Joshua, Judges and Ruth*. 2d ed. NCBC. London: Marshall, Morgan & Scott, 1986.
Greenspoon, L. J. *Textual Studies in the Book of Joshua*. HSM 28. Chico: Scholars Press, 1983.
Hasel, G. F. "Books of Chronicles." Pages 666–73 in *The International Standard Bible Encyclopedia*. Vol. 1, *A–D*. Edited by G. W. Bromiley. Grand Rapids: Eerdmans, 1979.
Hawk, L. D. *Every Promise Fulfilled: Contesting Plots in Joshua*. Literary Currents in Biblical Interpretation. Louisville: Westminster John Knox, 1991.
Hobbs, T. R. *2 Kings*. WBC 13. Waco: Word, 1985.
Holmes, S. *Joshua, the Hebrew and Greek Texts*. Cambridge: Cambridge University Press, 1914.
Japhet, S. *I &II Chronicles*. OTL. London: SCM, 1993.
———. *The Ideology of the Book of Chronicles and Its Place in Biblical Thought*. 2d ed. BEATAJ 9. Frankfurt am Main: Lang, 1997 (1989).
Jobling, D. Review of R. Polzin, *Samuel and the Deuteronomist*. *Interpretation* 44 (1990): 416.
Johnson, B. L. Review of R. Polzin, *Samuel and the Deuteronomist*. *WTJ* 54 (1992): 368–70.
Johnstone, W. Review of A. G. Auld, *Kings Without Privilege*. *SJT* 50 (1997): 256–58.
Kang, S. M. *Divine War in the Old Testament and in the Ancient Near East*. BZAW 177. Berlin: de Gruyter, 1989.
Kautzsch. E., and A. E. Cowley, eds. *Gesenius' Hebrew Grammar*. Oxford: Clarendon, 1909.

Keating, J. Review of R. Polzin, *Samuel and the Deuteronomist*. *Faith and Mission* 7 (1989): 89–90.
Keller, C. A. "Über einige alttestamentliche Heiligtumslegenden." *ZAW* 68 (1956): 85–97.
Kenyon, K. *Digging Up Jerusalem*. London: Benn, 1974.
Kittel, R. *Geschichte des Volkes Israel*, vol. 2. 6th ed. Stuttgart: Kohlhammer, 1925.
Klein, R. W. *1 Samuel*. WBC 10. Waco: Word, 1983.
———. *II Samuel*. WBC 11. Waco: Word, 1989.
Knoppers, G. N. *I Chronicles*. 2 vols. AB 12A and 12B. New York: Doubleday, 2004.
———. "Hierodules, Priest, or Janitors? The Levites in Chronicles and the History of the Israelite Priesthood." *JBL* 118 (1999): 49–72.
———. *Two Nations Under God: The Deuteronomic History of Solomon and the Dual Monarchies*. 2 vols. HSM 52–53. Atlanta: Scholars Press, 1993–94.
Kucova, L. "Common Source Theory and Composition of the Story of the Divided Monarchy in Kings with Special Emphasis on the Account of Josiah's Reform." Ph.D. diss., University of Edinburgh, 2005.
Langlamet, F. *Gilgal et les récits de la traversée du Jourdain*. Cahiers de la Revue Biblique. Paris: Gabalda, 1969.
Lemke, W. E. "The Synoptic Problem in the Chronicler's History." *HTR* 58 (1964): 349–63.
———. "Synoptic Studies in the Chronicler's History." PhD diss., Harvard University, 1963.
Leuchter, M., and J. M. Hutton, eds. *Levites and Priests in Biblical History and Tradition*. SBL 9. Atlanta: Society of Biblical Literature, 2011.
Long, B. O. *1 Kings with an Introduction to Historical Literature*. FOTL 9. Grand Rapids: Eerdmans, 1984.
———. *2 Kings*. FOTL 10. Grand Rapids: Eerdmans, 1991.
Macy, H. R. "The Sources of the Books of Chronicles: A Reassessment." Ph.D. diss., Harvard University, 1975.
Margolis, M. L., ed. *The Book of Joshua in Greek According to the Critically Restored Text with an Apparatus Containing the Variants of the Principal Recensions and of the Individual Witnesses*. Part 1–4, *Joshua 1:1–19:38*. Publications of the Alexander Kohut Memorial Foundation in Trust at the American Academy for Jewish Research. Paris, 1931–38.
Mazor, L. "A Nomistic Re-Working of the Jericho Conquest Narrative Reflected in LXX to Joshua 6:1–20." *Textus* 18 (1995): 47–62.
McCarter, P. K., Jr. *I Samuel*. AB 8. New York: Doubleday, 1980.
———. *II Samuel*. AB 9 New York: Doubleday, 1984.
McKenzie, S. L. *1–2 Chronicles*. Nashville: Abingdon, 2004.
———. "The Books of Kings in the Deuteronomistic History." Pages 280–307 in *The History of Israel's Traditions: The Heritage of Martin Noth*. Edited by S. L. McKenzie and M. P. Graham. JSOTSup 182. Sheffield: Sheffield Academic, 1994.
———. "Cette royauté qui fait problème." Pages 267–95 in de Pury, Römer and Macchi, eds., *Israël construit son histoire*.
———. "The Chronicler as Redactor." Pages 70–90 in *The Chronicler as Author: Studies in Text and Texture*. Edited by M. P. Graham and S. L. McKenzie. JSOTSup 263. Sheffield: Sheffield Academic, 1999.
———. *The Chronicler's Use of the Deuteronomistic History*. HSM 33. Atlanta: Scholars Press, 1985.

———. "The Divided Kingdom in the Deuteronomistic History and in Scholarship on It." Pages 135–45 in Römer, ed., *The Future of the Deuteronomistic History*.

———. "Mizpah of Benjamin and the Date of the Deuteronomistic History. " Pages 149–55 in, eds., *"Lasset uns Brücken bauen ...": Collected Communications to the XVth Congress of the International Organization for the Study of the Old Testament, Cambridge 1995*. Edited by K. Schunck and M. Augustin. BEATAJ 42. Frankfurt am Main: Lang, 1998.

———. "Postscript: The Laws of Physics and Pan-Deuteronomism." Pages 262–71 in Schearing and McKenzie, eds., *Those Elusive Deuteronomists*.

———. *The Trouble with Kings: The Composition of the Book of Kings in the Deuteronomistic History*. VTSup 42. Leiden: Brill, 1991.

McKenzie, S. L., and W. P. Graham, eds. *The Hebrew Bible*. Louisville: Westminster John Knox, 1998.

Min, K. J. *The Levitical Authorship of Ezra–Nehemiah*. JSOTSup 409. London: T&T Clark International, 2004.

Mitchell, Gordon. *Together in the Land: A Reading of the Book of Joshua*. JSOTSup 134. Sheffield: JSOT, 1993.

Moatti-Fine, J. *Jésus (Josué). Traduction du texte grec de la Septante, Introduction et notes*. La Bible d'Alexandrie 6. Paris: Eisenbrauns, 1996.

Morgenstern, J. "The Ark, the Ephod and the 'Tent of Meeting.'" *HUCA* 17 (1942–43): 153–266.

Nelson, R. D. *The Double Redaction of the Deuteronomistic History*. Sheffield: JSOT, 1981.

———. *Joshua*. OTL. Westminster: John Knox, 1997.

Noth, M. *Das Buch Josua*. 2d ed. HAT 1/7. Tübingen: J. C. B. Mohr, 1938. 2d ed. 1953.

———. *The Chronicler's History*. Translated by H. G. M. Williamson with an introduction. JSOTSup 50. Sheffield: Sheffield Academic, 1987. Originally published as the second part of *Überlieferungsgeschichtliche Studien: Die sammelnden und bearbeiten Geschichtswerke im Alten Testament*. Halle: Niemeyer, 1943.

———. *Das vierte Buch Moses, Numeri*. ATD 7. Göttingen, 1966.

———. *Das zweite Buch Mose: Exodus*. ATD 5. Göttingen: Vandenhoeck & Ruprecht, 1973.

Otto, E. *Das Mazzotfest in Gilgal*. BWANT 107. Stuttgart: Kohlhammer, 1973.

Peckham, B. "The Composition of Joshua 3–4." *CBQ* 46 (1984): 413–31.

———. *The Composition of the Deuteronomistic History*. Atlanta: Scholars Press, 1985.

Peltonen, K. *History Debated: The Historical Reliability of Chronicles in Pre-Critical and Critical Research*. 2 vols. Publications of the Finnish Exegetical Society 64. Göttingen: Vandenhoeck & Ruprecht, 1996.

Pisano, S. J. *Additions or Omissions in the Books of Samuel: The Significant Pluses and Minuses in the Massoretic, LXX and Qumran Texts*. OBO 57. Freiburg, Switzerland: Universitätsverlag, 1984.

Pitkänen, P. M. A. *Joshua*. AOTC 6. Nottingham: Apollos, 2010.

Polzin, R. M. "Curses and Kings: A Reading of 2 Samuel 15–16." Pages 201–26 in *The New Literary Criticism and the Hebrew Bible*. Edited by J. C. Exum and D. J. A. Clines. JSOTSup 43. Sheffield: JSOT, 1993.

———. *David and the Deuteronomist: A Literary Study of the Deuteronomistic History*. Bloomington: Indiana University Press, 1993.

———. *Moses and the Deuteronomist: A Literary Study of the Deuteronomistic History*. New York: Seabury, 1980.
———. *Samuel and the Deuteronomist: A Literary Study of the Deuteronomistic History*. San Francisco: Harper & Row, 1989.
Porter, J. R. "Old Testament Historiography" Pages 125–62 in *Tradition and Interpretation: Essays by Members of the Society for Old Testament Study*. Edited by G. W. Anderson. Oxford: Clarendon, 1979.
Propp, W. H. C. *Exodus 1–18: A New Translation with Introduction and Commentary*. AB 2. New York: Doubleday, 1988.
Rad, G. von. *Deuteronomy*. OTL. London: SCM, 1966.
———. *Holy War in Ancient Israel*. Grand Rapids: Eerdmans, 1991.
———. *Old Testament Theology*. Vol. 1, *The Theology of Israel's Historical Traditions*. Translated by D. M. G. Stalker. New York: Harper & Row, 1962.
———. *Studies in Deuteronomy*. London: SCM, 1953.
———. "The Tent and the Ark." Pages 103–24 in *The Problem of the Hexateuch and Other Essays*. New York: McGraw-Hill, 1966.
Rahlfs, A., ed. *Septuaginta. Id est Vetus Testamentum graece iuxta LXX interpretes*. Stuttgart: Privilegierte Württemberg Bibelanstal, 1935.
Rezetko, R. C. "Dating Biblical Hebrew: Evidence from Samuel–Kings and Chronicles." Pages 215–50 in *Biblical Hebrew: Studies in Chronology and Typology*. Edited by I. Young. JSOTSup 369. London: T&T Clark International, 2003.
———. "Source and Revision in the Narratives of David's Transfer of the Ark: Text, Language and Story in 2 Samuel 6 and 1 Chronicles 13, 15–16." Ph.D. diss., University of Edinburgh, 2004.
Rofé, A. "The Classification of the Prophetical Stories." *JBL* 89 (1970): 427–40.
Römer, T., ed. *The Future of the Deuteronomistic History*. BETL 147. Leuven: Leuven University Press, 2000.
Rose, M. "Name of God in the OT." *ABD* 4:1001–11.
Rost, L. *The Succession to the Throne of David*. Translated by M. D. Rutter and D. M. Gunn. Historic Texts and Interpreters in Biblical Scholarship 1. Sheffield: Almond, 1982.
———. *Die Überlieferung von der Thronnachfolge Davids*. BWANT 3/6. Stuttgart: Kohlhammer, 1926.
Rottzoll, D. U. *Abraham Ibn Esras Langer Kommentar zum Buch Exodus 1*. Berlin: de Gruyter, 2000.
Rudolph, W. *Der "Elohist" von Exodus bis Josua*. BZAW 68. Berlin: Töpelmann, 1938.
Saydon, P. P. "The Crossing of the Jordan, Josue 3 and 4." *CBQ* 12 (1950): 194–207.
Schearing, L. S., and S. L. McKenzie, eds. *Those Elusive Deuteronomists: The Phenomenon of Pan-Deuteronomism*. JSOTSup 268. Sheffield: Sheffield Academic, 1999.
Schicklberger, F. *Die Ladeerzählungen des ersten Samuelbuches: eine literaturwissenschaftliche und theologiegeschichtliche Untersuchung*. Würzburg: Echter, 1973.
Seebass, H. *Numeri*. BKAT 4/1. Lieferung 1. Neukirchen–Vluyn: Neukirchener Verlag, 1993.
Seow, C. L. "Ark of the Covenant." *ABD* 1:386–93.

Sipilä, S. *Between Literalness and Freedom: Translation Technique in the Septuagint of Joshua and Judges Regarding the Clause Connections Introduced by* ו *and* כי. Publications of the Finnish Exegetical Society 75. Göttingen: Vandenhoeck & Ruprecht, 1999.

———. "The Septuagint Version of Joshua 3–4." Pages 63–71 in *VII Congress of the International Organization for Septuagint and Cognate Studies: Leuven 1989*. Edited by C. E. Cox. Society of Biblical Literature Septuagint and Cognate Studies Series 31. Atlanta: Scholars Press, 1991.

Smelik, K. A. D. "The Ark Narrative Reconsidered." Pages 128–44 in *New Avenues in the Study of the Old Testament*. Edited by A. S. van der Woude. Leiden: Brill, 1989.

Smend, R., Jr. "Das Gesetz und die Völker. Ein 'Beitrag zur deuteronomistischen Redaktionsgeschichte.'" Pages 494–509 in *Probleme biblischer Theologie. Gerhard von Rad zum 70. Geburtstag*. Edited by H. W. Wolff. Munich: Kaiser, 1971.

———. *Die Entstehung des Alten Testaments*. Stuttgart: Kohlhammer, 1981.

Soggin, J. A. *Joshua*. 2d ed. OTL. London: SCM, 1982.

Steussy, M. J. *David: Biblical Portraits of Power*. Studies on Personalities of the Old Testament. Columbia: University of South Carolina Press, 1999.

Stipp, H.-J. "Textkritik Literarkritik Textentwicklung. Überlegungen zurexegetischen Aspektsystematik." *ETL* 66 (1990): 143–59.

Svensson, J. *Towns and Toponyms in the Old Testament, with Special Emphasis on Joshua 14–21*. CB[OT] 38. Stockholm: Almqvist & Wiksell, 1994.

Talshir, Z. "The Reign of Solomon in the Making: Pseudo-connections Between 3 Kingdoms and Chronicles." *VT* 50 (2000): 233–49.

———. "Textual and Literary Criticism of the Bible in Post-Modern Times: The Untimely Demise of Classical Biblical Philology." *Henoch* 21 (1999): 235–52.

Timm, H. "Die Ladeerzählung (1 Sam 4–6; 2 Sam 6) und das Kerygma des deuteronomistischen Geschichtswerks." *EvT* 29 (1966): 509–26.

Tov, Emanuel. *The Greek and Hebrew Bible: Collected Essays on the Septuagint*. VTSup 72. Leiden: Brill, 1999.

———. *The Text-Critical Use of the Septuagint in Biblical Research*. 2d ed. JBS 8. Jerusalem, 1997.

———. *Textual Criticism of the Hebrew Bible*. Minneapolis: Fortress, 1992.

Ulrich, E., F. M. Cross, S. W. Crawford, J. A. Duncan, P. W. Skehan, E. Tov and J. Trebolle Barrera, eds. *Qumran Cave 4.IX: Deuteronomy, Joshua, Judges, Kings*. DJD 14. Oxford: Clarendon, 1995.

Van der Meer, M. N. *Formation and Reformulation: The Redaction of the Book of Joshua in the Light of the Oldest Textual Witnesses*. VTSup 102. Leiden: Brill, 2004.

Van Seters, J. *In Search of History: Historiography in the Ancient World and the Origins of Biblical History*. New Haven: Yale University Press, 1983.

———. "Joshua's Campaign of Canaan and Near Eastern Historiography." *SJOT* 4 (1990): 1–12.

———. *The Life of Moses: The Yahwist as Historian in Exodus–Numbers*. Louisville: Westminster John Knox, 1994.

———. "The Pentateuch." Pages 3–49 in McKenzie and Graham, eds., *The Hebrew Bible*.

Vogt, E. "Die Erzählung vom Jordanübergang, Josue 3–4." *Bib* 46 (1965): 125–48.

Volz, P., and W. Rudolph. *Der Elohist als Erzähler: Ein Irrweg der Pentateuchkritik?* Giessen: Töpelmann, 1933.

Welch, A. C. "The Chronicler and the Levites." Pages 55–80 in *The Work of the Chronicler: Its Purpose and Its Date.* London: Oxford University Press, 1939.

Wellhausen, J. *Die Composition des Hexateuchs und der historischen Bücher des Alten Testaments.* 3d ed. Berlin: Reimer, 1899.

Wilcoxen, J. A. "Narrative Structure and Cult Legend: A Study of Joshua 1–6." Pages 43–70 in *Transitions in Biblical Scholarship.* Edited by J. C. Rylaarsdam. Chicago: University of Chicago Press, 1968.

Williams, J. C. "The Prophetic 'Father.'" *JBL* 85 (1966): 346.

Williamson, H. G. M. *1 and 2 Chronicles.* NCBC. London: Marshall, Morgan & Scott, 1982.

———. "Introduction." Pages 11–26 in Martin Noth, *The Chronicler's History.* JSOTSup 50. Sheffield: JSOT, 1987.

———. "A Response to A. Graeme Auld." *JSOT* 27 (1977): 33–39.

———. Review of A. G. Auld, *Kings Without Privilege. VT* 46 (1996): 553–55.

Winther-Nielsen, N. *A Functional Discourse Grammar of Joshua: A Computer-assisted Rhetorical Structure Analysis.* OTS 40. Stockholm: Almqvist & Wiksell International, 1995.

Woudstra, M. H. *The Book of Joshua.* NICOT. Grand Rapids: Eerdmans, 1981.

Würthwein, E. *Das Erste Buch der Könige, Kapitel 1–16.* 2d ed. ATD 11/1. Göttingen: Vandenhoeck & Ruprecht. 1st ed. 1977.

———. *Studien zum deuteronomistischen Geschichtswerk.* BZAW 227. Berlin: de Gruyter, 1994.

INDEXES

INDEX OF REFERENCES

HEBREW BIBLE/
OLD TESTAMENT

Genesis

1:2 138
1:9 32
6:16 103
7:20 103
9:8–17 174
9:11 174
15:19 168
15:20 57
17:1–21 174
17:14 174
18:14 102
19:20 102
19:27 102
20:8 102
21:14 102
22:3 102
26:31 102
26:33 100
28:18 102
30:14 103, 155
31:2 101
31:48 100
31:55 102
32:1 102
32:11 154
32:33 100
43:16 151
47:6 141
47:26 100
48:15 100
50:26 70

Exodus

3:8 168
3:10 57
3:17 168
3:20 102
4:15–16 203
4:20–24 203
5:7 101
5:14 101
7:20 137
8:16 102
9:3 101
9:13 102
10:6 100
12:8 168
12:26–27 173, 174, 185
12:26 173, 174
12:27 173, 174
12:37 163
13:3–10 61
13:5 57, 168
13:8–10 173, 174, 185
13:8–9 173
13:8 173
13:9 173
13:10 173
13:14–15 158, 173, 174, 185
13:14 61, 174
13:15 174
13:17–14:31 13, 21, 135, 136, 138, 139, 141–43, 145, 146, 171, 179, 191
13:17–22 141, 142
13:18 63, 137–39, 141, 145, 176
13:20 141, 163
13:21–22 144
14 143, 145, 146, 179
14:1–4 141, 142
14:2 142, 163
14:4 139, 141
14:6 139, 141
14:7 139, 141
14:8 137, 145
14:9 139, 141, 142
14:14 139, 141
14:16 137, 142, 146
14:17 139, 141
14:18 139, 141
14:19 144
14:20 139, 141, 144
14:21 136, 138, 142, 143, 145, 146
14:22 137, 142, 143, 146
14:23 139, 141, 142
14:24 139, 141, 144

28:14 207
28:36 207
28:64 207
29:3 100
29:25 207
29:26 207
30:9 160
30:11 102
30:17 207
31:2 154
31:9 165
31:15 104
31:18 207
31:20 207
31:25 165
31:26 70, 165
32:34 104
34:6 100

Joshua
1–12 23, 30
1–6 156
1 10, 30, 156, 163, 164, 166, 186, 190, 202
1:1–5:15 29
1:1–9 37
1:2 38, 150, 154
1:3 38, 151
1:4 38
1:5 7, 38, 167, 186
1:7 7
1:9–12:24 37
1:10–11 7, 164, 186
1:11 154, 161, 163, 206
1:12–15 176, 190
1:14 176
1:16–18 177
1:17–18 167, 186
2–8 37
2 26, 36, 38, 163, 164, 206
2:1 164
2:10 179
2:11 169
2:16 164
2:22 164
2:24 38
3–8 36
3–4 1–5, 7–14, 17, 20, 22, 25, 28, 33, 38–43, 53, 54, 66, 68–71, 76–78, 82, 83, 85–87, 94, 98, 101, 103, 106, 110, 128, 129, 133, 135, 136, 138–43, 145–50, 155, 160–63, 165, 179, 184, 191, 193, 204–206, 208–11
3–4 LXX 10
3 6, 18–20, 26, 59, 169, 185, 189, 207, 208, 210
3:1–5:1 17, 19, 209
3:1–4:24 26, 36, 40, 181, 184
3:1–4:19 145
3:1–4:14 19, 21, 210
3:1–17 182, 183
3:1–16 5
3:1–11 191, 199–202
3:1–8 161, 189
3:1–4 185
3:1 3–7, 18, 26, 36, 38, 43, 51, 54, 66, 102, 103, 106, 131, 138, 149, 150, 156, 160, 162–64, 180, 181, 185, 186, 189, 192, 193, 199–201, 204–206, 208
3:2–11 179, 181, 182, 184, 204, 208
3:2–5 36, 38
3:2–4 3, 6, 164, 186
3:2–3 4, 5, 163, 166, 170, 188
3:2 6, 7, 17, 20, 38, 43, 94, 138, 140, 141, 161, 163, 185, 193, 206, 210
3:3 4, 6, 7, 43, 52, 54, 66, 77, 80, 82, 84, 86, 87, 134, 149, 150, 156, 160, 164–66, 185, 192, 193, 199–201, 204
3:4–5 5

Joshua (cont.)

3:4 3, 4, 6, 7, 43, 52, 55, 101, 106, 156, 157, 160, 165, 166, 185, 186, 193
3:5–6 3, 166, 167, 186
3:5 4, 6, 7, 33, 44, 52, 55, 66, 101–103, 106, 150, 155, 156, 160, 166, 186, 193
3:6–13 36, 38
3:6–10 3
3:6–7 5, 161
3:6 4, 6, 7, 38, 44, 56, 63, 65, 66, 80, 86, 94, 139, 149–51, 165–67, 186, 190, 192, 193, 199–201, 204
3:7–11 3, 167, 186
3:7–8 167, 186
3:7 4, 6, 7, 26, 44, 52, 53, 56, 59, 66, 139, 149–51, 154, 167, 177, 186, 187, 192, 194, 200, 201, 204
3:8 4–7, 44, 52, 56, 66, 80, 86, 142, 150, 157, 165, 167, 186, 187, 194
3:9–13 170
3:9–11 4, 5, 187
3:9–10 6, 167
3:9 6, 44, 52, 56, 57, 66, 151, 156, 157, 160, 167, 168, 186, 194, 206
3:10–13 26
3:10 3, 6, 32, 45, 52, 57, 66, 140, 149, 151, 156, 160, 167–69, 171, 186, 192, 194, 199–201, 204
3:11–12 18
3:11 6, 7, 45, 52, 57, 59, 66, 77, 82, 149, 151, 157, 160, 165, 167–70, 186, 188, 192, 194, 199–201, 204, 206
3:12 3–6, 18, 45, 56, 58, 66, 149, 152, 159–61, 169, 180, 181, 185, 187, 191, 192, 194, 199–202, 204–10
3:13–17 7, 179, 181, 182, 184, 187, 191, 199–202, 204, 208
3:13–16 5
3:13–14 165
3:13 3, 4, 6, 7, 45, 58, 66, 77, 80, 86, 103, 142, 143, 146, 149, 151, 157, 165, 167, 169–71, 187, 188, 192, 194, 199–201, 204, 206
3:14–17 3, 36, 38, 39
3:14–15 158
3:14 4, 6, 7, 38, 39, 45, 52, 58, 67, 80, 86, 149, 158, 160, 165, 170, 187, 188, 192, 194, 199–201
3:15 4, 6, 7, 46, 58, 66, 67, 73, 80, 86, 103, 129, 143, 149, 150, 155, 158, 170, 178, 187, 188, 192, 195, 199–201, 204
3:16–17 189
3:16 4, 6, 46, 52, 58, 59, 67, 103,

140, 142, 143, 146, 149–51, 158, 160, 170, 171, 176, 178, 187, 188, 192, 195, 199–201
3:17–4:8 5
3:17 4–7, 18–20, 26, 46, 59, 60, 66, 67, 80, 86, 136, 145, 149–51, 158, 160, 165, 170, 171, 175, 178, 179, 187–89, 191, 192, 195, 199–201, 204
3:20 161
3:21–24 161
3:24 66
3:26 142
4 20, 26, 169, 172, 185, 207, 208, 210
4:1–24 183
4:1–14 182
4:1–10 36, 38
4:1–9 188, 191, 199–202, 204
4:1–8 6, 18, 19, 21, 159, 160, 169, 171, 175, 179–81, 185, 187, 189, 191, 204, 206–208, 210, 211
4:1–5 3, 5, 175
4:1 3, 4, 26, 38, 47, 59, 65, 67, 149, 151, 158, 171, 172, 175, 188, 192, 195, 199–201, 204
4:2 4, 6, 18, 47, 59, 60, 66, 67, 149, 152, 169, 171, 187, 188, 192, 195, 199–201, 204, 206, 207, 209, 210
4:3 3, 4, 6, 19, 47, 52, 59, 60, 62, 66, 67, 86, 149, 150, 152, 164, 171, 172, 188, 189, 192, 195, 199–201, 205, 210, 211
4:4–5 4, 172
4:4 47, 67, 149, 152, 159, 171, 188, 192, 196, 199–201
4:5 6, 47, 60, 62, 66, 67, 77, 137, 146, 149–53, 159, 172, 175, 188, 189, 192, 196, 199–201, 205, 211
4:6–8 3
4:6–7 4–7, 158–60, 173, 174, 185
4:6 3, 47, 61, 67, 103, 106, 150, 154, 172, 173, 188, 196
4:7 3, 4, 7, 48, 53, 67, 142, 149, 150, 165, 172–74, 188, 192, 196, 199–201, 205
4:8 3–5, 48, 59, 62, 66, 67, 150, 159, 160, 172, 175, 188, 189, 1964:9–14
18
4:9–10 5, 39
4:9 3–7, 20, 22, 39, 40, 48, 60, 62, 63, 67, 80, 86, 100, 149, 150, 152, 153, 159, 165, 175, 180, 181, 185, 188, 189, 191, 192, 197, 199–201, 204–209
4:10–14 5, 181, 189, 191, 199–202, 204

Joshua (cont.)
4:10–11 21, 175, 179, 181, 184, 189, 204, 208, 211
4:10 3–7, 19, 20, 49, 53, 63, 67, 73, 80, 86, 104, 106, 138, 139, 149–51, 153, 159, 175, 176, 180, 181, 185, 186, 190, 192, 197, 199–201, 204, 205, 208
4:11–15 39
4:11–14 38
4:11–12 4
4:11 3–6, 18, 20, 26, 38, 49, 63, 66, 67, 73, 82, 138, 149, 150, 158–60, 165, 175, 176, 180, 181, 185, 189, 190, 192, 197, 199–201, 204, 208, 210
4:12–14 5, 6, 177, 190
4:12–13 3, 94, 176, 177, 180, 181, 185, 204, 208
4:12 3, 6, 7, 49, 63, 64, 94, 137, 138, 140, 141, 145, 176, 189, 190, 197
4:13 3, 4, 6, 49, 53, 64, 66, 67, 94, 140, 141, 149, 158, 176, 189, 190, 192, 197, 199–201, 205
4:14 3, 4, 6, 7, 26, 49, 53, 56, 67, 139, 149, 154, 160, 167, 177, 179, 181, 184, 186, 189, 192, 197, 199–201, 204, 208
4:15–5:1 19, 21, 210
4:15–19 5
4:15–18 3–5, 18–21, 38, 210
4:15–17 6, 165
4:15–16 177, 179–81, 185, 190, 191, 199–201, 204, 208
4:15 38, 49, 50, 65, 151, 177, 190, 197
4:16–18 139
4:16 6, 7, 50, 63, 64, 67, 77, 78, 80, 86, 150, 165, 177, 179, 190, 197
4:17–19 177–79, 181, 182, 184, 190, 191, 199–202, 204, 208
4:17 50, 86, 176, 177, 190, 197
4:18 6, 7, 36, 39, 50, 53, 58, 64, 65, 68, 80, 86, 101, 106, 136, 138, 142, 145, 149, 151, 153, 158–60, 165, 177–79, 189–92, 198–201, 205
4:19–5:1 18
4:19–24 21, 36, 38
4:19 3, 4, 6, 7, 11, 17, 20, 50, 53, 94, 150, 177, 190, 198, 210
4:20–24 5, 21, 40, 171, 178–81, 185, 188, 191, 199–201, 204, 208
4:20–23 6
4:20 3, 4, 50, 53, 65, 159, 160, 172, 178, 189, 191, 198
4:21–5:8 11

4:21–24 3, 4, 6, 7, 32
4:21 3, 4, 51, 56, 65, 68, 103, 106, 149–51, 154, 178, 191, 192, 198, 199, 201, 205
4:22–24 42
4:22–23 6
4:22 3, 42, 51, 53, 65, 68, 137, 149, 154, 160, 178, 179, 191, 192, 198, 199, 201, 205
4:23 42, 51, 54, 68, 137, 138, 142, 150, 156, 160, 178, 179, 191, 198
4:24 3, 6, 51, 54, 65, 68, 101, 106, 150, 156, 160, 174, 178, 179, 191, 198
5 156
5:1 17, 21, 33, 36, 38, 41, 42, 53, 168
5:2–12 10, 36, 42
5:9–12 178
5:9 100
5:10–11 210
5:10 178, 209
5:11 156, 178, 209
5:12 64, 156
5:13–6:26 36
5:13–15 36
5:13 36
5:15 62, 159
6 29, 36, 69–71, 76, 78, 82, 83, 85–87, 93, 96, 98, 99, 129, 130, 132, 134, 156, 164, 190
6:1–27 129
6:1–20 129
6:1–3 132
6:1 132
6:2–5 36
6:3–4 130
6:3 130, 132
6:4 73, 86, 96, 98, 130, 132
6:5–6 132
6:5 96, 98, 99, 130, 132
6:6–10 36
6:6 73, 80, 86, 96, 98, 132
6:7 61, 73, 94, 129, 132, 153
6:8 82, 86, 96, 98, 130, 132, 165
6:9 94, 129, 130, 132
6:10 99, 131, 132
6:11 73, 79, 80, 82, 94, 132, 164
6:12 73, 80, 86, 102, 103, 106, 131, 163, 185
6:13 61, 73, 86, 94, 96, 98, 129, 130, 132, 153
6:14 94, 132
6:15 102, 103, 106, 131, 132, 185
6:16–20 36
6:16 86, 96, 98, 99, 130, 132
6:17 36, 132
6:18–20 132
6:18 94
6:19 104, 131
6:20–21 36
6:20 96, 98, 99, 130, 132
6:22–23 132
6:23 94
6:24 104, 131, 132
6:25 100, 132
6:26 36, 131, 132
6:27–8:29 36
6:27–7:1 36
6:27 132, 169
7 29
7:2–5 37
7:3 36
7:6–25 37
7:6–15 36
7:6 61, 70, 72, 153
7:11 26
7:13 26, 167
7:16 102, 131, 163, 185
7:21 153
7:23 153
7:26 100
8:1–29 10
8:1–9 36
8:4 60
8:9 164

4:1–7:2 13, 69–71, 76, 78, 80, 82–84, 86, 89, 90, 92, 93, 98, 101, 107, 126–28, 133, 135
4:1–5 76
4:1 89, 92–94
4:2 92
4:3 73, 80, 89, 92, 94, 165
4:4 70, 73, 80, 89, 92, 165
4:5 73, 80, 89, 92–94, 99, 131, 165
4:6 73, 80, 89, 94, 99
4:7 89, 92, 94
4:8 89, 92, 101, 106, 166
4:9 89, 94
4:10 89, 92
4:11 73, 76, 80, 89, 92
4:12 92
4:13 73, 89
4:14 89, 92, 104, 106
4:15 89
4:16 89
4:17 73, 80, 89, 92
4:18 73, 89, 92
4:19 73, 80, 89, 92
4:21 73, 80, 89, 92
4:22 73, 80, 89, 92
4:23 89
4:24 89, 92
5 76
5:1 70, 73, 80, 89
5:2 73, 80, 82, 89
5:3 73, 89, 102, 103, 106, 131, 163
5:4 73, 89, 101, 102, 103, 106, 151, 163
5:5 100
5:6 89, 101, 106
5:7 73, 76, 80, 89, 92, 101
5:8 73, 76, 79, 80, 82, 89, 92
5:9 80, 89, 101, 106
5:10 70, 73, 80, 82, 89, 92
5:11 73, 80, 82, 89, 92, 101
5:12 73, 80, 89, 92
6 73, 89, 90, 92
6:1–7:2 73
6:1 73, 82, 89, 93
6:2 73, 82, 89
6:3 73, 79, 82, 89, 92, 101
6:4 79
6:5 89, 92, 101
6:7 89, 92
6:8 73, 78, 80, 82, 89, 92
6:9 89, 101
6:10 92
6:11 73, 82, 89
6:12 70, 89
6:13 73, 82, 89, 103, 129, 155, 170
6:14 89
6:15 73, 82, 84, 86, 87, 89, 128, 134
6:16 89, 92
6:17 89
6:18 73, 82, 83, 89, 92, 100, 134
6:19 73, 82, 89, 92, 94, 129
6:20 73, 79, 80, 89, 92
6:21–7:2 99
6:21 73, 80, 82, 89
6:23 92
6:24 89
6:25 92
6:26 89
6:27 89, 92
7:1 70, 73, 80, 82
7:2 73, 80, 82, 89, 92
7:13 101
8:8 208
9:26 102
10 73
10:11 73, 101
11:4 208
11:10 208
12:2 100
12:5 100
12:15 101
12:17 103, 155
13:23 152
14:1 152
14:4 152
14:6 152

1 Samuel (cont.)
14:9 208
14:11 152
14:15 152
14:18 70, 72
14:21 101
15:12 102
17:20 99, 102, 131
17:26 168
17:52 99, 131
19:7 101
19:21 208
21:5 167
21:6 101
26:19 208
27:6 100
28:8 208
29:3 100
29:6 100
29:8 100
29:10 102
29:11 102
30:25 100

2 Samuel
1:5 116
1:16 116
1:17 116
1:26 102
2:7 141
4:3 100
5:2 101
5:11–6:23 93, 133
5:11–25 87, 94, 95
5:11 116
5:12 88, 91, 93, 116
5:13 116
5:14 116
5:17 91
5:18 117
5:19 88, 117
5:20 88, 117
5:21 117
5:22 117
5:23 88, 117
5:24 88, 117
5:25 88, 117
6 13, 69–72, 76, 81, 84, 87, 88, 91, 94–97, 101, 105, 107, 111, 113, 114, 126, 127, 135, 184–86, 202, 204
6:1–11 72, 95, 126, 157, 166
6:1 91
6:2 76, 83, 88, 91, 100, 114
6:3 72, 79, 81, 83, 88, 115
6:4 72, 88, 115
6:5 88, 91, 96, 97, 113, 115, 126, 135
6:6 72, 81, 83, 88, 115
6:7 72, 88, 115
6:8 100, 115
6:9 72, 83, 88, 115
6:10 72, 74, 81, 83, 88, 116
6:11 72, 79, 83, 88, 116
6:12–19 126
6:12 72, 79, 88, 120
6:13 72, 79, 83, 88, 120
6:14–20 72
6:14 88, 120
6:15 72, 79, 83, 88, 91, 96, 97, 99, 113, 120, 126, 131
6:16 72, 79, 83, 88, 121
6:17 72, 79, 81, 83, 88, 91, 121
6:18 88, 91, 93, 121
6:19–20 124, 126
6:19 91, 93, 121
6:20–23 95, 125, 126, 135
6:20 91
6:21 88, 91
6:25 88
7:2 70, 72
7:6 100
11:1 93
11:11 70, 72
13:2 102
15:2 102
15:24 70, 72, 74, 84
15:25 70, 72
15:29 70, 72
18:18 100
23:14 152
24:14 101

1 Kings
1:42 141
1:52 141
2:3 77
2:26 70
3:15 70
5:17 151
5:27 93
6:19 70, 74, 165

1 Chronicles (cont.)
12:38 95
13–16 13, 69–72, 76, 79, 81, 84, 85, 87, 88, 90, 91, 93–97, 99, 105, 107, 113, 114, 126, 133, 135, 184, 185, 202, 204
13 72, 76, 90, 95, 100, 186
13:1–4 114, 126
13:2 84, 85, 87, 88, 91, 95
13:3 72, 76, 79, 88
13:4 91
13:5–14 157, 166
13:5 72, 79, 88, 91, 114
13:6 72, 79, 83, 88, 91, 99, 100, 114
13:7 72, 79, 81, 83, 88, 115
13:8 88, 91, 96, 97, 113, 115, 126, 130, 135
13:9 72, 81, 83, 115
13:10 72, 88, 115
13:11 88, 100, 115
13:12 72, 79, 83, 88, 115
13:13 72, 81, 83, 116
13:14 72, 79, 88, 116
13:15 97
13:16 97
13:20 97
13:21 97
13:28 130
14 94, 95
14:1 116
14:2 88, 91, 93, 116
14:3 116
14:4 116
14:5 116
14:6 116
14:7 116
14:8 91, 116
14:9 117
14:10 88
14:10 117
14:11 88, 117
14:12 88, 117
14:13 117
14:14 88, 117
14:15 88, 94, 117
14:16 88, 94, 117
14:17 88, 118, 126
15–16 72, 90
15 76
15:1–24 94, 95, 118, 126, 135
15:1 72, 88
15:2 72, 79, 85, 88
15:3 72, 79, 88, 91
15:4 85
15:11 85
15:12 72, 76, 79, 85, 88, 91, 101, 167
15:13 88
15:14 72, 76, 79, 84, 85, 88, 91, 101, 134, 167
15:15 72, 79, 85, 88
15:16 85, 96, 97, 113
15:17 85
15:19 96, 97, 113
15:20 96, 113
15:21 96, 113
15:22 85
15:23 72
15:24 72, 85, 88, 96, 97, 113, 130, 134
15:25 74, 79, 88, 91, 120, 165
15:26 74, 79, 85, 88, 120, 165
15:27 72, 79, 85, 120
15:28 74, 79, 83, 88, 91, 96, 97, 99, 113, 120, 126, 130, 131, 16515:29 74, 79, 83, 88
15:29 121, 165
16:1 72, 79, 81, 83, 88, 121
16:2 88, 91, 93, 121
16:3 91, 121
16:4–42 94, 95, 121, 126, 135
16:4–7 126
16:4 72, 85, 88, 91

16:5 96, 97, 113
16:6 74, 85, 88, 96, 97, 113
16:7 88
16:8–22 126
16:8 88, 91
16:9 102, 106, 167
16:10 88
16:11 88
16:12 102, 106, 167
16:13 91
16:14 88
16:17 91
16:20 91
16:23–33 126
16:23 88
16:24 88, 91, 102, 106, 167
16:25 88
16:26 88, 91
16:28 88, 91
16:29 88
16:31 88
16:33 88
16:34–36 126
16:34 88
16:35 88
16:36 88, 91
16:37–42 126
16:37 72, 74, 88, 165
16:39 85, 88
16:40 88, 91
16:41 88
16:42 88, 96, 97, 113
16:43 91, 93, 124
17:1 70, 165
17:5 100
20:1 93
21:13 101
22:19 70, 165
26:20 104
26:22 104
26:24 104
26:26 104
27:25 104
27:27 104
27:28 104
28:2 70
28:12 104
28:18 70, 165
28:19 101
29:8 104
29:17 77
29:18 151

2 Chronicles
1:1 53
1:4 70, 72
2:16 93
3:3 55, 156
4:4 103
5 13, 69–71, 76, 78, 83, 93, 96, 105, 111, 113, 133–35, 184, 185, 202, 204
5:1–6:2 111
5:1–14 76, 79, 81, 85, 87, 88, 91, 97, 111
5:1 88, 104, 111
5:2 74, 76, 83, 88, 91, 111, 165, 208
5:3 91, 111
5:4 72, 76, 85, 91, 93, 111, 206
5:5 72, 79, 84, 85, 112, 134
5:6 72, 76, 91, 112
5:7 74, 83, 85, 87, 88, 112, 165
5:8 72, 76, 103, 112
5:9 72, 100, 112
5:10 72, 76, 88, 91, 112, 206
5:11–13 111, 113, 135
5:11 85, 87, 101, 112, 167
5:12 85, 96, 97, 112
5:13 96, 97, 104, 105, 112
5:14 85, 87, 88, 104, 105, 113
5:15 104
6:11 70
6:41 70
7:4 93
7:5 93
7:19 207
7:22 207
8:8 100
8:11 70
9:4 138
10:18 93
10:19 100
11:11 104
12:9 104
13 88
16:2 104
16:41 72
18:20 138
18:21 138

Index of Authors

Ackroyd, P. R. 108, 127
Ahlström, G. W. 127
Auld, A. G. 2, 4, 8, 11, 12, 42, 53–55, 57–65, 68, 73, 76, 90, 93, 95, 110, 126–28, 130, 132, 136, 138, 142, 143, 152–60, 162, 163, 165–67, 170–72, 176–78, 185, 209

Beek, M. A. 140
Begg, C. T. 94, 111, 113
Bieberstein, K. 2, 58, 63, 155
Blenkinsopp, J. 127
Boling, R. G. 2, 5, 54, 65, 150, 152, 163, 164, 168, 172, 189
Butler, T. C. 2, 54, 57, 59, 129, 154, 163, 165–67, 171, 177, 179, 187, 188

Campbell, A. F. 90, 100, 126, 127, 133, 165
Childs, B. S. 137, 141, 144, 171
Coats, W. 133, 141, 163, 171
Cody, A. 84
Coggins, R. J. 110
Cooke, G. A. 3
Cowley, A. E. 55
Cross, F. M. 11, 71, 108

Davies, G. H. 165
Davis, M. T. 1
De Vries, S. J. 111, 113
De Wette, W. M. L. 107
Dietrich, W. 11
Driver, S. R. 3
Dus, J. 4, 129

Edelman, D. 1
Eichhorn, J. G. 107
Eissfeldt, O. 3

Fokkelman, J. P. 127
Fritz, V. 6, 129, 163, 165, 168, 169, 172, 185

Gertz, J. C. K. 12, 173
Gibson, J. C. L. 166
Gray, J. 2, 57, 139, 140, 166, 170, 186
Greenspoon, L. J. 2

Hasel, G. F. 108
Hawk, L. D. 1, 22, 26
Hobbs, T. R. 139, 140
Holmes, S. 2, 7, 54, 56, 150
Hutton, J. M. 55

Japhet, S. 76, 93, 94, 104, 105, 111, 113
Jobling, D. 1
Johnson, B. L. 1
Johnstone, W. 110

Kang, S. M. 99, 131
Kautzsch, E. 55
Keating, J. 1
Keller, C. A. 4
Kenyon, K. 129
Kittel, R. 90
Klein, R. W. 71, 80, 90, 100
Knoppers, G. N. 11, 71, 84, 100, 107, 110
Kucova, L. 107

Langlamet, F. 4, 157, 169
Lemke, W. E. 108
Leuchter, M. 55
Long, B. O. 111, 113, 139, 141

Macy, H. R. 108
Margolis, M. L. 51
Mazor, L. 129
McCarter, P. K. 71, 100
McKenzie, S. L. 76, 95, 109–11, 113, 126, 128
Min, K. J. 84
Mitchell, G. 1, 29, 30, 32
Moatti-Fine, J. 2, 55
Morgenstern, J. 165

Nelson, R. D. 1, 6, 7, 11, 99, 129–31, 166–72, 176–78, 186, 189, 190
Noth, M. 3, 9, 94, 129, 132, 133, 142, 144

Otto, E. 129

Peckham, B. 1, 6, 11, 129
Peltonen, K. 107
Pisano, S. J. 100
Pitkänen, P. M. A. 161
Polzin, R. M. 1, 14, 40, 127, 128, 148, 209
Porter, J. R. 108
Propp, W. H. C. 141, 142

Rad, G. von 99, 131, 133, 165
Rahlfs, A. 51
Rezetko, R. C. 93, 108, 127, 128
Rofé, A. 140
Rose, M. 87
Rost, L. 90, 126, 133, 165
Rottzoll, D. U. 137, 142, 177
Rudolph, W. 3, 12

Saydon, D. U. 1, 3, 169, 176, 187
Schicklberger, F. 127
Schmid, K. 12
Seebass, H. 132
Seow, C. L. 77, 177
Sipilä, S. 2, 9, 10, 58, 61, 65, 151, 152, 154
Smelik, K. A. D. 127, 128
Smend, R., Jr. 11
Soggin, J. A. 2, 5, 54, 56, 60, 61, 156, 157, 164, 167, 168, 172, 176, 178, 186, 190, 209
Steussy, M. J. 127
Stipp, H.-J. 63
Svensson, J. 1

Talshir, Z. 110
Timm, H. 127
Tov, E. 2, 8, 9, 59, 61, 63, 65, 132, 150, 152–54

Ulrich, E. 172

Van Seters, J. 5, 12, 127, 129, 141, 144, 145, 163, 164, 176
Van der Meer, M. N. 2, 10, 11, 55, 56, 64, 65, 129, 131, 150, 153, 154, 172, 178
Vogt, E. 4
Volz, P. 12

Welch, A. C. 84
Wellhausen, J. 129
Wilcoxen, J. A. 129, 156
Williams, J. C. 140
Williamson, H. G. M. 76, 90, 108
Winther-Nielsen, N. 1, 2, 34, 35, 37, 40
Witte, M. 12
Woudstra, M. H. 163, 165, 168, 170, 172, 179, 185, 189
Wright, G. E. 2, 5, 54, 65, 150, 152, 163, 164, 168, 172, 189
Würthwein, E. 11, 139, 140